INFORMATION SYSTEMS DESIGN

INFORMATION SYSTEMS DESIGN

CYRIL H.P. BROOKES
PHILLIP J. GROUSE
D. ROSS JEFFERY
MICHAEL J. LAWRENCE

Department of Information Systems
University of New South Wales

PRENTICE-HALL OF AUSTRALIA

Prentice-Hall of Australia Pty Ltd, Sydney
Prentice-Hall International Inc, London
Prentice-Hall of Canada Ltd, Toronto
Prentice-Hall of India Private Ltd, New Delhi
Prentice-Hall of Japan Inc, Tokyo
Prentice-Hall of Southeast Asia Pte Ltd, Singapore
Whitehall Books Ltd, Wellington
Prentice-Hall Inc, Englewood Cliffs, New Jersey

Typeset by Abb-Typesetting Pty Ltd,
Collingwood, Victoria
Printed in Great Britain by
Butler & Tanner Ltd, Frome and London

4 5 86 85

National Library of Australia
Cataloguing-in-Publication Data

Information systems design.

Includes index.
ISBN 0 13 46485 1
ISBN 0 7248 0642 3 Paperback

1.System design. I. Brookes, Cyril H.P.
(Cyril Henry Putnam), 1938–.

001.6

To Diana, Margaret, Cas and Sarah

CONTENTS

PREFACE

The discipline of information systems design is both ancient and modern. When did it become an important aspect of human activity? Construction of the wonders of the ancient world — the Egyptian pyramids, the Hanging Gardens of Babylon or the Colossus of Rhodes — must have been supported by management information systems. More recently, most large organizations have instituted 'organization and methods', 'clerical work study' or similar activities in the period following World War 2. Some observers may link the beginnings of the formal practice of systems design to milestones in computer hardware development such as Babbage's 'Analytical Engine', ENIAC or UNIVAC 1, or even IBM's 1401 or System 360. Still others could nominate starting or major transition points by less concrete events or products such as a realization of the similarity between information systems and engineering design procedures or the publication of IBM's Study Organization Plan or NCR's Accurately Defined Systems.

This much is certain, however, that systems design for applications using computers as the information-processing tool is now a major activity in all organizations. If the scope of information systems is defined to include all forms of information collection, storage, retrieval, processing and communication, then it is clear that an effective organization relies on having well-designed systems. Hence, the study of information systems design and implementation should form a significant component in any discipline concerned with effective organizational structure or operation.

Our book is intended to serve as a text for those who wish to become familiar with the tools, techniques and practice of systems design. It covers material normally found in both Master's and undergraduate programs. We believe it will suit courses both in specialized programs, such as computer science, and in user disciplines, such as accounting or librarianship. It will also serve as a handbook of design procedure for practitioners.

With the maturation in the discipline which has been evident since the early 1960s, it has become clear that a basic set of tools and techniques can now be defined which provide a framework for the activities of the systems analyst and designer. This framework is presented in some detail in the chapters dealing with systems design, file and database specification, on-line systems, project management, audit and control, and implementation. Although we have made these basics central to the theme of the book, we have felt it appropriate to provide extensions in a number of areas. These sections are intended to show students the degree of complexity which can arise in systems design and also to build a 'bridge' between basic and more advanced courses.

Examples of this extension, or 'enrichment', material include: complex file structures in the appendix to Chapter 3, distributed database concepts in Chapter 9, cryptography in the appendix to Chapter 10, and decision support systems in Chapter 13. At the risk of being accused of adopting an uneven treatment of the subject, we have deliberately highlighted the fact that systems design tasks are not merely the application of 'basic' technique. For example, reporting from files may need consideration of DSS concepts, security of data communication may present a problem requiring the use of cryptography, or the data may be spread over a number of processing centres necessitating an understanding of distributed databases. We envisage instructors may use this extension material in a number of ways, such as a basis for class discussion on more complex issues, as a means of challenging the better students, or as the basis of advanced systems design courses where recent journal articles are set as supplementary reading.

Our approach to the subject is oriented towards practicality, with emphasis on issues, guidelines and procedures. In developing a text such as this an author has a choice between taking a conceptual line — for example, considering the general question of the nature of information systems within organizations — or following a 'hands on' approach which is largely prescriptive. While we do develop a wide range of conceptual questions in later chapters, the initial focus is on what must be done by persons involved in the systems analysis and design task and what their objectives ought to be at each stage of the project.

In common with the problem of developing many other human performance skills, the acquisition of systems design competence can only be achieved through 'doing'. For this reason we have included a wide range of case studies and it is intended that these should be used as soon as the students have commenced work on the relevant section.

Naturally we welcome comments, suggestions or criticisms of the book which may assist us in improving later editions.

Cyril Brookes
Phil Grouse
Ross Jeffery
Michael Lawrence   January, 1982

1 INFORMATION SYSTEMS AND THE ORGANIZATION

PART A — INTRODUCTION TO INFORMATION SYSTEMS

1.1 INTRODUCTION

Information systems are the organization's instrumentation. They inform decision makers at all levels about those variables which represent the state of the organization (e.g. cash held at bank, order backlog, inventory holdings, total debtors, staff numbers) and about those which represent changes, or rates of change, in variables affecting the organization (e.g. production rates, cash flow, stock received, profit and loss, employees' weekly pay).

Of course not all information systems, nor all parts of the one system, are computer based; even so, similar design principles hold for all types of system. However, the technology of computers, communications, and data storage brings special problems to the design, implementation, and effective operation of computer-based systems. This technology provides both opportunities for and limitations to the scope, scale, and flexibility of information systems. It is well known that high processing speed and large data-storage capacity lead to a wide variety of options in the design of an information system's environment. Indeed, processing capacity in excess of that required for just the basic processing tasks has encouraged the development of generalized database management systems and of other software products which further extend the range of options so that systems designers can now integrate the processing and data storage of a wide range of applications. But it is less well known that the options made possible by new

1

technology lead to particular problems in the control of the system-development process. The large number of and the wide differences in the alternatives open to a systems designer mean that it is difficult to consider them all, let alone determine the potential consequences of any one possibility. On the one hand computer specialists are often unaware of the significance of the changes that new technology may bring to their organization, and their preoccupation with technical matters can lead to the design of systems which do not fit well within the organization's structure. On the other hand non-technical managers are often reluctant to become involved in evaluating the different options because of their inadequate training or experience in the essential technical concepts.

Loss of flexibility is probably the main general source of dissatisfaction with information systems. At the start of an information system project many things are possible, within the limits of cost and technical feasibility, but as the design proceeds the available options are narrowed down; and once programming is complete and the system is being implemented, any possibility of change has virtually disappeared. This situation contrasts markedly with that for manual-based information systems in which the procedures and practices can be altered at very short notice. This difference in flexibility is illustrated in the following two scenarios.

1. *Manual production-costing systems are being used.* The general manager says to the chief accountant, 'Fred, I want to get regular daily reports from 8 A.M. tomorrow, detailing marginal and fixed costs on the new production line, for all product groups, comparing them with the old facility and highlighting fuel usage. These summarized figures are no use to me while the fuel shortage continues.'

    Fred then asks Reg, the production costing clerk, to change his reports from the next day. The likely result is a set of handwritten reports presented next day, which are broadly along the lines required, and which can be adapted as time proceeds to fit the real needs of the general manager.

2. *A computer-based system is installed.* The computer services the general ledger, production, and product manager areas with weekly reports and daily summaries. The general manager makes the same request as in Scenario 1.

    This time Fred calls on Bill, the DP manager, who calls on Julie, the systems analyst, who liaises with John, the programmer. Jenny, the program librarian, is also involved, as is Frank, the data clerk who coordinates input controls and data entry. It may take some time to specify the information flow and write the programs, especially if the original request is not specified in detail, or if all the interpersonal communication involved results in errors. If new data types are needed, it may also be necessary to change the formats of the files of stored data. A possible result is a delay of a few days and then the lack of any daily report at all due to bugs introduced by the programmer when rewriting the procedures.

So it can be seen that computer systems may lack flexibility, resulting in increased costs when alterations are needed. On the other hand, the main source of benefit following the implementation of an information system can be this same inflexible character — a transaction can be processed in only one way, the way programmed into the computer, and hence good procedures are always followed.

In this chapter the information systems environment is developed further, concentrating on the part that general management, management of computer-using departments, and the team of systems analysts should each play within it.

1.2 COMPONENTS OF AN INFORMATION SYSTEM

Every information system is made up of a number of components or modules, which are usually connected as shown in Figure 1–1. Data enter the system by means of an input function, and are 'cleansed' by passing through an edit-and-validate module before entering the true data-processing section. The DP section usually comprises reading a file, carrying out some processing, and updating a file. The information which results from the processing is then made available to the outside world through an output module. Usually some form of control balancing takes place so that those in charge of the system can be sure that all the data have been processed. A more detailed description of the various components follows.

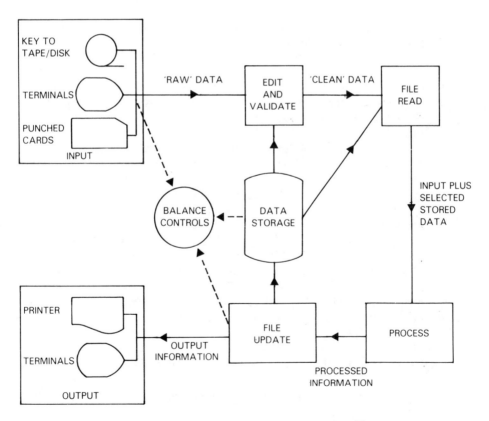

Figure 1-1 Components of an information system

Input function. Transaction data (e.g. hours worked by employees, goods received, invoices issued, inquiries) are converted from human- to machine-readable format. These data are 'raw', in that they may contain errors or omissions.

Edit and validate. The raw data are checked or 'cleansed' by reference to (1) format, range, and other criteria (editing), and (2) data held in the storage device (validation).

File read. The frequently performed task of accessing the data storage either to obtain additional data relevant to the processing function or to satisfy an inquiry (e.g. previous payroll totals, inventory balances, customer details) is the first function in the DP section. In simple systems there may be no need for this function since all necessary data are provided by the input function.

Process. Calculations are performed on the input and stored data to produce information which is to be output or returned to the data storage.

File update. The content of the data storage is altered to agree with those results of the processing which are required for subsequent reference, processing, or output.

Output. The required information is transformed to human-readable form.

Controls. A series of checks on input, output, and stored details are performed, involving (in part) counts of transactions and totals of specific entities (e.g. a check that the total hours worked, as entered to the system, balances with the total hours paid on the printed pay dockets).

Data storage. Although the data-storage unit is not an 'active' element in this system representation, it clearly plays a central role in linking the different components, and the results of earlier processing with current operations. It also provides a 'bridge' between different categories of systems (e.g. payroll, costing, and general-ledger systems use common data elements but are processed at different times).

The emphasis placed on each of these subsections of the system naturally depends on the particular application. For example, a transaction file update requires very careful consideration being given to cleansing the data and to the processing to make sure that erroneous information is not entered on files, and that appropriate output is generated. The control balancing is also vital for this type of application. At the other end of the spectrum is the example of an inquiry for a management information system. In this case the main emphasis is on the file-read and output modules, the first ensuring that appropriate data are selected from the files, and the second that output is presented in such a way that the person seeking the information can readily determine its importance. Here the control-balancing operations may be trivial indeed — restricted simply to ensuring that all messages input to the systems do, in fact, receive a reply.

1.3   ATTRIBUTES OF AN EFFECTIVE INFORMATION SYSTEM

Information in the information system environment has two important requirements:

- It must have surprise value
- It must be relevant

The first characteristic implies that the information was unknown to the recipient before the system produced it (or at least its significance was not apparent). The second entails an attempt by the system's designer to ensure that the information contained in output reports is only that which needs to be acted on or is essential background briefing.

To produce information having these qualities, an information system requires certain attributes. These attributes are:

- Decision-oriented reporting — meaning that the output from the system is designed to facilitate decision making by those persons who receive the output. Note that a choice to take 'no action' is effectively a decision in this context.
- Effective processing of the data — indicating that the checks and controls on input and output are appropriate, system timing is meaningful in the context of the application, and the utilization of the hardware and software environment is efficient.
- Effective management of the data — e.g. requiring attention to be paid to: the timing of file updates, the accuracy of input data, controlled redundancy, the maintenance of integrity once data are stored within the system, the security requirements while the data are being used and on disposal, and appropriate back-up facilities.
- Adequate flexibility — i.e. it is possible to meet changing needs of the organization because the system can be updated as new computing technology becomes available, and can adapt to changes in the behavioural characteristics of those persons associated with it.
- A satisfying user environment — those responsible for the system's design make sure that the machine–people interfaces are appropriate for the tasks involved.

PART B — INTERFACING THE INFORMATION SYSTEM WITH THE ORGANIZATION

1.4   THE IMPACT OF INFORMATION SYSTEMS

The expectation of economic or performance-related benefits has often led to the rapid penetration of computer-based information systems into all facets of an organization's activities. While the benefits given by increased productivity, reduced working-capital needs, etc. are obviously prime planning targets, the capability of increasing production, services, or turnover without proportional staff increases is seen as a major objective for many businesses and government departments.

The criteria used for selecting information system projects are discussed in some detail in Chapter 12. However, it is valuable at this stage to outline some of the less specific effects that information systems have on organizations. The following comments are drawn partly from research reported in *The Human Side of Information Processing* (Bjorn-Andersen, 1980).

1.4.1   Frequently Observed Results

Organizational structure. Computers eliminate routine work to a greater extent than they create it. There is also a reduction in the number of clerks and their supervisors relative to the quantity of work performed. Thus productivity is increased. The number of administrative levels is reduced, presumably because middle management requires less time for information reporting, and there are fewer people to control.

Job content. Tasks tend to become more routine at the clerical and supervisory levels, but more challenging and demanding of skill at the more senior levels. However, computers also permit solution of problems that cannot be attacked manually, with a consequent increase in job satisfaction at the relevant levels.

Decision making. While the provision of more timely, accurate, and comprehensive information does not necessarily improve decision making (see Chapter 13), there is a trend towards the integration and consolidation of decision systems. This is because it becomes increasingly possible to base reports on data drawn from related and yet different operating areas or functions. In addition, there is often more formality in the decision-making process, as action rules are made explicit for design purposes.

1.4.2   Results Conditional on the System's Design and Management

Interpersonal communication. The amount and quality of communication possible between people after the implementation of a computer system depends greatly on the design philosophy adopted. While it is frequently contended that computers reduce interaction between people, it certainly is not a required or inescapable result.

Decentralization or centralization. Many observers similarly condemn information systems as being instruments of centralization — especially in the decision-making area. However, it is obvious that a computer's information reporting can support any organizational structure, depending on how the information flow is designed. Thus the net effect depends on the organization's management style.

Decision making. The introduction of a computer system can change the emphasis in individual decision making from the case-by-case approach to the setting of criteria and threshold levels for 'system' decisions. That is, the computer system can take over many structured decision responsibilities. The alternatives for the designer are to increase or to decrease rigidity and inflexibility in the decision area. Admittedly, including flexibility does usually require extra design creativity and effort and, in the absence of such effort, it is likely that a more rigid system would result.

User satisfaction. There is no inherent characteristic of computer-based information systems which increases either satisfaction or dissatisfaction for the system's users. Considerable criticism has been made of the approach taken by designers who focus attention on the technical and financial aspects of a project to the detriment of the human interface design. These issues are discussed more fully in Chapter 12.

1.5 ADMINISTRATION OF THE INFORMATION SYSTEMS FUNCTION

The administration of the information systems function within any organization requires coordination at the policy, applications, and technical levels. Thus a triad, comprising general, departmental, and information systems managements, as shown in Figure 1–2, is involved. Communication between the three management areas is essential if an effective and efficient environment is to be established and maintained.

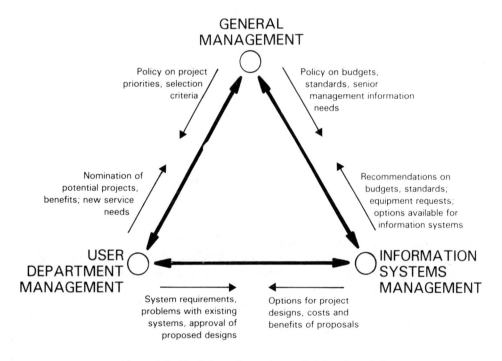

Figure 1–2 The information systems administration triad

1.5.1   General Management

In industry, commerce, and government the picture of senior management involvement with computer projects has been poor. Nevertheless, there is mounting evidence which shows that it is important for senior executives to play an active role in setting the scene within which computer projects are selected and developed for their enterprise. Surveys carried out over a ten-year period show a strong relationship between the success of computer projects and senior management involvement. Although this connection between the involvement of senior executives and the success with projects is well known, there is far less awareness of the appropriate nature of that involvement and how it can be facilitated and encouraged.

With what aspects of computer systems ought senior managers to be involved? Clearly they would have no desire, nor would it be possible for them, to be involved in the detail of the various projects because their interests lie with the broader issues and policy questions. It follows that policy determination is the key area; normally it is the task of information systems management to propose the options for consideration. The issues with which it is important that senior management are involved include:

1. Setting organization-wide objectives for the use of computers (e.g. staff reductions, decentralized decision making)
2. Specifying criteria to be used for project selection and approval
3. Reviewing the implications of technical developments to ensure advantage is taken of them
4. Setting up a mechanism to review regularly the effectiveness of current activities
5. Specifying broad project management policy parameters; some examples:
   - Who is responsible for making each type of decision?
   - On what basis should that person make decisions?
   - Is there to be a limit on total annual expenditure on computing?
   - What constraints should be placed on systems designers regarding the impact of computer systems on people and procedures?
   - What is the best permissible degree of departmental autonomy with respect to the selection of computer projects and the approval of equipment and software purchases?
   - What standards are required for computer project work, data management equipment, and audit procedures within the organization, and who should set them?
6. Establishing procedures which ensure that there is adequate communication within the enterprise about the progress on computer projects, the difficulties being encountered, and any conflicts arising

The other major area in which senior management must take an active part is the selection of projects. It is most important that a master plan of potential computer projects be agreed upon at senior management level at least once every six months. The purpose of this project master plan is to make sure that the work being developed by the technical specialists in the engineering, data-processing, and other areas which may be involved with computer projects is an appropriate use of the available financial and staff resources. Preparation of such a project master plan requires each key area of the enterprise being studied to determine how computer systems can be used to improve corporate performance by removing or relieving constraints on the organization's activities. Normally there are many more projects which pass the project approval criteria than there are people or computer equipment resources to carry out development and implementation. Given the constraints on expenditure which have been set within the computer policy it is therefore necessary to determine a sequence of projects which best suits the overall objectives. These issues are further developed in Chapter 12.

1.5.2   User Department Management

A reluctance to become involved with the underlying technical concepts of computers is also exhibited by managers in control of departments which are, or will be, making use of information systems. Just as a well-defined policy environment is critical for success, so it is equally important to have the active participation of those responsible for operating the system once it is implemented.

Six general reasons for the failure of a system to achieve its objectives are proposed by Oliver Wight (1974) in his book *The Executive's New Computer*. In summary they are:

- The system's design is over-sophisticated and too ambitious for the project scope — i.e. a conspiracy for sophistication has been allowed to gain control, and technical excellence becomes more important than practical utility.
- The application is not appropriate — i.e. poor project selection techniques have been used.
- The system's designers have assumed, or user management has abdicated, responsibility for the system's design — i.e. proper control over broad system design procedures has not been applied.
- The system is designed to supplant, not support, the user — i.e. the system's designers have failed to appreciate the role of the user.
- The implementation of the project has been over-optimistically planned — i.e. management has not recognized the impact of the design on the department, and the amount of change involved cannot be absorbed.
- The department is incapable of managing with any new system — i.e. the project should not have been attempted because the application environment is not healthy.

All of these problem situations are in the province of the user manager and they demonstrate the type of involvement needed. Therefore, management of the user department ought to play a prime role in:

- Project selection, which includes considering modifications to existing systems — by nominating candidates which fall within the overall policy guidelines, for inclusion in the master plan.
- Approving the technical approach proposed by the system's designers — after reviewing the implications for the application, especially the operator interface and cost effectiveness aspects.
- Project management and control — in particular monitoring aspects relating to the user interface, the attainment of performance objectives, and the implementation schedule.

To be able to take part in these activities, the department management needs the technical advice of the computer specialists. The best form for this advice is in the nature of recommended options with an explanation of the technical implications of each option.

It is sometimes proposed that a representative of the user department assume the project manager role — and accept full responsibility for success or failure of the entire project. As users become more familiar with system design techniques and become experienced in system operation, there will be increasing numbers of people qualified to take on this task. For the present (1982), most organizations are content to have a technical specialist in charge of projects with more junior user representatives acting in advisory capacities. Chapter 12 gives more details on options for user participation in the project.

1.5.3   Information Systems' Department Management

The technology of computers clearly has a dominating influence on the information systems' administrators. Developments in hardware, systems software and, more recently, applications development aids and packages all provide 'solutions' looking for 'problems'. Thus as new approaches become available the range and scope of options open for new and existing computer applications increases.

Ideally, it is the responsibility of those leading the information systems function to keep both general management and users aware of the potential impact of technical developments on the organization — by recommending changes to policy on standards, equipment selection, and projects. The desirable role of information systems managers in the policy environment has already been covered (Sections 1.5.1 and 1.5.2). It is particularly important that the 'leave it to the experts' syndrome be avoided by actively encouraging user participation, otherwise there is a real risk of the resulting system designs proving unacceptable.

1.6   THE STAGES OF INFORMATION SYSTEM MATURITY

Richard Nolan (1979) has hypothesized that each organization passes through six stages in its progression from initial involvement with computers to a mature information systems environment. The hypothesis suggests that the rate of progression is likely to be different for each organization depending on many factors including industry classification, management style, and size. The six stages nominated by Nolan (see Figure 1–3) are:

1. Initiation. A period during which the first computers are acquired and early attempts to develop applications are made — the projects are not necessarily the most cost effective, but are more likely to be those close to the hearts of the people who originally proposed the computer acquisition. This is a period in which the technicians tend to dominate decision making on project control and equipment/ software configuration. Rate of expenditure growth is relatively slow.

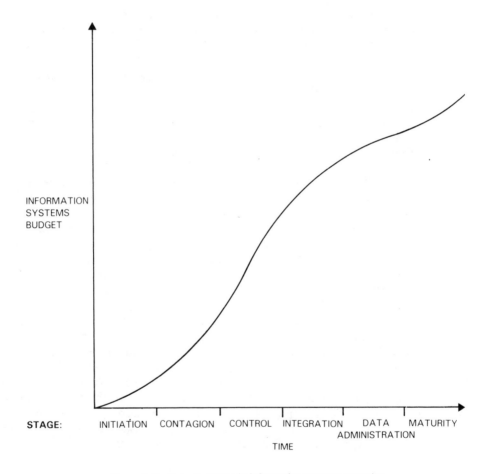

Figure 1-3   Nolan's stages in information systems maturity

2. Contagion. At some point the potential of computer-based systems becomes apparent, and systems development commences on many applications perceived as contributing to the organization's performance. The growth in expenditure on staff and equipment accelerates sharply as enthusiasm develops —

rather like a disease! While the technical specialists still dominate project decisions, the role of users starts to develop, initially among the less conservative executives and supervisors.

3. Control. With rising expenditure levels and the surfacing of problems concerning underestimation of project resources, user dissatisfaction with systems, and disagreement over priorities, it becomes clear that a greater degree of control is necessary. Computer systems are perceived as not being automatically profitable ventures, and the situation is often regarded by senior executives as being out of control. As a result, a number of constraints on computing activities are rapidly imposed. These frequently include:

- Steering-committee formation at policy and project selection levels
- Stringent budgetary controls and expenditure approval procedures
- Effectiveness audits of existing applications and management standards

4. Integration. It takes some time for an organization to modify the control measures it adopted in Stage 3 to the point at which an effective environment is created. Steering committees take time to find their true role while their members come to understand the issues involved, and the whole information systems function needs to adjust from the heady uncontrolled days of Stage 2 to the relative austerity of the more stable Stage 4. User involvement in policy and project management gradually increases as experience is gained.

5. Data administration. The concept of the set of data being a major corporate resource becomes well accepted as experience with the sharing of data across applications increases during Stage 4. The increased ability of the organization to store and control its data resources, resulting from the development of large-capacity disk units and database management software, soon requires the data-processing management to focus attention on data management. Data become a key factor in planning. Note that all data may not be physically or logically under the control of one DBMS (database management system), but the administration of data is standardized.

The database administrator is appointed, which often results in additional controls being placed on designers and users while codes, data definitions, etc. are rationalized. In many ways, this results in problems similar to those of Stage 3 when budgetary and project management controls were introduced.

6. Maturity. Perhaps this nirvana is never reached. In this stage: users assume an appropriate shared but dominant role in project management; data resources are controlled but flexible; the flow of information within computer systems reflects the 'real-world' applications; and the planning goal is to reach a condition where the best possible use, for overall effectiveness, is made of the data resources.

PART C — THE INFORMATION SYSTEMS PROJECT

1.7 THE SYSTEMS LIFECYCLE

1.7.1 Description

Once a project has been chosen, the systems development cycle commences. Every project passes through a series of phases in much the same way as a building project is conceived, designed, specified, constructed, and finally fitted out for occupation (Figure 1–4). Within each phase there are a number of tasks which must be performed before it is possible to proceed to the next phase. The various phases in the system's development cycle are frequently referred to as the *systems lifecycle.* The lifecycle is closely related to the system design and development methodologies.

In addition, the lifecycle forms the basis for project control, since the project managers tend to monitor the output of the design team at the completion of each phase — these forming natural checkpoints.

There are many different methods for representing the lifecycle, but all contain essentially the same components, the main differences being in the boundaries which the various authors perceive as important. The representation of the lifecycle used in this book is:

Phase 1 — Statement of the terms of reference and specification
            of requirements
Phase 2 — The feasibility study
Phase 3 — Systems analysis
Phase 4 — The logical design of the new system
Phase 5 — The physical design of the new system
Phase 6 — Programming
Phase 7 — Implementation
Phase 8 — Post-implementation review

See also Figure 1–4. Each of these phases are now dealt with in more detail.

Terms of reference and initial requirements specification. The best starting point for any project is a statement of requirements and expectations by the system's users. Sometimes this is prepared after consultations with information systems management about the applicability of computing technology to the problem area involved, and the general order of costs which would be incurred. This statement must be converted to a specification before detailed work can commence.

The amount of effort needed to complete the requirements specification varies greatly. It depends upon such factors as the complexity of the target area, the users' knowledge of their environment, the risk and the cost of failure, the technical capability of the computer specialist, and the data volumes. If there is any uncertainty, special approaches may be necessary to limit the scope of work to manage-

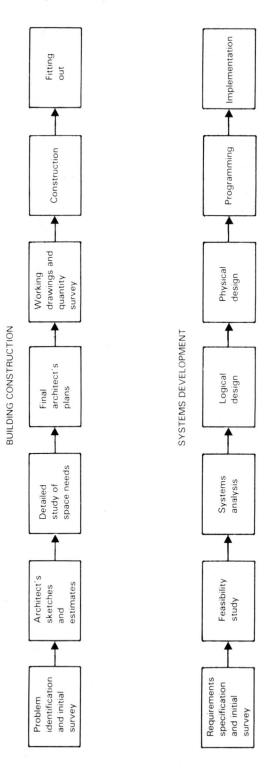

Figure 1–4 Comparison of the stages in building construction and the systems development lifecycle

able proportions. Sometimes a pilot study or some other form of simulation or experimentation is necessary.

The feasibility study. A preliminary analysis of the problem area should be carried out in sufficient detail to determine what options are available to meet the requirements stated in the terms of reference. This phase is critical because it determines the overall architecture of the new system, and hence the project controllers need to review the range of options, and their implications, carefully. Once the design proper commences it becomes much harder to alter direction.

Systems analysis. This step involves an analysis of the existing system in full detail, paying particular attention to the physical flow of data and information through the system, and highlighting any bottlenecks or other constraints on improvement in performance.

The logical design of the new system. This phase consists of the preparation of a user specification for the flow of data and information both within the system and at the interface between the user and the computing environment. In this phase it is important to determine *what* it is that the computer system will be doing, rather than *how* the solution is to be implemented on the computer.

The physical design of the new system. In this phase the system designer explores the means for implementing the logical design on the computer system by designing files and the details of computer program modules.

Programming. Programming involves the design and coding of programs which cause the computer to follow the steps outlined in the physical design. This phase also covers the testing of the programs to make sure that they are working within specifications.

Implementation. In this phase the complete system and its implementation in the user environment are tested. Frequently this includes a cut-over period during which the old procedures and the new system are both operating to verify that correct results are obtained from the new procedures.

Post-implementation review. A review of the performance of the system after it has been in operation for approximately six months is desirable. This review determines if the system is successfully meeting the requirements stated in the terms of reference, and whether the anticipated benefits are being obtained.

1.7.2   Resource Allocation

The actual proportion of resources spent on each phase of the systems lifecycle depends very much on the nature of the project. For example, a system which involves the creation of a large and complex data file with relatively little reporting will have great emphasis in the logical and physical design areas, whereas the implementation and testing phases will be relatively inexpensive in resource terms. By contrast, a project which makes use of an existing data file to provide comprehensive production-scheduling facilities may require a large part of the resources to be given to implementation, as production operators are trained to use the new procedures. And in the case of a system designed to assist decision making at middle-manager level, it may not be at all clear exactly what information is needed, how it should be provided, or even whether the system will result in better performance after it is completed. This is the type of situation in which extra effort needs to be spent on requirements specification and feasibility studies. Table 1–1 gives approximate proportions of resources generally used in each of the lifecycle phases.

Phase	Proportion of resources %
1. Terms of reference and initial requirements analysis	1–5
2. Feasibility study	8–15
3. Systems analysis	10–15
4. Logical design	15–20
5. Physical design	15–25
6. Programming	10–20
7. Implementation	15–30
8. Post-audit review	1

1.8 SYSTEM DEVELOPMENT METHODOLOGY

Although the systems lifecycle is a useful framework within which to consider the whole systems analysis–design process, those persons responsible for carrying out the tasks need a more detailed representation or methodology to follow. Without an adequate methodology, less experienced analysts/designers may have difficulty knowing what aspect of the project should be worked on at any given time. In addition, it is usually important for all the individuals working on systems development within the one organization to follow the same procedures in terms of the sequence of steps and the means for documenting the results of their analysis and design work to assist in both project control and the interchangeability of staff.

This need for a formal representation or methodology was perceived fairly early in the development of information systems, and the first such methodology to become widely known was the Study Organization Plan (SOP). SOP was developed at IBM in the 1960s, and is described in detail in the book *Management Systems* (Glans *et al.*, 1968); it is a system which depends on a number of forms. The forms are filled in by the analyst/designer, and they cover the present business activities, the requirements of the new system, and the design process itself.

Another 'forms-driven' system was developed by NCR and titled Accurately Defined Systems, or ADS (Lynch, 1969). This system lays particular emphasis on the physical design phase and the later stages of the logical design phase of the lifecycle. Its particular merit is the way that the different sets of forms are cross-referenced to minimize errors of omission resulting from the designer neglecting either to provide for input of information which is to be subsequently output, or to specify an essential processing activity.

Since that time a wide range of development methodologies have been introduced, all based on a detailed set of steps and subtasks to be performed in each of the lifecycle phases, together with appropriate documentation specifications. A particular set of subtasks for the phases of the systems development lifecycle are proposed in this book and are detailed in Chapter 12.

More recently there has been a trend towards specifying new conceptual approaches to design methodology, approaches which generally fall under the term 'top-down structured design'. These approaches fit within almost any sequence of subtasks, but frequently they require particular documentation techniques to be used, for example the data flow diagram tends to be a requirement for the structured analysis and design procedures. More detailed discussions of these methodologies are given in Chapters 2 and 6.

Note that most of these approaches to the design project are appropriate when the requirements are well specified and the problem area is structured, i.e. the project has a fairly stable environment and there are known sets of rules to govern activities. When uncertainty surrounds the project, other types of lifecycle and methodology may be more appropriate. These are discussed in Chapter 13, which considers the design of decision support systems.

1.9   THE ROLES OF THE SYSTEMS ANALYST/DESIGNER

The title 'systems analyst', or sometimes 'systems analyst/designer', is usually given to the person responsible for the analysis and design tasks associated with the development of an information system. A consideration of the tasks to be performed in the systems lifecycle, and of the relationship which should exist between the technical specialists and systems users, shows that the systems analyst has to assume a variety of roles throughout the project. Among these roles are:

- Analyst — studying the existing system in detail, with meticulous attention to critical aspects
- Designer — proposing new procedures for information flow, reporting, and computer processing
- Technical writer — documenting the results of the design effort; different versions may be needed for the non-technical users of the system and for the other team members who may be responsible for subsequent aspects of the design or for maintenance following implementation
- Consultant — advising options available to users, and indicating the implications that each of these options has for the performance of the system
- Team member — being a member of the design team, the analyst needs to work with other computer specialists and user department representatives towards achieving a common goal
- Behavioural scientist — attempting to design an interface between the system's users and the computer so that the design itself and its method of implementation results in users being satisfied with the final result

Consequently, to be effective, the analyst needs to combine a variety of skills, some technical and some social, at a level of detail which varies from the broad overall picture at the start of the project to the detailed and precise considerations of the analysis and physical design phases. It is not an easy assignment and it is no wonder that it is frequently done poorly.

REFERENCES

N. BJORN-ANDERSEN (ed.), *The Human Side of Information Processing*, North Holland, Amsterdam, 1980.

T. B. GLANS, B. GRAD, D. HOLSTEIN, W. E. MYERS & R. N. SCHMIDT, *Management Systems*, Holt, Rinehart and Winston, New York, 1968.

H. J. LYNCH, 'ADS: A Technique in Systems Documentation', *Data Base* vol. 1, no. 1, Spring 1969, pp. 11-23.

R. L. NOLAN, 'Managing the Crises in Data Processing', *Harvard Business Review*, March–April 1979, pp. 115-26.

CASE STUDY — INTERNATIONAL TRANSPORT COMPANY

In 1979 the International Transport Company decided to review its data-processing operations. This move was initiated by the Director of Finance Mr J. B. Hendricks, who was responsible for the data-processing function, because he judged that the performance of the company in this area had deteriorated in terms of value for money, that the company was not making the best use of the potential of information systems, and also that his fellow executives' attitudes towards computer systems design and operations were not sufficiently constructive. Mr Hendricks set the following objectives for the formal study into the computer operations of the company:

1. To identify corporate and division information requirements in terms of type and frequency
2. To establish the current status of data-processing facilities and the adequacy of design of current systems
3. To determine the tasks necessary to provide the information indicated by objective 1 that is not currently available
4. To report on shortcomings of existing corporate computing policy
5. To present a plan, which covers both the short and the long term, indicating the resources required for the tasks determined by objective 3

Background

The following background notes were prepared by Mr K. Joy, the Data Processing Manager, to help the consultants prepare for the review.

ITC is a transport company providing a wide range of transportation services including long distance haulage by road, rail, sea, and air, intracity courier services, security services, and specialist transport services for certain industries in all states of Australia. The company has recently been reorganized on a functional basis along the lines shown in Figure 1–5. The operating divisions of the company are:

- Long Distance Haulage: intercity and interstate transport by road, rail, sea, and air.
- Courier Services: metropolitan taxi trucks and intracity parcel distribution.
- Security Services: armoured car transport for cash and other valuables.
- Specialist Transport Services: bulk commodities, refrigerated transport services, and international services such as storage, customs clearing, and international freight forwarding.

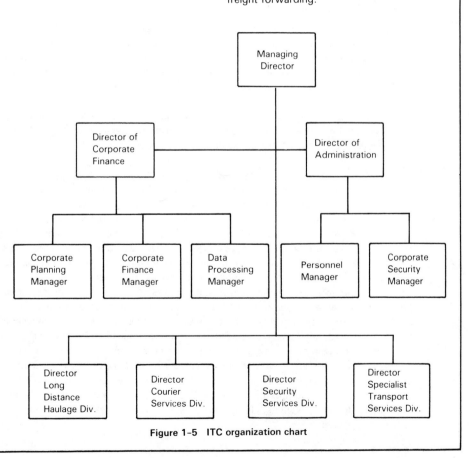

Figure 1–5   ITC organization chart

Financial statistics

A brief summary of the financial position of the company is given in the table.

	$ million		
	1976	1977	1978
Turnover	95	108	150
Net profit	3.0	4.5	5.8
Total asset used in the business	69	75	97
Profit in cents per $ turnover	2.8c	3.2c	3.0c

Data processing history

The growth evidenced in the financial statistics for the years 1977 and 1978 was achieved mainly by acquisition of smaller transport companies. Although the number of acquisitions in earlier years was somewhat smaller, the history of data processing in the organization has always been one of the problems associated with absorbing the companies which have been taken over into the computer system set up for the parent company.

Data-processing operations in the company commenced in 1964 when a IBM 1401 machine was installed to handle vehicle maintenance costing and, later, the debtors' system. In 1978 the systems operating are:

- *Motor vehicle costing:* This was the first system introduced in 1964 and is designed to report on costs incurred by individual equipment items — originally only motor vehicles but now any asset of either a capital or an operational nature. Originally designed for the 1401, it now runs in 'emulation mode' on the current computer. Thus it is a kind of combined asset register and costing system. It is written in Assembler language and only rarely does it operate without failure during the monthly production run. A new costing system has been specified but not implemented due to pressures of other work.
- *Debtors' system:* The present debtors' system is designed to produce monthly statements, but only minimal reporting is made for management use. The current system is written completely in COBOL and was first implemented in 1972, but is based on the old design implemented in 1965. The editing system is unwieldy, but its major problem centres around the customer name and address files, of which there are two, one for the Long Distance Haulage Division and the other serving the needs of all other divisions. This resulted from a change in corporate policy in 1976, and hence there are, in effect, two separate debtors' systems. This system is the major consumer of computer resources.

- *General ledger system:* This system currently provides most of the financial reporting of both an operational and a balance sheet nature. Its major function is the computerization of accounting procedures because the reports are usually received in final form too late for decision-making purposes. In ordinary months the general ledger system tends to be run at least twice to facilitate posting of late accounts and the posting of last-minute interdivision transfers. At the end of each six-month period, as many as six or seven runs may be performed in order to tidy up the interdivision transfers. Steps should be taken to improve the effectiveness of the posting procedures for these transfers.

- *Creditors:* An old system is used by most divisions of the company and has been operating since 1966. Essentially it is the same design as the earlier debtors' system with a reversed sign. The programs are written in Assembler. A new system has recently been introduced but has been used by only one section of the company. This is also based on a reverse debtors' principle, but it does include a capability of printing cheques. There are no linkages between the old system and the general ledger and costing systems. Other divisions are being urged to join the new system, but are reluctant since it will involve them in a greater responsibility for data entry.

- *Automatic invoicing preparation:* Because of the large number of individual transactions handled by the company it has long been felt desirable to implement an invoicing system which can automatically extend the details on freight consignment dockets and issue the invoice. The system would create an input file for use with a new, or the existing, debtors' systems. At this time the system is operating for the Security Services Division and a system has been designed and programmed for the Long Distance Haulage and Courier Divisions. The first trial implementation of this second system was not successful. Modifications are being carried out. Excessive editing rejects and inadequate reporting were the main reasons for failure of this trial.

- *Other systems:* Smaller systems are operating for share register procedures and provide minor reporting services, such as cheque reconciliation, for some divisions.

Currently installed equipment

The company currently has installed an IBM 370-148 computer with 1.5 Mbyte central memory, 500 Mbyte of disk storage, 4 tapes, printers, etc. Its loading is three shifts per day, five days per week for half a month and two shifts per day for the remainder of the month. Implementation of the automatic invoicing system will use up most of the remaining available time.

Current staff

Systems and program personnel currently consists of three maintenance programmers, three business system analysts and two programmers.

Current budget

The budget for computing services is $850 000 for 1978, made up of $240 000 for key punching, $410 000 for computer operators and $200 000 for systems programming.

Corporate Management Requirements

The consultants, J. Davidson and R. Brown, first interviewed the Managing Director Mr Turner, and the Director of Corporate Finance Mr Hendricks, to determine their attitudes towards the needs of corporate management for information from the company's computer systems.

Q: What do you regard as the basic objective of ITC's computer systems?

MR TURNER: In our business it is important for the organization to operate in as decentralized a manner as possible. The managers of all of our sections need to be encouraged to run their businesses by direct contact with clients. The information systems must be designed to reflect this need for section managers to be able to manage relatively independently and must also be flexible so that we can regroup our sections without requiring changes to the computer systems. At the same time it must be possible for division managers and corporate executives to be able to rapidly obtain the picture concerning the profitability and the trends in costs and revenues as they occur. We also need to direct our management more towards a return on investment objective, which means they need up-to-date figures with respect to their profit in relation to assets employed.

MR HENDRICKS: Our key information requirements centre around profit and loss and return on investments. We must have weekly profit-and-loss figures which are up-to-date and accurate. Currently our systems are only available on a monthly basis and are not accurate, and usually need to be adjusted several times to account for accrued revenues and costs as well as interdivision transfers. We need to be able to spot weaknesses quickly and we must be able to reconcile easily from individual sectional results through to divisions and to the corporate results.

Q: How do you regard the adequacy of the general ledger system which is currently prepared by the data-processing department?

MR HENDRICKS: The general ledger system is virtually useless for decision-making purposes since it has to be altered a number of times before the various division directors will accept that the figures represent the real situation. That may take six weeks. At present anyone can raise a debit or a credit on any account in the system and, consequently, we face much buck-passing, particularly at the end of six-monthly periods. We must move to a situation where weekly and monthly profit-and-loss figures are available within a few days of the end of the month and where monthly balance sheets are also prepared. Cleaning up the posting procedures is a high priority.

Q: Where should the responsibility for data control and the timeliness of data input and editing procedures lie?

MR TURNER: This must be the responsibility of the individual section managers who supply the data. In fact, perhaps they should operate their own computers.

Q: Are you proposing then that the company should move towards a totally decentralized computer system?

MR TURNER: I don't care whether we have a centralized or a decentralized system as long as it meets our objectives, and section managers come to rely on the computer system for their records on profitability, turnover, etc. And it must be simple for the clients to determine from the system output how much they owe the company and for what services. Some of the other executives have stronger opinions on this — like Mr Hendricks.

MR HENDRICKS: I believe data is a corporate resource, hence decentralization of data storage would be undesirable. Separate computers are out, but distributed data entry and file access are OK.

Q: Do you have a standard chart of accounts and standard coding systems?

MR HENDRICKS: At this stage we have neither. A standard chart of accounts is currently being considered by the Corporate Finance Department but there are problems in having it accepted by the divisional managers. We had a policy of standard coding systems for customer names and addresses but this was not enforced and now I believe we have at least two sets of customer names and addresses.

Q: Do you have a corporate data-processing plan?

MR TURNER: We want to implement any computer system which can be justified in economic terms. However, I am not sure our current systems meet this criterion.

MR HENDRICKS: Our plan at present is to implement the automatic invoicing system for Long Distance Haulage and Courier Services. Beyond that we must move to the preparation of profit-and-loss, balance sheet, costing, asset register, and capital expenditure systems.

Q: How about a purchasing system?

MR HENDRICKS: Yes, that too.

Q: You only have three business analysts, and that doesn't seem enough for the program you just outlined.

MR HENDRICKS: Once we've set up our plan we will hire more if necessary.

Q: What time frame are you looking at?

MR HENDRICKS: Profit-and-loss figures within twelve months and the rest as soon as possible after that.

MR TURNER: Yes, that seems reasonable.

Q: How do you evaluate project proposals?

MR HENDRICKS: All our projects are treated the same way, they must meet the investment hurdle D.C.F. rate of 25 per cent.

Q: Who evaluates the costs and benefits?

MR HENDRICKS: The computer people, of course, look after the cost side and we ask the operating divisions to estimate benefits.

Divisional Management Requirements

Ms Davidson and Mr Brown interviewed all the directors of the operating divisions. The information requirements seen as being common were: weekly profit-and-loss figures, broken down for each section within the division and against budget estimates; sales analyses by type of customer and type of business, also weekly on some kind of exception-reporting basis; automatic extension of freight consignment notes for invoicing purposes was essential for rapid reporting; and costing systems for all operating costs.

The directors of the four divisions also gave their individual perceptions.

Mr K. Green, Director of the Long Distance Haulage Division: 'Our division is the major revenue earner but uses about 70 per cent of the assets and thus is not as profitable when judged on a return on investment basis.

'The computer systems people from head office did a poor job on the automatic invoicing system and it was unable to handle the volume of information. Automatic invoicing will solve many of our problems when it is operational. The decisions I make, which affect profitability, nearly all centre around the information it could provide — if it works. We need to control our own data-processing installation and our own systems analysts and programmers because we can't rely on head office people. We should do our own edits in the office, rather than send to the sections for corrections. The operators out there are unreliable, some of them are just out of jail. Give them more than half-an-hour for lunch and they need retraining.

'Hendricks and his lot seem intent on controlling all the information for power play reasons. We only want to get on with the job of making profits.

'It is absolutely critical for us to be able to allocate customer codes rapidly and, therefore, we cannot operate within the system which was proposed for corporate control of customer coding. It is more important to serve the needs of the customer and the operating divisions than to satisfy the requirements of head office people.

'The motor vehicle costing system is virtually useless and our division makes little use of it. The figures are usually wrong and arrive late. Costs are only important on a monthly basis, revenue is our problem variable. The general ledger system is also of little use due to the fiddling that occurs and the fact that it is so late.'

Mr E. George, Director of the Security Services Division: 'The Security Services Division is the most profitable in the company, based on a return on assets.

'We get good results from the motor vehicle costing system because we take a great deal of care over the input we submit to it. It gives me a good handle on our cost movements each month. But the general ledger system is not satisfactory because it is always late and because other divisions tend to try to obscure the figures by accruing revenue and costs when it suits them. Our division requires much better sales analysis figures than we get now from automatic invoicing but current customer-coding systems don't allow us to break down details of consignees or consignors; they only refer to invoicing addresses.

'We generate relatively few new customers each month and so are happy with the concept of centralized customer-coding allocation system.'

Ms D. Thomas, Director of the Courier Services Division: 'Our business generates new customers almost every minute and therefore we must be able to allocate customer codes ourselves. The debtors' system is too inflexible in that we cannot produce anything other than monthly statements even though many of our customers only use us once every two or three years, if that. It is accurate though — as far as it goes. We do a large amount of subcontracting work for the other divisions, and since we operate on a profit-centre basis we must be able to enter divisional transfers into the general ledger and profit-and-loss systems.

'The motor vehicle costing system is useless — even this desk is classified as a motor vehicle and we get a printout every month telling us how much petrol it uses. I understand Security Services make better use of the system but their environment is much more static.

'Sales statistics are vitally important for us. These statistics could be given by the new automatic invoicing system but it hasn't been designed for this and it's only useful as an input to the debtors' systems. Even then it doesn't work properly because editing procedures are inadequate, and the people in the sections don't take enough care in filling in the forms. In our class of business we will never solve the data-input accuracy situation unless input is checked at its source. Green is right on this point, we should do our own thing.'

Mr G. Huntley, Director of the Specialist Services Transport Division: 'Our division operates in a totally different manner to all the others, providing a large range of services, often on the basis of contract quotes. Even though monthly profit-and-loss and balance sheet figures are good enough for us, Corporate Finance is trying to force weekly profit-and-loss reporting down our necks but it has no relevance for us since many of our contracts take much longer than that to run.

'I was talking to an executive of a small computer company at the club last week. It seems his systems would suit our needs well for much less than Joy charges. I've asked for a price.'

Data Processing Management

Ms Davidson and Mr Brown then interviewed the Data Processing Manager, Mr K. Joy, and the Computer Operations Supervisor, Mrs U. Johnson.

Q: Why do you have so much computer disk storage given over to the customer file?

MR JOY: The operating divisions are unable to agree on the procedures for allocating customer codes and so we need to hold two copies of the customer files although the same names appear twice in a high proportion of cases and the same code often refers to different customers in the two files. The disk-storage usage could be halved if we could get around this problem but nobody takes any notice of our requests on this matter.

Q: Many of the users have mentioned difficulties with the timing of reports and with their accuracy. Have you got any comments on this?

MRS JOHNSON: The users provide us with very bad service on data input — 90 per cent of the data input arrives for key punching and editing on the last four days of the month and the first five days of the next month. In spite of repeated requests the situation has been like this for some years. Then 80 per cent of our input batches of data fail to pass the edit procedures, and it is impossible to continue processing a batch until all edits have been fixed. Often sections never respond to our request for corrections to errors such as non-existent customer numbers, service codes, etc. In many cases we simply print invoices without names and addresses and return them to the originating section in the hope that they will fill in the appropriate name and address, since otherwise they keep sending back the forms with the same wrong customer number.

MR JOY: Yes, the situation is really bad, there appears to be nothing we can do to fix it and we muddle on as best we can. Senior executives are not prepared to discipline the divisions over DP matters.

Q: I understand you have problems with the motor vehicle costing system each month. Some users comment that their results are useless.

MRS JOHNSON: That would be the Long Distance Haulage Division. Half the time they don't provide us with any operating costs for their assets and in this case we just calculate depreciation figures, and so on. Other users, such as the Security Services Division, are very careful with their data input and the system works well for them. It is a very old system and really should be replaced by a proper costing system, but all our staff are fully engaged on maintenance, or implementation of the automatic invoicing system for the Long Distance and Courier Divisions.

Q: I understand that the automatic invoicing system is regarded as being extremely important.

MR JOY: Yes, it is. Unfortunately, the system was designed five years ago by the previous Data Processing Manager and is only directed towards providing an input to the debtors' system. Much of the information they now want is difficult to provide because of the file structure. In addition, the clerical staff in the sections are of a low standard and they seem incapable of filling in the new form without error. We are currently revamping the system in order to make it easier to input data and to bypass edit errors and at the same time to try to provide some of the information. Our problem is that we find it hard to talk to the executives of the two divisions since they are only rarely available and they keep changing their minds about what figures are important.

Q: How would you rate the quality of your staff and their work?

MR JOY: Most of them are well-experienced DP people. We find it hard to get on with the transport operations people sometimes. Our financial systems were much more adequate before decentralization. I think that was a mistake.

MRS JOHNSON: Yes, they really are dedicated. The maintenance programmers are here all weekend at the end of the month, fixing problems as they occur.

Q: Do you charge the divisions for your services?

MR JOY: All operating costs are charged out to users on the basis of time or volume of data. Systems development costs are also charged out as incurred. We made a profit of $100 000 on our services last year.

Q: You charge out at a rate higher than your costs then?

MR JOY: Yes.

Q: How are new projects selected for design?

MR JOY: We are flat out at the moment anyway, so nothing is really being planned. Ostensibly, the project is approved by Mr Hendricks if it costs more than $10 000. In fact, the division managers decide if they want a system and usually it is approved. Before we decentralized, the DP manager made most of the decisions on projects.

Q: Who is responsible for planning the company's future policy on EDP matters?

MR JOY: Before decentralization I used to decide what I felt was necessary and put this up to corporate executives, who usually approved my ideas. However, you will have noted that most of these systems were in the finance area and did not greatly affect any operating departments. Under the decentralized organization everything affects operating departments, even finance systems, and as a result I am unable to develop a plan in the same way. In addition, some of the newer staff in the operating divisions have their own ideas about how our computer systems should be developed and it is hard to coordinate these.

Q: Do you feel the company is going to suffer because of the lack of a plan?

MR JOY: We have already seen the effect of lack of standardization in coding systems and now with all this talk of minicomputers for data collection, truck-scheduling systems and the like, I believe we are in some danger of ending up with a wide range of unrelated equipment which will be impossible to integrate for database management purposes.

Q: What corporate policy changes do you feel are most important if the company is to get the most out of its computing?

MR JOY: Management must take a firm hand with executives in charge of operating divisions to make sure they don't get their own way in the design and implementation of computer systems. Why, last week I discovered the Long Distance Haulage Division were negotiating with a firm of consultants over the installation of a key-disk data-preparation system which was able to do some sales analysis reporting. We didn't know anything about it. They called it an 'office-communications' system, but it's really a computer. We don't have enough computing resources to be able to distribute them in a decentralized manner and so all computer projects will have to come under my direct control to make sure the company optimizes its return on investment. Besides data is a corporate resource — Green doesn't 'own' his numbers.

ASSIGNMENT

1. Comment on the current status of the data-processing effort within ITC. What stage, using Nolan's terminology, has it reached in its development? What are the major problem areas?

2. Are the attitudes of senior managers within ITC appropriate? Compare those of Mr Hendricks and Mr Green.

3. Comment on the attitudes and performance of Mr Joy and Mrs Johnson.

4. What action would you recommend be taken by ITC to improve the EDP environment?

5. Comment on the ownership-of-data controversy and the related decentralization-of-computers issue.

6. Following receipt of the consultants' report, Mr Hendricks has suggested a number of immediate changes to be made to the ITC information systems environment. These include the following steps:

   (a) In order to improve the data entry accuracy and to provide a database for reporting sales statistics prior to the full implementation of automatic invoicing, it is proposed that all data collected at the freight terminal sections will be encoded at those locations onto magnetic media, probably cassettes. During the evening, dial-up facilities will be used to allow the computer to receive the day's encoded information from each of the sections. These data will be processed through the editing stages of the systems and any edit rejects will be returned via a printer connected to a dial-up modem ready for corrections to be performed the first thing each morning. In this way it is expected that data will be no more than 24 hours behind the actual transactions and hence corrections should be made much more easily. This will also remove most of the data entry bottleneck which is currently being experienced.

   (b) A set of reporting programs will be written to analyze these data and prepare sales analysis statistics for each division. Consultants will be engaged to develop the automatic invoicing systems and implement them for Courier and Long Distance Haulage Divisions.

   (c) The costing system will be revamped according to the existing design so as to provide more comprehensive figures. Responsibility for data entry associated with the costing system will lie with the divisions. It will be encoded on local data entry equipment and forwarded via magnetic tape or floppy disk to the central processing centre.

   (d) A project steering committee comprising nominees of the directors of each division plus Corporate Finance will be set up to prepare a master plan of projects for ITC following completion of the above projects.

   (e) A ban will be placed on the procurement of any type of computing equipment by divisions without the approval of the Director of Finance. This will ensure that the integrity of the corporation's data remains intact since the installation of independent systems is likely to lead to the establishment of databases which cannot be integrated into a corporate information system.

Case Study — International Transport Company

Comment on the proposals of Mr Hendricks and indicate whether you believe they are likely to solve the problems you have identified in Question 1 of this assignment.

2   TOOLS OF THE ANALYST AND DESIGNER

2.1 INTRODUCTION

The development of 'tools' to assist the systems analyst and designer in their tasks has received considerable attention in the past, and is continuing. Many of the tools currently being developed are in the area of software support for the analysis/design tasks, such as requirements definition processors, or are en-capsulated in new software design methodologies. This chapter covers only those tools which are useful regardless of the design method chosen. The related design methodology material is given in Chapter 6. The tools and techniques available to the systems analyst range from behaviour-based techniques such as interviewing to more technically precise methods closer to those used by programmers (e.g. system flowcharting).

2.2 FACT-FINDING METHODS

2.2.1 Interviewing

One of the most important skills of the systems analyst is the ability to conduct a successful interview. However, it is a skill which is developed mainly through practice because it depends on the interviewer's ability to communicate with people of different personalities, attitudes, skills, and motivations. The interview is used throughout the systems lifecycle to gather up-to-date information and to share information with the system participants, but it is chiefly used in the analysis stage. There are two categories of interview in the analysis environment:

- Information gathering
- Information feedback

The information-gathering interview attempts to collect information not only on objective facts, such as the number of people in a department, but also on peoples' attitudes, plans, personalities, and values. It is only when analysts can appreciate the people in the system that they can begin to identify the truly objective information as opposed to information coloured by the personal biases of the interviewee.

The aim of an information-feedback interview is to notify people, to share ideas with them, or to negotiate with them. In this situation the analyst is often exploring possibilities and observing the interviewees' reactions or looking for suggestions to problems. The feedback of information is a very important tool in the interview process. Summation during and at the end of an interview is necessary to ensure, first, that all the information presented has been noted and, second, that it has been correctly understood.

In conducting an interview there are two basic sequences which can be followed: general to specific, or specific to general. Each approach has advantages in different environments. If the analyst feels that the respondent does not have a well-formulated point of view, then, by starting with specific questions, the respondent can be helped to consider various parts of the system, and assisted in grasping the total picture of the system under study. If, however, the reverse is the case, then, by starting at a general level, the respondent is free to focus the interview on those aspects which he or she considers to be of prime importance.

Similarly, each question can be one of two types: open or closed. An open question is one that cannot be answered by a Yes or No response. In the early stages of an interview it is best to use open questions, as they require a sentence in reply, which is much more likely to create an atmosphere for effective communication than a series of Yes and No responses. Other situations in which it is best to use open questions are: when the aim is to explore a particular subject; when the subject matter is ill-defined; or when the analyst or respondent does not know very much about the subject area.

Before attempting an interview the analyst must plan for it. Planning should include:

- Defining the purpose of the interview — knowing the objective of the interview and exactly what is to be accomplished
- Obtaining background information — this information should include the system area, the technology requirements, and the people involved; without this information the interviewer will in all probability be perceived as 'not knowing the field', which will hinder the task at hand
- As a general rule, planning the interview sequence top-down — in other words starting with upper management and working down the organizational hierarchy

- Making interview appointments and communicating the purpose of the interviews to the respondents before the interviews

During the course of the interview there are several points for the analyst to keep in mind:

- The aim is to help, and to be helped, and so conduct and appearance should ideally conform to social norms.
- The respondent can be given time to relax, if necessary, by starting with non-controversial questions.
- The interview is best paced to suit the respondent, but at the same time the interview objectives and time constraints must be remembered.
- The interview must be controlled by the analyst, but not so that the respondent is dominated, or forced into an uncomfortable situation, unless it is to achieve a planned purpose.
- An awareness of non-verbal communication is very useful. Body language, both the analyst's and the respondent's, is an integral part of the communication process.

An analyst needs to be aware that interpersonal communication is a multichannel medium. There are a variety of body-language channels which can frequently communicate more information than spoken words themselves. At the very least, the information conveyed by body-language channels will help the analyst:

- Interpret the words which have been spoken
- Determine the general attitude of the interviewee to the issues currently being discussed
- Evaluate the general confidence of the interviewee both in his surroundings and in dealing with the target area of the system.

Body-language communication has been the subject of a number of books and articles. A useful article that relates it specifically to the situation of an information systems analyst is by Jenkins and Johnson (1977). In this text, we can only summarize the main elements of body-language communication under the following headings.

- *Hand movements.* Hand movements are relatively easily controlled by the speaker and so may not necessarily add information to the spoken message. However, in general, any hand movement which indicates a defensive attitude can be taken to indicate a degree of discomfort on the part of the speaker. An example would be clenched fists held close to the body, much as if the interviewee was getting ready to defend himself. Conversely, an 'open-handed' attitude, with the arms extended in a non-defensive manner, indicates that the interviewee has a fair degree of confidence in the issue currently being discussed. Hand movements such as eye scratching, nose picking, etc. probably indicate a high degree of detachment on the part of the interviewee, possibly even boredom with the subject under consideration.

- *Facial expression.* It appears that most people are less able to control their facial movements than gestures. For example, a trace of smile that accompanies some words of pity for another's misfortune may better indicate the speaker's feeling about the event than the spoken message.

- *Eye contact.* The eyes can be an important means whereby the persons engaged in verbal communication exchange cues regarding speaking turns. The eyes can also indicate to another person the degree of intensity of your feeling about the current issue.

- *Posture.* Posture can give a good indication of the degree of interest that an interviewee, or the interviewer for that matter, has in the current proceedings. For example, a person leaning back with arms folded is clearly expressing far less interest in the meeting than one who is leaning forward with elbows on the table, poised to leap into the conversation as soon as there is a break in the flow of words.

- *Proxemics.* This term has been used by some authors to refer to the manner in which the person handles the space around him or her. Most people have a so-called 'personal distance zone' which is the space around them that they like to keep clear from intrusion by other people, other than those that they know on an intimate basis. The size of this zone naturally tends to increase when the person is feeling defensive or uncomfortable, and vice versa. Something can also be learned about the interviewee by examining the way that this person places himself during the interview. For example, if he seeks a refuge behind his desk when there are other alternative seats available, this may indicate a degree of defensiveness, or possibly a feeling of superiority.

- *Body rhythms.* It is often interesting to observe how the participants in an interview move their bodies, that is, change posture. For example, it might be expected that a managing director and his advisers might all lean forward and lean back together if they all hold the same views about questions being considered (the 'yes-men syndrome'). A person whose body-posture rhythm is out of phase with the other people in the room could well be expressing disagreement or disinterest in the proceedings.

Obviously body language does play an important role in the interview process and a special emphasis needs to be placed on the additional 'soft' information that can be conveyed via these channels. This is a major reason why all interviews should be conducted on a face-to-face basis rather than by telephone, except where certain reasons make a telephone interview absolutely necessary.

In the systems analysis activity, information is required on the inputs, outputs, operations, and equipment used in the system, and consequently categorizing along these lines may help in structuring an interview. For an input, the facts needed are: when it originates, how it is derived, in what format, from where it originates, who is responsible, and what is done with it. Similarly, for an output: what it is and to where it is directed, the purpose of that output, and the timing must be determined. The respondent's satisfaction with the current inputs and outputs should also be explored. With regard to the current operations: what is done, who does it, how, where, and why it is done, the time taken, and any decision rules or conventions that are currently used all need to be determined. Again, the respondent's ideas and feelings about the current system can provide valuable insights into possible improvements or requirements. Equipment capacity and workload information then completes the picture given by this respondent.

As several people are interviewed, inconsistencies and disagreements not only about how the system should function but also about how the system presently functions may be found, and so other forms of data collection are also necessary.

2.2.2 Questionnaires

The questionnaire is a method of data collection which can be used by the analyst in situations where it is impossible to interview all desired respondents because either the physical distances or the number of desired respondents are too large. It can also be that the nature of the information required lends itself to this form of collection.

Questionnaires can be conveyed to respondents by mail, telephone, or in person. Interviewer contact with the respondent has the advantages of allowing explanation of questions and increasing the likelihood of accurate responses. A mailed questionnaire usually has a lower response rate than the other two methods.

In constructing a questionnaire three types of questions may be used:

- Open ended (or free format)
- Fixed format
- Mixed format

An *open-ended question* is one which simply asks for a response, whereas a *fixed-format* question provides a range of responses from which a choice is to be made. The *mixed-format* question combines the free and fixed formats within the one question. Examine the examples given in Figures 2–1, 2–2, and 2–3. Care should be taken to make sure that an open-ended question can be answered quickly, briefly, accurately, and in common terminology. If the question requires an essay in response then it should not be on a questionnaire. When structuring fixed-format

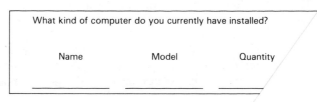

Figure 2–1   Example of an open-ended que~

questions the response categories should be balanced between affirmative and negative, and one response should allow for self-disqualification from the question. Self-disqualification from the entire questionnaire should also be possible, so that a person who feels unable to answer with any knowledge of the subject area can still return the questionnaire and indicate the reason for non-completion.

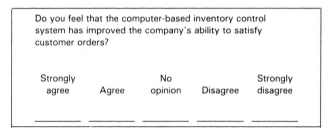

Figure 2-2   Example of a fixed-format question

This project took longer than estimated because of:

1. Inaccurate original time estimate
2. Unforeseen software difficulties
3. Unforeseen hardware difficulties
4. Inadequate staff levels
5. Other (please explain)

_____

_____

_____

_____

Figure 2-3   Example of a mixed-format question

Regardless of the type of question used, the questionnaire should conform to the general rules:

- It should not be too long. The longer the questionnaire, the less likely people are to complete it.
- Confidentiality of responses (where necessary) should be ensured and communicated to the respondents.
- The use and purpose of the questionnaire should be explained to the respondents.

The way in which potential respondents are selected is critical to the value of the results. Clearly, when the sample population is small compared with the total, that sample must be as representative as possible. For example, it would be useless to rely on a telephoned questionnaire if the survey concerned the unemployed. Considerable care must be taken to ensure uniformity (where these items may interfere) in demography, application area, ethnic backgrounds, etc.

2.2.3 Searching Records

In the interview and the questionnaire the analyst can derive information on both the formal and informal systems of the organization. By searching company records only the formal systems can be discovered, but this is often the source of the only complete description of many of the organization's activities. The analyst should remember, however, that these records are often out of date and not always completely accurate. The types of records used are:

- Company policy and procedure documents
- Organization charts
- Files of reports and forms currently used
- Systems documentation

Company policy and procedure documents can provide information ranging from the general (company aims) to the specific (job description), and can therefore be of considerable use as background information before any interviewing commences. Organization charts provide a picture of the structure of the organization. This structure may be in terms of responsibility and authority, or it may be in terms of reporting structures. Again, these form a background to the interview environment and should be checked for accuracy during the interviews.

Files of reports and forms currently in use provide much information on the current system's inputs and outputs and are, consequently, a very good starting point for analyzing the current system. The analyst needs to determine the use or non-use of these forms and reports in the interviews and by personal observation, as well as to determine their perceived strengths and weaknesses. Where computer-based systems are being used, much information on the system is contained in the system documentation. This should provide the analyst with at least a system overview, input and output layouts, program specifications, file layouts, and user procedures.

2.3 SYSTEM REPRESENTATION METHODS

Many tools have been developed over the years to assist the analyst in the analysis and documentation of systems and logic. This section describes two of these tools: systems flowcharting and data analysis.

2.3.1 Systems Flowcharts

Although there are obvious graphical similarities, systems flowcharts are a completely different genre to conventional logic flowcharts. Systems flowcharts are concerned with the inputs, process, and outputs of system components. The interconnecting lines describe the flow of information, unlike logic flowchart lines, which indicate what-to-do-next. The boxes in systems flowcharts represent records, files,

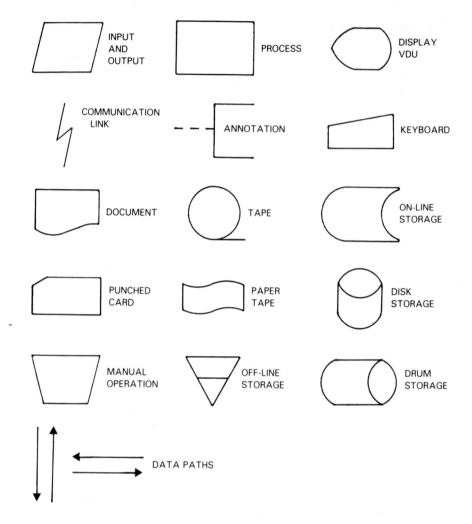

Figure 2–4   Standard systems flowcharting symbols

databases and processes; logic flowcharts are an appropriate means of describing the sequence of events within those processes. Each logic flowchart has a starting point, a termination point, and various decision points. None of these should appear in a systems flowchart. The basic outlines which form the permissible 'grammar' of systems flowcharts are given in Figure 2–4.

The systems flowcharting symbols reflect the essential input-process-output nature of systems design. Each *processing* box may be 'exploded' in a program flowchart. *Off-line storage* may refer to the physical storage of output media in some form of manual retrieval system, such as cards in card drawers or magnetic tapes in a tape library. *Manual operation* is an operation not requiring mechanical aid. The *communications link* represents the transmission of information to or from remote locations by means of some electronic or optical line. The *annotation flag* clarifies another symbol by adding descriptive or explanatory comments. The flag connects to the point concerned by a broken line. When the general *input/output* symbol is used, the chart is expressing the essential fact of information transfer without indicating how the transfer is performed. The specific media and devices which perform information transfers may be expressed by other symbols. Three of these are worth special mention. *Keyboard* input refers to entry of data through an on-line keyboard such as a console typewriter used for control purposes, or a remote keyboard device located at some point of data origination, e.g. a bank teller's desk. *Visual display units* show information in printed or graphic form. They may also permit input operation if equipped with a light pen or other sensing device, but these devices are usually represented by some specific symbol other than that used for the visual display. Examples of visual displays are the graph plotter and the TV or video display tube. Most computer firms supply both hardware and software to enable visual displays to be incorporated into an information system. *External on-line storage* refers to the storage of information on units which are under the direct control of the CPU such as drum, disk, or other 'random access' or on-line device.

Guidelines for drawing flowcharts are:

- A flowchart should be drawn to suit the reader. For example, wording that is incomprehensible to a particular person should not be used if the chart is meant to communicate with that person.
- Identification must be used consistently. If, for example, a file is labelled IN-06 in one chart, exactly the same identification should be used elsewhere.
- Clarity is the aim in the flowchart presentation. This includes: breaking the chart at sensible points to continue over the page; showing a complete system segment on each page; avoiding crossing lines; minimizing the number of lines entering or leaving any particular symbol; using annotation so the reader can understand the chart easily; and using only standard symbols.

2.3.2 Data Analysis

Another way of looking at the system under study is by documenting the data used in the system and the flow of that data. This technique is different from flowcharting in that the symbols do not show the equipment or media used, but the focal point is the set of data. Many analysts feel that this is the logical starting point for analysis because the data are the design pivot. The set of data is the fundamental element of any information system, and if all of the existing and required data can be identified, then the beginning of a good design process is at hand.

One technique used for data analysis is the data dictionary. The data dictionary is a tool which can be used throughout the systems lifecycle, but in this section it is discussed only in relation to the analysis task. A *data dictionary* is a file containing data about data items — a list of data items and their properties such as:

- Data item or record name
- Alternative names used
- Capture and storage formats
- Where kept (both logically in records and physically)
- Origin
- Uses
- Volume per period of time
- Access restrictions
- Comments

By compiling a data dictionary the analyst builds a picture of the data which currently exist in the system. This picture can then be used to gain an understanding of the present system and to highlight its deficiencies. The dictionary may be kept manually or be computer based.

The second element of data analysis is an investigation of the data flows in the system. The data flow diagram (DFD) is a tool which has been developed for this task. Four basic symbols are employed; they are shown and explained in Figure 2–5. An example of a logical data flow diagram is given in Figure 2–6. The logic represented is a function-booking system for a club. The step-by-step narrative description may help readers to follow the diagram.

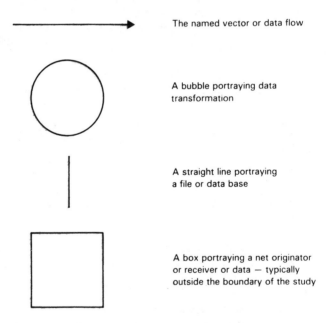

The named vector or data flow

A bubble portraying data transformation

A straight line portraying a file or data base

A box portraying a net originator or receiver or data — typically outside the boundary of the study

Figure 2-5   Data flow diagram symbols

1. Customers make an inquiry, a booking, provide firm details of bookings, or cancel a booking. These data are labelled TRANSACTIONS on the data flow diagram.

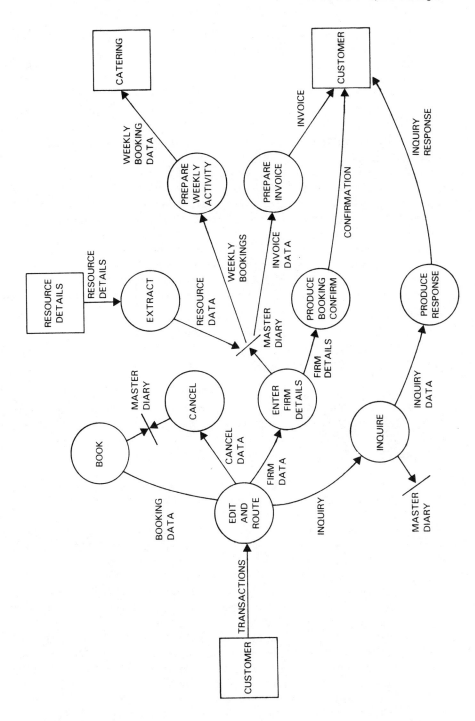

Figure 2-6   Sample logical data flow diagram

2. A clerk then directs the data according to their nature, after making sure that the data are suitable for this system.
3. Inquiries, bookings, cancellations, and firm details are all entered in a master diary.
4. Resource details are used to complete the master diary for bookings with firm details, and a weekly activity sheet is prepared and sent to catering.

In this example all the processes are manual, but the diagram can equally be used for automated processes. Similarly, the files may be manual or computer based. It should also be noted that in this example one diagram alone has been used to show the logic of a simple system, but in practice many DFDs are used, in a hierarchical form, to display the data flows. An example of this is given in Figure 2–7 in which a two-level structure outlines the flows for a simple production-scheduling and control system.

To summarize, the technique of data analysis shows the data flows in a system graphically, without placing emphasis on the physical or control aspects, and does not reveal any timing considerations in that system. These are significant advantages to the analyst/designer because they allow the logical system attributes to be considered separately from the physical attributes.

2.3.3 Forms Design

Apart from designing report layouts, the analyst also needs to design input and output forms to interface the system with the external environment. The layout and content of these forms can greatly affect overall system efficiency, reliability, and controllability. Some suggested guidelines are:

- Each form must carry its own clear identification, in particular, a title, name of the organization, a form number, and any necessary controls (such as serial numbering, coloured multiparts, etc.).
- If instructions on filling out the form are necessary, they should be positioned so that they do not interfere with the body of the form, yet be clearly identified so that the user can see them easily.
- The form should be designed to facilitate the entry of data. For example, if data are to be entered by hand, sufficient space must be allowed for a person to write them in, or if a form is to be filled in by typewriter, the number of starting positions should be kept to a minimum.
- The form should facilitate effective use of the data. In many forms horizontal or vertical lines or other separations make it difficult to recognize the response or data area on the form which relates to the preprinted question or description of the data item.
- The arrangement of the form should be logical. Related data should be grouped together, and non-related data shown appropriately. Quite often a form consists of three basic parts: the introductory data, the body of the form, and the conclusion such as signatures.

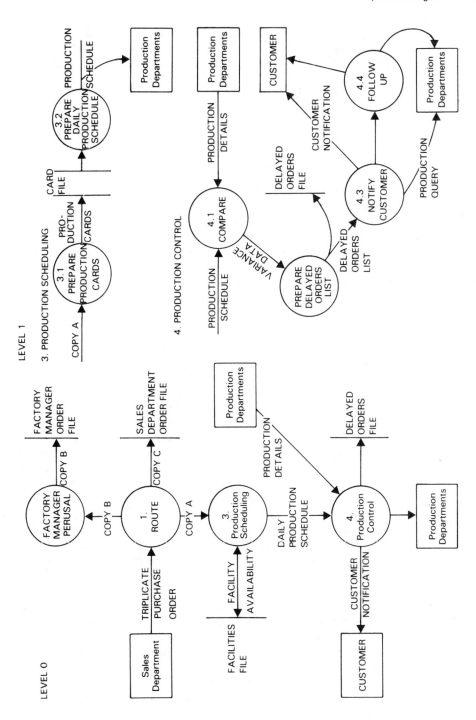

Figure 2-7   A two-level data flow diagram

- Major data items should be highlighted and easy to find.
- If multiple copy documents are necessary, the identification of each copy should be obvious, which can be effected using colours or obvious copy headings.
- If the form is to be stored, then the form identification should be placed to facilitate its retrieval from the file mechanism.
- All fixed data should be preprinted on the form.

2.4 PROCEDURE SPECIFICATION METHODS

Two common techniques for procedure specification — decision tables and logic flowcharts — are described in this section. Both techniques can be used at the overview level or at the final detail level, the latter being suited more for the specification of programs. Unless the analyst is also involved in program specification, the primary interest is in their use as documentation aids; they are useful either in the analysis of existing systems (e.g. in interview recording) or in designing the sequence of events for a new system.

2.4.1 Flowcharting

The flowchart is a time-honoured graphical technique used in both the macro- and micro-expression of procedures or information systems. It is possible to program a simple operation without first constructing a flowchart. However, as business operations become, in practice, quite complex, it is usually necessary to precede the coding phase with a more-or-less formal problem definition phase.

A program flowchart can be constructed at two levels of complexity: a language-oriented and a problem-oriented level. A *problem-oriented flowchart* is a systematic technique for describing an operation in non-technical terms. It is generally constructed without regard for the actual machine or language to be used. As its name indicates, the problem-oriented flowchart is derived directly from the problem definition, necessitating a full understanding of the problem or operation under analysis. It is at this point that the analyst must exercise the talents of logical understanding and creativeness.

Unless a problem-oriented flowchart can be constructed, there can be no possibility of coding an operation. Assuming, however, that the required analysis has been performed and flowcharted, the ensuing process of coding (i.e. specifying the actual machine instructions) is a fairly routine matter. The construction of an intermediate language-oriented flowchart is a considerable help in the coding process when a lower level language is to be used, usually resulting in a more efficient and smaller program. The language-oriented flowchart forms a valuable meeting place for the basic concepts of the operation and the peculiarities of the computer language employed for its implementation. That two distinct levels of flowchart may be required highlights the need for computer languages which are not quite so removed from the world of operations. This need has been the stimulus behind the evolution of the so-called problem-oriented languages such as FORTRAN, ALGOL, COBOL, and PL/I. By means of such languages, the programmer is able to encode an operation directly from a problem-oriented flowchart, leaving the translation into machine language as a routine job for the computer itself.

Both the problem-oriented and the language-oriented flowcharts are methods for describing the inner sequential workings of some specific operation. The boxes describe the sequence of basic processes such as addition, storing, accumulating, input, and output. Accordingly, the term 'program flowchart' (or 'logic flowchart') is usually applied to both forms collectively. Since it is used to describe only one of the many interconnected operations in a given information system, the program flowchart becomes the micro-expression, dealing with only a portion of the overall system. The flowchart which expresses the flow of information between operations is a system flowchart (see Subsection 2.3.1). Thus a complete information system may be described by an overall system flowchart, in which the individual boxes refer to specific operations, each detailed in separate program flowcharts.

Flowcharting techniques need not be confined to computer systems. An activity such as order processing, which involves non-information operations such as packaging of stock and the mailing of invoices, can also be described in terms of a flowchart. Essentially, a flowchart consists of a network constructed from boxes, each containing brief descriptions of certain operations, interconnected by directional lines which indicate the next operation in the sequence. In a program flowchart, one box is designated as the first to be processed or 'obeyed'; another as the last. The former is referred to as the 'entry point', the latter as the 'exit point'. These operations are usually described in rounded boxes (see Figure 2-8). Other boxes may describe arithmetic, input/output, testing, predefined procedures and connectors to other flowcharts.

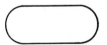

Figure 2-8   Terminal box

Before 1963 there were no standards for the shapes of the boxes used for the different kinds of operation. Every computing establishment or programmer did what was thought best, with a consequent interorganizational communication barrier. All felt the need for some measure of standardization, but few were prepared to relinquish their individually established practices. In 1963 the American Standards Association (ASA) Committee on Computers and Information Processing proposed a set of flowchart symbols — it is now called the American National Standards Institute (ANSI). These symbols were revised in 1966 and have now been widely accepted. The shape, not the size, of the symbol defines its purpose. Programming templates which conform to ANSI specifications are readily available. The standard symbols used in system flowcharting and their meanings have already been described (Figure 2-4). Figure 2-9 describes the symbols used in program flowcharting.

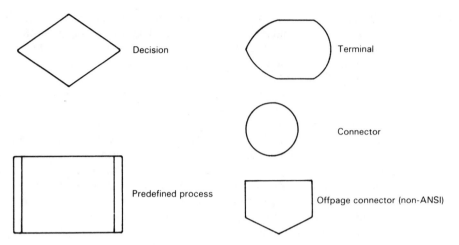

Figure 2-9 ANSI program flowchart symbols

The *decision* symbol is used when the program may take different paths depending on the result of a test, a comparison, or the existence of some condition. The condition to be tested may be written within the symbol while the various responses possible are marked on the emerging lines. The responses may be a simple Yes or No, or two expressions may be compared with three possible outcomes: less than, equal to, or greater than. In this case the comparison is indicated by the form $A:B$ where A and B represent the two expressions while the symbols $<$, $=$, and $>$ mark the three responses lines.

The *predefined process* identifies a program or subprogram not detailed in this flowchart. A subroutine or subprogram is simply a group of instructions which may be obeyed (by transferring to it from the main program), performing some generally useful operation such as the extraction of a square root, and which provides for the automatic return of control to the instruction following the original transfer.

The *connector* is used as an entry from or exit to another part of the program on the same page. Connectors are usually identified by capital letters. *Offpage connectors* link pages of flowcharts when the chart extends to more than one page. These connectors cross-reference each other, specifying both page and entry/exit point on the page. In spite of its not being an ANSI symbol, it is included in this list because of its wide acceptance and value.

Figure 2-10 is a sample program flowchart for a popular sorting technique — the Shell sort (so named after its designer). All the interconnecting control lines are marked with arrows showing the direction to follow. In this example, COUNT is the number of items to be sorted. SPAN is a working variable (always an integer). The expression int|SPAN/2| means the integer result of dividing SPAN by 2 (i.e. the quotient, the remainder being ignored). I, LIM, HI, and LO are also integer work variables. A second example (file updating) is discussed at the end of this section.

In summary, the benefits to be expected from flowcharting are:

- *Quicker grasp of relationships.* The flowchart provides a very effective

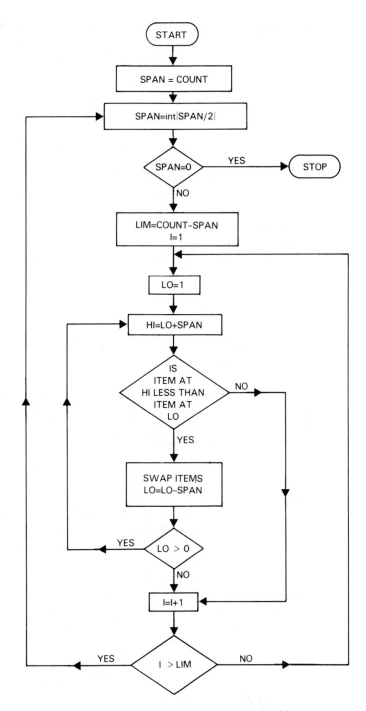

Fig. 2-10   Flowchart for the shell sort algorithm

shorthand description of logical procedures, with the benefit of clarity and conciseness. This means that the flowchart reader can comprehend the relationships much more rapidly, and also that the person preparing the chart can do so much more quickly than if the logic were to be expressed in pages of written notes.

- *Effective analysis.* The clarity of expression provides an effective model which highlights the particular components of the chart that require further study.
- *Effective synthesis.* The flowchart allows the reader to understand the whole task and all the interrelationships within it.
- *Communication.* Provided the symbols used are in accordance with an accepted standard, the flowchart is a worthwhile aid in communicating problem resolution logic.
- *Documentation.* Any system or program must be adequately documented so that the methods and knowledge of the designer can be retained, in a communicable medium, for future use. This documentation is used whenever modifications are needed, or new staff are to be educated in the logic of current operations, or the same logic is applied to future problems, or the logic needs to be checked. It also ensures that the logic of operations is not 'lost' if the designer leaves the organization.
- *Efficient coding.* The program flowchart specifies all the functions which must be carried out for a computer program. It is therefore a 'blueprint' for coding, and a control device for checking that all necessary functions have been coded.
- *Program testing.* The situation can arise in which either the program fails to run, or the program fails to produce the correct results from data for which the correct answers have been precalculated. In either case the program flowchart can assist in identifying any mistakes that have been made.

The main limitations of conventional flowcharting include:

- *It is essentially for external documentation.* The shapes of the ANSI symbols are suitable as support to internal program documentation. They are generally unsuitable for including in the source program as comments (i.e. as internal documentation). Accordingly, the logic specification may easily become detached from subsequent machine-readable program listings, and not be updated as the program is modified.
- *Difficulty of updating.* A minor change in logic necessitates some redrafting of a logic flowchart. Many 'live' systems rely only on the comments in the program listings because it is easier to update program comments than the flowchart.
- *It is not geared to structured programming.* The expressive power of conventional logic flowcharting allows unskilled program designers to use an uncontrolled coding style which may not conform to generally accepted structured programming conventions.

2.4.2 Decision Tables

The process of designing a good flowchart from a description of the program's requirements requires a reasonable degree of insight, ability, and experience on the part of the analyst. A knowledge of the application of flowcharting standards will no more produce a good flowchart than will the knowledge of English grammar, syntax, and spelling enable the automatic production of fine literature. However, other techniques are available which impose more rigour on the designer. The best known of these is the decision table.

The chief value of the decision table lies in the fact that business data-processing problems are essentially decision oriented, i.e. certain processes depend on the outcome of certain decisions. For example, the notification which a particular debtor may receive depends on certain criteria such as the amount shown in the over-ninety-days figure of his or her statement. In complex processes, flowcharts become unwieldy and difficult to construct, and although branches from a single decision symbol are easy to follow, the situation changes quite drastically if the number of decisions is large. In these cases it can be advantageous to replace part or all of the flowchart by one or more decision tables. Figure 2-11 gives the basic format of the decision table. The table is divided into four, the upper two sections describing

Table heading	Decision rules								
	1	2	3	4	5	6	7	8	. . .
CONDITION STUB				CONDITION ENTRIES					
ACTION STUB				ACTION ENTRIES					

Figure 2-11   Decision table format

The number of condition and action lines as well as rules is adjusted to suit the application.

conditions, the lower two describing actions; the lefthand sections are descriptive stubs, those on the right are 'entries'. In addition, the whole table is given a name in the area labelled 'table heading' in Figure 2–11, while the individual columns in the entry side are numbered, starting with 1. An entry column is also called a 'rule' and rules are referred to by their column number. While it is possible to use preprinted decision-table forms such as those supplied by the leading machine manufacturers, it is usually better to draw up a special form which allows for the specific number of conditions, actions, and rules the particular decision requires.

The method of use is best illustrated with an example. Consider an accounts-receivable process in which customers' accounts are examined with the purpose of producing a statement and a possible reminder, of variable severity, for each account. The analyst's first step is to decide upon the set of criteria applicable. By questioning the appropriate people, three (unrelated) possibilities are discovered: (1) the within-thirty-days amount exceeds $500, (2) the within- sixty-days amount exceeds $200, and (3) there is still an amount to be paid on goods purchased more than sixty days ago. In the following description, these are referred to as AR1, AR2, and AR3 respectively. The conditions to be written in the condition stub therefore become:

> AR1 $500
> AR2 $200
> AR3 $0

The possible answers to each of these questions is a simple Yes or No in each case. Consequently there must be a maximum of $2^3 = 8$ rules, corresponding to the possible combinations of answers. These are placed in the condition entry section of the table, one per decision rule column. There is no significance attached to the order in which the rules are written, provided that all possible entries are recorded. As shall be seen, it is sometimes possible to combine two or more rules if it is known that the ensuing actions are all identical.

By further questioning, the analyst establishes the complete list of all possible actions and writes them in the action stub, one per line. Suppose that, by the time this section of the system is 'activated', a preliminary operation has bypassed all those customers not needing a statement, and has already produced a statement for those to whom one is due. The only task remaining is to produce one or more of:

- A moderate reminder (LETTER A)
- A more severe reminder (LETTER B)
- A very terse POSTSCRIPT to either letter (the same in each case)
- A special report on the customer for the sales manager (called EXCEPTION REPORT)

These actions are written in the four lines of the action stub. The order in which the actions are recorded must correspond to the order in which they are required to take place. Thus the POSTSCRIPT must follow the LETTERS. These letters however may be placed in either order since only one letter is to be sent to any one customer. The REPORT will no doubt be produced on some unit other than the one which will print the letters and may consequently be produced anywhere in the action sequence.

To be quite explicit, a terminal action which directs to the next operation to be performed could also be included (i.e. GO TO xxx, where xxx is the name of some other decision table).

The required set of actions applying to each individual rule can now be established. The action entries are simply crosses which mark the lines of the actions to be performed. The analyst simply determines the required actions as dictated by the table: no action is to be taken in the first two cases (in which there is no amount owing for more than thirty days); LETTER A only is produced for rule 3; LETTER A and POSTSCRIPT are sent in rule 4; in all cases in which there is an amount owing for over sixty days, LETTER B must be sent (rules 5, 6, 7, and 8); and in the special case of rule 8, the customer also receives the POSTSCRIPT with management receiving the EXCEPTION REPORT. All this is recorded by making the appropriate marks in the action entry section of the table. The completed decision table is shown in Figure 2–12.

A/R LETTERS	DECISION RULES							
CONDITION STUB	1	2	3	4	5	6	7	8
AP1 $500	N	Y	N	Y	N	Y	N	Y
AP2 $200	N	N	Y	Y	N	N	Y	Y
AP3 $ 0	N	N	N	N	Y	Y	Y	Y
ACTION STUB								
LETTER A				X	X				
LETTER B						X	X	X	X
POSTSCRIPT					X				X
REPORT									X
GO TO NEXT	X	X	X	X	X	X	X	X

Figure 2-12   Decision table example

Before discussing the question of writing a program from this table, it is worthwhile noting the orderly nature of the inquiries into which the analyst is led. This is a most valuable discipline, tending to regularize the otherwise random questioning which may occur. Secondly, it can be seen that some degree of horizontal compression is possible in certain cases. Thus instead of having two lines — one for LETTER A and one for LETTER B — having one line headed simply LETTER, and writing A or B or leaving a blank in the action entry area, as the case may be, could be used. Because this method effectively extends part of the action definition into the entry area, it is referred to as 'extended entry', as distinct from the 'limited entries' used in Figure 2–12. Conditions may also be extended in a similar way. A table consisting entirely of limited entries is called a 'limited' table, whereas one consisting entirely of extended entries is an 'extended' table. Where a table has both kinds of entry it is known as a 'mixed' table.

Vertical compression of the rules is also possible in some cases. In the example it is clear that the actions for rules 1 and 2 are identical. Accordingly, this fact could have been expressed by deleting reference to the redundant first condition and using only one rule headed with a rule number of 1, a blank as the condition entry corresponding to the first (redundant) position, with N in both the condition entries for the second and third conditions. The same process may be applied to simplify rules 5, 6, and 7. In more complex cases, Boolean algebra may be used in the simplification process, but it is frequently possible to simplify intuitively.

Having expressed the table in as concise a form as possible, the programmer can now proceed directly with the encoding process, or use the table to construct a formal flowchart which may then serve as a basis for coding. Coding from a decision table is as much a routine matter as coding a program from a program flowchart. In some respects the process is even simpler. Because of this it is possible to automate the coding function. There are translation programs which take a decision table as input, and produce as output a program written in a language such as FORTRAN, COBOL or PL/I, or compiled code. Examples of this are the Rand Corporation's FORTAB and IBM's Decision Log Translator, both of which produce FORTRAN programs; DETAB/65 produces a COBOL program.

In summary, the decision table is a powerful analytic tool when applied to complex business procedures. Compared to the flowchart, it is less likely to allow the omission of a logical possibility. In addition, it can provide for better communication between interested parties.

2.4.3   File-updating Methods Example

An example — a sequential file update— is worked so that the two tools, decision tables and program flowcharts, can be compared.

Updating a file involves adding, deleting, and replacing selected records. This is one of the most frequently performed basic data-processing operations, and therefore demands careful planning. The technique selected must take into consideration such matters as: file security; recovery techniques (i.e. is the operation failsafe?); the nature of incidental reports to be produced as by-products of the operation; the form in which the data for the 'variations' has been supplied; whether or not the variations have been edited for validity of format and content; the organization (sequential or random) of the original file, new file, and the variation file; and the storage medium employed in each case. In the case of a direct access file, updating is simply a matter either of locating the appropriate record and then carrying out the required action (deletion or change), or of adding any new records to the appropriate address in the file. In the updating of sequential files, this direct operation upon individual records is not used. The usual sequential update involves three physically distinct files: (1) the original file, (2) the new file, and (3) the file containing the variation records. The update procedure uses the first and third files (referred to as OLD and VARN respectively) strictly as input, and produces the second file (NEW) as output.

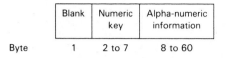

	Blank	Numeric key	Alpha-numeric information

| Byte | 1 | 2 to 7 | 8 to 60 |

Figure 2–13   Record format for file 2 and file 4

In the example, a sequential update is to be programmed to update FILE 2 to FILE 4, both to hold 60 character records with the format shown in Figure 2–13. Variations are on FILE 3, these also conforming to the format of Figure 2–13, with the exception that the first byte indicates the nature of the variation as follows:

First character	*Action*
A	*A*dd this whole record to NEW after replacing the first byte with a blank.
D	*D*elete the record in OLD having the same key as this variation. If the record cannot be found in OLD, issue a diagnostic message on the printer.
C	*C*hange the record in OLD having the same key as this variation to the information supplied in the variation record. If the record cannot be found in OLD issue a diagnostic message. The record to be written must have a blank as the first byte.

Both the OLD and VARN data sets (FILE 2 and FILE 3) have been arranged in ascending key sequence. The update procedure must retain this sequence for NEW (FILE 4). VARN has undergone an editing procedure to check sequence validity and correctness of record contents.

The first step may be to prepare a decision table which describes the operation in detail. As the decision table, Figure 2–14, shows, there are eleven distinct rules to be considered. For example, if the operation has not just commenced (i.e. it is under way), and if the last records read from the input files OLD and VARN were not end-of-file indicators, and if the VARN record has a key less than that of the OLD record, and if the TYPE of the VARN record (found in the first byte) is A, then this means that a new record is to be added to the NEW file from the VARN file. Accordingly the information from the VARN file is PUT (into NEW) and a new VARN record is read. This is all summarized in rule 6 of the decision table. Readers should check each of the remaining rules before comparing the resulting flowchart with the table.

In the flowchart, Figure 2–16, the decision box shown in Figure 2–15 asks the question 'did the last GET operation on file VARN read the end-of-file marker?'. If the answer is Yes, the saying is 'the ENDFILE condition has been raised for that file'.

	1	2	3	4	5	6	7	8	9	10	11
START	Y	N	N	N	N	N	N	N	N	N	N
OLD FINISHED		Y	N	Y	Y	N	N	N	N	N	N
VARN FINISHED		Y	Y	N	N	N	N	N	N	N	N
VARN: OLD						‹	‹	=	=	=	›
TYPE				A	$\bar{A}$	A	$\bar{A}$	A	C	D	
PUT*			O	V	E	V	E	E	V		O
GET OLD	X		X						X	X	X
GET VARN	X			X	X	X	X	X	X	X	
STOP		X									

* O = OLD, V = VARN, E = ERROR MESSAGE

Figure 2-14   Decision table for worked example

Are all the logical possibilities covered?

Figure 2-15   Endfile condition

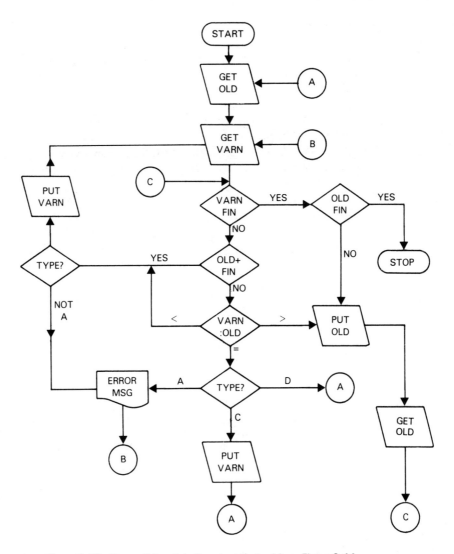

Figure 2-16 Sequential update flowchart derived from Figure 2-14

Follow the chart rule of the decision table. Can this flowchart be simplified further?

REFERENCES

R. BARNETT, *Forms for People*, 2nd edn., Cyber Management Services, Sydney, 1978.

T. DE MARCO, *Structured Analysis and Systems Specification*, Yourdan Inc., New York, 1978.

C. GANE & T. SARSON, *Structured Systems Analysis*, Prentice-Hall Inc., Englewood-Cliffs, N.J., 1979.

A. M. JENKINS & R. D. JOHNSON, 'What the Information Analyst Should Know About Body Language', *Management Information Systems Quarterly*, September 1977, pp. 33-48.

3   FILE CONCEPTS

3.1 INTRODUCTION

Files are organized collections of data which, in most production systems, are stored on magnetic disk or magnetic tape. One of the most significant factors affecting a system's capability and efficiency is the manner in which data are organized in files and, consequently, the decision on how the data are to be organized is one of the most important in the design of computer-based systems.

A primary objective, when deciding the most appropriate method of organizing data in files, is to provide write and retrieval efficiency, because access to data on secondary storage is slow in comparison with other computer functions. The factors which affect the selection of file organization are:

- Volatility
- Activity
- Size
- Growth
- File medium available

Volatility. This term refers to the number of additions, deletions, and/or changes to the records in a file.

Activity. The amount of activity is the proportion of records which has to be processed in any given computer run; a payroll file has high activity as each record is usually processed, often on a daily basis. The manner in which the file is organized (arranged) should assist in locating a particular record as quickly as possible. The activity ratio is the number of records processed compared to the total number of records in the file. This is also referred to as the 'hit rate'.

Size. If a file is very large it is sometimes desirable to alter its organization and processing in certain ways to achieve retrieval efficiencies. For example, where each record in a file contains a large number of data items, it may be desirable to maintain two files. One file — known as the 'abridged file' — contains the data items which change frequently (e.g. invoice amounts, daily wages) and the other is a complete file of all data items. The abridged file is processed more frequently than the complete file, and is used to keep the latter up-to-date. This procedure conserves space in the computer main storage during processing and allows faster processing to be carried out.

Growth. The potential growth of the file must be considered, and planning must include arrangements as to how the anticipated growth in the size of the file is to be handled in the future. Many problems arise if not enough care is taken in planning the growth of a system to meet the increased information needs of an organization.

3.2   FILE ORGANIZATION AND RETRIEVAL

Basically there are two types of file organization: sequential and random. As the name suggests, a *sequential file* is one in which contiguous records follow a predetermined (usually key) sequence. A *random file* is one in which there is no simple relationship between contiguous records.

In many of the file organizations discussed in this chapter, the basic technique of chaining is used, and so a brief description is necessary. *Chaining* refers to the use of pointers to indicate the logical relationship between records. Thus, if necessary, the location of the next logical record in a sequence can be indicated by a pointer which directs the retrieval process to the address indicated by the pointer.

3.3   SEQUENTIAL ORGANIZATION

3.3.1   Sequential Access

Sequential access to files, defined as retrieving each record in sequence, is applicable for large files which have low volatility and high activity in their processing runs. An organization's payroll file is a much-quoted example because each payday the entire file is read in order to print pay cheques and advices. Thus, nearly every record in the file is 'hit' (high activity), but alterations are infrequent (low volatility). To illustrate, in a sequential file maintenance update using magnetic tape as the medium, a new tape is written as a result of (1) copying records unchanged from the old file, (2) adding new records, and (3) deleting specified records. In this example, the master file contains details of inventory held, minimum balance, reorder quantity, and unit cost. The update file consists of three possible transaction types, as printed in the transaction code column:

1. An addition to the master file

2. A deletion from the file
3. A change to the file

Sections of the master file and the update file are shown in Figure 3–1.

To create the new master file, both the old master file and the update file must be read, one record at a time, and the keys compared. The first update transaction (item number 1876) is greater than the first two item numbers on the old master, and consequently records 1011 and 1326 are copied without change on to the new file. On reading 2487 from the old master, update record 1876 must be written on to the new file first, and so on. Thus the process of key comparison creates the new file in correct sequence.

Old master file

Item number	Balance on hand	Minimum balance	Order quantity	Unit cost
1011	220	300	200	2.75
1326	1768	1500	750	13.52
2487	487	250	250	6.87
3215	52	25	50	3.28
3637	168	65	100	28.50

Transaction (update) file

Item number	Transaction code	Balance on hand	Minimum balance	Order quantity	Unit cost
1876	1	100	50	100	13.75
3215	2				
3637	3	188	65	100	28.50

Figure 3–1   Sequential-file update example

3.3.2   Direct Access

Direct access is defined as the ability to go directly to any wanted record. Clearly, direct access would not always be possible in a sequentially organized file. However, two methods for achieving direct access have been developed — addressing and indexing.

Addressing

Direct access to a sequential file (stored on a suitable medium) can be facilitated by establishing a relationship between the record's key and the record's actual address. This technique is known as *self addressing*, and is feasible when keys of fixed-length records form a complete or almost complete range of consecutive numbers. As a simple example, suppose that the keys are numbered from 1001 to

9999 and so the relative location 351 holds key number 1351. If there are, say, eight records to a block and the first block is number 2000, then the address of record 1351 can be calculated from:

$$(1351 - 1001)/8$$
$$= 350/8$$
$$= 43 + 6$$

This means that the desired record is in block 2043, and it is the (6 + 1), i.e. the seventh record in that block. This form of organization and access provides the significant advantage of a single seek and read retrieving the desired record. However, applicability is limited by the need for fixed-length records, and the need for a full key sequence even if not all the keys are used.

These limitations can be partly overcome, at the expense of using more than one read, if *partial addressing* is used. This method allows for fixed-length or variable-length records, preferably of low volatility, but requires a fairly even spread of keys in the file. The use of an average block spread allows for much the same logic as for self addressing. Suppose the desired key is 4281 and the keys used span 3501 to 5500; furthermore the blocks used are 300 to 499. Then the average block spread is:

$$= \frac{5500 - 3501 + 1}{499 - 300 + 1}$$
$$= 10$$

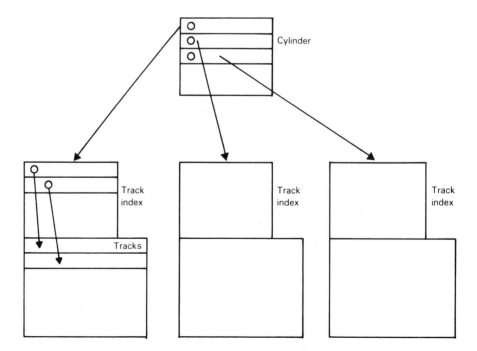

Figure 3-2   Indexes on an ISAM (Indexed Sequential Access Method) file

So the desired record (4281) resides at or near to relative block (4281 − 3501)/10, i.e. relative block 78. This is then block 300 + 78, or 378.

Indexing

Another method of accessing a sequential file which is stored on a direct access medium is to set up an index file. This file contains pointers to keys held on the data file, and therefore provides a system which allows both sequential and direct access to the data file, without the restrictions of self or partial addressing. This form of organization is called *indexed sequential*, and the table of contents to this book, which contains page-number pointers to the sequentially numbered and arranged chapters, is a good illustration.

An example: access to a particular record is by way of a cylinder index and a track index. The cylinder index contains pointers to the track index, and there is one track index for each cylinder in the file, as shown in Figure 3–2. Assume, for simplicity, that the data are stored one record per block, and that the file is organized in alphabetical sequence. The first block in each cylinder contains the track index for that cylinder, as is shown in Figure 3–3 for cylinder 73.

	1	2	3	4	5	6
7300	track index	FA	FC	FL	FN	FR
7301	FT	GD	GG	GK	GR	GW
7302	HB	HD	HI	HL	HP	HT
7303	HX	HY	IC	ID	JD	JF
7304	JG	JK	JP	JT	JW	KE
7305	KF	KG	KJ	KK	KL	KP
7306	KT	KV	KY	LE	LF	LG
7307	LH	LJ	LL	LM	LN	LP
7308	LQ	LR	LV	MC	ME	MJ
7309	@	@	@	@	@	@

Figure 3-3   Contents of cylinder 73

The tracks on cylinder 73 are numbered 0–9 and the blocks 1–6. Thus block 73001 contains the track index. The contents of this block are shown in Figure 3–4. The first data item is an overflow pointer (73091) which indicates the first block available for overflow use, since in this example all of track 7309 is set aside for overflow. The four columns store: the normal highest key in the track, the first block, the highest key in overflow, and the first overflow block. Thus the first entry indicates that FR is the highest key in track 7300 and data are stored from block 73002 on. Because overflow space is not used at this stage, the third and fourth columns are copies of the first and second respectively.

To see how this works, assume that a new record, JM, is to be added to the file. The cylinder index directs the search to cylinder 73. In the track index JM is greater than JF but less than KE, and, therefore the record should go in track 4. After the insertion KE has been moved to overflow as shown in Figure 3–5. The track index

overflow pointer 73091			
FR	73002	FR	73002
GW	73011	GW	73011
HT	73021	HT	73021
JF	73031	JF	73031
KE	73041	KE	73041
KP	73051	KP	73051
LG	73061	LG	73061
LP	73071	LP	73071
MJ	73081	MJ	73081

Figure 3-4   Track index for cylinder 73

now makes use of the overflow pointers. The overflow pointer indicates 73092 as the first available overflow block, JW is the highest key in track 4, KE is the highest key in the sequence, and 73091 is the first overflow block used for this sequence (Figure 3-6). If a further record, JV, is added, then after insertion the tracks and track index will be as shown in Figures 3-7 and 3-8.

7304	JG	JK	JM	JP	JT	JW
7309	KE	@	@	@	@	@

Figure 3-5   Affected tracks after insertion of JM

73092		
JW	73041 KE	73091

Figure 3-6   Parts of track index after change

7304	JG	JK	JM	JP	JT	JV
7309	KE	JW	@	@	@	@
	73091					

Figure 3-7   Affected tracks after insertion of JV

When a record is deleted from the file the record is flagged but not physically eliminated. The record is eliminated only if it would otherwise be bumped into overflow because of other additions. The flagging is shown in Figure 3-9. The major disadvantage of this form of organization is that as new records are inserted, overflow chains grow and therefore, until the file is reorganized, search performance deteriorates.

An alternative indexed file organization, which overcomes the overflow

			73093		
JV	73041		KE	73092	

Figure 3-8   Parts of track index after change

chaining problem of the indexed sequential organization illustrated in this section, is the B-tree data structure and variations thereon. This is discussed in the appendix to this chapter.

7306	KT	KV	KY¢	LE	LF	LG

Figure 3-9   Delete KY

3.4 RANDOM ORGANIZATION

Unlike sequentially organized files, random files have no simple relationship between contiguous records. The method of organization is based on a computed relationship between the record key and the location at which the record is stored. Thus instead of using say an index to indicate the record's address, a computation is made on the record's key to transform it into a disk address. This process is illustrated in Figure 3-10. Methods available for generating an address from the record key include:

- Division
- Extraction
- Folding
- Squaring

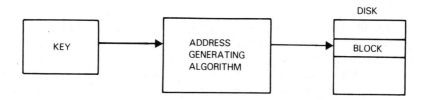

Figure 3-10   Storing and retrieving records in a random file

The *division* method involves dividing the key by a prime number close to the number of blocks available on the disk. Thus if there are 200 blocks, divide the key by 199 and the remainder becomes the relative address of the record.

Extraction, as the name suggests, involves a process of extracting digits from the key to use as the basis for the relative address. Thus if in a key 48573 the first, third, and fourth digits are extracted, and there are 200 blocks available, the relative address is:

$$457 \times 0.2 = 91\text{st block}$$

In *folding*, the key is split into parts and the sum of the parts (or some part of the sum) is used as the address, whereas *squaring* involves taking the square of the key and using some of the digits as the basis for the address.

In a performance simulation study by Lum, Yuen & Dodd (1971) on these and other address-generating techniques, the conclusion reached was that the division method, using a relatively large prime number gave the best overall performance.

A significant advantage that random file organization has over indexed sequential files is that the same procedure is used for the initial loading of the file and for subsequent insertions. It also requires no sorting prior to creation, and no index is used for direct access. This leads, in general, to faster access speeds when searching for a particular record. The disadvantages include:

- Wasted space on the file medium, since packing density is generally less than 85 per cent
- Synonyms leading to overflow use even at file creation
- The average seek time can be less in a sequentially organized file if the file activity is high

3.5   OVERFLOW HANDLING

In an indexed sequential file it is not necessarily possible to physically insert a record in its correct location, and consequently it must be placed in an overflow area with chains established to link the overflow position to the proper home address (Subsection 3.3.2). This situation occurs either because a variable length record expands and so cannot be accommodated in its home address, or because a new record needs to be inserted but there is insufficient space for it at its home address. The indexed sequential example worked in Subsection 3.3.2 shows how the home address is chained to the overflow area by a record in the track index. This chain record indicates where the records which have overflowed are located.

With random files overflow is needed for a different reason. The address-generating algorithm may calculate the same address for different records with different keys, and when eventually insufficient space is left at the home address, the other records have to be placed into an overflow area. How often this occurs depends on the address-generating algorithm. Thus, in a random file, overflow areas may be used at the time the original file is created, whereas in an indexed sequential organization overflow areas are only used under the two cases already mentioned: when new records are added to the file, or when variable-length records expand for some reason.

The overflow areas may either be located in the same cylinder as the home address or, alternatively, separate cylinders may be allocated for overflow. The former has the advantage that no disk arm movement is necessary in order to read records in the overflow area.

One method of handling overflow in random files uses a technique called 'open overflow'. Under this approach, when the capacity of an address is reached, subsequent records are stored in the first consecutive address with an available empty slot. This is illustrated in Figure 3–11, in which the arrival sequence of the records is $C_1, B_1, D_1, A_1, A_2, C_2, D_2, A_3, A_4, B_2, C_3, A_5, C_4, C_5, D_2$. Thus there is no chaining of overflow records, and if a record is not at its home address then each following bucket on the cylinder must be tried to locate the wanted record.

Address

A	A_1	A_2	A_3
B	B_1	A_4	B_2
C	C_1	C_2	C_3
D	D_1	D_2	A_5
E	C_4	C_5	D_2

Figure 3–11   Open overflow

An alternative to this approach is to use tags. A tag, pointing to the location where the record is actually stored, replaces the record in the home address.

3.6 CHAINS

A *chain* is a file structure in which the logical relationship between records is conveyed by means of pointers. In this approach, physically adjacent records may bear no logical relationship to each other. The pointer in the record is a field which 'points to' a second logically related record. The three main types of pointers are:

- *Machine address.* This gives the fastest operation but if files are relocated or reorganized in any way all of the pointer fields must be changed.
- *Relative address.* This type of pointer gives the relative position of the record with respect to some fixed point, often the first record in the file. It is almost as fast as the machine address, and has the advantage that the relativity is not upset if a file is physically moved.
- *Record identifier.* This gives the slowest operation because the machine address needs to be found by, say, looking up an index or using a hashing algorithm. It does however provide independence between the two data sets, allowing data to be reorganized or relocated without affecting the pointers.

One method of setting up a chain or linked list is as shown in Figure 3–12. In this approach, each record contains a field which indicates the next record in the linked list. Deletion of records under this structure involves changing the pointers, so that if, for example, record B was deleted from Figure 3–12, then the pointer in record A would have to be changed to d. A problem occurs if there is more than one linked list within a file, as that can give rise to intersecting chains. In that case, which pointer to comply with must be known if the correct linked list is to be followed. Furthermore, if one of the records is corrupted, then, with this one-way pointer system it is very difficult to determine the next record in the linked list. It should also be noted that the starting record in any chain must be known to get into the file in the first place.

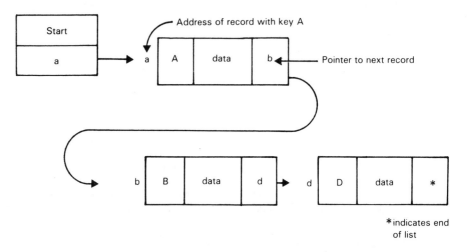

Figure 3–12 A linked-list data structure

In Figure 3–12 the pointers are shown as fields within the records. Another approach is to physically remove the pointers from the records and store them in a directory such as that illustrated in Figure 3–13. The advantage of this approach is that the pointers themselves may be traversed rapidly in the directory, which means that if a particular record is being sought there could be considerable time savings, particularly as much of the directory may be pulled into main memory for the searching process. Furthermore, the directory itself may be efficiently organized for searching.

Key	Logical follower key	Pointer
Start	A	a
A	B	b
B	D	d
D	*	*

Figure 3–13 A linked list using directory pointers

An example of the use of chains is given in Figure 3–14, in which the first record contains account data such as the account number, name, address, and balance, and then pointers to the month's transactions against that account. As new transactions occur they are chained to the previous record under that account number.

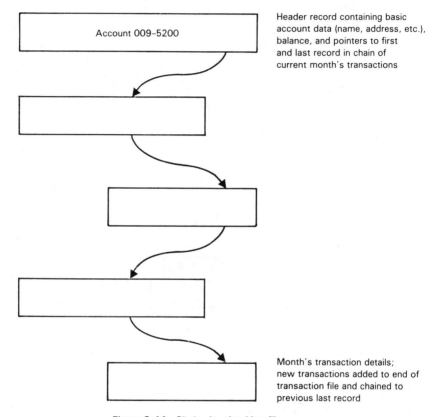

Header record containing basic account data (name, address, etc.), balance, and pointers to first and last record in chain of current month's transactions

Month's transaction details; new transactions added to end of transaction file and chained to previous last record

Figure 3-14   Chains in a banking file

The example in Figure 3–15 shows the chaining of records concerning an employee within a personnel data system.

3.7   RINGS

A *ring* is a list of records linked by pointers in a similar way to chains, but with the last record in the list pointing back to the first, as illustrated in Figure 3–16.

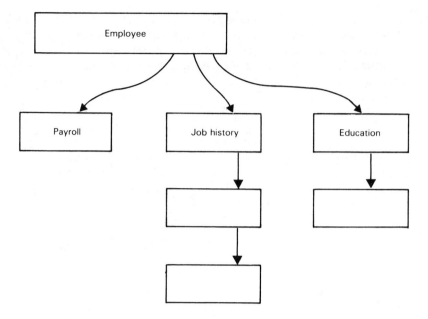

Figure 3–15   Personnel chains

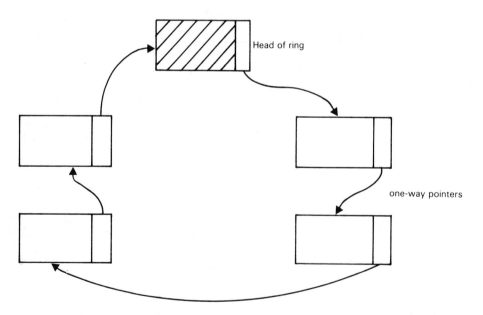

Figure 3–16   Ring structures

The ring structure may make use of bidirectional pointers as illustrated in Figure 3–17. Having such two-way pointers greatly reduces the problem which arises when a break in the ring occurs, for any reason. Thus the security of the data is greatly increased, as the chain can be read in the reverse direction. Two-way pointers can also speed up search time by allowing access from either end of the ring.

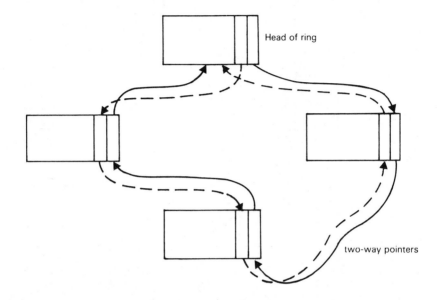

Figure 3–17   Bi-directional pointers

3.8 SKIP-SEARCHED CHAIN

To increase the speed of searching a chain, a system of two-way pointers can be arranged as illustrated in Figure 3–18, which allows skipping over a number of records to access a particular record. Thus if record 6 in this list was wanted, access would be from record 1 to record 4 to record 7, using the forward pointers, and then back to record 6.

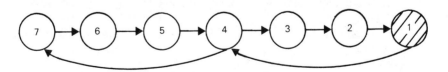

Figure 3–18   Skip-searched chain

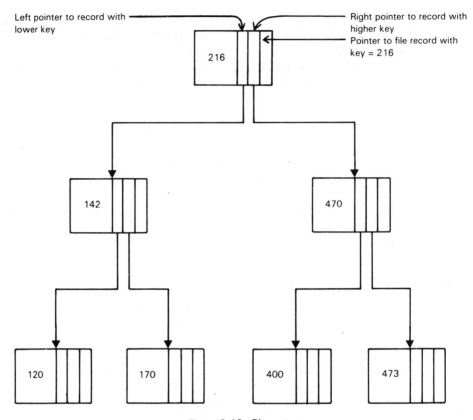

Figure 3-19   Binary tree

3.9   TREES

A tree is organized as a hierarchy of records or nodes, the highest of which is referred to as the root node. Each node at the lowest level in the tree is referred to as a leaf. A tree is illustrated in Figure 3–19, which shows that any node can have only one parent node. A parent can have any number of children in a tree structure; however the example shown is a binary tree in which each parent node has two children nodes, and each node contains a pointer to a record with a lower key and one with a higher key.

A particular type of tree known as the B-tree is discussed in the appendix to this chapter.

3.10   INVERTED FILES

In the file structures looked at so far, each record consists of a key followed by attributes of the particular entity. In an inverted file structure, each value that an attribute may have in a particular field has an ordered subfile. In other words, the subfile shows the attribute value, followed by a list of the records which contain that value. This is illustrated in Figure 3–20. This technique can be particularly useful when searching for an entity with given attribute values because the process is one of searching for the records which contain the desired attributes.

Normal file

Reference	Author	Title	Topic
658.403/164C	Senn	*Information Systems in Management*	Information systems
001.642/164	Cohen	*Data Base Management Systems*	Data base
621.38041/3B	Fitzgerald	*Fundamentals of Data Communication*	Data communication
657.02854/8	Cushing	*Accounting Information Systems*	Information systems
658.054/41A	Condon	*Data Processing Systems Analysis*	Information systems
001.528/13	Kroenke	*Data Base Processing*	Data base

Topic inverted list

Information systems	657.02854/8
	658.054/41F
	658.403/164C
Data base	001.528/13
	001.642/164
Data communications	621.38041/3B

Figure 3–20   An inverted file

This file is partly inverted, whereas a fully inverted file is one in which all attributes are included as lists; that is, every field is inverted.

3.11   INDEXED NON-SEQUENTIAL FILES

Subsection 3.3.2 shows how an index can be constructed to provide a direct access capability to a sequential file. However, the situation can arise in which access to a sequential file or even to a random file by some means other than the primary key is wanted. In this situation, another index can be similarly constructed to give access to the desired file. If the file is sequential on a primary key then it obviously cannot be sequential also on a secondary key and, therefore, an index to a non-sequential file is being constructed. For example, if a customer file is sequential on customer number it is unlikely that the file would also be sequential on customer name. If access on customer name is wanted, an index containing a reference to every record on the file could be constructed so that direct access either on the customer number or on the customer name would be possible.

Another application of this approach is shown in Figure 3–21. In this case access to a stock file is required, by the stock code, or by the bin number, or by the

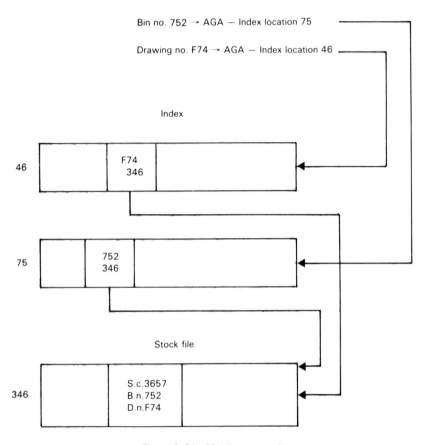

Figure 3-21   Multikey accessing

drawing number of the inventory item. The organization of the stock file is based on the primary key being the stock number. Access using the bin number or drawing number is by a combination of an address-generating algorithm and the use of indexes.

The search for a particular bin number or drawing number takes the number into an address-generating algorithm to determine an index location. This index record then indicates the address of the stock record in the stock file.

3.12 SEARCHING AN INDEX

If an index is sequentially organized then it may be searched serially, using a block search, or by binary chopping. A *serial search* simply reads every record starting at the beginning of the index. Therefore the average number of records read to find a given record is the number of entries in the index divided by two. A block search is similar to skip searching of a chain described in Section 3–8. The optimal block size is equal to the square root of the number of records in the index, and the average number of records that must be read is also equal to the square root of the number of records. In *binary chopping* the search method goes to the middle of the index and compares the wanted key with the key of the record found. This then identifies which half of the index contains the wanted record, and the process is repeated until the record is found. The process is illustrated in Figure 3–22.

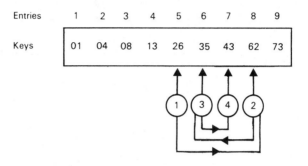

Figure 3-22   Binary chopping

To compare the three methods, the average number of probes required to locate a wanted record in an index of 600 entries is: 8 for binary chopping, 24 for a block search, and 300 for a serial search.

A random index can be searched efficiently by using binary trees. Each index record is arranged in the form of a key, a pointer to the record of that key in the file, and two pointers to two records in the index with a lower and higher key respectively, as shown in Figure 3–19. If a delete flag is included in the index entry then the capability of not breaking links in a highly volatile file is added.

APPENDIX TO CHAPTER 3 — TREE-INDEX SEQUENTIAL

The B-tree is a generalization of the binary search tree, discussed in Section 3.9. Each node of a B-tree of order d must contain between d and $2d$ keys and between $d+1$ and $2d+1$ pointers. This is illustrated in Figure 3–23. A B-tree should always be balanced, that is, have all its 'leaves' at the same depth. To see how this is achieved, consider the following examples of insertion and deletion in a B-tree of order 2. Note that the root node may contain fewer than two keys.

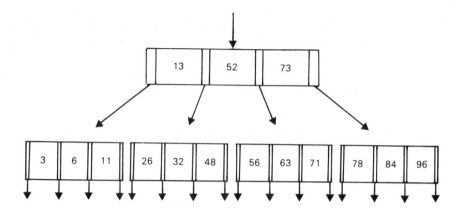

Figure 3–23 *A B-tree with three keys and four pointers per node*

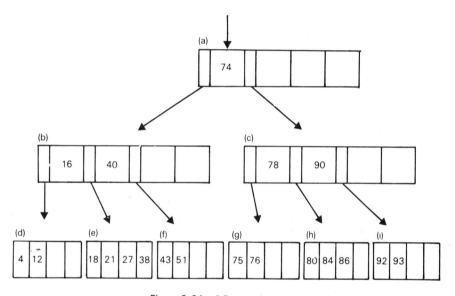

Figure 3–24 *A B-tree of order 2*

If key 53 is inserted in the B-tree illustrated in Figure 3–24, the seek comparison would go from the root node (a) to node (b) (53 < 74), to node (f) (53 > 40). Thus node (f) would become as shown in Figure 3–25. If key 24 is inserted, the seek comparison would go from the root node (a) to node (b) (24 < 74), to node (e) (24 > 16 but < 40). However this node already contains the maximum number of keys. In this situation what is known as a 'split' occurs, which is illustrated by Figure 3–26. Key 24 cannot fit in the leaf and consequently the leaf splits and an extra key is added to the previous node. If node (b) were to contain four keys also, the number of keys in node (a) would have to increase. Similarly if the root node (a) were full, the tree would increase in height by one level.

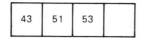

Figure 3-25   Leaf (f) after insertion of key 53

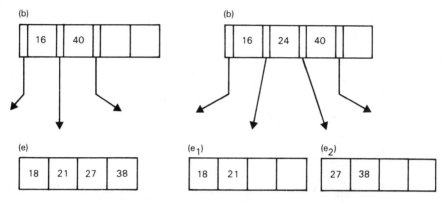

Figure 3-26   Before and after insertion of key 24

Returning to the original B-tree of Figure 3–24, assume now that key 12 is to be deleted. The deletion of key 12 results in fewer than the permitted number of keys in leaf (d) (underflow), and therefore a redistribution of the keys is necessary. In this case, sufficient keys are left in (d) and (e) for a redistribution which still satisfies the minimum-number-of-keys requirement. If there had been, say, only three keys left in (d) and (e), then the keys would be combined into one node.

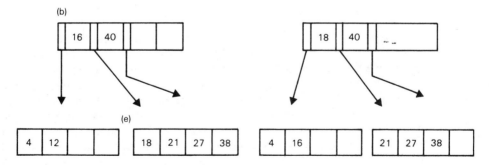

Figure 3-27   Before and after deletion of key 12

Variations on this approach have also been developed, one of which is IBM's VSAM, which makes use of a variation known as B+-trees. In a B+-tree there is a B-tree index pointing to a sequence set which contains the highest keys in each control interval. The sequence set is linked to provide a sequential access capability.

The sequence set, in VSAM files, then points to the actual data. This is illustrated in Figure 3–28.

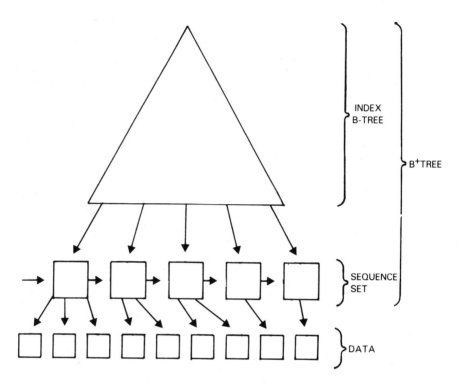

Figure 3-28   A VSAM file

Figure 3–29 illustrates the sequence set and actual data of a file. The index is called into main memory as needed by using virtual memory capabilities. Figure 3–29 shows the sequence set with keys 57, 73 and 97, which are stored on the same cylinder as the data and point to the control intervals. There may be several control intervals per track, or several tracks per control interval. Each control area must fit on one cylinder of the disk device. On the insertion of records into the file, control intervals and control areas split as required, in order to insert the new records in sequence. Thus, if records with keys, say, of 50, 53 and 54 were added, the file would then appear as shown in Figure 3–30. If more records are added to the sequence such that the control area could no longer fit the required records, then the control area splits, and two control areas are used, as shown in Figure 3–31.

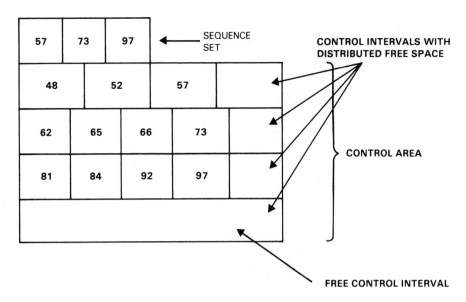

Figure 3-29 VSAM file data as loaded

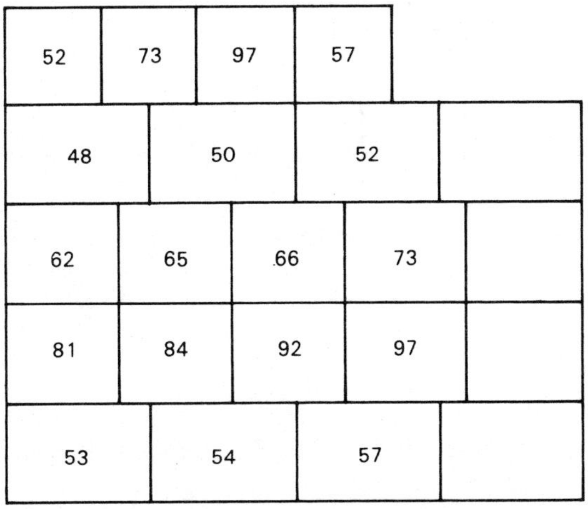

Figure 3-30 Control area after a control interval split

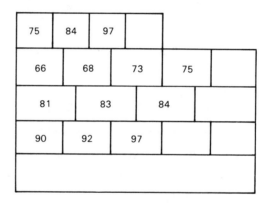

Figure 3-31   Control area split

REFERENCES

D. COMER, 'The Ubiquitous B-Tree', *Computing Surveys*, June 1979, pp. 121-37.

M. ELSON, *Data Structures*, Science Research Associates, Chicago, Ill., 1975.

C.C. GOTLIEB & L.R. GOTLIEB, *Data Types and Structures*, Prentice-Hall Inc., Englewood Cliffs, N.J., 1978.

T.G. LEWIS & M.Z. SMITH, *Applying Data Structures*, Houghton Mifflin, Atlanta, Ga., 1976.

V.Y. LUM, P.S.T. YUEN & M. DODD, 'Key-to-Address Transform Techniques: A Fundamental Performance Study on Large Existing Formatted Files', *Communications of the ACM*, April 1971, pp. 228-38.

CASE STUDY — UNION RECIPE SYSTEM

A large university catering division, which satisfies the requirements of students and special functions, has sales of over $1.5 million each year. The margin on meals prepared is very low, and consequently recipe costing and adjusting the selling prices to reflect changes in ingredient costs are key areas of management control.

A standard recipe system has been designed to provide Union management with an accurate and up-to-date cost of producing a cooked meal serving in the Union's kitchens. Each meal is prepared to a recipe, or a standard 'material mix', in which set proportions of ingredients are combined in some preset manner to produce the food. The cost of the serve is the total of materials used, labour, and an overhead charge. This system was designed because it was felt that the prices charged were failing to cover costs during periods of inflation — due to the slowness in repricing to reflect raw material cost changes. For example, if beef suddenly increased in price, the Union would want to adjust the prices of all serves which had beef as an ingredient.

The system involves two files, one of ingredients and their costs, the other of the organization's standard recipes. Periodically, the current cost of materials of each recipe is calculated and this cost is compared with the cost on the last occasion on which prices were reviewed. This report provides the basis for decisions concerning changes to selling prices. In this system there are approximately 60 different recipes and 400 different ingredients. Many ingredients are used in more than one recipe.

An overview of the system is given in Figure 3–32, the system flow is shown in Figure 3–33, while Figures 3–34 and 3–35 give the input layouts and file layouts respectively.

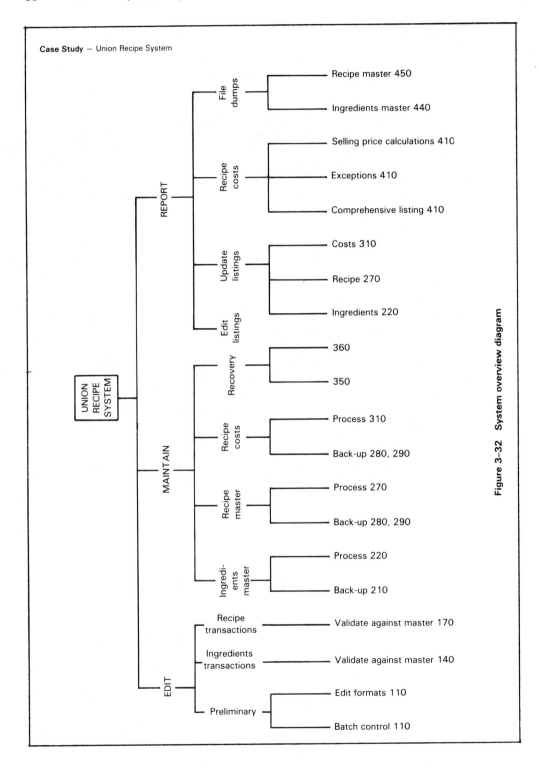

Case Study — Union Recipe System

Recipe master 450

Ingredients master 440

Selling price calculations 410

Exceptions 410

Comprehensive listing 410

Costs 310

Recipe 270

Ingredients 220

360

350

Process 310

Back-up 280, 290

Process 270

Back-up 280, 290

Process 220

Back-up 210

Validate against master 170

Validate against master 140

Edit formats 110

Batch control 110

Figure 3–32   System overview diagram

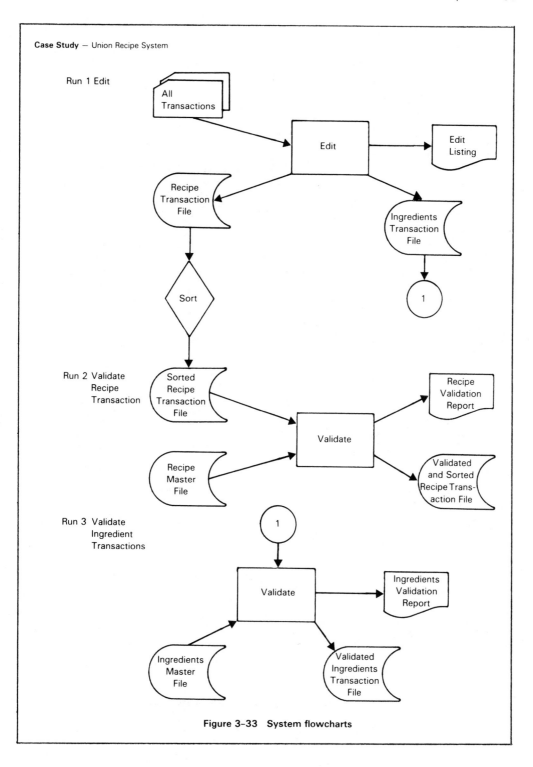

Figure 3-33   System flowcharts

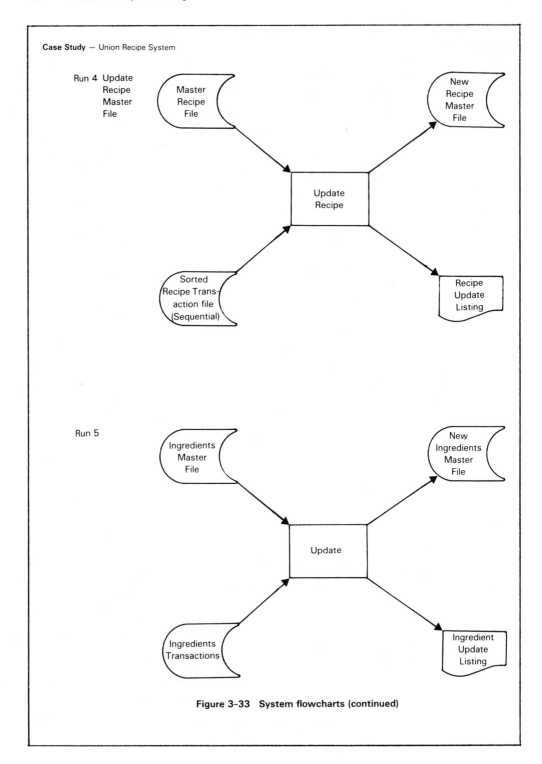

Figure 3-33   System flowcharts (continued)

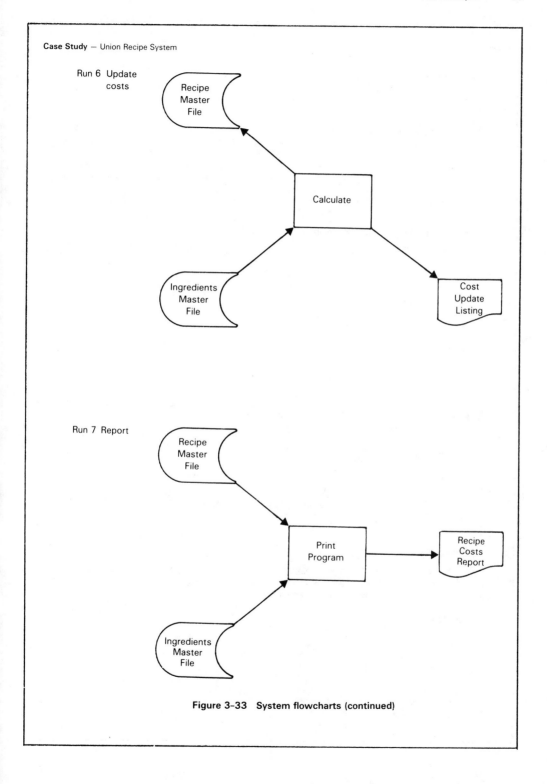

Figure 3-33   System flowcharts (continued)

Case Study — Union Recipe System

Ingredient transaction formats

Field	Picture	Insert	Amend	Delete
Key Ingredient no.	9(5)	√	√	√
Transaction type	999	110	150	190
Unit of measure	xx	√	*	spaces
Cost per unit	999v999	√	*	zeros
Description	x(30)	√	*	spaces

* At least one of these fields must contain meaningful data
√ Denotes the presence of this field

Recipe transaction formats (for recipe record)

Field	Picture	Insert	Amend	Delete
Key Recipe no.	9(4)	√	√	√
Ingredient no.	9(5)	zeros	zeros	zeros
Trans. type	999	210	250	290
Recipe name	x(30)	√	*	spaces
Current cost	999v999	√	*	zeros

* At least one of these fields must contain meaningful data

Field	Picture	Insert	Amend	Delete
Key Recipe no.	9(4)	√	√	√
Ingredient no.	9(5)	√	√	√
Trans. type	999	310	350	390
Quantity	999v999	√	√	zeros
Unused	x(30)	–	–	–

Figure 3–34   Input layouts

Recipe file

The recipe-master-file format has been designed for a computer system which only handles fixed-length records within one file. This file contains two types of records: the first for recipe details, and the second for ingredient details.

Recipe record

Key fields Recipe no.	9(4)	
Ingredient no.	9(5) value zeroes	
Record type	999	
Recipe name	x(30)	
Current cost	999v999	
Last reported cost	999v999	
Date last reported	9(6)	

Case Study — Union Recipe System

Ingredient record

Key fields   Recipe no.   9(4)
              Ingredient no.   9(5)
              Record type   999
Quantity   999v999
Unused space   42 characters

The file is organized sequentially on the key fields. Thus each recipe is completely defined by the recipe record and a number of following ingredient records, one for each ingredient used in that recipe.

Ingredient file

This is a random file accessed by the key fields.

Key fields   Ingredient no.   9(5)
              Record type   999
Unit of measure   xx
Cost per unit of measure   999v999
Description   x(30)

Figure 3-35   File layouts

ASSIGNMENT

Develop three alternative designs for the system, using magnetic tape files only. The system must provide the recipe cost report shown in Figure 3-36. Show any alterations to the file layouts necessary, and flowchart any altered runs. Assume that the main memory is very limited and therefore only very small tables can be stored there.

Union Recipe Cost Report
99/99/99   page 99

Recipe number	Recipe name	Ingredient number	Ingredient name	Ingredient cost	Current cost	Last cost	Date last reported
4567	Goulash	13874	Beef	7.456			
		26871	Onion	0.381			
		34827	Capsicum	0.283	2.871	2.695	27.3.81

Figure 3-36   Recipe cost report

4 SYSTEMS ANALYSIS

4.1 OVERVIEW OF SYSTEMS ANALYSIS AND DESIGN

Systems analysis is the study of a system's problems, including the identification and analysis of various alternative solutions. In *systems design* the particular broad solution chosen is elaborated, and an appropriate detailed design produced ready for programming. This distinction between analysis and design is not rigid, but does suggest the primary foci of these two phases of systems development activity. Aspects of analysis and design work are performed throughout both these phases. Thus the analysis phase involves a component of design in the creation of alternative solutions, while the design phase involves analysis in, for example, detailing output specifications. Although this chapter specifically examines systems analysis, it begins with an overview of both analysis and design to establish an overall perspective in which to discuss analysis in detail.

The detailed analysis and design of an application system involves a range of skills, including interviewing and fact finding, political compromises, collection and analysis of a bewildering array of data, and finally preparing a design (or a number of alternative designs). It is not a cut and dried progression through a number of defined stages but is iterative in nature, as each stage is cycled through to improve the understanding of areas not sufficiently explored earlier.

4.1.1 A Model of Systems Analysis and Design

The activities carried out in the analysis and design phases can be represented diagramatically as in Figure 4-1, and this framework forms the basis of the dis-

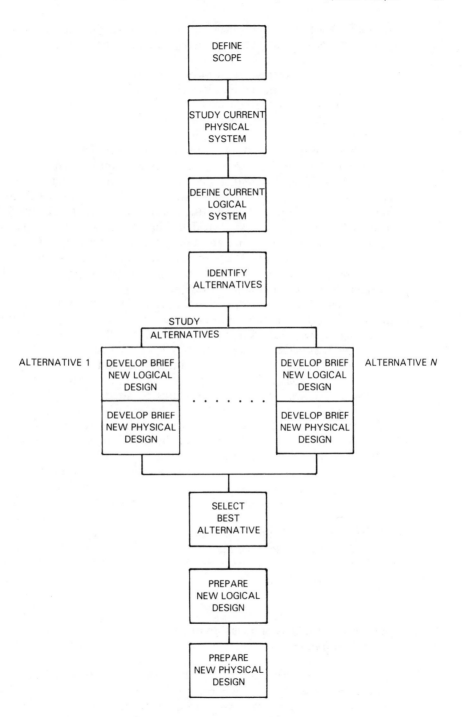

Figure 4–1   Steps in the analysis and design of a new system

cussion in this and the following chapter. Figure 4–1 illustrates the basic model of systems analysis and design as consisting of four components:

- The study of the current physical system
- The study of the current logical system
- The design of the new logical system
- The design of the new physical system

Although the content of these steps is spelt out in greater detail later (Subsections 4.5, 4.6, 5.2, and 5.4), a brief description is given here.

Current physical system study. The starting point of analysis is the current physical system. The word 'physical' denotes that all relevant details of the actual implementation of the system and its environment are captured and studied. This includes, for example, the kind of data filing and retrieval systems used in the departmental boundaries which affect the system, and the attitudes and perhaps the cognitive styles of the users. The purposes of studying the current physical system are both to discover the present system's strengths and weaknesses and to develop an understanding of the logical system requirements.

Current logical system study. At the physical system level the interest is in the identity of the information processor and the 'how' of the current system. The current logical system study investigates the 'what' of the current system: it distils the mass of detail gathered in studying the physical system to obtain the underlying logic of what is happening. At this basic level there is frequently little difference between a manual and a computer-based system. Thus the product of the current logical system study is a specification for the procedures required to fulfil the same business objectives as the present system. As well as forming a foundation for the system's design, this stage enables the current logic to be analyzed for weaknesses.

New logical systems design. Here the users' objectives for changes to the systems functions are incorporated into the design. The changes may range from extra reported information to whole new operational procedures which were previously uneconomical given the current system's technology.

New physical systems design. The new logical design communicates the functions to be carried out, while the physical system's design shows how they are to be implemented. Thus the physical design translates and packages the logical design for the chosen technology: computer processor, data-base or file-management system, communications-network access method, local terminal intelligence, peripheral storage capacity, etc.

4.1.2 Tasks in the Analysis and Design of an Information System

Initiating the systems study. Ideally, systems analysis is preceded by a request incorporated in a terms of reference for the study, which specifically lays out the objectives of the systems analysis exercise, the scope of the study, and management's perceptions of the problems present with an expression of the benefits that they hope to realize. In some cases, systems analysis is preceded by a less formal document, or maybe only a verbal communication, in which management express the feeling that a certain area of the business may lend itself to study because they suspect better technology or better systems design may lead to some cost savings or other desired benefits. Indeed, apart from projects involving minor modifications to an existing system, it is rare for a user to be very definite about what needs to be done, or even what the scope of the system study should be. Whatever the nature of the start of the project, it is essential that the user management support the work, and that they believe there is a possibility of improving on the present system.

Analysis. Following the receipt of the terms of reference, the current system is studied at the physical and then at the logical level. This thorough study of the current system and its environment permits the analyst to work effectively with the user to define the user's objectives and to draw, where appropriate, from the organization's long-range plan for identifying alternative solutions. This is the creative heart of the analysis exercise and can only be well executed if both user and analyst have mutual trust and sufficient knowledge of each other's area to be able to communicate freely and work as a team. All too often distrust, excessive pride, secrecy, and not understanding the need for team work prevent this user/analyst cooperation ever emerging. Some techniques which assist in building this level of mutual cooperation are dealt with in Section 4.2.

Feasibility study. In the feasibility study segment, each of the proposed alternative solutions are examined by first developing a brief new logical design and then a brief new physical design. This omits much of the detail and is principally directed at establishing the size, type, and cost of the required hardware resources, including files storage, computer processors, communications, and input/output devices. These steps are required to examine the economic and technical feasibility of the proposal. When all alternatives have been studied the selection can be made. The cost/benefit data contribute significantly to the decision, but a number of subjective areas are also very important, highlighting the extent of user contribution needed at this stage.

Preparing the design. Following the selection of the most attractive alternative solution, the analyst sets to work on the system's design. Many facets of the system need to be defined precisely before the detailed specification can be developed. This stage is a careful examination of the overview design prepared earlier, filling in all the holes. Chapter 5 considers this design stage in detail.

4.2 FORMING A CREATIVE TEAM

A number of studies have been carried out to identify the most important success factors of a computer-based information system. Some of these studies have examined failed systems to determine what went wrong (e.g. Lucas, 1975), and others have sought the opinions of computer professionals and managers (e.g. Carter, Gibson & Rademacher, 1975). A conclusion common to all these studies is that the identification of the information needs of management and the involvement of the user in the project are two of the most important factors associated with successful information systems development. These two factors are, in reality, mutually inclusive and dependent. Effective user involvement ensures good requirements definition, while without user involvement it is almost impossible to define requirements accurately. The issue is, then, one of finding the best means to develop the systems analyst/user team. Setting up the team is, desirably, the first step taken in a project.

Both the user and the systems analyst need to prepare themselves before they can work together effectively. The user needs to become familiar with computer systems, and the systems analyst needs to learn about the user's job. If users are not sufficiently prepared for their role, they are not able to approach the tasks of defining requirements and of identifying possible alternative solutions creatively. For example, an inventory clerk, whose only experience is working with a manual system which updates inventory cards once a week, may feel very bold when defining a requirement for an update every second day. People's expectations and requirements are greatly moulded by their understanding of what is feasible from an economic and technical standpoint. Another example, which illustrates erring on the side of excessive expectations, is that of a sci-fi enthusiast inventory clerk who lists as a requirement a system with two-way human-computer voice communication capability for customer ordering and for inventory interrogation and reporting. But in this case at least the user is motivated to think creatively about the job and the role that computer technology can play in assisting a better job to be done. This is the user frame of mind necessary for successful requirements definition. The term 'unfreezing the user' has been used to describe the task of preparing users for requirements definition by exposing them to a number of exciting alternative ways in which computer systems can assist them.

One way that unfreezing can be accomplished is for the user to visit a number of organizations with varying systems implementations, or to view technology in an area where it is relatively advanced. For example, seeing an advanced colour-graphics-based computer design system may stimulate managers to think of ways of receiving information other than through printed reports. Each project needs its own carefully thought-out approach to unfreezing the user. Obviously some users are well aware of current technology and alternative systems approaches, and no preliminary work is needed. However, in the case where the user is firmly entrenched in the current system, the price often paid for not unfreezing the user is a computer system which is a copy of the manual system and, later on, a stream of enhancement requests because the user is dissatisfied with the low level of the system, possibly due to seeing other, better systems.

Systems analysts have typically shied away from exposing users to advanced systems, possibly because they fear losing control of managing the user's expectations and requirements. What is needed is for the systems analyst to recognize the legitimate and necessary role of the user in defining requirements, and that the proper role of the systems analyst is as catalyst, organizer of information, project secretary, and technical advisor. The systems analyst needs to learn about the user's job environment, the current system, and its business impact before being able to interact creatively with the user. This is accomplished by the steps in Figure 4-1 called 'study current physical system' and 'define current logical system'.

4.3 DEFINING THE SYSTEM'S SCOPE

The first step of the systems team is to establish and obtain agreement on the scope of the systems study. This is an important exercise and embraces both political and technical issues. If the problem area is wholly under the control of one user, the political aspect is likely to be minor, but if the area overlaps a number of responsibility areas or is to be a common system for a number of users, the political question is likely to dominate. As computer systems always bring change, there are usually in the power stakes a number of winners and losers. The losers may be exampled by the department manager whose staff level is reduced following the implementation of a system, or by the accountant who previously had responsibility for preparing the management information reports, which are now to be prepared on the computer. The winner is often seen as being the EDP department, which is why this department is often viewed with a certain amount of suspicion by users. If the systems analyst fails to recognize the political nature of defining the system's scope, significant problems can ensue. These problems may be either in obtaining agreement on the system's scope or, worse still, in securing cooperation with implementing the completed system.

This scope needs to be broad initially, and narrowed down as successive areas are omitted during the study. This procedure ensures that the scope eventually selected is well understood by the users. Some points that should be considered in arriving at the best scope for a study are:

- The temptation to widen the system boundary excessively is best resisted. Systems analysts are trained to have a systems-wide view, which may lead them to err on the side of defining too large a scope for the system. An example of this is the case of an organization requesting a new inventory system, but the analyst setting the scope of the system feels, after examining them, that order entry and invoicing should also be included because they involve the entry of data to the inventory system. And, after checking on the receipt of purchased goods, the accounts-payable system may also be included in the scope. And so on. However, since many small problems are much easier to solve than one large one, it is simpler to carry out a number of separate systems analysis studies, integrating each one with the preceding work, than to attack one large project encompassing them all at one point in time. Wherever possible, it should be the aim of the systems analyst to decouple systems so that they can operate, as far as possible, independently. In this way, the effect of errors and omissions can be localized, and subsequent maintenance work is easier. This does not mean that systems should not be integrated, but rather that the boundaries between systems be tightly managed to ensure that they are simple and pass the minimum necessary data.
- The system's scope should be such that the system can be implemented within a reasonable period of time (which may be around six months) —

before the user's enthusiasm declines to a point at which success is
jeopardized.
- The system must be provided with hooks for linkage to future systems so
that a narrow scope does not lead to problems with integrating new systems.
This means that the systems interface requirements have to be included in
the project scope.
- The scope should be chosen to maximize the potential benefits.

4.4 DEFINING THE TECHNICAL OBJECTIVES

Concurrently with defining the scope and objectives of the system, the
technical objectives need to be decided. These objectives are additional to the user's
performance and functional objectives. They need to be made explicit, as they
influence design decisions and the cost/benefit trade-off decisions which are
constantly being considered by the members of the project team during the design
stage of the project. The objectives can be grouped under eight headings:

- Flexibility/maintainability
- Schedule and cost
- Efficiency
- Integration
- Security
- Reliability
- Portability
- Simplicity

However, these technical objectives cannot be considered singly because many
overlap, and they can be in conflict with one another. Consequently, a balance needs
to be struck depending on their relative importance in a given situation. An obvious
example of this is a conflict between the goal of providing, say, portability of the
design to different system software and hardware environments and the goal of
efficiency when running in a given environment.

Flexibility/maintainability

Flexibility and maintainability have been grouped together because they both
relate to the need for and the ease of modifying the system. Any system is subject to
pressures for change, over a period of time, by which enhancements or modification
to the original system are called for. Therefore, when designing, the analyst should
attempt to predict the directions in which the system may evolve and so design to
minimize the trauma of future changes. The more successful the analyst can be in
this area, the greater is the expected life of the system. For any system, the point is
reached where the changes required to the system are so great that the most effective
solution is to redesign, or in other words, to begin the lifecycle again. If, by designing
for flexibility and maintainability this point can be deferred without extra costs, then
the total long-run cost of the organization's systems can be reduced.

Another example of the need for a flexibility objective is the situation where a system is being designed for one division of a multidivision organization. In this case it may be possible to design a system which can be used by many divisions. The system may contain more facilities than required by any one division, but the cost advantage to the total organization may be considerable when compared with the alternative of separate but similar systems for each division. This approach can have an effect on user requirements by requiring standardization across divisions on such matters as the chart of accounts, code design, and perhaps input and output data contents, so that other objectives such as efficiency can be met.

Schedule and cost

In some situations the schedule or cost constraints may be of overriding importance and act as a significant factor in making design decisions. An example of a schedule constraint is the case of a government department entrusted with introducing a new health insurance scheme which the government has promised the public will commence on a certain date. An objective to minimize cost is frequently held in one-off limited-life systems and leads to short cuts which, under other circumstances, would not be acceptable.

Efficiency

Efficiency for a system can be defined as the resource usage needed to run the system. Efficiency was an important objective in the 1960s and early 1970s when, motivated by high computer costs, designers would trade many hours of design time for marginal improvements in a system's efficiency. Today, in many organizations, efficiency is not given great weight as it is considered cheaper to utilize hardware inefficiently than expanding costly software development resources to tune application systems finely so they run more efficiently. Nevertheless, in some circumstances efficiency is very important, particularly in a real-time application where efficiency measures such as terminal response time are important.

Integration

When designing, the analyst must remember that the system is a part of the total organization and is, therefore, a subsystem which must fit with the other subsystems in that organization. Regardless of the nature of the system under study, the output of this system provides input to some other system. Consequently, the designer must decide on the means and the extent to which the new system is to mesh with other systems. This can affect the output provided, input used, as well as the manner in which the data are stored and aggregated. Examples of systems options, in order of increasing level of integration, are:

- The same data are input to more than one system (no integration)
- Printed output is coded and key entered (manual integration)
- Output tape file provides connection (tape file integration)
- Master file is updated by one system and accessed by another module (disk master file integration)

- Module-level integration, when one system calls the module of another

Security

The design of a secure system involves many facets including system controls and physical security. The important point is that adequate control must be built into the system from the beginning, as attempts to add controls after the design is complete are usually unsuccessful and expensive. For this reason many designers welcome the assistance of audit personnel during the design stage to give expert advice on the level of security required and the controls necessary for the system. The need for security differs markedly from system to system. For example, a cash-dispensing system or an electronic funds transfer system have a far greater need for security than, say, a production control system in a cement plant. Refer to Chapter 10 for a further discussion on security.

Reliability

System reliability has many aspects, including accuracy of the stored data, recovery and restart capability, hardware reliability, and application and system software reliability. Furthermore, increasing reliability incurs increasing costs and, therefore, decisions on the cost/benefits of providing increased reliability in a given situation are necessary.

A common example is in a critical real-time environment, such as an on-line banking system, where system failure can interrupt customer withdrawals and so may severely disrupt and damage the organization. Because the processing is critical, hardware is duplicated to ensure as close to 100 per cent hardware reliability as possible. Reliability of application software is increased through comprehensive testing by various methods, and by providing ways to back out transactions which would cause a 'systems crash'. Also, the design philosophy must allow easy testing. An unnecessarily complex design makes the testing more difficult and, therefore, increases the likelihood of flaws in the system.

Portability

Although it is rarely possible for a system to be completely portable from one hardware environment to another, choices made throughout the system lifecycle influence the degree of portability attained. The concern for portability arises from uncertainty about future computer suppliers and from the need for compatability with other computers within the one organization. When a system is being designed, the differences between manufacturers should be recognized and taken into account if manufacturer-unique facilities are considered for the design. Unfortunately, the use of the more advanced manufacturer-supplied system software, such as data-base management systems and transaction-processing software, has reduced the degree of application systems portability. When portability is an important objective, a standard high-level programming language should be used, and file access and storage strategies kept simple.

Simplicity

Just as some of the most effective inventions have been the simplest, so too do simple solutions to system problems provide the most effective answers. Unwarranted complexity in the design may boost the ego of the designer, but it does so at the expense of the user and the people who implement the system. For any system designed to be operated by untrained users, simplicity of the user interface is a very important consideration.

4.5   STUDYING THE CURRENT PHYSICAL SYSTEM

After defining the system's scope and objectives, the next step in analysis is to thoroughly understand and document the current system at the physical level. An important distinction in this methodology is that between the physical system and the logical system. The physical level contains complete details of not only what is happening but also how it is being carried out. The logical level focuses attention only on the 'what' and omits the 'how'.

A simple example may help to make this point. Suppose an analyst wants to draw a physical data flow diagram (DFD) of a manual stock-recording system (refer to Chapter 2 for a discussion of DFDs). Jan B. is the stock issue clerk and Jackie F. handles stock receipts. The stock receipts and stock issue documents are sent to Fred W. who sorts and batches them before updating the stock file which is held on cards in product name sequence. The physical DFD is illustrated in Figure 4–2. The physical details here are:

- The names of the people responsible for activities
- The sort and batch procedures
- The sequence of the stock file

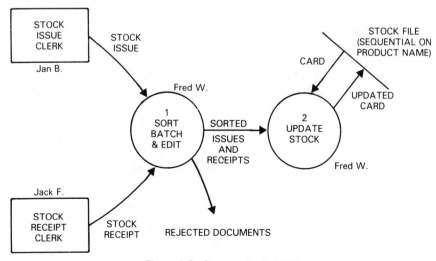

Figure 4–2   Current physical DFD

The logical DFD is obtained by removing the physical details or else replacing them with their logical equivalent. This gives rise to Figure 4–3. Note that the edit, which is a logical procedure, has also been deleted. This could have been left in but has been omitted because all input data must always be edited, and so the edit procedure contributes no additional information to the DFD. At the logical level, only the necessary procedures which transform the input data into output data are represented.

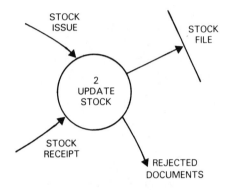

Figure 4–3   Current logical DFD

For simple systems it may appear a waste of time to plod through all the details of the physical system and draw the DFD, but experience shows that it is all too easy to omit important considerations such as, for example, the effect of a new system on the users because no one has bothered to find out in detail how the current system operates. Furthermore, a detailed knowledge of the current system is needed to plan the appropriate change strategy for implementing the new system. Drawing the physical DFD forces the analyst to consider every possible aspect within the scope of the new system, and simplifies the user's job of understanding the documentation and spotting any errors.

After drawing the DFD, all the information flows need to be defined in detail in a data dictionary, and the accuracy of the source data audited by sampling. All codes used in the system should be included and their structure given. An example of how all the data items in Figure 4–2 can be defined in this dictionary is:

Stock issue   = date + job no. + {product code + quantity}

     the {} mean a repeating group or iteration

Stock receipt   = supplier code + order number + date
                + product code + quantity

Product code   = 5 digits unstructured

Stock issue no.   = 4 digits unstructured

Supplier code   = First two alphas of customer name + 6 digits

Order no.   = 6 digits + check digit modulus 11

Brief notes explaining the nature of each of the DFD procedures ('bubbles') should accompany the DFD. These notes should explain the actions taken to process the incoming data to each bubble and convert it to the output. In addition, copies of all the forms used in the current system must be collected and identified with the relevant section of the DFD. Some authors (e.g. De Marco, 1980) favour the writing of the DFD procedures in a form of pseudo-code they call 'structured English'. Except in very complex situations this level of detail does not appear to be warranted.

Although the broad methodology for documenting the system is presented in terms of data flow diagrams, other documentation tools such as flowcharts could be used if preferred. The DFD has the advantage over other tools of the symbols used having no physical connotation, and hence it is relatively simple to proceed from the physical to the logical view of the system. The physical descriptions are provided by notes attached to the DFD symbols, and these can be removed and the diagrams reorganized fairly simply when drawing the logical DFD. The DFD has two other advantages over other documentation tools — it is simple to draw freehand, and its levelled hierarchical nature encourages a top-down design strategy in which detail is progressively revealed without redrawing higher level or preceding diagrams.

As well as the physical flow of data through the system being documented, the transaction volumes for each data input document and the number of records to be stored for each file need to be measured and recorded. Care must be taken to record transaction rates at peak times so that both the average rate and the peak rate are known. This is particularly relevant for on-line systems, where there is little opportunity to smooth the load. It is also a consideration with some batch systems which have strong monthly and/or seasonal fluctuations in volume, such as in the retail industry.

Obtaining the detailed data on a system, and organizing and presenting the information, are tedious and time-consuming tasks which call for much patience on the part of the analyst. The length of time spent is partly due to the large number of people who must be interviewed, since no one person understands the system, and the time needed to obtain information in each interview. Most systems have a multitude of special rules (e.g. 'this is what we do unless it is the last Friday of a month when we handle it differently') which also add to the difficulty, as do conflicting accounts of what happens.

4.6 THE CURRENT LOGICAL SYSTEM

The data flow diagram of the current logical system is derived from the current physical system by removing all physical information to obtain a DFD which shows only the transformations necessary to process the data from input to output. No change is made to the system in drawing the current logical DFD other than removing references to physical aspects. Hence, in Figure 4–3, which gives a simple example of a current logical DFD, the file contents are unaltered but the access method is not referred to.

At the logical level there is generally very little difference whether a system is manual, computer batch, on-line real-time, conventional files, or data base. Note that all these descriptions refer to alternative physical processing means. Since the current logical DFD expresses necessary actions on the data, it forms the foundation for constructing the new system. For an operation-type system like order entry, purchasing, or debtors, the current logical DFD relates to standard business practice which almost certainly needs to be performed in the new system. For higher level systems like an MIS, the current logical DFD may form less of a framework for the new system. The data dictionary developed in documenting the current physical system is also applicable to the current logical system, and normally needs only checking but no modification between these stages.

4.7   DEFINING THE USER REQUIREMENTS

Defining the user requirements accurately and completely is probably the most essential task in the whole systems project, and the one most critical to its success. If discovered during implementation, small errors or omissions made in defining a system's requirements may be impossible to rectify without a complete rewrite of the system. Section 4.2 covers the important aspect of building a creative team capable of developing a sound and imaginative requirements definition. Broadly, this team should analyze the current system and the business environment spanned by it to identify the problems which can be overcome and the opportunities which can be exploited by the new system.

4.7.1   Problems of the Current System

Deficiencies of a technical or efficiency nature are probably the easiest problems to define with regard to a current system. These inadequacies may be associated with problems caused by the type of input media used, or by the volume of processing either overloading certain areas of the organization or exceeding the capacity of the current system and so leading to late reports and delayed processing. Also quite easily identified are the control problems of the current system. Auditors frequently draw these to the attention of management as a result of the financial audit.

Timing, completeness, or the arrangement of the current system's reports are problem areas frequently cited by users. New data items can be identified, preferred timing of reports specified, and data rearranged. However, the analysis team should be careful not to settle too early on such requirements because often they are fairly superficial and tend not to represent the major potential benefits of the new system.

4.7.2   Opportunities

The more difficult but more potentially rewarding area for user requirements lies in identifying the opportunities for a new system to make a major impact on a key area associated with the success of the business. An example can illustrate this. A team was involved in carrying out an investigation for a new payroll system. Initially, the system's requirements were summed up as the need to carry out the same logical functions as in the current system. Minor clerical savings were identified but it was unlikely that they would have much impact on the organization. Then the analysis team widened the scope of their investigation to consider ways in which a system containing employee data might help the organization accomplish its objectives. This revealed a problem the organization had been having in employee record keeping and in identifying employees with wanted skills. Extending the system to meet this need represented a very significant benefit to the organization.

There is no easy recipe for spotting significant systems opportunities. What can contribute to the likelihood of their being spotted is members of the analysis team and its steering committee thoroughly understanding the business in which their organization is engaged, and its strategic plans.

4.8 WORKED EXAMPLE

As an example of the use of data flow diagrams to model the current physical, current logical, and new logical systems, an enhancement to the Union Recipe System (introduced in the Chapter 3 Case Study) is carried out. This is a very simple enhancement and the methodology would probably be somewhat abbreviated in practice.

4.8.1 Problem Statement

The Union has taken over a large catering business and now has 400 recipes and 2000 ingredients on file. It employs 50 chefs to prepare the recipes, each chef being a specialist in the 5 to 10 recipes allocated to him. To enable the chefs to study the recipes they are responsible for, the recipe cost report produced by the Union Recipe System is now to be printed in alphabetical order by chef's name. Therefore the recipes are to be listed under the responsible chef's name in recipe-number sequence. A sample sketch of the desired report is given in Figure 4–4.

Chef	Recipe no.	Recipe	At last report		Current
			date	cost/serve	cost/serve
ABEL, Aaron	0342	BEEF GOULASH	5.5.79	0.84	0.96
	0864	CHICKEN A LA KING	30.3.79	0.73	0.86
EDGELL, Janet	0952	CHICKEN AND PEAS	15.8.79	0.82	0.89
	1214	BEEF CURRY	15.5.79	0.25	0.32
SANDERS, Col	0386	FRIED CHICKEN	3.3.79	0.65	0.81
	0941	CHICKEN LEGS	3.8.79	0.52	0.59

Figure 4–4   Union recipe cost report

Recipe Changes

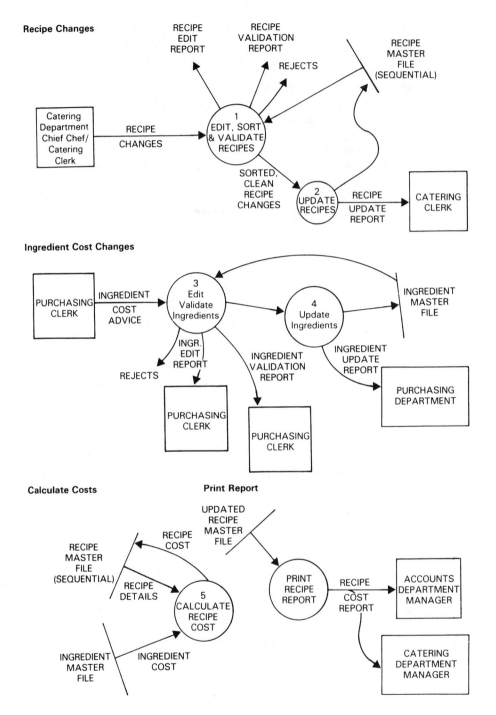

Figure 4–5   Union recipe system: current physical DFD

4.8.2 Current Physical Data Flow Diagram

The current physical DFD is given in Figure 4–5. It is broken up into the major activities needed to produce the recipe cost report:

- Update recipe changes
- Update ingredient costs
- Calculate new recipe costs
- Print recipe cost report

The DFD is drawn at quite a high level. Should more detail be required, any of the bubbles could be broken down into the next level of detail. Note that, for clarity of presentation, no mention is made of the supporting manual procedures. Normally they would be included. The data dictionary for the physical DFD is given, for this computer system, by the input and output formats, and the file formats are given with the Union Recipe System documentation (see Chapter 3).

4.8.3 Current Logical Data Flow Diagram

This DFD is obtained from the physical DFD by removing all physical references in the system, and is given in Figure 4–6. Note that the editing and validating steps have also been eliminated, since all data must be edited on entry to a system. The data dictionary for the logical DFD is:

Recipe changes = recipe no. + transaction type [add, change, delete] + (recipe name) + (sale price) + (ingredient no. + transaction type [add, change, delete] + quantity)

    Note: ( ) marks an *optional field*, [ ] *either, or* and, { } *iterations of.*

Ingredient cost advice = ingredient number + transaction type [add, change, delete] + (unit of measure) + (cost per unit) + (description).

    Note: A decision table would probably be advisable to show which fields are required with which transaction types, or else use the format given in the case study.

Recipe master file = recipe no. + recipe name + current cost + last reported cost + date last reported + {ingredient no. + quantity}

Ingredient master file = ingredient no. + description + unit of measure + cost per unit of measure.

New recipe cost = recipe no. + current cost

Recipe cost report = recipe no. + recipe name + {ingredient no. + ingredient name + ingredient cost} + current cost + last reported cost.

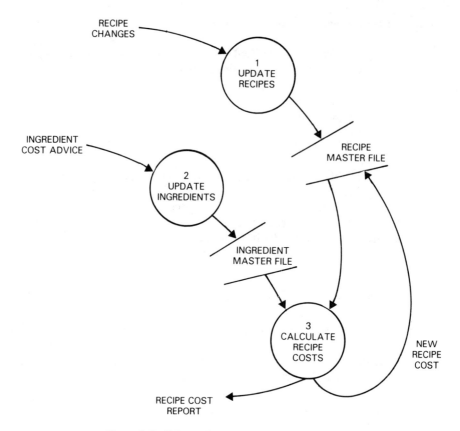

Figure 4-6   Union recipe system: current logical DFD

4.8.4   New Logical Data Flow Diagram

The current logical DFD now has to be modified to embrace the requirements of the new Union recipe cost report. Since each chef is exclusively allocated a number of recipes, it seems reasonable to include the relevant chef code on the recipe master file. The new recipe master file will be:

Recipe master file   =   recipe no. + recipe name + chef code + current cost + last reported cost + date last reported + {ingredient no. + quantity}

A new file is needed for the chefs:

Chefs' master file   =   chef code + chef name + (chef address + other chef data).

The changes required to the current logical DFD concern only bubble 3 of Figure 4-6. Figure 4-7 illustrates these changes. The data dictionary entry for the modified cost report is obvious and so has been omitted.

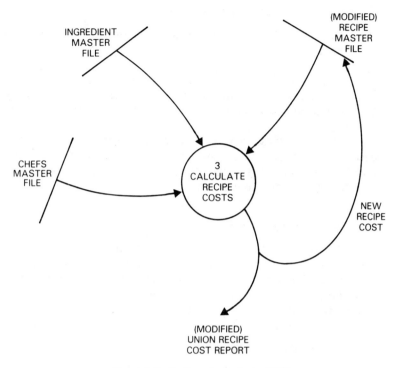

Figure 4-7   Portion of new logical DFD

4.9   IDENTIFYING THE DESIGN ALTERNATIVES

There are usually many solutions to a given specification of user needs, each alternative differing in some significant way from the others and also in terms of costs and benefits. Never should any one solution be put forward without specifying and analyzing a number of potential answers to the requirements. Only by following this maxim can the analysis team be sure that the most attractive solution has been selected. Clearly, if the range of potential solutions proposed by the team is too narrow then the recommended solution may be deficient, so it is important that a sufficiently broad set of solutions is considered. This can be helped by recognizing some of the main decision variables in developing any solution, including:

- The location of data input, output, and processing
- The response rate of the processing
- The mode and medium of data input
- The style and medium of data output
- The system's human–computer boundary
- The level of data aggregation in the system.

In addition, the technical objectives covered in Section 4.4 have a major bearing on the identification, analysis, and selection of design alternatives.

Location of input, output, and processing

The broad classes of solution alternatives which depend on the location of equipment are:

- Centralized data input, processing, and output
- Decentralized input and output with centralized processing
- Decentralized input and centralized processing and output

For each of these solution alternatives, the data communications between the decentralized source of data and the central office can be handled in a number of possible ways including leased line telecommunications facilities, overnight mail bag, dial-up line, and courier.

The processing response rate

Processing can be instantaneous, as in on-line real-time processing where each transaction is edited and its contents update the relevant files in real-time. An alternative is to carry out the editing in real-time but to perform the updating on a batch-processing basis. The slowest alternative is to enter and process the data in a batch mode, with a number of possible run frequencies.

Mode and medium of data input

There are a number of systems in use today which provide clever solutions to the problem of data input. An example is the on-line automated grocery-checkout counter at which bar-coded products are read by a scanner, the purchases totalled, and the inventory file updated. As systems move further into the factory and ware-house, data input becomes a more difficult aspect, calling for new initiatives.

Data output

Output of data can be: full listings, exception reports, ad hoc or on request; by voice, on paper, on visual display units with or without a hard copy device, or microfiche; in color or black and white; in pretty pictures or in numbers. There are many posssibilities to help the user best profit from the information produced by the system.

Human–computer boundary

Many different boundaries between the manual and the computer system can be drawn, each one presenting a different cost/benefit trade-off.

Data aggregation

At many points in a system, decisions can be made concerning the level of data aggregation. Some of these decisions affect the type of reports produced; others affect the future usefulness of the historical data for analysis purposes; and many affect the level of aggregation of the data input, and the coding and data entry costs.

Many retail systems operate by aggregating input and reports on a department basis to reduce coding and data input costs. While there is a trend to enter and store data on the lowest level, there are many situations where this is an expensive luxury, unjustified by the use which the data have.

4.10 ANALYSIS OF DESIGN ALTERNATIVES

After identifying a number of design alternatives, the next step is to narrow down the search by applying broad decision criteria, and so reduce the list to a manageable number of alternatives. What is manageable depends on the resources available for the analysis and the importance of the project. In some cases perhaps two alternatives are analyzed in detail, while in others four or five may be considered.

The general structure suggested for the analysis is, for each alternative, to: (1) develop a brief new logical system design, and (2) a new physical system design. There is not time to develop a complete physical design for each of the alternatives, so only the key points can be established. These key points need to be the facets of the system which have a governing influence on the way the alternative functions, and on its cost and benefits. In general, the use of a certain physical component which dominates the cost/benefit equation for the system may be the key point. An example of this is using a point-of-sale terminal to capture cheaply the product codes of goods sold.

When the new physical system for each alternative has been designed, (3) the technical feasibility and selection of the hardware and systems software proposed has to be argued, (4) the size and speed of the communications facility must be established, and (5) the various personnel and staffing levels need to be considered. A checklist for the points to be considered is given in Chapter 12. Finally, (6) each alternative's impact on the organization and its business needs should be carefully analyzed as it is on this analysis that the system's success depends.

Chapter 5 considers design in detail and should be read to understand the nature of the preliminary design task undertaken in this stage. Chapter 12 discusses the details required in the feasibility study report, which is the climax of the work of the analysis team on a project, and gives specific details of techniques which can be used to carry out the cost/benefit analysis of the design alternatives.

REFERENCES

D.M. CARTER, H.C. GIBSON & R.A. RADEMACHER, 'A study of critical factors in management information systems for the U.S. Air Force', *National Technical Information Service AD-A-009-647/9WA*, NTIS, Springfield, Va., 1975.

H.D. CLIFTON, *Business Data Systems*, Prentice-Hall Inc., Englewood Cliffs, N.J., 1978.

T. DE MARCO, *Structured Analysis and Systems Specification*, Prentice-Hall Inc., Englewood Cliffs, N.J., 1980.

C. GANE & T. SARSON, *Structured Systems Analysis*, Prentice-Hall Inc., Englewood Cliffs, N.J., 1978.

H.C. LUCAS, *Why Information Systems Fail*, Columbia University Press, New York, 1975.

S.J. WATERS, *Computer Systems Design*, NCC Publications, Manchester, U.K., 1974.

CASE STUDY — UNION RECIPE
SYSTEM ENHANCEMENT

Refer to the Union Recipe System case study in Chapter 3. The Union now wants to enhance its recipe costing system to produce an ingredients-used Report.

Date DD.MM.YY

page 99

(Week ending) DD.MM.YY
(Month ending)

Ingredient code	Ingredient description	Qty used	Unit of measure	Current unit cost $	Cost of materials $
00287	POTATOES	250	kg	0.80	416.00
00369	AVOCADOS	2	ea	0.70	1.40

— report sequence: ingredient cod·
— total at end of report on cost of materials

Figure 4–8   University union ingredients-used report

Requirements

Weekly collection of the sales of each recipe, input to the modified system to produce the new ingredients-used report, the format of which is given in Figure 4–8

- The report produced on a weekly and a monthly basis, with the monthly report being the total of the weekly reports falling in the month; this means that some months have four weeks and some have five weeks
- Note that the cost of materials is calculated on a weekly basis, using the unit ingredient cost current at the close of the week

ASSIGNMENT

Prepare a system design by amending the current Union Recipe System to satisfy the requirements. Show:

1. New logical data flow diagram.
2. New systems flowchart of the physical system, showing only the altered sections.
3. Format of new input fields, new master files, new work files and new intermediate reports produced (where applicable), and organization of new files.
4. Format and organization of existing files if they have been amended.

Explain and justify your answer where appropriate.

CASE STUDY — PURCHASING DATA FLOW DIAGRAM

The current purchasing subsystem of a manufacturer does not involve any computerization. At present the following procedures apply:

1. At the beginning of each year, vendors of standard items are reviewed on the basis of price, service, and payment terms, and a list of approved vendors is prepared by Barbara Hassel the purchasing officer. This list is then approved by the factory manager.

Purchase requisitions are raised by operating departments and sent to the purchasing section, which enters each requisition in a purchase requisition register under purchase requisition number.

When a purchase requisition for a standard item is submitted to the purchasing section by one of the operating segments, one of two procedures is followed. If the cost is $500 or more the purchase requisition must be approved by the factory manager. If the cost is less than $500 the purchasing officer approves. After approval and selection of a vendor (vendor code entered), all requisitions are sent to the accounting section where the account to be charged is entered as a code and the requisition returned to purchasing. Any requisitions not approved by the factory manager or purchasing officer are returned to the originating operating segment with the reason for disapproval written in.

Purchase requisitions for non-standard items are prepared on a special requisition form and must be approved by the factory manager. If the anticipated cost of the order is less than $500 then Barbara Hassel selects a vendor and records the vendor's name and address on the requisition. If a requisition is for $500 or more Hassel then prepares a 'request-for-bid' form which is sent to two or three possible suppliers, and the lowest bidder accepted and entered on the requisition.

2. After the purchase requisition is returned from the accounting section, a prenumbered purchase order is prepared and distributed as follows:
   (i) original to the supplier, after updating purchase requisition register
   (ii) copy to open order file with purchase requisition (filed alphabetically by vendor), and entered in the purchase order journal (held in the purchasing department) in order number sequence
   (iii) copy to originating department
   (iv) copy to receiving store
3. When the goods are received, a receiving report is prepared by the receiving store, showing the supplier's name, items received, quantity, and indicating any damage or deficiencies. The original of this report goes to purchasing, and a copy is filed (alphabetically by vendor) by the receiving store.
4. In the purchasing department the receiving report, purchase order, and invoice are compared for quantity and price and, if satisfactory, are sent to the accounting section. If there is a price or quantity difference, the purchasing department initiates an investigation into the reasons for the difference. When orders are completed an entry is made in the purchase order journal to indicate the completion.

Each month the purchasing department prepares reports on:

   (i) outstanding requisitions, listing all requirements for which an order has not been placed
   (ii) outstanding orders, listing all purchase orders unfilled
   (iii) orders received report, showing all orders filled during the month

Case Study — Purchasing Data Flow Diagram

ASSIGNMENT

Draw this logic in the form of data flow diagrams, and comment on the advantages and disadvantages of this form of analysis and documentation. It is suggested that you separate the logical data flow diagrams into three sections:

- The order cycle — covering the distribution of the purchase orders
- The receiving cycle — covering the receipt of goods from the supplier
- Monthly processing — producing monthly reports

5 APPLICATION SYSTEMS DESIGN

5.1 INTRODUCTION

After presenting an overall framework for systems analysis and design in Section 4.1, Chapter 4 deals with systems analysis. This chapter continues where Chapter 4 finishes, and considers specifically the design of a new system after the analysis and requirements definition have been carried out. Thus the stages of designing the new logical system and designing the new physical system are dealt with, along with their supporting activities. The strategy of first designing the logical system and then the physical system reduces the complexity of the development and allows an easy progression through the design.

5.2 DEVELOPING THE NEW LOGICAL SYSTEM

Thexnew logical system is a design which includes all the user's logical requirements and shows — by means of the data flow diagrams (or other technique), the data dictionary, and supporting documentation — the network of logical steps required to transform the input data to the output reports, documents, and file data.

While the user's requirements are largely defined in the feasibility study, the definition continues through the design stage as the user participates in the development of the design and sees ways in which the utility of the system can be increased. While one part of the user's requirements is logical in nature (e.g. reports, inputs, file updating), there is another part which is physical (processing volumes and speeds, input media objectives, response times, machine size restrictions, reporting frequency, and file sizes). These physical requirements are considered at the physical design stage after the logical design has been completed.

It is important that the probable general shape of the future physical environment is available to the design team before they embark on designing the new logical system, as there is a relationship between the logical system's requirements and the physical means used to accomplish these requirements. For example, a user may well dictate different information requirements under different assumptions about reporting frequencies and form of presentation. The feasibility study, containing abbreviated new logical and physical designs for each solution alternative, should normally provide an adequate framework of the selected physical system for the new logical systems analysis and design to be carried out. However, this needs to be reviewed, and any ambiguities resolved before commencing the logical design.

There are three parts to developing the new logical system:

- Developing the new logical DFD
- Designing the files
- Updating the data dictionary

Clearly, these three parts must move together. For example, the new DFD cannot be drawn until it has been decided what the files and their contents will be.

5.2.1   Developing the New Logical Data Flow Diagram

For most data-processing systems, business practice dictates that the current logical system forms the basis for the new system. Thus the logical design stage consists of superimposing the user's logical requirements on the current logical DFD. This results in extension and modification of current DFDs, but in most cases preserves the broad structure of the diagram. For an example of developing a new logical DFD, consider the current logical DFD for the elementary (manual) order entry system shown by solid lines in Figure 5–1. It is assumed the new requirements can be summarized as:

- Place this system on the computer
- Produce listings of orders and back orders

These new requirements, shown in Figure 5–1 by dotted lines, produce only minor modifications to the current logical system. They also require additional data to be captured on the files, and a number of modifications to the data dictionary and to the detailed procedure specifications.

5.2.2   Designing Files

Designing the files for the new logical system requires grouping into like classes the objects or entities for which the system needs to maintain or store information.

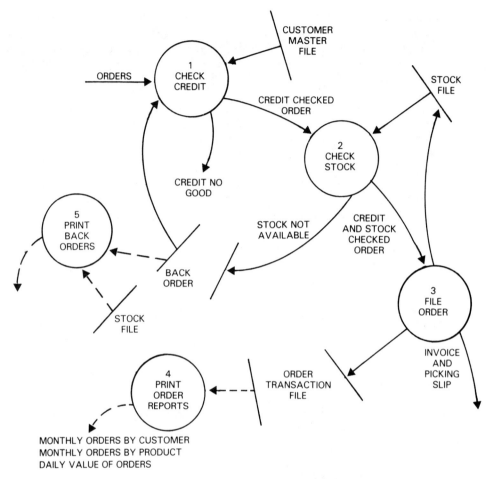

Figure 5-1   Order entry system logical DFD

Examples of entities typically encountered in business systems are customers, products, employees, sales orders, machines, back orders, assets, and general ledger accounts. Some of these entities relate to groups of transactions and would be stored on a transaction file, while others relate to entities which are relatively long lived (e.g. customers, products) and would be stored on master files. In this chapter it is assumed that the data structures are not complex. In Chapter 7 this whole question is investigated in much more detail, and approaches to file design for more complex data structures are investigated.

In most cases the individual records need to be identified either individually (e.g. master file records), or as a member of a group (e.g. transaction file records). Examples of group membership are:

- All the order transactions in a certain batch
- All the orders for a certain product
- All the orders from a certain customer for a certain product

A record is identified by the unique record key which is composed of one or more data items on the record. For example, a customer number is normally the data item which acts as the key for the customer file. As the key constitutes the unique identifier for a record it should be carefully designed. A key may be chosen from one of three classes: structured, unstructured, or partially structured.

Structured or speaking keys have certain positions within the key structure designed to communicate coded information. For example, 1150N may indicate a 50mm, 11-gauge nail. Here the first two high-order digits give the gauge, the next two the length in millimetres while the final character of the key indicates we are dealing with a nail. These keys used to be popular with unit-record-oriented systems when much sorting was necessary because only sequential files were available, and record storage was very much at a premium since record length was generally preferred to be shorter than the 80 characters of a punched card. Another example of a structured key is the airline three-alphabetical-character airport code. Thus SYD is Sydney, SFO is San Francisco, LON is London, and NYK is New York Kennedy Airport.

Unstructured keys contain no information apart from the fact that they refer to a certain object. When unstructured keys are used all the data concerning the object are kept as attribute information within the data items of the record. Hence, if the nails just referred to were given an unstructured key the length, gauge, and product type would be held as data items within the record.

Partially structured keys contain some unstructured information. For example, a student identification number may hold the year of first registration in the leading two fields, with the remaining fields unstructured.

Desirable properties of keys are: they should be brief, not subject to change, unique, and simple.

Brevity. Keys should always be as short as possible, consistent with uniquely identifying all the objects, and allowing for growth and turnover within the objects. This last point refers to the situation where entity records are being deleted and added but the deleted keys are not to be reused for some years to avoid errors. If keys are longer than necessary, extra clerical time is taken transcribing and entering the key data, additional errors are made, and storage space is needlessly occupied.

Unchangeability. This characteristic applies principally to structured keys, which should not hold data that are likely to change over time since it is a major undertaking to change a key for all the history, budgets, and other data that relate to the object. An example of a poorly designed code is a product code with a leading field which indicates the selling division responsible for that product. If, at a later stage, the organization wishes to reorganize the selling responsibility for its products, its coding structure would be a barrier.

Uniqueness is an obvious requirement for a key that is to provide an identification of a single object.

Simplicity can relate to both the key structure and its length. Keys should desirably all have the same number of fields to avoid the problems of right or left justification and of recognizing when a character of the key has been unintentionally omitted. It makes for a simpler key structure to have all fields either numerical or alphabetical characters. Mixed alpha and numerics cause confusion between such pairs as 7 and T, 2 and Z, 6 and G, 5 and S, and a number of others. One has only to try to decipher the postcode on a hand-written English letter to see the problem.

5.2.3 The Data Dictionary

The data dictionary defined for the current system now needs considerable expansion to include the additional data elements, new files and records, and new data flows that may have been included on the new logical DFD. The data dictionary has one or more entries for each input document, each output document, each unique data flow identified on the DFD, and for each of the files. For systems of an average commercial scale this makes it quite a large document containing hundreds of entries. Hence it is a prime candidate for being placed on a computer to simplify the continual updating and revision made to it during the development effort. Ideally, for a large project both the data dictionary and the DFDs should be held on a computer database which automatically, by reference to the data dictionary, makes sure that all the DFDs are consistent, and which can print a number of useful reports including a 'where used' listing for each data element. These reports would assist both in the ongoing development and in the later maintenance and enhancement phases of the project which, in terms of the total effort invested over the lifecycle of a project, generally exceed the initial development effort.

One of the important activities in checking the new logical DFD is making sure that the diagram is internally consistent. That is, for each bubble in the diagram, all the data that comes out of a bubble also goes in. Consider the example in Figure 5–2. In the dictionary the data flows are defined as:

purchase invoice details	= product code + date + quantity received + total cost
old stock details	= product code + b.f. quantity on hand + b.f. average cost
new stock details	= product code + c.f. quantity on hand + c.f. average cost

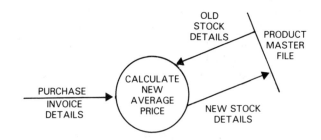

Figure 5-2 Consistency check example

The documentation for the bubble 'calculate new average price' shows that:

$$\text{c.f. average cost} = \frac{\text{(b.f. average cost x b.f. quantity on hand)} + \text{total cost}}{\text{c.f. quantity on hand}}$$

c.f. quantity on hand = b.f. quantity on hand + quantity received

A check such as is shown in Table 5–1 can prove the bubble flows consistent by demonstrating that each of the output data items can be traced, either directly or through a calculation, to input data. Such a check is needed for all the non-trivial bubbles in the DFD, and for all flows to and from files. This helps prevent the module and program interface problems which normally contribute so significantly to errors found in program and systems testing.

Table 5–1   Consistency check of bubble 'calculate new average price'

Output data items	Input data items used (if a calculated field)	Source
new stock details = product code + c.f. quantity on hand +		purchase invoice details
	b.f. quantity on hand	old stock details
	quantity received	purchase invoice details
c.f. average cost	b.f. average cost	old stock details
	b.f. quantity on hand	old stock details
	total cost	purchase invoice details
	c.f. quantity on hand	source already specified

Data integrity controls for input, files, and outputs should be specified in this stage. The principles for designing these features are discussed in the data controls Sections 10.3 to 10.6.

5.3   IMPLEMENTATION PLANNING

5.3.1   The Need for an Implementation Plan

A careful and well-devised plan for the implementation of a new system needs to be made before finally settling on the physical design. An important reason for this concerns the effect of the system on the user — the need to design the system so that the changes can be introduced in a way that is most likely to lead to the system's acceptance. A bad impression created during the system's implementation by poor training, excessive errors, long breakdowns, or any other reason may jeopardize user support and cooperation and require much work to overcome the loss of support. Any system introduces change to its users, and research shows that the way the change is introduced is as important as the change itself in influencing attitudes to the system. Bostrom & Heinen (1977) give a good summary of this research. The process of introducing change starts at the project initiation and reaches a climax during implementation, when the users gain their first impression of the operating system. Planning a smooth introduction for a new system is often a major and complex activity, especially when a considerable number of people are involved in the changeover. It can present a challenging design task which ranks equally with the initial design.

Some other reasons why the implementation needs careful advance planning are:

- The need to design and build-in the capability of rapidly identifying, diagnosing, and correcting errors that may be found during the implementation
- The high cost of system implementation
- The time-critical nature of many of the implementation activities in the total project timetable
- The need to have a fall-back position in case the system fails to operate successfully

The chief activities during the installation of a new system are:

- Checking to make sure the new system is producing the right information within the specified time frame
- Completing the training of users, key entry operators, and computer operators
- Training management in the use of the information reports produced by the system

Developing the plan for implementing a project cannot wait until after programming is complete, as it may then be found that the system cannot support the desired implementation plan. Three examples are given to illustrate this point.

For the first example, consider the task of preparing an implementation plan for an organization which is developing an on-line order entry system to replace its current batch system. The old system uses sequential customer and product master files on tape. It is estimated that ten operators will be required to enter orders on the new system's on-line terminals. The current system includes eight clerks and operators batching and controlling documents and using key equipment to enter the batched orders. The common strategies for implementing a new system include parallel running and phased changeover. In this case, parallel running would involve hiring (or transferring) eight new operators, training them on the old system, training the present staff on the new system, running the two systems in parallel, and then laying off the newly trained staff. This is clearly an unattractive option. Phased changeover, involving phasing the new system in and the old system out, appears more attractive. This alternative involves training a few of the current clerks or key operators on the new equipment and then cutting them across to the new system.

This process is repeated a number of times as the new system is phased in. During the phased implementation, invoices and transaction files are produced from two sources, and customer and product master files have to be kept in duplicate. This latter point is due to the current system using sequential master files, while the on-line system requires direct access. Under these circumstances, checking credit and stock availability is a complex manual task requiring access to both systems. This task needs assistance from special features provided in the new system specifically for this purpose. It would not be possible during changeover to provide automatically the credit and stock-checking functions as they will be after the implementation is complete. Also, maintaining and reporting inventory status is a more complex task during changeover. Thus the changeover itself generates a set of special user requirements which have logical as well as physical design implications. It is necessary to carry out a detailed systems analysis of the implementation strategy for the new system (considering a number of alternatives, then selecting the best) and provide features in the system to ease the manual burden during the changeover period.

The next example is drawn from a case study prepared by one of the authors. A large international oil company developed a new capital assets system to give better control over its widely distributed assets of service stations, bulk depots, refineries, offices, plant, and equipment. The new system, an advanced database application, was to replace a simple sequential file application which had served the corporation for more than ten years. No thought was given to the implementation of the new system during the design phase, as it was believed that parallel running of the two systems would be straightforward. The unexpected problem which occurred in the implementation was the extreme difficulty of reconciling the two systems. Since all the reports had been changed it was very difficult to trace imbalances in totals, except by laborious manual searches through file dumps. Some 30 clerks were co-opted for three weeks each month to reconcile the two systems' monthly reports in order to prove the new system correct. After three months of parallel running the chief accountant could not stand the strain on clerical resources any longer and, despite the fact that a number of errors were still being located, decided that the new system had to be satisfactory. In fact quite a number of the errors located were due to problems in the old system, not the new system. Had thought been given to the task of reconciliation, special computer-prepared reconciliation reports could have been provided for in the system and the manual effort almost entirely eliminated.

The last example concerns a very large personnel records system, developed for a government body, and capable of maintaining all personnel records (pay, history, leave, and skills) for around 50 000 employees on a distributed on-line basis. After the design had been completed, the equipment purchased, and programming well under way, an independent review of the project found that no implementation plan had been prepared and the only way the designed system could be implemented was by completing the entire system, installing the full communications network, and placing the 50 000 employees on file. Thus no phased changeover was feasible with the system as designed. Since it was recognized as being impossible to implement such a large system at one time, and to run it in parallel with the existing system, consequently a major change to the design was necessary to permit phased implementation.

5.3.2 Changeover Approaches

The changeover approaches which generally form the basis for implementation plans are:

- Parallel running of new and old systems
- Phase in new system and phase out old system
- Pilot study of new system
- Start up new system and stop old system

These four methods are illustrated in Figure 5–3.

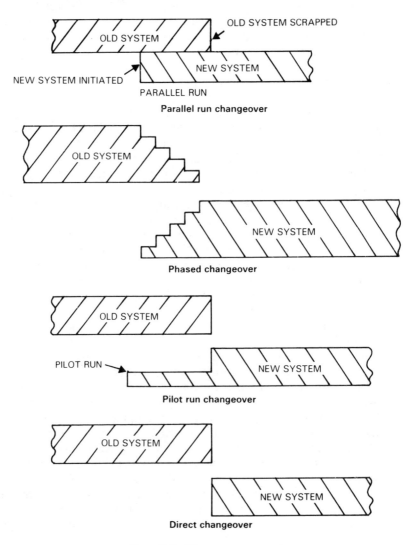

Figure 5-3 Changeover approaches

Parallel running

In this approach both the new and the old system are in parallel for a number of cycles until the new system has been proved to be operating reliably and correctly. This changeover approach is generally suitable where the new system is not very labour intensive so that operating both systems together does not over-tax employee resources.

However, it is inevitable that parallel running will involve a number of staff in operating two systems concurrently, and the implementation plan must provide for temporary staff and/or overtime to catch up on the extra workload. Because parallel running involves starting the whole new system up at one time, it is only suitable for small-to-medium-sized systems. For large systems, subsystems need to be implemented progressively both because of the effort required to get a system going, and also to localize problems to a smaller more manageable segment.

Phased changeover

Phased changeover is the process of progressively cutting small segments of the old system across to the new system. This may be done by periods of parallel running for each segment before cutting across or, alternatively, cutting a segment across directly without running in parallel first. Deciding whether to run in parallel depends on the scale of the segments, the difficulty of returning to the old system should the new be unsatisfactory, and the impact on the organization of the system being down for a time.

This changeover approach is most suitable for large projects and for projects involving a significant number of personnel, when it is impractical to consider operating the old and new systems in parallel. The phased changeover is particularly suitable for installing a system where there are natural segments in the user population such as provided by an organization structure. For example, when installing a new payroll system for an organization based on a divisional structure, it may be decided to phase the system installation by division.

Pilot run

The pilot run method uses the new system to rerun data from a previous period, thus allowing reconciliation of the data. Alternatively, sampling a selection of the current data may be used as input to the system.

As the name implies, this method is, in essence, a further system test on live data. When the system has been proved to be working correctly and the staff are comfortable with operating it, the new system can be started up and the old stopped.

Direct changeover

The direct changeover method is to stop the old system on, say, the last day of the week, month, or year, and start the new system up. In some circumstances there is no alternative to this method. However, it must be borne in mind that direct changeover is risky unless the old system can be easily revived and used as a fall-back position. This is often impossible as the old system's files are out of date. Generally, if this method is required, a period of pilot running should be considered to first test and prove the system under operating conditions.

A number of companies in Australia have been in very great difficulty as a result of using direct changeover for their accounts receivable systems. Faced with the new system not working, they were unable to send statements to their customers for a period of some months, thus placing the whole organization at risk.

5.4   INPUT/OUTPUT MEDIA SELECTION

The choice of input and output media can have far-reaching cost implications for the system designed. Frequently the costs of input data capture and output and dispersal are a significant proportion of the total operating cost of a system. In some cases the specialized and efficient nature of the data capture system is the key to the cost effectiveness of the entire system. Some point-of-sale systems are good examples of this. Other reasons for taking care in designing the input and output systems are:

- Poor input design leads to input errors and user dissatisfaction
- The variety of input devices available provides many alternatives, one of which may afford a very creative solution to input problems
- The range of choice offered in output media is not as great as for input media; careful design chiefly falls into the category of producing the most informative and compact reports

5.4.1   Input Media

Batched input

Batched input is probably the most commonly used method of input. It affords good opportunity to verify and control input, but its disadvantage is that it isolates the users from data preparation and introduces time delays between data entry, data processing, and output. This makes error correction more difficult and reduces user motivation for careful data entry. The main methods used for batched input can be divided into keyed input or direct reading devices.

Keyed input is still the most commonly used method, and can produce punched cards, magnetic tape, or magnetic disk. The use of punched cards is now rare but the methods used in the past were either cards wholly punched from input documents (80 or 96 column cards), or prepunched or partly prepunched cards. This latter form of input is generated by prepunching a card, its return indicating that the transaction is complete; it is called a turnaround card. Another possibility is to prepunch some of the data onto the cards (e.g. product code, invoice numbers), and then to pull the cards from a 'tub file' and complete the punching of the transaction (this form of input is largely outdated).

Key entry onto tape or disk has many advantages over punched card. These include factors in the physical environment such as silent operation, faster computer reading of the medium, simple storage and handling of the medium, and faster keying rates because of the elimination of card transport time in the card punch. Other advantages are due to the inclusion of buffer memory and logic capability in the key device. This means that simple edit checks and batch controls can be carried out while data entry is in process. Furthermore, because the whole record is normally carried in buffer memory until it is completed to the operator's satisfaction, then if the wrong key is depressed (80 per cent of errors fall in this category) the error can be corrected immediately.

For high-volume data-entry applications, minicomputer-based systems are often used. They enable many (from 5 to 50, say) operators to key data which is then stored on a central disk unit. Batches are written to magnetic file for input to the main computer. This is illustrated in Figure 5–4. The main advantages, in addition to those already discussed, are:

- A high degree of format keying support
- Extensive edit checking of input data
- Statistics and status reports prepared on-line for supervisor
- Operators do not have to handle media
- Cheaper system per key station
- Verification control can be simplified
- Automatic batch control checks

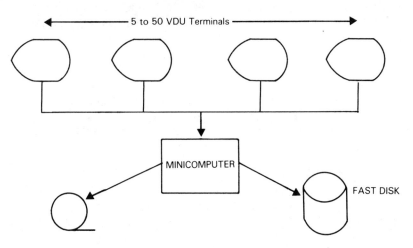

Figure 5–4   High-volume data entry system

The main disadvantage is:
- All key stations become inoperable if the controlling minicomputer goes down

The objectives of all the direct-reading devices are to decrease the time taken to input data to the system, and to reduce the number of errors occurring in the data input activity, and consequently the use of these devices is increasing.

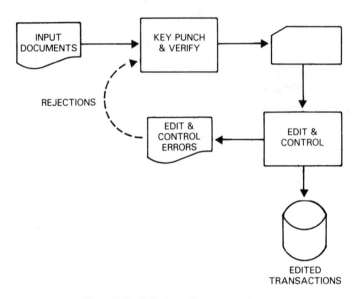

Figure 5-5   Fully keyed input procedures

Optical character recognition (OCR). OCR devices can read mechanically formed or precisely written hand-printed characters. They are therefore well suited to turnaround documents such as utility accounts, having the advantage of being both computer and human readable. A major problem, however, is read errors which give rise to increased system activities. This can be seen by comparing Figure 5-5 with Figure 5-6.

If fully keyed input is used, then only one procedure applies to the data entry task, but if OCR input is used there is still a need for keyed input when input documents cannot be correctly read or are not available. Thus the automated and manual procedures are both necessary, adding to the system's complexity.

Magnetic ink character recognition (MICR). This technique is used mainly in the banking industry. The MICR characters are preprinted and provide very low error rates, but at an increased cost.

Bar code. This code is read by a document reader, and can be used as an alternative to OCR characters on turnaround documents. The chief disadvantage is its lack of human readability.

Hand marked mark sense. These devices operate on the basis of sensing a mark in a specific location on the document, and as such can be used for many forms of coded data. They cannot be used for free-form data.

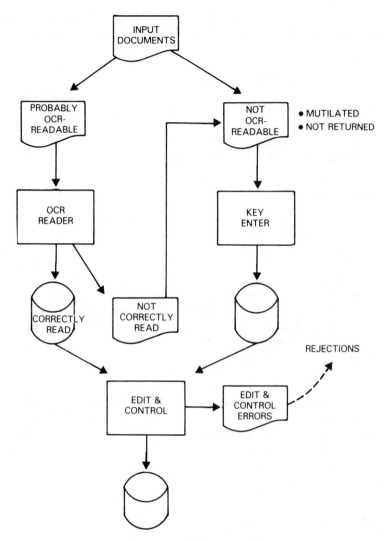

Figure 5-6   OCR input procedures

On-line input

On-line input means terminal devices which input data to a computer and update files or write edited and verified transaction records for later updating. The big advantage of on-line data entry is the ability to correct data at time of input and to update files in real time. The main on-line input device alternatives are:

Key-printing terminals. By producing a hard copy, the key-printing terminal can serve both for input and output.

Visual display unit (VDU). A VDU uses a TV-like screen to display text. It operates much faster than a printing terminal, allows for selective and simple editing of data formats, and allows a whole screen of data to be assembled before communication. However, if printing is required for documents or reference, a separate printing terminal must be employed.

Card and badge readers. These readers are typical of special-purpose terminals for point-of-sale, library systems, time-clock systems, etc.

Special-purpose process control. In some manufacturing applications the machines can be instrumented and attached to an input device to input automatically data such as production quantity.

Special-purpose input

Tags. Some merchandising systems use machine-readable tags which are punched (now outdated), OCR, or bar coded, and attached to the merchandise. The tag is separated at sale time and input to a special-purpose reader for recording, usually on magnetic tape attached to the cash register, or input directly to the computer.

Bar code or OCR wand scanners. These input devices can be as portable as small tape cassette machines and may also allow input from a small numerical key pad. They are finding a number of applications in merchandising, including readers for point-of-sale terminals, product replenishment for supermarkets, and library book-recording systems.

Card and badge readers. These readers are similar to the on-line devices already mentioned, but they may also be off-line.

Voice recognition. There are systems on the market today which recognize human words and convert them into digital computer input. The equipment must be 'preprogrammed' for each voice by each operator reading in the set of words. Some of these machines can store the voice patterns of up to twenty operators. They have been used in production and distribution systems, where operators input data to the system by voice while they work with their hands.

5.4.2   Location of Input Devices

This topic is covered in detail in Chapter 9. The discussion here is limited to saying that input devices may be located centrally or decentralized to the user site where the data originates. If a centralized approach is taken it is possible to achieve higher data-capture speeds and tighter control. However, decentralizing data capture reinforces the user's responsibility for the provision of data and provides an environment in which the user sees more of the computer system and so may be motivated to provide more accurate data input.

Each of these alternatives offers significant advantages, which is no doubt why both procedures are being employed in industry and commerce.

5.4.3 Output Media

The primary means of output available to the systems designer are printers, VDUs, voice, and microfilm/microfiche. With the exception of voice, they are all used extensively in current systems.

Printers can be classified in four ways:

- Impact *v.* non-impact
- Dot matrix *v.* shaped character
- Line *v.* character
- Speed

With respect to speed, a wide range is available:

- Low speed — 10 characters per second
- Medium speed — up to 200 characters per second
- High speed — 200–2000 lines per minute
- Very high speed — 4000–18 000 lines per minute

The wide variation in speed arises because of the different technologies used by different printers. Impact line printers usually work by filling a buffer with an entire row of characters before printing the line, using a chain or drum mechanism. A chain-type line printer provides fair quality print at maximum speeds of around 1000 to 2000 lines per minute. A character printer, as the name suggests, prints one character at a time across the page. It may use a ball, a cylinder, or a daisy wheel mechanism to strike the page. Another form of impact printing uses a dot matrix of five by seven or seven by nine to form the characters. Non-impact printers use ink-jet or xerographic principles. Ink-jet printers spray charged ink particles through an electrostatic field to direct them onto the paper. Xerographic printers image the characters onto a printing surface, which is then toned, i.e. the ink particles are attached and then transferred to paper. Both of these methods provide very fast printing speeds. For example, an ink-jet could provide up to 45 000 lines per minute using multiple jets.

Voice output is largely used in special applications such as airport flight announcing and telephone number information. Computer output to microfilm/microfiche (COM) is widely used for price lists, parts lists, libraries, ledger account balances, etc., because it provides very high output speeds with compact information delivery.

5.5 DEVELOPING THE PHYSICAL SYSTEM

Having developed the logical system, it becomes necessary to operate that logic on the selected hardware and in the organizational environment. This requires the further specification of input, output, files, and processing methods and requirements. The result of this activity is the physical design specification, which provides the basis for system implementation.

5.5.1 Input

The logical design results in draft formats for the input, such as documents or screen layouts. These formats must be connected to their final form, which can be used (1) to set up the document printing in the case of hard copy, or (2) as part of the specifications for programming in the case of screen layouts. If a document is being used, factors such as exact character positioning, type font, paper quality, paper colour, and wording of instructions must be resolved. Similarly with screen layouts, factors such as exact positioning and method of display must be decided in accordance with the terminal and system software characteristics of the target hardware environment.

5.5.2 Output

Here again, the draft outputs must be converted to their final form, be it computer listings, screen layouts, or partly preprinted documents. For computer listings, printer layout sheets showing the exact positioning, and sample entries provide the necessary specifications for programming, while in other cases the requirements are the same as discussed for input.

5.5.3 Files

A proposed set of files with the record key(s) and contents will have been documented as a result of the logical design. They now have to be (1) confirmed or altered in accordance with the capabilities of the target computer environment, and (2) fully documented. The final decision on a file's organization, content, and access paths must be made in the light of the system's processing requirements, which must therefore be considered in parallel. Leaving this aside for the moment, however, the system software capabilities play a major part in determining the physical form of the files. Thus IMS or DL1 database segments and almost exclusive use of VSAM files might typically be found in an IBM environment. This is not to say that organizations do not move outside the provided file management software, but that the cost of doing so may not be easily justified because of the increased risk of failure and the increased expertise required by the designers and, most importantly, by those responsible for implementation.

Once the physical organization, content, and access paths have been determined, file documentation should be established showing the fully defined record contents in terms of the fields and their pictures, key field, volumes, and organization.

5.5.4   Processing

This stage of the design involves packaging the bubble procedures into programs, and specifying the systems security, control, and back-up provisions in the light of the chosen hardware, file organization, input, and output. Breaking down tasks into program modules is covered in detail in Chapter 6. However, some of the broad principles which can be used to guide the program packaging (run subdivision) activity are:

- Keep programs small and homogeneous in function and data, as this reduces programming time and later maintenance effort
- Provide for the completion of all editing before any updates are begun
- Be more concerned with the ease of subsequent maintenance than with run-time efficiency

5.6   DOCUMENTATION

Different types of documentation are shown in various chapters of this book (see Chapters 2, 4, and 6). This is because the documentation methods of the systems analysis and design task are often also tools of the various activities. Thus documenting the existing system is a task of the analysis stage, and the form of the documentation depends on the tools and techniques used by the analyst.

However any developed system needs further documentation to provide a record of the characteristics of that system, and to provide the basis for the system implementation (see Chapter 11). Once a system has been implemented it is subject to continuing maintenance and enhancement, which require accurate documentation of the system. Another purpose of this documentation is to act as a communication vehicle for the system's users so they can gain an understanding of their interface with the system. The types of document illustrated in this section are:

- Report layouts
- Screen layouts
- Program specifications
- System specifications
- User instructions

5.6.1   Report Layouts

The contents of all reports are determined during the logical design. It is now necessary to prepare an exact specification of the layout of all reports produced by the system. The use of a 'printer layout worksheet' marked with, say, 136 columns and 67 rows, enables the report format to be precisely defined, and forms a part of the program specifications. Figure 5-7 is an example of such a worksheet. Once the system is operating it is advantageous to compile a folio containing both descriptions and computer-produced examples of all reports in the system, such as illustrated in Figure 5-8.

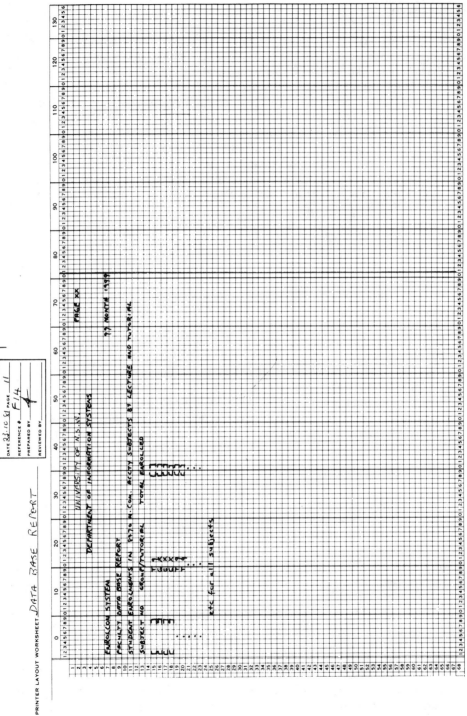

Figure 5-7 A printer layout worksheet

Trial balance

FREQUENCY: Monthly
FUNCTION: Accounting aid
SUMMARY: This is a register of debit and credit balances by branch as
                         at month end.
INFORMATION SUPPLIED: Account number
                         Account name
                         Balance amount

XYZ LIMITED (SYDNEY BRANCH)
TRIAL BALANCE AS AT 24/10/81   PAGE 1

Account no.	Account name	Debit	Credit
0347-021	LOANS INCOME		45 325.42
0373-025	PENALTY INTEREST		273.67
1764-021	SALARIES	17 364.78	
1768-023	STAFF ALLOWANCES	435.56	
2317-314	AUDIT FEES	240.00	
2474-056	ADVERTISING	1 745.00	

Figure 5–8   Illustrative report folio entry

5.6.2 Screen Layouts

As with report layouts, the designer must precisely define the screen contents
for the programmer, usually using a worksheet similar to the report worksheet of
Figure 5–7, but reflecting the size of a screen. A detailed discussion of screen-layout
types is given in Chapter 9. Once again, to provide a complete documentation set for
the operating system, a folio of all panels should be compiled using the computer to
generate a hard copy of the layouts, such as that shown in Figure 5–9. This example
illustrates the main menu for an accounts-receivable system, showing which key to
depress to gain access to any particular part of the system.

PRESS RESPECTIVE KEY FOR REQUIRED FUNCTION
ENTER -INQUIRY -BY CONTRACT NUMBER
PF1 -INQUIRY -(SUPPLIER)
PF2 -NEW ACCOUNTS / ADDITIONS /
PF3 -AMENDMENTS
PF4 -CLOSE ACCOUNTS / DELETIONS
PF5 -POSTING
PF6 -DAILY BALANCE SUMMARY

Figure 5–9   Menu screen

5.6.3 Program Specifications

To design and code each program the programmer needs a description of the
program, which should contain: the program number, program name, overview
description, system flowchart, files required, input and output layouts where

relevant, and processing requirements. An example of a program description is given in Figure 5-10. In addition to this form of program documentation, a complete list of all programs in the system should be compiled, showing information such as program number, program description, screen numbers used, and report numbers generated. This list provides cross references between input, program, and output, and makes it easy to determine the function of each program in the system quickly.

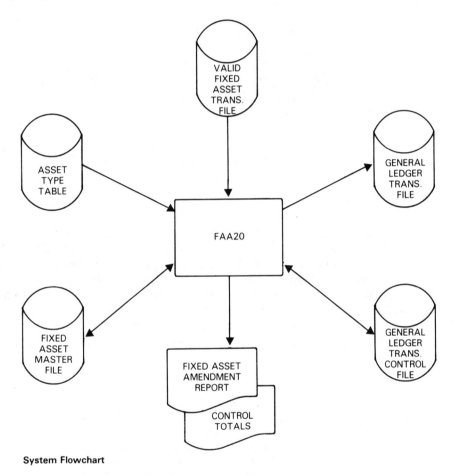

System Flowchart

FIXED ASSET ACCOUNTING   OCTOBER 1981

Program no.:   FAA20

Program name: FIXED ASSET AMENDMENTS

Program overview:

FAA20 reads the Valid Fixed Asset Transaction File created by FAA10 and updates the Fixed Asset Master File. The accounting entries generated are output to the General Ledger Transaction file and all additions, deletions and adjustments to the Master File are listed on the Fixed Asset Amendment Report.

File layouts
1. *Input Files*
    (i)   Valid Fixed Asset Transaction File
          — Refer Data Dictionary,
             page 3.2/6
    (ii) Asset Type Table
          — Refer Data Dictionary,
             page 3.2/7
2. *Input-Output Files*
    (i)   Fixed Asset Master File
          — Refer Data Dictionary,
             page 3.2/4
    (ii) General Ledger Transaction
          Control File
          — Refer Data Dictionary,
             page 3.2/3
3. *Output Files*
    (i)   General Ledger Transaction
          Multifile
          — Refer Data Dictionary,
             page 3.2/2

Report layouts
An example of a report layout is given in
Figure 5–8

Processing requirements
- When S. Switch = '0' process all
  records
- When S. Switch = '1' process only
  Sydney
- When S. Switch = '2' process only
  Melbourne

Figure 5-10   Program description

Note that this is only an example; normally the processing requirements would
be much more detailed.

5.6.4   System Specification

The system specification document outlines the whole system at a broad level,
and consists of a logical data flow diagram, system flowcharts, input documents,
output documents, general description, controls and security, and implementation
plans.

5.6.5   User Instructions

It is vital to have a set of computer-use instructions wherever a user makes
contact with the system, as in decentralized data entry. These instructions assist user
understanding and ensure the smooth operation of the system. Once again, this type
of documentation is best explained through an example, in this case an on-line
accounts-receivable system. Figure 5–11 shows the first panel displayed — the main
menu.

```
SCREEN 1                          MAIN MENU                        COMPANY XYZ

                                                                      SYSTEM 32

PRESS RESPECTIVE KEY FOR REQUIRED FUNCTION
            ENTER   - INQUIRY -BY CONTRACT NUMBER
            PF1     - NEW ACCOUNTS / ADDITIONS / VERIFY NO. ACCOUNT
            PF2     - AMENDMENTS
            PF3     - CLOSE ACCOUNTS / DELETIONS
```

Figure 5-11   First panel display

To proceed with an inquiry relating to an account, the instruction displayed on the panel is followed, i.e. PRESS RESPECTIVE 'PF' KEY FOR REQUIRED FUNCTION. When the ENTER key is pressed, the result is 'proceed to inquiry menu screen 2' — Figure 5-12.

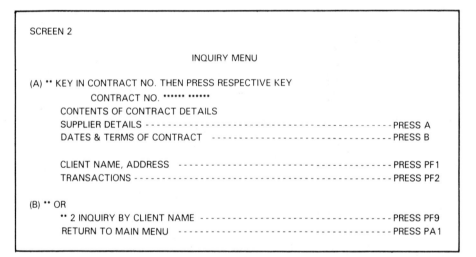

Figure 5-12   Inquiry menu 2

There are two methods by which inquiries can be furthered:

• The contract number (option A)
• The client's name (option B)

Note: At all times if you wish to discontinue your inquiry (at whatever panel is on display), it is simply a matter of returning to the inquiry menu or main menu.

Method 1. If the contract number is known, Option A is used — KEY IN FULL CONTRACT NO.

Method 2. The second method of inquiry is via the client's name, i.e. from the inquiry menu, Option B is taken and the instructions followed: PRESS 'PF9'. The result is 'Proceed to INQUIRY BY CLIENT NAME', shown in Figure 5-13.

```
SCREEN 3

                          INQUIRY BY CLIENT NAME
                   KEY IN CLIENT NAME THEN PRESS ENTER
                          ••••••••••••••••

INQUIRY BY THIS SCREEN WILL CAUSE THOSE ACCOUNT NOS FOR THE CORRESPONDING
NAME TO BE DISPLAYED.

RETURN TO INQUIRY MENU  ------------------------------------------------- PRESS PF10
RETURN TO MAIN MENU  --------------------------------------------------- PRESS PA1
```

Figure 5-13   Inquiry by client name

5.7 ESTIMATING RUN TIME

It is frequently necessary to estimate the time a system will take to run on a particular computer. This may be needed to:

- Compare the operating efficiency of two alternative physical designs
- Calculate the total run time for machine-scheduling purposes
- Estimate the response time for a real-time system
- Provide an external indication of the efficiency of a completed system

Two methods of time estimation are discussed in this section:

- Estimation from the systems design documentation prior to programming
- Estimation using pilot-run data

5.7.1 Design Estimation

Before programming, a system run-time estimate can be made from knowledge of the necessary input-output activity of the individual programs, by calculating the run time for each program and hence, by addition, the system run time. For commercial systems it is assumed that the run time is determined by the time to input and output the data to the CPU. This simplifying assumption is made because the CPU cycle time is around 1000 times faster than the peripheral storage input-output time. However, for programs carrying out extensive logic or arithmetic this assumption would not be valid.

The method used can best be illustrated by means of an example. An estimate is required of the run time for a program which is to read 800 order transactions from a disk file, update a direct-access product master file on disk and, for each record read, write a record out to a file on the same disk as the input transaction file is stored on. A systems flowchart is given in Figure 5–14.

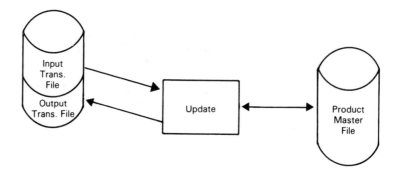

Figure 5-14   Systems flowchart of estimation example

The relevant data from the manufacturer's publication and the systems design documentation are:

Disk hardware	Performance	
seek time	maximum	55 milliseconds
	average	30 ''
rotational latency	maximum	18 ''
	average	9 ''
disk transfer rate	1.2 megabytes per second	
supervisor overhead	2 milliseconds per read or write	

Input file

size	800 records
record length	120 characters
blocking	6 records per block

Output file

size	800 records
record length	60 characters
blocking	unblocked

Product master file

file organization and access	index sequential
size	4000 records
blocking	unblocked
record length	250 characters

The *seek time* is the time for the disk read/write heads to be positioned over the track to be read. The maximum time of 55 milliseconds (ms) is the time for the heads to move across the entire disk pack, while the average of 30 milliseconds assumes the disk read/write head moves halfway across the disk.

The *rotational latency* is the time taken for the wanted data to rotate under the read/write head. The maximum time is for a full revolution of the disk, while the average is for half a revolution.

The *disk transfer rate* is the maximum rate of the communications link between the disk read/write head and the CPU. The *supervisor overhead* is a machine overhead incurred each time a disk read or write operation is initiated.

For calculating the estimated run time, it is assumed that no buffering is used for the input-output except that required for the blocked input file. The effect of this assumption is explored later in this subsection. To process the input records, the input-output steps are:

- Read block of input data
- Read matching record from product master file
- Write record to product master file
- Write record to output transaction file

Note that only after processing six records is it necessary to read again another input block. The estimated times in milliseconds are calculated in the following way.

1. Read input block of six records

supervisor overhead	2
disk seek time (assume average)	30
disk latency	9
disk transfer time 720/1200	0.6
	41.6

Hence, average time per record = 41.6 ÷ 6 = 6.9, say 7 ms.

2. Read matching record from product master file

To access index

supervisor overhead	2
disk seek time (assume average)	30
disk latency (assume average)	9

To access track index and record

supervisor overhead (× 2)	4
disk seek time	30
disk latency (× 2)	18
disk transfer time — negligible	—
total =	93 ms

3. Write record to product master file

For the write operation after the read, there is no seek time, hence total time is due to latency and supervisor overhead and = 11 ms.

4. Write record to output transaction file

There only needs to be a seek after each read of the input file; hence seek time per record = 30/6 =   5 ms.

supervisor overhead	2
disk latency	9
disk transfer time — negligible	–
	16 ms

5. Final calculation

Thus time to process each record =
$$7 + 93 + 11 + 16 =$$ 127 ms.

∴ time to process 800 records = 127 × 800 =   101 seconds

If a greater degree of buffering is provided, the various input-output operations could proceed almost independently, so that the time for the program with 100 per cent buffering would be the time for the longest input or output operation. With a large amount of buffering on the product master file, records would not be written physically to the disk until space was needed in the buffer. This may mean that active records stay permanently in the buffer and are updated there, greatly reducing the amount of physical input-output activity. One of the greatest sources for error in run-time estimation is due to inaccuracies in estimating the number of physical input-output operations. The estimates provided by this method may also be in error due to inefficient programming which unnecessarily causes the computer to perform redundant input-output and logic operations.

The time taken for standard utilities like sort, merge, and copy, can be estimated using tables provided by the software supplier.

5.7.2 Pilot-run Estimation

Frequently, run times need to be estimated based on the results of a pilot run or benchmark test. This situation arises when a package is being investigated or new computer equipment is being considered to run existing systems. Since it is generally impossible to carry out a full-scale live run with operating-size files, normal transaction volumes, and full outputs, a pilot run is carried out, which involves an extract of the various master files and a sample of the input volume specially selected to fall within the range of the files. The pilot run is timed and the production run time estimated on this basis.

This approach has the potential of yielding far more accurate time statistics than the design calculation discussed in Subsection 5.7.1, but great care is needed when designing the pilot run to ensure that it is indeed representative of the production environment, primarily with respect to physical input-output activity. This requires making an estimate of the production environment physical input-output activity. It generally results in a number of pilot runs being performed to generate results for different levels of physical input-output activity, and so bracket the estimated production input-output level.

A different level of physical input-output activity can be provided for each pilot run by modifying the buffering conditions, by modifying the file placing to change the level of disk contention, and by modifying the input transactions. For example, if all files are placed on one disk drive, are unblocked and have one record buffer per file, each read or write instruction to a new record must result in a physical read or write operation with generally a disk seek to locate the wanted track. Using the statistics generated by the various pilot runs an estimate can be made for the time to run the live system in a defined operational environment.

5.7.3 Time-estimation Issues

Multiprogramming. When a computer is processing more than one job simultaneously, the time taken to complete the processing of one job depends on the demands placed on the computer by the other concurrent jobs, and the additional supervisor overhead incurred. Thus the run-time estimate prepared by either approach may not give an accurate estimate of the elapsed time of the job. However, if concurrently run jobs are well matched so that peripheral and CPU contention is minimized, then the increase in run time for each job may be quite slight.

Coding efficiency. The code quality can have a substantial effect on the execution time of the program. Thus estimates made on the basis of the design documentation may turn out subsequently to be quite inaccurate if the program is badly coded. On the other hand they may help to identify poorly performing programs which are candidates for efficiency tuning.

Location of computer files. The location and distribution of the files between the disk drives has a marked influence on the number of read-write head seeks needed. For example, consider a program which is reading alternately from two sequential files. If both these files are placed on the one disk drive a head seek is needed for each read. Alternatively, if the files can be placed on two independent drives no head seeks are necessary.

Performance data. The manufacturer-supplied performance data that serves as the basis for estimating from the design documents (e.g. disk speed, printer speed, card reader speed) are calculated under somewhat more ideal conditions than those experienced in practice. For example, a line printer rated at 600 lines per minute rarely performs at that speed, even when printing directly from a print file. Thus a certain degree of optimism is injected into the estimates when using the manufacturer's published data, and some allowance needs to be made for this.

REFERENCES

T. DE MARCO, *Structured Analysis and Systems Specification*, Prentice-Hall Inc., Englewood Cliffs, N.J., 1980.

C. GANE & T. SARSON, *Structured Systems Analysis*, Prentice-Hall Inc., Englewood Cliffs, N.J., 1978.

CASE STUDY — SPEEDY SEED COMPANY

Background

The Speedy Seed Company (SSC) packages and markets a range of some 400 seed-based products. They also market a range of 100 small gardening implements. Seed, their main product line, is purchased from growers in standard 50 kg packs and by blending they produce the colour variety, seed quality, and mix to meet home gardeners' requirements. The SSC is particularly interested in a totally new concept of producing mixtures of flowers and/or vegetables which thrive symbiotically by resisting disease and bug attack, and produce a pleasant appearance and good yield. They have a number of these products, called SYMBIOSEED, and are a world leader in this new environmentally safe approach to agriculture.

Stock control

The manufacturing method is based on a set of 20 blending/mixing machines which feed a small attached packaging machine. Two employees, a leading hand and an assistant, operate each machine and generally each packaging run takes from two hours to one day. The formulae for the blends are determined by the R & D Department and are kept in a recipe file ordered on product code.

Work orders are issued by the Stock Control Department who are responsible for ensuring that there are enough finished goods on hand to meet expected orders. The Stock Control Department access the recipe card file and write the recipe for the finished goods on the work order for the setting of the blending machine. As well, they calculate the raw material seed requirements and write these on the work order.

When the leading hand receives a work order, the required quantities of raw materials are obtained from the store with the authority of the work order, which is marked to show the issue, and a copy is kept in the store as a record of the issue. At the end of each run the leading hand completes the work order showing total time expended by class of labour, number of packs produced (which may vary slightly from the number requested in the work order), and quantity of raw materials consumed. Any raw materials left unused are returned to the store, and the work order and its copy marked for the record.

The work orders are then sent back to the Stock Control Department for the updating of stock records — both finished goods and raw materials (both files are kept on cards filed sequentially). Copies of the work order are sent to the Sales Department for calculating the cost of goods sold and the sales price.

When raw materials reach their predetermined reorder points, the Stock Control Department raises a purchase order with the Purchase Department and this is sent to the supplier. On receipt of ordered materials, the warehouse checks quantities with those listed in the accompanying delivery docket, and the marked-off docket is sent to the Purchasing Department for filing with the copy of the purchase order. When the invoice is received by the Purchasing Department it is checked against the purchase order and goods received note, and approved for payment. These, together with statements of account, are sent to the Accounts Department for payment.

Costing

The costing for both raw materials and finished products is based on the average cost of goods in stock. Hence when raw materials are received into stock their cost is averaged with the cost of the goods already in stock to produce the new average cost. Likewise, when finished goods are produced their cost is calculated and averaged with the cost of finished goods in stock.

Speedy Seed works on a direct-cost system. Finished products are costed at the sum of the raw material components (seeds and packaging material) plus the cost of direct labour used in the mixing, blending, and packaging operation. There are no in-process inventories; all stock is either in the raw or finished state.

Pricing

Sale price is calculated at direct cost plus 75 per cent. The 75 per cent figure has been arrived at after considering manufacturing and office overheads, research and development, and the need to allow for a return on investment and risk.

Processing customer orders

As a result of Speedy Seed's direct-sell philosophy, their customers, about 5000 in number and spread throughout Australia, are mostly retailers (e.g. hardware shops, variety stores, nurseries, and garden shops). Recently though there have been some quite large orders placed by international seed dealers. This large customer base results in an impressive invoice volume of some 1500 per month. Average number of lines per invoice is five, with an average value per invoice of about $100.

Orders are processed for availability against the finished goods file by the Sales Department and invoices are prepared. The original goes to the Accounts Department and a copy is issued to the warehouse as authorization for filling the order and delivery. The marked-off copy of the invoice is then sent to the Stock Control Department for the updating of stock records. Out-of-stock orders and partly filled orders are held in a back-order file by the Sales Department and notification is sent to the customer and to Stock Control. When the finished goods become available the order is removed from the file and the invoice prepared. Completed invoice copies from the warehouse are then sent to the Accounts Department who then issue the original invoice to the purchaser and retain a copy in their records.

Speedy Seed have recognized the necessity of having an efficient finished-goods warehouse operation so that customer orders are rapidly and economically filled. To this end they have created a special code for each product, in which the first three characters of the product code give the warehouse location. Specifically the first three characters are:

- The warehouse aisle code, A–E;
- E or W for the East or West side of the aisle
- The section number (1–5) along the aisle

Thus the warehouse location code BE5 refers to the east side of B aisle in the fifth section. The fourth character of the warehouse code refers to the product group; a '1' refers to 'seed' and a '2' to 'other products'. There are three additional characters in the code, to construct a unique code for each product.

The position of the products in the warehouse has been determined generally on product activity, with the most active products in aisle A section 1 and the least active products in aisle E section 5. This idea was suggested some years earlier by a distribution consultant and has certainly worked out well, saving much needless time in picking orders.

In all but very special situations, orders received up to lunchtime are invoiced and assembled in the afternoon ready for shipment first thing next morning. The SSC manual system used to operate quite efficiently; but of late, due to a rapidly increasing level of business, several problems have surfaced, the chief ones being:

- With production working overtime, updating of stock records from receipts to finished goods has fallen behind — sometimes by three or four days.

Case Study — Speedy Seed Company

- Downdating inventory for sales shipments has likewise fallen behind by some days.
- The inaccuracy of the stock files has led to very real difficulties for the order takers, who receive the majority of orders by telephone. Customers placing orders like to be informed whether the goods are in stock and have, as a consequence of being given incorrect information, complained to the managing director.
- The time taken to process orders has frequently been so long that the warehouse staff have had to work overtime.

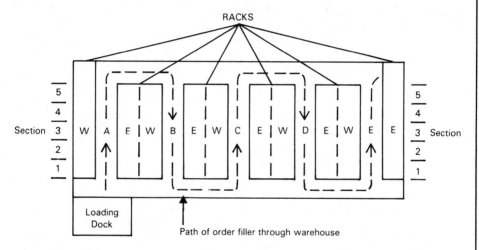

Figure 5-15   Speedy seed warehouse layout

The Need for Change

When orders first started climbing from the level stabilized at for the preceding five years, Speedy Seed management believed it was probably a temporary phenomenon caused by current high prices for vegetables and cut flowers. As the trend has now been apparent for over two years, with current sales running at twice the level of a year ago, Mr Giles Gillespie, the Managing Director, has decided that there has been a definite expansion in the market. More Australians appear to be getting out into their gardens and growing plants. Particularly significant in the sales increase are the SYMBIOSEED products, some of which are rapidly becoming the largest selling products. A few years back they held a position of relative insignificance.

After talking to some friends with computers, Gillespie has decided to investigate the introduction of a computer to handle order entry, stock pricing and control, accounts receivable, and maybe later on general ledger. In broad terms, his suggestions for the order entry, stock pricing and control system are:

- The present situation, whereby orders received before noon are shipped first thing next morning, is preserved.
- Customer credit must be checked before processing orders. This has not been done previously, but the increasing bad debts suggest it as a high priority.
- If the product ordered is not in stock, it should be back-ordered and filled at the first opportunity.
- A current finished-goods stock level and price report should be prepared at the end of each day's invoicing run. This report will be used by the order takers to inform customers of the stock position. The stock report should show, for any product which has zero stock level, the total of back-orders against the product and the number of days the product has been out of stock. In addition, an out-of-stock report should be prepared daily, showing those products that ran out of stock on today's processing and had to be back-ordered.
- Finished-goods price and quantity on hand need to be updated daily for receipts to stock (either from manufacturing or purchase), customer returns, and stock adjustments, before invoicing customers.
- Invoice transactions are to be recorded on a transaction file which will interface with the future accounts receivable system.
- Picking and assembling the orders in the warehouse may have some possibility of being further simplified by producing, for each invoice, a 'picking slip' arranged in the sequence that the order filler moves through the warehouse. The picking slip for each invoice should contain: product code and warehouse location, product type, product name, and quantity ordered. Obviously if the same product code is used in the new system, product type and warehouse location, being part of the code, need not be separately indicated. However, there is no constraint to maintain the present structured code if compelling reasons exist for changing it. The picking slip can be produced with the invoice.
- The present customer code is structured with the first three characters representing the first three significant characters of the customer's name, the next character indicating the discount category (1 = no discount; 2 = 2 per cent off for payment within 30 days of statement date), and the last three characters being unstructured for unique identification. This code may be changed if it appears unsuitable for a computer system.

Case Study — Speedy Seed Company

ASSIGNMENT

Before talking to any computer manufacturers, Mr Gillespie has employed a consultant to design, in broad detail, the application systems listed. In this case study *only* the order entry, invoicing, pricing, and raw materials and finished-goods stock-control system are of interest. Put yourself in the consultant's shoes, and answer the following questions:

1. Briefly comment on the advisability of retaining the present product, customer, and warehouse location code structures. Redesign if you feel it is needed.

2. Draw the physical DFD of the current manual system and define the data dictionary.

3. Draw the logical data flow diagram for the current system and indicate on the DFD (by means of, say, a different colour pen) the modifications (if any) necessary to provide the logical system features required to satisfy the objectives listed by Mr Gillespie. Where necessary, update the data dictionary to include any new data flows.

4. Draw and briefly describe the system flowcharts for the physical system which meets Gillespie's requirements. Make sure input and output document names correspond to entries in your data dictionary.

5. Give the layout and organization of each file, using, where appropriate, data names defined in the data dictionary.

CASE STUDY — SOUTH COAST HOSPITAL

The South Coast Hospital, owners of a powerful small business computer, are following a plan to computerize their main accounting and clinical information systems. Their fixed asset system is next in line for systems analysis and design. At present, their fixed asset records are maintained in a subsidiary ledger on plant record cards of the general form shown in Figure 5–16. The asset number is a unique code with its leading two digits being an asset-type code and the following five digits allocated sequentially within each asset-type code. The asset-type code indicates the nature of the asset:

01 Patient amenities
02 Operating theatre equipment
03 Recovery room equipment
04 Ward equipment
05 Patient transport

.
.
.

46 Office furniture
47 Visitor amenities

Asset No.		Cost Centre	Cost	
Description			Est.Life	
Depn Method		Depn Rate	Resid. Val.	
Date	Details	Annual Depn	Accum. Depn	Book Value

Figure 5-16   Plant record card

The hospital is divided into 20 administrative cost centres (e.g. maternity wing, emergency unit, John Collins' geriatric wing, pediatric unit). The hospital administrator (perhaps somewhat unadventurously) feels that the current system is adequate except for the great effort required each year to calculate the depreciation and prepare the reports. The new system should continue to produce the current reports:

- *Listing of all fixed assets.* Report sequence: asset type, asset number. The listing shows: asset type, description, asset number, description, cost centre, original cost, brought forward book value, carried forward book value, current depreciation charge. On change of asset type, each of the

Case Study — South Coast Hospital

dollar value fields (e.g. original cost, b/f book value, c/f book value) are totalled and grand totals are given at the end of the report.

- *Value of assets by location cost centre.* Report sequence: cost centre, asset number. This shows: cost centre, asset number, description, original cost, brought forward book value, current depreciation charge, carried forward book value. There is a total line on change of cost centre.

Data-preparation equipment is a key-to-disk machine. The computer configuration includes two disk drives of adequate capacity, and a fast line printer.

ASSIGNMENT

1. Provide logical data flow and a data dictionary for the requested system. Attention must be paid to the consistency of the data flows.

2. Discuss the files you propose for this system. Detail the contents and organization of each file.

3. Give a *specific* recommendation for ensuring the integrity of the files, and the data processed by the system. (Note: a general discussion of techniques is not sufficient.)

4. Draw a systems flowchart of the physical system, showing all details. Be sure to include:

   - All file layouts
   - All output report details (including control reports)
   - Input documents
   - Brief notes explaining each computer program

5. Discuss the approach to the implementation you propose. Include your suggestions for:

   - A conversion plan from the existing procedures
   - Training for those who will use the new system

Please note: The system you are called on to design is relatively elementary. What is wanted is a good, *complete,* and well-documented design with no loose ends.

CASE STUDY — DINGO DENIMS: INPUT SYSTEM DESIGN

Note: Read the background and system description in the Dingo Denims case study of Chapter 7.

The Dingo Denims Company conducted a modest trial of credit marketing. They allowed their branch stores to extend credit to selected customers, provided they controlled the accounts themselves with no staff increase. This proved such a success, both in terms of increased sales and number of credit customers, that nearly all the stores were pushing up against the limit of their staff time for preparing statements, receiving cash, banking, reconciling accounts, etc.

Accordingly, a study team was set up to propose an improved system for handling credit sales, together with the accounts receivable system. Alternatives explored included:

- Branch preparation of statements with centralized cash receipt
- Central control of accounts receivable and receipt of cash

It was anticipated that volume would increase to an average of 600 active credit customers per store (60 stores total) charging two transactions per month. Dingo Denims considered and rejected the alternative of using Bankcard, as they felt this was too impersonal and would not further the close customer contact on which they felt the success of their business depended. The study team could ascertain no objection to centralizing the accounts-receivable and credit-control functions using as sales invoice input the cash register tape containing, for credit sales, the customer's number and invoice number. They next designed a suitable system in outline so they could arrive at comparative costs. They decided that perhaps the most important unresolved feature of the system was that of data preparation for cash receipts, and they considered the following alternative methods of data input:

- Papertape, punchcards, magnetic tape, or direct input keyed by an operator. The variation in volume of input appeared to present problems and in addition this alternative seemed quite expensive.
- A card, prepunched by the computer and sent with the statement. The team anticipated difficulties in associating the correct punch card and related notice, and also thought that a high proportion of cards might be mutilated.
- A card prepunched by the computer, which would also be printed with statement particulars. They were unaware of any equipment for rental

that could produce this particular form of document. There also was a likelihood of mutilation.

- A counterfoil attached to the statement precoded by the computer for mark sense or bar code reader. This alternative also appeared open to mutilation by customers adding extra bars or extra marks.
- A counterfoil attached to the notice precoded by the computer for an optical character reader. OCR equipment could be rented quite readily by the hour at a neighbouring site and this equipment was able to read machine written or constrained hand-written figures. The price per hour was quite reasonable and the chief disadvantage would be the need to provide protection against misread characters. It was felt that mutilation would be a much less significant problem with this form of input.

ASSIGNMENT

1. Design, in outline, the input system for centralized receipt of cash, using the last alternative. The system should cover both the aspects:

   - Manual procedures for opening envelopes, removal and handling of counterfoil cheques or cash, and batching of documents
   - Computer system for input to accounts-receivable system and its reconciliation to banking

2. Assess the last alternative and compare it with the first alternative. For this exercise assume the following data:

   OCR thruput rate — 150 documents/minute
   OCR rental cost — $80 per hour (includes operator)
   Percentage of customers returning OCR counterfoil — 95
   Percentage of OCR documents not able to be read by OCR — 1.5
   Cost of key punch operators (including overheads) — $900 per month
   Rental cost of key punch machine — $200 per month
   Key punch operator speed — 60 000 key strokes per day

3. Which alternative do you recommend?
   Under what circumstances would the first alternative be the preferred option, and under what circumstances would the last alternative be preferred?

6   DESIGN METHODOLOGIES AND TECHNIQUES

6.1   INTRODUCTION

There has been a growing feeling that the art or craft of systems analysis, systems design, and program design need to be transformed into an 'engineering-type' discipline. The rigour and clearly defined techniques used by hardware designers have been often contrasted to the individualistic and frequently undisciplined approach of the software developers. Furthermore, the declining cost and improved reliability of hardware is additional fuel for such comparisons when faced with the high cost and low reliability of software. The feeling that there has to be a better way has sprouted a large number of techniques and methodologies which have, at their core, proposals for achieving one or more of:

- Improving the documentation and visibility of the analysis and design phase
- Standardizing the approach taken to systems analysis and design
- Improving the predictability of the design (i.e. increasing the probability that two individuals faced with the same problem will produce the same design)
- Improving the efficiency of subsequent maintenance and enhancement through readable, predictable, and well-structured systems and program design
- Improving communication between users, analysts, designers, and programmers through the use of a disciplined and commonly understood approach
- Reducing the scope for ego-tripping experimentation

- Improving the tools for bug finding and testing
- Reducing the complexity of design by appropriate segmentation
- Automating the analysis, design, and documentation

The emergence of analysis and design methodologies has been a gradual process, building on precomputer techniques developed as early as the 1920s, and it is still continuing. The methodologies/techniques can be broadly categorized into five overlapping groups based on the software tools of: checklists, forms, data structure, data flow, and computers.

6.1.1 Checklist

This is by far the largest class of methodologies and involves a standard procedure which specifies the sequence and content of the steps to be followed by the analyst during each stage of a project. Most organizations have a standard which details the systems lifecycle to be used, and the reporting guidelines and milestones. In fact this approach is so widely accepted today that many EDP people would not even call it a methodology, reserving that word for the more detailed prescriptive methodologies or techniques. Examples of this checklist type are the methodologies given in Chapter 12, and the commercially marketed packages like SPECTRUM and PRIDE.

6.1.2 Forms Driven

A number of techniques, such as ADS, rely heavily on standard forms to guide the analyst in the collecting and analyzing of data, and in preparing the design. The forms are used within an overall planned sequence of activities, making forms-driven methodologies a subgroup of checklist-based methodologies. Indeed the distinction is not hard and fast, but is intended to suggest that the primary orientation of the forms-driven technique is the use of standard forms for the organization and documentation of information. Two early methodologies, NCR's Accurately Designed Systems (ADS) and IBM's Study Organization Plan (SOP), both widely used in their time, are forms-driven, as is the more recent HIPO, which appears to have been less successful.

6.1.3 Data Structure

In contrast to the checklist and forms-driven methodologies, which leave the actual design work to the creative talent of the analyst, the data-structure methodology proposes a detailed prescription for designing systems and programs based on analysis of the structure of the input and output data. This is a problem-oriented approach, with the problem expressed in the mapping of the input data structure to the output data structure. The solution, or the means of transforming the data from input to output, emerges from the application of the method. This approach is a break from most other techniques as it infers that the system and program function is implicit in the data structures. Examples of these methodologies are those proposed by Jackson (1975), Warnier (1974), and Orr (1977).

6.1.4 Data Flow

The data-flow-based methodologies are directed at the same objective as the data-structure-based methodologies: that of providing a technique to guide the analyst through the design of a system, at both the system level and the program level. These techniques use data flow diagrams to provide a top-down segmentation of the system into programs, and then a segmentation of the programs into modules. Examples of these methodologies are contained in the works of Yourdon & Constantine (1979), Myers (1978) and De Marco (1980).

6.1.5 Computer-based Software Tools

The fact that the computer is generally not used as an aid in systems analysis and design has prompted interest in the development of computer-based tools for this purpose. These range from special-purpose tools such as those under development at General Telephone and Electronics (USA) for electronic switching systems (Davis, 1979), to the more general Problem Statement Language/Problem Statement Analyzer (PSL/PSA) system, which is intended for use in all software development settings.

6.2 CHECKLIST AND FORMS-DRIVEN METHODOLOGIES

Since forms-driven and checklist-based methodologies have great similarities they are treated together in this section. This also enables a chronological presentation which, by focusing on the progression of the development of these approaches, allows a better view of their likely future. The methodology presented in Section 12.7 is an example of the current (1981) state-of-art of these methodologies.

6.2.1 Study Organization Plan (SOP)

SOP, the first widely disseminated computer systems analysis methodology, was developed and promulgated by IBM in the mid-1960s. It is based on three major phases, with each phase divided into a number of states. SOP, reflecting the mood of the mid-1960s, is chiefly oriented to the overall MIS 'systems study' of an organization, which has as its objective the development of an integrated set of systems requirements for all the activities of the organization. Although the methodology is presented with its scope embracing the whole enterprise, it could equally be applied to a single self-contained segment (e.g. a division). The three major phases of SOP are:

- Phase 1 — Understand the present business
- Phase 2 — Determine and define the system requirements
- Phase 3 — Design and communicate the new system

Phase 1, which is broken into three stages, embraces the study of the current physical and logical system. It commences, in stage 1, with information gathering carried out by searching manuals and documentation, and interviewing key user personnel. Stage 1 is oriented towards providing the analyst with a clear under-standing of the organization, its competitive environment, industry background, business objectives and goals, major policies and practices, and relevant government regulations. The second stage of phase 1 describes the business in terms of an input-output model (see Figure 6–1). The inputs are the materials and suppliers, and

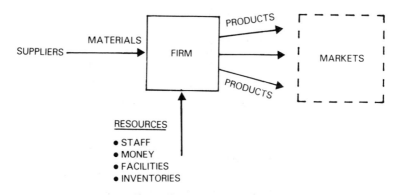

Figure 6-1   The firm as an input-output model

the resources of staff, money, facilities and inventories. The outputs are the products and the markets in which they are sold. The third stage uses five basic documents to gather operational data which describe the activities of the business. These documents are schematically illustrated in Figure 6–2. The message sheet contains details of inputs and outputs to a specific processing operation. The file sheet describes the stored data required to carry out the processing. The relationships between the input, processing, output, and file data are contained on the operation sheet. All operations are summarized on the activity sheet. The resource usage sheet shows the relationship of the system to the organization and its business environment.

Phase 2 is concerned with defining the systems requirements. It consists of five stages:

- Stage 1 — Identify the business goals
- Stage 2 — Determine the impact of goal changes on activities

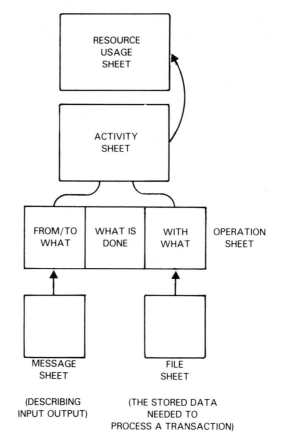

Figure 6-2 SOP Phase 1 Stage 3 documentation

- Stage 3 — Analyze each activity in terms of inputs, processes, outputs, and resources
- Stage 4 — Construct a measure of effectiveness for each activity
- Stage 5 — Document the requirements

Stages 1 and 2 explore the goals of the organization and their effect on its activities. Understanding the relationship between goals and activities means that the system's requirements can be defined so that they are directly relevant to the decision maker's job of achieving the organization's goals. Stage 3 is akin to developing a new logical data flow diagram for the organization. Stage 4 tackles the tough task of defining criteria for measuring the effectiveness of each activity; this is the measure by which each activity is assessed, and should form a central focus for the information system of that activity.

Phase 2 uses a number of preprepared forms including an input-output sheet, required information sheet, and resource sheet to assist the systems analysts in their tasks.

Phase 3 is concerned with the physical design of the new system and includes system selection, costing, programming, and the development of the implementation schedule.

6.2.2 Accurately Designed Systems (ADS)

ADS is concerned with the systems lifecycle steps of new logical design and new physical design (NCR, 1968). It largely assumes that the broad requirements have been defined and starts with the required systems output. ADS is largely a forms-driven methodology comprising five forms:

- Report layout (form 1)
- Input media layout (form 2)
- Computation definition (form 3)
- History definition (stored data) (form 4)
- Logic definition (form 5)

Each output data item on the report form 1 is linked to input data items on form 2, file-data items on form 4, to computations on form 3 (where the data items used in the computations are themselves defined by their association with input or file data) or to logic (e.g. a decision table) performed on certain defined data items (form 5). By exhaustive cross-references, the origins of all the data on the output reports are fully specified.

The advantages of this approach include the highlighting of omissions and contradictions by the chaining process wherein each data element is assigned a tag and linked at each occurrence. The disadvantages of ADS include the relative difficulty of making alterations to the design because of the chaining, and also the limitation that the methodology encompasses only the design portion of the systems lifecycle. This is highlighted when compared with SOP, which covers both analysis and design.

6.2.3 Business Systems Planning (BSP)

BSP, published by IBM in the early 1970s, is an extension of SOP, with greater emphasis on:

- Building a working team, comprising top management and the systems analysts, to undertake the study
- A database orientation
- Integration of the MIS with the organization's strategic plan

BSP is founded on three principles:

- Establishment of a business-wide perspective
- Top-down analysis and bottom-up implementation
- System and data independence

The BSP study is sponsored by a senior manager who appoints a business executive as a team leader. The team also includes a data-processing manager or a senior systems analyst. These two then compile background material for the study team on the organization structure, environment, current plans, financial and product reviews, market analysis, profile of information systems, and results of previous related studies. The BSP methodology of top-down analysis comprises six steps:

- Identify strategic business objectives and problems
- Define the business processes (products, markets, etc.) which service the business objectives
- Define the business organization which has been developed for the processes to pursue the strategic objectives
- Determine the information and computer applications required
- Determine the data entities
- Determine the major data items

BSP is implemented by a bottom-up process, starting with the data items developed in the last step of the top-down analysis. The implementation steps are:

- Define the database
- Determine the information systems required to process the database
- Apply the systems to the business processes
- Define the effect the systems will have on the strategic business objectives

It should be noted that the implementation excludes mention of the business organization. This is done with the idea that the information systems primarily support the business processes, regardless of change in the organization.

From this brief overview it can be seen that BSP is oriented to the broad systems requirements definition of the firm. It does not consider the stages of the systems lifecycle concerned with the detailed analysis and design of a specific application.

6.2.4   Current Commercial Checklist Methodologies (e.g. SPECTRUM, PRIDE)

A number of commercial firms are marketing (generally for a price in the range of $10 000–80 000) methodologies which lay out in great detail the sequence of steps to be undertaken in a systems project, and the project control system to be followed. Typically these systems contain standards relating to:

- Steps for initiating a project and securing top management and user participation

- The roles of the user, the analyst, the project leader, and the EDP manager
- The detailed content of each of the major reports
- A structured approach to systems development which involves, for example, for SPECTRUM, three major phases divided into 13 subphases which are in turn further divided into 15–20 tasks per subphase
- Estimating guidelines for determining the resource requirements for each phase
- The project status reporting guidelines
- The sign-off procedures for the tasks, subphases, and phases
- Checklists for the analyst for each task in the project

A number of well-established DP departments in major companies have recently purchased these packaged methodologies despite previously having their own in-house standards, which had grown up over the years, and which related to most of the areas covered in the new methodology. A central reason for their purchase appears to be that the in-house standards were inconsistent and hard to follow as a result of progressive modification over the years, and it looked cheaper to buy and train the organization to use a new approach than to rework their current methodology.

6.2.5   Hierarchy plus Input-Process-Output (HIPO)

HIPO was developed by IBM as a design aid and documentation technique which attempts to (1) provide a structure by which the function of a system can be understood, (2) state the functions to be accomplished, and (3) provide a visual description of the input, process, and output for each function. A HIPO package consists of the visual table of contents (hierarchy diagram), and overview and detail diagrams (input, process, output diagram). An example should clarify the approach.

Consider the modest computer-based stores inventory system illustrated in the systems flowchart in Figure 6–3 (note that file maintenance is not included). Figure 6–4 shows the visual table of contents (VTOC) for this system. It both acts as a hierarchy chart for the functions to be performed and contains a reference, on the boxes, to the number of the diagram which displays the detailed processing description in terms of an input-process-output (IPO) diagram. The VTOC segments the system into three major functions: transaction input, inventory update, and inventory reporting. Figure 6–5 presents the overview IPO diagram (diagram 1–0). The inputs, major processing functions, and outputs are displayed. As an example of a lower level IPO diagram, Figure 6–6 illustrates 'edit stock issues' (diagram 2–1).

It can be seen that HIPO gives a logical rather than a physical view of a system. For example, the program view given in the Figure 6–3 systems flowchart is not reflected in Figure 6–4. This can be seen in the edit and update being separate functions in Figure 6–4, whereas in Figure 6–3 they are included together in the one program.

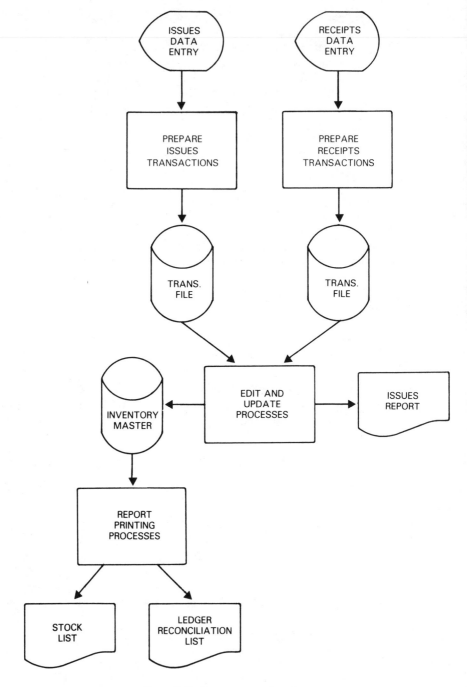

Figure 6-3   Stores system flowchart

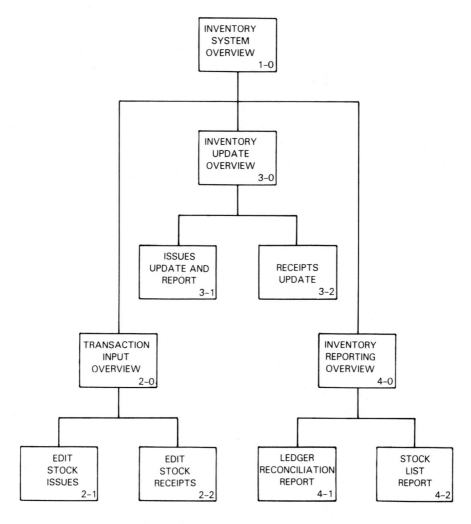

Figure 6-4   Stores visual table of contents (VTOC)

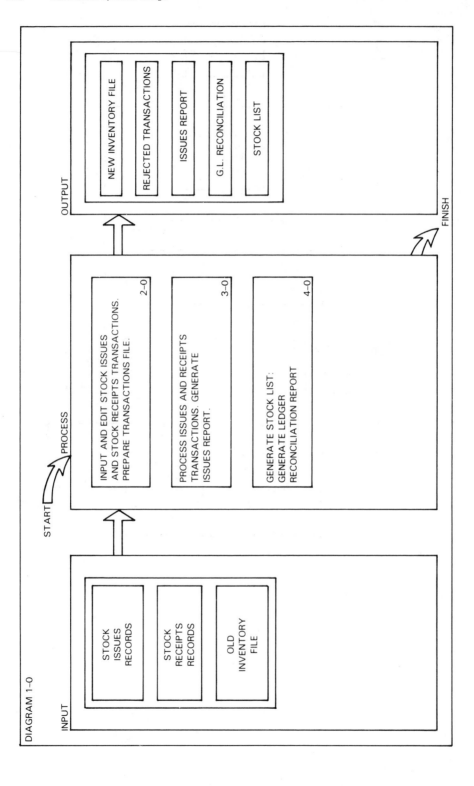

Figure 6-5 Overview diagram

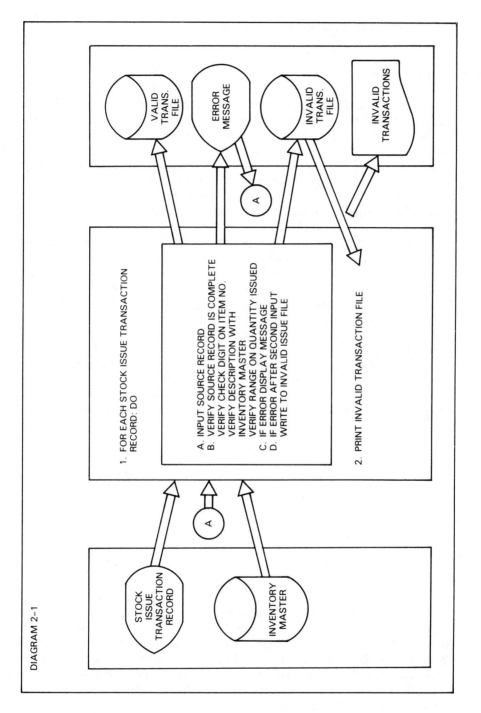

Figure 6-6   Example detail

6.3   DATA-STRUCTURE-BASED METHODOLOGIES

6.3.1   General Description

The data-structure-based methodologies are founded on the principle that the structure embodied in the systems or program should correspond to the structure of the data being processed. While this principle has a certain appeal, it cannot be established as correct by proof, nor has it been empirically established. It remains a statement of faith on which potential users must make their own decision. This section discusses the program design technique only, as it is better understood, more widely used, and similar in style to the data-structure-based systems design technique. The technique discussed is also called the Jackson technique or methodology after its chief exponent Michael Jackson (1975).

Correspondence between the program structure and the data structure is achieved by modelling the program and data structures using the same set of constructs. Four constructs or components are used for both data and program to model the structure. These are elementary, sequence, iteration, and selection.

An *elementary* component is atomic and cannot be further dissected. A *sequence* component has a number of parts, each of which is executed or appears once only and in order. For example, a program may consist of a sequence of three paragraphs of code, B, C, and D, which are executed once in that order. Alternatively, for data, a deck of cards A may consist of a sequence of one B type card, one C type card and one D type card. Further examples of sequences are a form which consists of a header, a body, and a total line, and a record which consists of a number of fields. Diagrammatically this sequence component is represented by Figure 6–7.

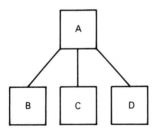
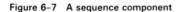
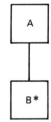

Figure 6–7   A sequence component   Figure 6–8   An iteration component

An *iteration* component is performed or occurs zero or more times. For example, A may consist of a paragraph of code B which is performed zero or more times. Typical programming constructs used to execute an iteration are DO, DO WHILE and PERFORM ... TIMES. Examples of iteration data structures are a deck of cards A which consists of one or more B cards, and a variable-length record which has zero, one, or more fields following a header field. Figure 6–8 illustrates an iteration. The asterisk on the B box designates an iteration of B.

A *selection* component has a number of parts, only one of which is present in each occurrence of the selection component. Figure 6–9 shows an example of a selection where A is a selection of B, C or D. A CASE construct or IF condition are typical examples in a program. In data, a selection component may be used to represent a valid or an invalid card. Another example is a card deck where each card contains either a credit note or an invoice. The symbol used in Figure 6-9 to represent a selection is a small circle.

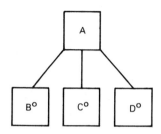

Figure 6-9   A selection component

The application of this technique to program design is best illustrated by an example. An edit program is to read an input file consisting of a header record H followed by an arbitrary number of transaction records of type T. The edit program is to print a report showing title, date, etc., and a body containing a listing, by batch, of all the input data. Each batch listed is headed by the batch number, followed by a line for each input record, and an appropriate designation if the record is invalid. The last line of each batch listing is a total line, and the last line of the report is a grand total of all the input. The input and output data structure is shown on Figure 6-10. The input file is shown as an iteration of batches, with each batch comprising a sequence of a header record H followed by an iteration of T records. Each T record is a selection of either a valid or an invalid record. The output is a sequence followed by an iteration of batches in much the same pattern as the input.

After establishing the input and output data structures, the methodology calls for finding a one-to-one correspondence between them to develop a program structure based on the structural correspondence. If a one-to-one relationship cannot be found, intermediate data relationships are defined to bridge the gap. In this simple example, a one-to-one correspondence is easy to establish and is shown by the dotted lines in Figure 6-10. The program structure based on this correspondence is given in Figure 6-11.

Note that the output report could have been validly shown on the diagram as a selection of the possible output print lines, as in Figure 6-12. Also, the input could have been validly portrayed as a selection of either an H or a T record, as shown in Figure 6-13.

Although the two data structures are logically correct they do not contain all the relationships which are relevant to the problem, and a correspondence could not be established between the two. The example problem requires information on batches, but the input data structure has ignored this aspect. For a very simple problem, say a listing of the input record by record, Figure 6-13 may represent a

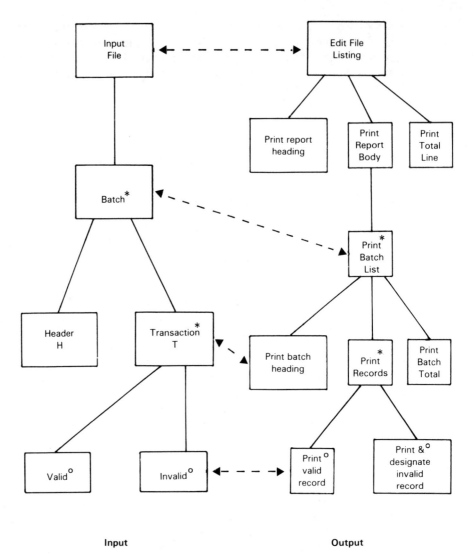

Input   **Output**

Figure 6-10   Correspondence between input and output data structures

suitable structure. The point is that it is not enough for the data structure to be correct as a data structure, it must also express all the relationships which are relevant to the problem.

If the required output is changed to reflect valid and invalid header cards, it would be necessary to show the header H input as a selection of either a valid or an invalid card. Consider another example: suppose there is a new requirement to sum all input records where the value field is $1000 or larger, and report on the total sum. To reflect this report requirement in the input data structure, the valid T record is now shown as a selection based on the value, as illustrated in Figure 6-14. This

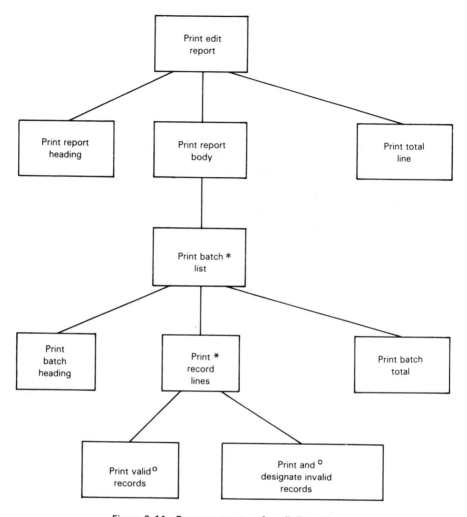

Figure 6-11   Program structure for edit list program

lowest level of the data structure would correspond to a function on the program structure 'sum value field where value $\geqslant$ \$1000'. This dependence of the data structure on the problem to be solved means that, as the problem changes, so too does the data structure, even though the same set of cards may be input to the program. If the data is to be used differently, say, to print more information on the report, then the output data structure must be modified to reflect this change as well as the input data structure.

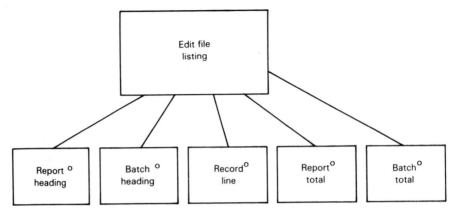

Figure 6-12 Alternative output data structure

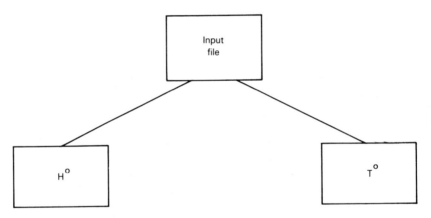

Figure 6-13 Alternative input data structure

6.3.2 Structure Clash

In more complex situations, a problem may be faced where no one-to-one correspondence between the input and output data structures can be established. This is called a structure clash, and is resolved by introducing an intermediate data structure. This situation very frequently occurs in processing sequential files, when the sequences do not match. The intermediate data structure is achieved by sorting one file to establish a structure correspondence. A structure clash may also occur when the two files are in the same sequence but a physical constraint on one file prevents a correspondence being established.

Jackson's example of the structure clash in processing a telegram file is briefly summarized here to illustrate this form of structure clash. The problem involves reading an input file on paper tape containing the text of a number of telegrams. The tape is read by a 'read block' instruction which reads a variable-length block (less than 100 characters) into memory. The block is delimited by an EOB character. Each

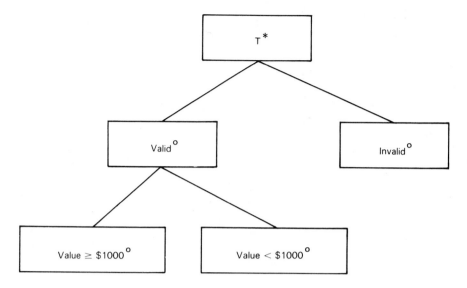

Figure 6-14   Modified transaction data structure

block contains a number of words separated by spaces (one or more). Each telegram, which may span a number of blocks, is terminated by the special word 'ZZZZ'. Telegrams may start and finish anywhere in a block so there is no relationship between block and telegram. The file is terminated by a special null telegram before the end-of-block indicator. Figure 6–15 illustrates a small section of this file.

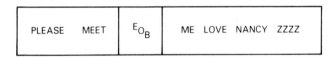

Figure 6-15   Section of telegram file

A report showing the number of words in each telegram and the number of words with more than 12 characters is required. Figure 6–16 shows what the report will look like, and the input and output data structures are shown in Figure 6–17. Since telegrams can span blocks, and a block can contain a number of telegrams, there is a structure clash between the input and output structures. The block structure of the input file is the problem. A simple way to resolve the clash is to set up an intermediate file which can be read a word at a time, so eliminating the block structure. Figure 6–18 gives the new file which is output from the telegram file in the first stage of processing. Figure 6–19 gives an alternative view of the new file, now seen as the input to the program which will prepare the telegram report. The structure correspondence between the input data structure and Figure 6–18, an iteration of words, is obvious, as is the correspondence between the output telegram-report data structure and Figure 6–19.

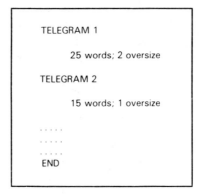

Figure 6-16   Telegram file report

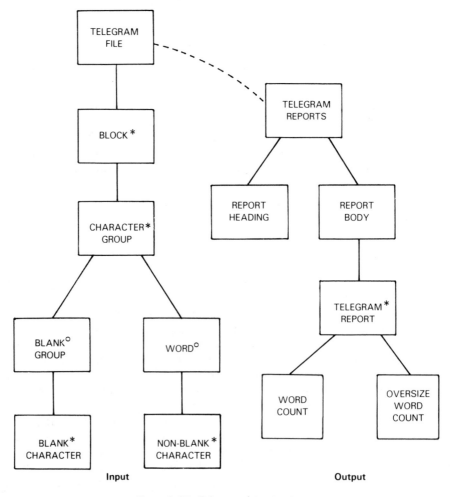

Figure 6-17   Telegram data structures

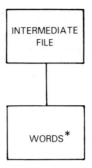

Figure 6-18   New file as output for the telegram file

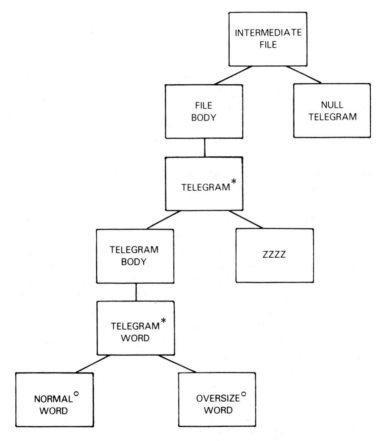

Figure 6-19   New file as input to create the telegram report

This solution removes the structure clash caused by the blocked telegram file, by writing the paper tape file to an output file and removing the block characters so this file can be read one word at a time. However, it suffers from the disadvantages of having unnecessarily increased the system size and introduced needless processing inefficiency. Jackson proposes a way around this problem by 'inverting' one of the programs and having the other program call it. Thus, if the first program is inverted, it becomes 'obtain next word'; hence every file read in the second program becomes a call to 'obtain next word', and every 'write to the file' in the first program becomes a 'return to the second program'. Unfortunately, this solution suffers from a number of disadvantages, the chief one being the necessity to resume the inverted program at the point where it last left off. This is difficult to achieve in a language like COBOL without maintaining a state variable and using a GOTO at the top of the inverted program. It would appear that other solutions may be more elegant and simpler to use when faced with problems such as these.

6.3.3 Summary

A major strength of the data-structure-based technique, both for systems design and for program design, is that it leads to standard and reproducible designs. If two analysts set out to design the structure of a program, there is a high probability that they will both design it the same way. This is a very significant factor in program maintenance, since it means that the programmer performing the maintenance, even though not the program designer, is able to understand the program as though she or he were the designer. This advantage would seem to indicate greater productivity in maintenance, provided the program structure has not been jeopardized by corner-cutting during previous maintenance work by putting in patches.

An interesting aspect of the data-structure-based techniques is that they are problem oriented. By this is meant the program's (or system's) structure is specified by considering only the problem statement (e.g. design a program to process the input and produce the output). This aspect distinguishes the data-structure-based techniques from all others which seek to define a solution for the problem (e.g. first open the file, then read the input record and check the contents, before writing to the output, etc.) and then a structure based on the solution. The techniques have been in use since 1975 and have attracted some very ardent supporters (see Menard, 1980). However, the number of programmers using them appears to be quite low. Criticisms have been voiced concerning the applicability of this data-structure approach to other than sequential-file-based programs or systems (Peters, 1977), although it would appear that Menard has not experienced this restriction.

6.4 DATA-FLOW-BASED METHODOLOGIES

6.4.1 Overview

A number of systems analysis and design methodologies are based on analyzing the flow of data through the system. This section first looks at the program design method proposed by Yourdon & Constantine (1979) and by Myers (1978). This technique is called Structured Design by Yourdon & Constantine and Composite Design by Myers. Then follows a brief look at the application of data flow diagrams and other supporting techniques that De Marco has brought together under the title *Structured Analysis and System Specification* (1980). The De Marco methodology is similar in style to SADT (Structured Analysis and Design Technique) which was developed by Ross of SofTech Inc. (Ross, 1977).

6.4.2 Structured Design

Structured Design (SD) is concerned with developing the best partitioning of a program into modules. With everything else equal, the best partitioning is a hierarchical structure of loosely-coupled modules, with the code within each module tightly connected in the data it manipulates and the function it provides. This is best because, intuitively, it gives the most easily maintained and enhanced code, since it isolates potential changes in data or function to as few modules as possible. The objective of SD is to produce a non-complex design that is robust in its performance and can be maintained and enhanced in the simplest possible way.

A *module* is defined to be a closed subroutine which can be called from any other closed subroutine and is capable of being independently compiled. It is generally felt by authors in this field that modules should be about one page of code, to allow easy and complete comprehension within a normal programmer's span of attention. (But there is little empirical evidence to support this belief.)

In none of the current data-flow methodologies is code execution efficiency specifically considered in the design. This is a deliberate omission, because execution efficiency is felt to be unimportant in relation to the ease of development and ease of maintenance. And with current cost and price trends, execution efficiency will become even less important in the future. For those applications where efficiency is important due to tight performance requirements, such as might be encountered in a critical real-time system, performance can be optimized after a first design has been developed. This enables the performance/maintenance trade-offs to be examined, and rational design decisions taken.

To motivate the discussion, a model is presented which gives the thrust of the basic assumptions. Assume that each line of a program's code can be associated with both a data structure and a function, and that the data pairs can be plotted on the space represented by the data-function axes. This would give a picture such as in Figure 6–20. A clustering of the points into groups would bring together the points representing lines of code which use similar data and perform similar functions. These groups would form a good basis for defining modules since:

- Potential change to the program's function would be likely to affect only the module containing that function
- Potential modification to the data processed by the program would be similarly restricted

Partitioning a program into modules (modularization) is only beneficial if the partitioning is well performed. Note that a completely random partitioning of the program into modules would most likely require modification of all modules if a change in the program was required. Bad partitioning would greatly increase the structural complexity of the product and increase its development and testing time, as well as degrading its future maintainability.

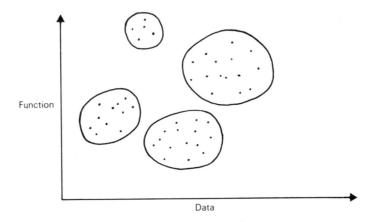

Function

Data

Figure 6–20   Model of program partition

Two concepts concerning the partitioning of a program into modules are important. The first is that of *module cohesion*, which refers to the degree of relationship between elements within a module. In Figure 6–20, the lines of code which clustered together would exhibit strong relationships to one another and could be said to have high cohesion. The second concept is *module coupling* which refers to the coupling or the bonds between two modules. The design goal of SD is to partition the program into modules which have high cohesion and low intermodule coupling, and to do this by:

- First, proposing a classification of different levels of cohesion and coupling to help the analyst recognize and understand the difference between good and bad designs
- Second, using a methodology to generate a first pass design which can be improved by the analyst using the knowledge gained from the first step

Module cohesion

Module cohesion is defined as the relationship between elements within a module. The terms 'binding', 'strength', and 'functionality' are also used to express this same concept. A discussion and ranking of different classes of module cohesion from weak to strong is given to demonstrate the concept and the important criteria used to assess the level of module cohesion.

Coincidental cohesion. This is the lowest form of cohesion and describes a near-randomly partitioned module in which:

- The function of the module cannot be easily described except by referring to a list of what the module does
- The module performs multiple, completely unrelated, functions on unrelated data

Time-related cohesion. This cohesion level brings together in one module a number of possibly unrelated functions that must all be done at the one time, say at the start of a program; for example, the functions in a start-up module may be:

- Open transaction file
- Set summary table at initial conditions
- Print report headings
- Rewind file

The main problem with this type of module is that its relationship to other modules is not clear.

Procedural cohesion. This term describes a module which performs multiple sequential functions, where the relationship between the sequential functions is implied by the problem, but there is no data relationship between functions. For example, on invalid command:

- Print message to terminal
- Checkpoint the log file
- Skip to next transaction in queue

Functional cohesion. Here the module performs a single specific function on a single data structure. Note that what is a single specific function is a matter of convenience of definition and concept. Some examples might be:

- Update customer record
- Write message to user

Module coupling

If two modules are completely independent of each other, each can be understood without having to refer in any way to the other. Conversely, if two modules are very highly dependent, say, referring to common variables or flags, both need to be understood in order to understand either one. It is suggested that a design goal for producing easily understood and easily modified code is to make modules as independent as possible. The degree of interconnection between two modules is referred to as module coupling.

Some of the factors to be considered in assessing module coupling are:

- The means provided for data sharing, e.g. global variables, local variables
- The type of connection, e.g. GOTO, CALL

- Complexity of module interface
- Whether information passed between modules is data or control information

The best form of coupling is where all data are local to a module and parameters are explicitly passed between modules.

Initial partitioning

The desirable properties of modules have been presented in terms of their internal cohesion and their coupling to each other. The designer who understands these properties is able to appraise a design and assess its merits in comparison with an alternative. They give a means of making consistent design decisions which reflect the importance of controlling complexity and improving maintainability.

A key activity in the design process is breaking down the program into modules. Some methodologies have been proposed for this and they are summarized here. However, the designer must never accept the modules from these techniques without carefully thinking about how they can be improved. In SD the designer needs to adopt an intuitive or evolutionary process in which a number of preliminary designs are made, and then scrapped as better designs are conceived which overcome problems inherent in the earlier ones. The steps proposed for initial decomposition are:

1. Define the top module as the function of the program.
2. By viewing this function as a 'problem to be solved', break it down into modules which are the functions required to solve the problem. Techniques which can be used to carry out this decomposition are:
   - Source/transform/sink decomposition
   - Transactional decomposition
   - Functional decomposition
3. For each of the modules defined, repeat the process of decomposition, stopping when the function is simple enough and can be coded in about 50 statements. There is nothing magical about 50, but it does appear to represent the short-term memory span of a programmer.

Source/transform/sink decomposition. The motivation for this method is that, if the development of the program structure is based on the data flow in the problem at hand, then like functions operating on like data will group together. This technique, suitable where there is a clear flow of data through the system, breaks the problem into three modules: a source module, a transform module, and a sink module. (It is the use of this approach that gives this technique the title of 'data flow based'.) To summarize the technique:

1. Draw the data flow diagram
2. Identify the major stream of input data and the major stream of output data.
3. Identify the point in the DFD where:

- The input data stream last exists as a logical entity
- The output data stream first exists as a logical entity
4. Use the boundaries defined above to segment the problem into three functions: source, transform, and sink.

As an example, Figure 6–21 illustrates the DFD for a simple update procedure.

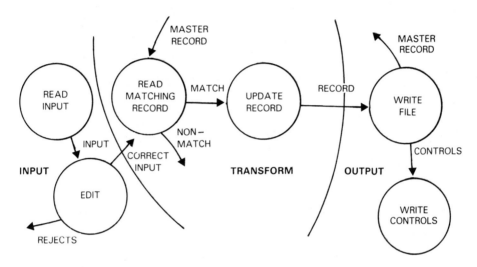

Figure 6-21   Source/transform/sink decomposition

The source/transform/sink (STS) technique leads to an initial source segmentation just after the edit, for beyond this point the input data is merged with the master file record and ceases to exist as a logical entity. The STS technique suggests a sink segmentation just before the write file, as the write file and write controls are parts of the one output record. The central segment is the transform, where the input is transformed to the output. The initial segmentation is given in Figure 6–22. Each of the modules shown in Figure 6–22 are then subjected to further analysis, maybe by the STS technique, to determine how they can be decomposed. The process stops when the modules are small enough and have good cohesion.

Transactional decomposition. This method applies to problems where the type of input data determines the nature of the function to be performed. To illustrate, consider a requirement to edit input transactions to accounts receivable file where transaction types are:

- Sales return
- Cash receipt
- Sale
- Sundry credit or debit

The decomposition here is based on a module for each transaction type, as shown in Figure 6–23.

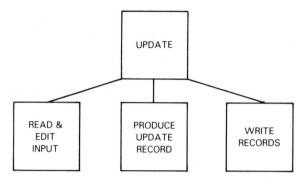

Figure 6-22   Initial segmentation of Figure 6-14

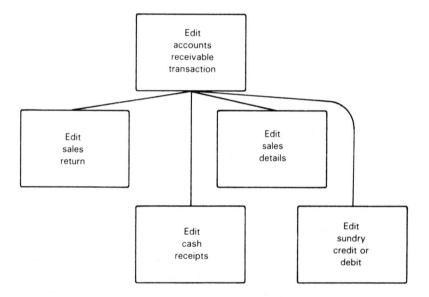

Figure 6-23   Transactional decomposition

Functional decomposition. Functional decomposition is an ad hoc procedure for breaking down a module in order to:

- Isolate common functions which, for example, may occur in a number of modules
- Decompose a too-large module which cannot be attacked with either STS or transactional decomposition.

6.4.3   Structured Analysis

De Marco (1980), who coined the term *structured analysis,* defines it as building a 'structured specification' by the use of the tools:

- Data flow diagrams
- Data dictionary
- Structured English
- Decision tables
- Decision trees

It is highly graphical and display oriented, and aims to eliminate words, wherever possible, by the use of pictures. Predominantly, structured analysis is a change in the documentation of the analysis phase and by so being, it is suggested, it introduces a change in the way communication concerning the analysis takes place, both between analyst and user and between analyst and analyst. The tools themselves have been available in some form for many years, and structured analysis is concerned with bringing their use together into a unified framework. Data flow diagrams and data dictionaries are defined in Subsection 2.3.2, and decision tables and decision trees are covered briefly in Chapter 2. Structured English is explained here, and then a short discussion of the steps of structured analysis is given.

Structured English

Structured English is De Marco's proposal for defining the functions represented by the bubbles in the lowest level of the data flow diagram. It aims to be a concise and precise way of describing a function, and is offered as a superior alternative to the more usual descriptive approach. It is concerned with describing the logical elements of the function, using simple English imperatives and indentation freely to mould the expression to the application by not formalizing the grammar or syntax. In short, it is shorthand documentation technique for writing a function specification which is equally valid for both manual and computer processing. Figure 6–24, an example concerning one part of a goods-received-note validation, should make the idea clear.

```
GOODS-RECEIVED-NOTE VALIDATE ONE

For each G.R.N. in G.R.N. Batch:

    Search Supplier-File for match on Supplier-Code
        If found Search Product-File for match on Product-Code
            If found Write Goods-Received-Data

    Otherwise Write Error Message to Print File
```

Figure 6-24   Structured English example

Structured English can be written at various levels of detail, and Figure 6–24 could perhaps be better written as shown in Figure 6–25. Figure 6–26 gives another example, this time involving a case statement. Note that file and data names included in the structured English text are defined entities in the data dictionary. The names of the functions should be descriptive and unique so they can be easily identified with the part of the data flow diagram they relate to.

```
GOODS-RECEIVED-NOTE VALIDATE ONE

For each G.R.N. in G.R.N. Batch:

        Search Supplier-File for Match on Supplier-Code and Product-File for match on
        Product-Code
                If both found Write Goods-Received-Data
                Otherwise Write appropriate error message
```

Figure 6–25   Alternative structured English example

```
                        DISCOUNT PROCEDURE

For each Order-Record in Order-File:

        Select the discount policy

        Case 1 (Cost-of-Order $1000) — Discount is 20%

        Case 2 (Cost-of-Order in range $50 to $999.99) — Discount is 12%

        Case 3 (Cost-of-Order $50) — Discount is 5%

        Write Discount to Invoice-Trailer
```

Figure 6–26   Case statement in structured English

Structured analysis steps

The approach of structured analysis is similar to that presented in Chapter 5, and is expressed by the following steps.

1. Describe the current physical system. The people, equipment and all features and details (including the idiosyncrasies) of the current system are described.

2. Abstract to the current logical system. The essential logical system is distilled from the physical, and all inessential and irrelevant aspects deleted. The data flow diagram approach assists greatly in identifying the logical system.

3. Redesign to give the new logical system. This is the heart of the analysis where the creativity of the analyst has full rein in reshaping the system to best realize the objectives defined for the project.

4. Define the new physical system. This stage involves establishing:

- The man-machine boundary
- The performance targets of the system
- The database and equipment needs

It may also involve the packaging of the system into programs and runs.

De Marco suggests that stage 4 should stop short of a completely physical description of the system in terms of program specifications, etc., as they excessively constrain the implementation team. The transition, in his view, is for the output of this stage to form the input to the structured design team, who use the techniques of source/transform/sink decomposition to obtain the modules directly from the data flow diagram. However, it would appear that some partitioning of the system into programs or functional processes is necessary before entering the program design stage. This partitioning is a systems analysis and design task which must precede the detail of the program module design, otherwise the system design is obscured by the detail involved in concentrating on the modules.

6.4.4   Structured Analysis and Design Technique (SADT)

SADT (Ross, 1977; Canning, 1979) is a proprietary technique marketed by SofTech Inc. It is claimed to significantly increase the productivity and effectiveness of systems project teams. Although based on data flow analysis, SADT encompasses a considerably wider ambit, including: division and coordination of team effort; methods for controlling the accuracy, completeness, and quality of work; planning and controlling team effort; and a technique for communicating and documenting the analysis and design. The documentation and communication tool uses a set of 40 constructs to graphically present a system which, SofTech claims, can also be used for graphically presenting anything, including itself.

Because of the generality and breadth of scope of the method, it is more complex and involved than, say, the De Marco method, and requires a training program lasting some weeks to fully master it.

6.5   COMPUTER-BASED DESIGN TOOLS

All the preceding methodologies are designed around manual techniques for collecting, recording, and organizing the data for the analysis, design, and implementation of a system. Some may use computer-based techniques for maintaining the data dictionary or for documentation text processing. But none have been explicitly designed, from the outset, to use the computer to assist in the analysis, design, and implementation stages. A number of efforts are currently underway with the bold long-term vision of having the computer take over the design and implementation of new systems once the analysis has been done. Davis *et al.* (1979) describe work at General Telephone and Electronics (GTE) to automate the requirements definition stage for telephone-switching software and to have the computer verify the internal consistency of requirements. The long-term plan at GTE (Davis, 1980) is to develop a software development facility which will produce efficient working code from an input of the requirements specification.

The ultimate aim of the Information Systems Design and Optimization System (ISDOS) project at the University of Michigan is to automatically produce working code from a problem statement for any information system. Currently only the front end, the problem-statement language (PSL) and problem-statement analyzer (PSA), are operational (Teichroew & Hershey, 1977). PSL/PSA, which was developed during the 1970s, is a computer-based analysis and documentation tool primarily intended to aid the logical system design process. The capabilities claimed for it are:

- Describing the key attributes of information systems in the problem-statement language
- Recording the descriptions in a computer database
- Allowing incremental adding to, modifying, or deleting systems components and segments from the database
- Analyzing the information system described in the PSL using the problem-statement analyzer
- Producing hard copy documentation

The problem-statement language is used to describe systems by way of objects which have certain properties and property values. Objects may be connected in a relationship. System descriptions may consist of the eight aspects:

- The system input-output flow
- System structure describing object hierarchies
- Data structure
- Data derivation describing data use in processes
- System size and volumes
- System dynamics
- Properties
- Project management describing personnel responsibilities and schedules

The PSA analyzes the PSL for correct syntax, and can:

- Produce data dictionaries and cross-reference listings
- Ensure completeness of relationships
- Indicate time-dependent relationships of data
- Analyze volume specifications

A number of commercial organizations have been using the PSL/PSA system for some years for their systems development. The benefits usually cited include:

- Improved documentation quality
- Simplified coordination among analysts
- Early identification of errors, inconsistencies, and omissions
- Easier maintenance

The plan of the complete ISDOS system is for the output from the PSA to be input to the System Optimization and Design Analysis (SODA) module, which produces source code for compiling, and input to a Data Organizer module. This module is to organize the data optimally on a database. Figure 6–27 shows the

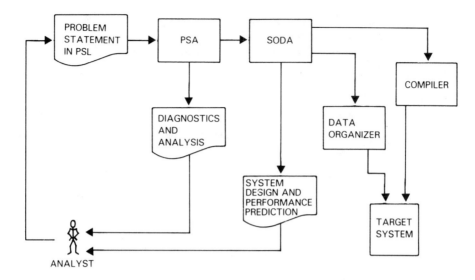

Figure 6-27 ISDOS system

module inter-relationships. The ISDOS project aims to go further than producing file/database designs and source code, as it intends to also determine the required systems configuration, including memory size and speed and input–output device requirements which satisfy the constraints of time and volume while minimizing cost.

The ten years put into the ISDOS project with only the front end having been produced is evidence that a general-purpose completely automated development system lies a long way in the future, especially on considering that the work required for the SODA and Data Organizer modules appears to be a quantum leap over that for the PSL/PSA segment. It seems that special-purpose development systems, such as that being undertaken at GTE for telephone-switching software, may provide an earlier indication of the viability of the concept.

REFERENCES

B. BEOHM, 'Software Engineering — As It Is', *IEEE Fourth International Conference on Software Engineering*, September 1979, pp. 11-21.

R.G. CANNING, 'The Production of Better Software', *EDP Analyzer*, February 1979.

R.G. CANNING, 'Program Design Techniques', *EDP Analyzer*, March 1979.

A.M. DAVIS, 'Automating the Requirements Phase: Benefits to late phases of the software life cycle', *IEEE Fourth International Computer Software and Applications Conference*, October 1980, pp. 42-8.

A.M. DAVIS, T.J. MILLER, E. RHODE & B.J. TAYLOR, 'RLP: An Automated Tool for the Processing of Requirements', *IEEE Third International Computer Software and Applications Conference*, November 1979, pp. 289-99.

T. DE MARCO, *Structured Analysis and Systems Specification*, Prentice-Hall Inc., Englewood Cliffs, N.J., 1980.

M.A. JACKSON, *Principles of Program Design*, Academic Press, London, 1975.

J. MENARD, 'Exxon's Experience with the Jackson Method', *Database*, Winter 1980, pp. 88-92.

G.J. MYERS, *Software Reliability*, Wiley, New York, 1976.

G.J. MYERS, *Composite/Structured Design*, Van Nostrand Reinhold, New York, 1978.

NATIONAL CASH REGISTER COMPANY, *A Study Guide for Accurately Defined Systems*, NCR, Dayton, Ohio, 1968.

K.T. ORR, *Structured Systems Development*, Yourdan Press, New York, 1977.

L.J. PETERS & L.L. TRIPP, 'Comparing Software Design Methods', *Datamation*, November 1977, pp. 89-94.

D. ROSS, 'Structured Analysis: A language for communicating ideas', *IEEE Trans. on Software Engineering*, January 1977, pp. 16-34.

D. TEICHROEW & E. HERSHEY, 'PSL/PSA: A computer aided technique for structured documentation and analysis of information processing systems', *IEEE Trans. on Software Engineering*, January 1977, pp. 41-8.

J.D. WARNIER, *The Logical Construction of Programs*, 3rd edn, translated by B.M. Flanagan, Van Nostrand Reinhold, New York, 1976.

E. YOURDON & L. CONSTANTINE, *Structured Design*, Prentice-Hall Inc., Englewood Cliffs, N.J., 1979.

CASE STUDY — STRUCTURED DESIGN

ASSIGNMENT

Design the edit program specified below according to the Jackson method and the Structured Design method. Compare the two designs from the standpoints of:

- Ease of the design job
- Ease of program development
- Maintainability

Edit Program

Objective

The edit program is to run on a small microcomputer in a distributed data collection and editing environment. Batches of invoices and batches of transfer documents are (1) entered, using a simple fill-in-the-blanks screen format, (2) edited and validated, and (3) written to an output diskette for later delivery by courier to the head office.

Flowchart

The flowchart for the program is given in Figure 6–28.

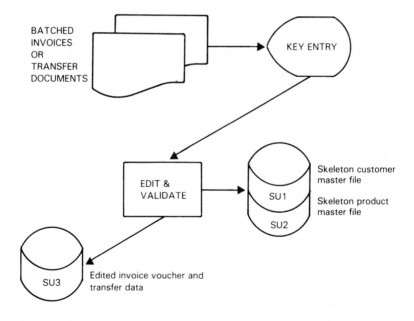

Figure 6-28   Flowchart for edit program

Input

    Terminal: Batch header
                    Batch of invoices or transfer documents

    Files: SU1 — skeleton customer master file (Figure 6–29)
                    SU2 — skeleton product master file (Figure 6–30)

Output

    File: SU3 — edited invoice voucher and transfer documents file

    Record sequence:
                Batch header
                Batch details
                End-of-batch marker

The output file contains all the data shown on the input documents. Note that batches of invoices and batches of transfers may occur in any order on the output file. A transfer document is given in Figure 6–31.

Processing frequency

    The diskette containing SU3 is to be ready for picking up each day at 4.30 P.M. Input should be keyed in during each day.

Processing details

    Edit and validate checks are to include:

- Format checks for all input data items
- Range check on quantity (between 0 and 1000)
- Product code by reference to SU2, returning description and unit of measure
- Supplier code (for invoice) by reference to SU1 returning supplier name
- For invoice, a check of calculated unit cost against cost on SU2; if variance is greater than 20 per cent, query for confirmation of accuracy
- For invoices, the calculated invoice value computed from the data input is to be compared with the total value shown on the invoice
- For transfers, the calculated hash total on quantity is to be compared with the hash total on the transfer document

The batch header will contain the number of documents in the batch and a total value for invoices and a hash total on quantity for transfers. If, after a batch has been key entered, the batch controls calculated by summing the input data do not agree with the batch header controls, provision should be made to read the batch from the file, record by record, and amend any incorrectly keyed data.

Invoice Data Entry

Data to be entered from each invoice will be:

- Cost centre number
- Date
- Invoice number
- Invoice date
- Supplier number
- Order number
- Invoice line data (up to eight invoice lines) consisting of product code, quantity, and amount
- Product discount
- Cartage charged
- Miscellaneous taxes and fees charged
- Invoice total value

Field	Description	Length
1	Customer code	8
2	Customer name	30
3	Customer city	15

Figure 6-29   SU1 — skeleton customer master file

Field	Description	Length
1	Product code	7
2	Product description	30
3	Unit of measure	4
4	Cost	6

Figure 6-30   SU2 — skeleton product master file

Case Study — Structured Design

No...............

Date.......................

RECEIVING COST CENTRE NO. ....

SUPPLYING COST CENTRE NO. ....

Product Code	Description	Quantity	Unit of Measure
	HASH TOTAL		

Issued by:	Goods Received by:

Figure 6-31   Interdepartmental transfer document

7 DATABASE MANAGEMENT SYSTEMS

7.1 INTRODUCTION

Generalized database management systems have been increasingly developed because it became apparent, during the early 1960s, that conventional data processing has a number of shortcomings, such as:

- Accessing data collected for a particular application area to satisfy the needs of a different application or to answer an ad hoc request is difficult. The main causes of this problem are: inconsistencies in data-storage formats; the early aggregation of data with the resulting loss of detail; poor data collection timing; and inadequate documentation about inquiry programs.
- Associating data, which relate to the same entity but are stored in different files, is difficult. This problem has proved an effective barrier to the implementation of many information systems because of inconsistent coding systems, incompatability of storage media and, probably most significantly, the inability of the system to access data without knowing the 'key' to the desired record.
- The cost of storing data relating to the same entity in a number of different files is excessive. For example, it may be necessary to keep name-and-address information on two or three files because file processing for a number of applications which use that name and address cannot be integrated.
- The cost of satisfying the stream of enhancement requests for installed systems, particularly those which affect the system's files, is high. A significant factor in the cost of these enhancements is the inflexibility

185

generated by conventional file structures and their tight binding to the application programs. There is a great need to make programs independent of the physical structure of the data they have to access.

- Managing and controlling the data resources of an organization, while safeguarding data integrity and ensuring rapid and secure access to data, is a difficult task.

Each of these difficulties grows directly out of the limitations of storing data in conventional application files. Consider an ideal database management system (DBMS) which could overcome these problems. This ideal DBMS is hypothesized as providing the user with the same kind of complete service that might be expected from a good accountant in a manual system, in which the manager, when asking for data, does not need any knowledge of the physical storage organization or access method adopted by the accountant. The accountant is responsible for managing the set of data (storage, update, and access), controlling its integrity, ensuring that confidential data are not disclosed to unauthorized individuals, and recognizing common aliases for data. Should the accountant decide to reorganize the data, add additional attributes to certain data entities, or file data under a new heading to improve access time, nobody in the organization need be told because only the accountant is concerned with this level of the record keeping. Users of the data only need to know what data are being collected. (This is called data independence.)

Conventional file systems, on the other hand, are analogous to having a dull-witted clerk looking after the data files. Every user (i.e. every program) who requires data needs to know exactly where the wanted data are located, how they are organized, the record layout, and, if more than one file must be used, the logic to apply to searching the multiple files. The user then directs the clerk to open a certain file drawer, search on a particular key or an index, and proceed until the wanted record is located. The whole record is passed to the user, who must be prepared for this and for identifying the particular data needed. Should any change be made to the contents of a file or to its organization all users wishing to obtain data from that file must modify their access procedure.

A number of objectives for a DBMS can be formulated from this discussion:

- Provide better tools for the programmer. A high-level data-manipulation language (also termed data-management language) to facilitate access and updating of stored data is an attractive means of improving programming productivity.
- Control data integrity. The ability to access data items easily by key and by relationship allows input data to be more completely validated before being stored. The standard interface to the data means that tight, consistent integrity controls can be set up.
- Facilitate quick answers to 'easy' data interrogation questions. Data-processing people have long recognized the considerable benefit that would accrue from a query facility which is simple enough to be operated by non-DP staff and which allows data to be extracted from any files, simple manipulations to be carried out, and then a report written. It has been felt that, since the substance of many queries can be expressed unambiguously

in a few lines, it should be possible, with a suitable language, to communicate this to a query processor and receive the report.

- Model data relationships. Few commercial programming language constructs are available specifically for modelling other than simple data relationships such as sequential list structures. Yet data relationships of varying complexity exist in practically all data that are processed. Employees may be related to department and projects; sales orders to customers and products; machines to departments, operators, and products; and so on. With suitable tools, these natural data relationships can be modelled and taken advantage of in systems design.

This chapter aims at laying a solid foundation for the concepts of database design and database management systems, irrespective of any particular piece of software. A historical perspective for the continuing development of DBMSs is outlined, and principles by which any particular DBMS may be judged are given.

7.2   DEFINING A DATABASE AND A DATABASE MANAGEMENT SYSTEM

It is difficult, in practice, to define 'database' and 'database management system' unambiguously, as the line which divides conventional application files using conventional file-access methods from databases using a DBMS is very blurred and indistinct. Some applications use a DBMS but have a systems design approach based on a trivial implementation of sequential files with sequential access. On the other hand, some systems employing conventional access methods are database in their philosophy. Perhaps the real crux of the distinction lies not in the DBMS or the access method but in the approach taken for the design of the database.

In Chapter 3, files organization and access methods are discussed in the light of the needs of the specific application for which the files are being designed. So, for a high-hit-rate, high-volatility application, sequential files are recommended, while for lower hit-rate applications direct access is indicated. This approach ties the file organization to the particular application. And, in normal systems design practice, the file record contents are designed to hold only the data needed for the particular application in hand. Thus, in content, in organization, and in access method, a file is designed to meet the specific identified needs of a given application. It is small wonder then, that when a new application is being developed, the existing files do not appear at all appropriate and so new files — involving duplication — appear to be the easy way around the problem.

Designing a database is approached from a more whole-system view of the organization's data needs. It is based on the principle of designing a logical database for an organization by considering only the organization's data and their interrelationships, and not considering the application systems that may be installed. After the logical design phase, there is a physical database design phase in which the implications of the physical environment are considered. But the primary thrust of database design is to consider at one time all the data types in the organization (or, for a large organization, an essentially self-contained sector of it) and to build a model for the data. Frequently this model involves complex data relationships, so a versatile DBMS is needed for its implementation.

But if it so happens that a simple data model results from this exercise, a model which can be handled by a conventional file-access technique like ISAM, then, it is argued, this is a database solution. This difficulty of definition has led some authors, e.g. Date (1981), and Kroenke (1977), to define a database merely as a collection of stored data used by the application systems of some particular enterprise.

The *database management system* (DBMS) is defined as the software which organizes the structure of the database (through the data-description language or DDL) and handles all access to the database (through the data-manipulation language or DML). User data-access commands in the DML are intercepted or passed to the DBMS where they are interpreted, and the appropriate actions taken on the physical database. Some DML commands may set in train a whole series of physical database accesses. In terms of the example used in Section 7.1, the DBMS provides many of the data-access, management, and control functions of the accountant in the manual system.

7.3 HISTORICAL EVOLUTION OF DATABASES

The modern database and database management system have grown out of early military command-and-control systems which were oriented to providing simpler access to the data. They were a giant step forward from earlier systems where programmers had themselves to write the code which performed all the input-output. By the mid-1960s the commercial versions of these early military systems had evolved to the point where two distinct paths, each based on the primary objective of the system, had emerged. One path gave rise to what is called the 'self-contained DBMS', oriented to providing data-interrogation facilities for the non-programmer. These systems generally work on the 'fill in the blanks' format or through a structured question-and-answer dialog on a terminal. The other path gave rise to the so-called host language systems which are oriented to providing facilities for programmers. 'Host language' implies that calls to these systems are embedded in a program written in a host language (COBOL, PL/I, etc.).

Many systems today fall exclusively into one or the other of these two categories, although there is an encouraging trend for the two objectives to be served by the one 'full' system. Some of the key differences between self-contained and host language systems are given in Table 7–1.

7.4 DBMS USERS

Three quite distinct classes of people need to have direct dealings with the database and to be catered for by the database management system. They are the database administrator, and programming and non-programming users.

Database administrator (DBA). The DBA is responsible for the database and the DBMS. Such tasks as database design and definition, database standards,

Table 7-1 Characteristics of DBMS systems*

	DBMS Type	
	Host language	Self-contained
Objective	Augment and extend usefulness of high-level host language (e.g. COBOL)	A complete stand-alone system for data storage and retrieval
Major user	Application programmer	Non-DP trained end user
Level of user interface	Record	File
Data models supported	Many	Flat or hierarchical
Control over physical processing	Program code fully controls physical operation	Code only controls logical operation: physical control is transparent to user
Flexibility	Very flexible	Limited to algorithms provided

* Adapted from G.C. Everest (1979)

database creation, database maintenance (redefinition of database structure), and database integrity and security (back-up, validation, and access control) are involved in the position. The DBA also acts as adviser on database access for programmers and systems design and user personnel, and monitors the efficiency of the database to determine when tuning modifications are required. Organizationally, the DBA generally reports within the data-processing group, often to the data-processing manager or one level down. Frequently, one or more systems programmers dedicated to the DBMS are employed within the DBA function.

The non-programming user. The DBMS needs a simple interface to permit the non-programming user to access and maybe to update the database. This requires a high-level and easy-to-use interrogation language, error messages which allow problems to be fixed easily, and a high standard of readable documentation.

The programming user. Both the systems designer and the programmer are responsible for the efficient use of the database through the medium of the application programs.

7.5 DATA INDEPENDENCE, SCHEMAS, AND SUBSCHEMAS

7.5.1 Data Independence

A significant problem with application files is the need to change every program which accesses a file when that file is modified. This requirement is due to each program carrying a copy of the data definition, in largely physical terms, for that file. Central to the database approach is having one definition of the database, with each program only defining and asking for the data it needs. In this section, the evolution of this concept, called *data independence,* is traced to the situation which prevails in today's DBMSs.

In early programs, and still at times today in programs written in low-level languages, the data-definition code, which describes the physical structure of the data that are contained on the files or are required as working storage, is distributed throughout the programs. Thus, if any record structure is modified, all the lines of code referring to that physical record structure need to be found and modified.

Languages like COBOL recognize that the data-definition code should be kept separate from the procedural code. This localizes modification to the data division if the record structures are changed. A further development is storing the data-definition code on a central library and using a COPY instruction to copy the version of the data definitions current at the time of program compilation. This means that only one file of data definitions is kept, which greatly reduces the effort required to adjust to revised record formats.

7.5.2 Schemas and Subschemas

The database approach takes this progression of storage independence of program and data one step further by setting up independent definitions of the data for both the program and the database. The database is logically defined by a database schema, i.e. a database model. This *database schema* defines the logical database, by defining record types, data items, repeating groups, the types of values a data item can take (e.g. alphabetical or numerical), and relationships between record types. The physical database is defined by the physical model, which describes the access paths in the database, the linkages provided between records, the formula used to calculate addresses, the means used to handle overflows, the representation used for numbers, and the other physical aspects of finding, retrieving, and storing records. Access to this level of the DBMS depends on the particular system used.

A program accessing the database has its own separate view of the data it requires. This view is necessarily a subset of the database schema and is called a *user subschema* (or user submodel). The user subschema disconnects the user's view from the database schema, allowing different data names and different user views of the data structure. In order to have program–data independence, the program must have its own definition of the data it needs, which can remain constant despite changes made to the database. Obviously, drastic changes to the database have the potential of damaging the user program. So the term 'program–data independence' is used in a relative sense.

For an example of a user subschema, consider the simple database consisting of a department entity containing department name and budget and an employee entity containing employee number, name, address, current and year-to-date pay and deduction details, job title, office location, and telephone number. The program which accesses the database to print the company telephone book would have a user subschema consisting of the employee name, office location, telephone number and perhaps department name. The program which updates pay details would have a user subschema consisting of employee number and current and year-to-date pay and deduction details.

Figure 7-1 presents a DBMS diagramatically as a series of mapping operations progressively transforming an application program's data request from the user-subschema-based DML through the schema and the physical storage model to the stored database. It is this series of mapping operations which provides for data independence between the application program and the database schema (program–data independence) and between the database schema and the physical storage devices (physical data independence). In most commercially available DBMSs the database schema serves as both a logical and a physical model of the database, thus dispensing with a separate physical model.

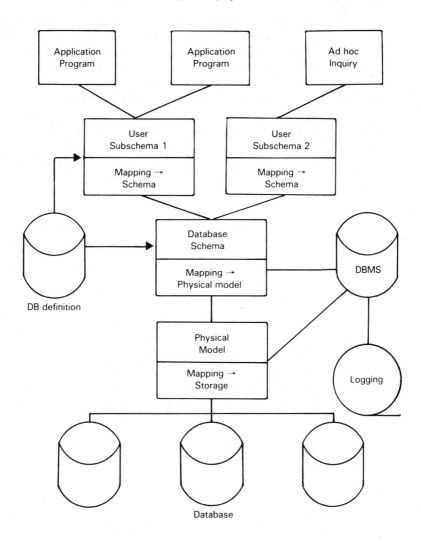

Figure 7-1   Schematic representation of a DBMS

7.6   DATA ENTITIES, ATTRIBUTES, AND RELATIONSHIPS

A *data entity* is a set of like objects for which the organization is interested in collecting descriptive data. An example is a customer entity where the set consists of all customers and the information typically collected for each customer is customer code, name and address, purchase history, and possibly accounts-receivable information. The information collected concerning an entity is called *attribute data.* Thus customer name and address are attributes of the customer who is designated by the customer code. Another example is an employee, designated by employee code and containing, as attribute information, name, salary, location, and phone number. The attribute information relating to a particular data entity is stored contiguously in a record.

Data entities are said to be related when one entity belongs in some sense to another entity. They may belong because an attribute of an entity is the key field of another entity. An example is given in Figure 7–2 where each employee is attached to a department. The underline indicates the key field. The double-headed arrow linking DEPARTMENT to EMPLOYEE is used to indicate that one department may own many employees while each employee belongs to only one department. This is an example of a one-to-many relationship in which one owner record (DEPARTMENT) owns many member records (EMPLOYEES). The department number DEPNO attribute of each employee record indicates the department to which the employee belongs. Note that when the relationship is drawn by means of the line connecting the two entities, it is possible to omit the DEPNO attribute from EMPLOYEE as it is now implied by the relationship.

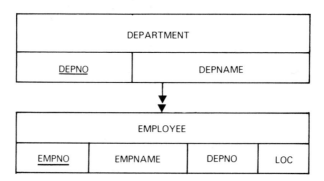

Figure 7–2   A one-to-many relationship

A one-to-one relationship is also possible, as in the case of the head of the department: each department has one head and it is assumed that an employee is potentially head of only one department. This entity relationship is drawn in Figure 7–3. In this case either EMPLOYEE or DEPARTMENT could be designated as the owner and the other entity as the member. This is another example of an entity relationship based on the attribute of one entity being the key of another entity. The implicit attribute here is the data item 'head of department' within DEPARTMENT which would contain EMPNO.

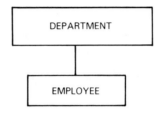

Figure 7–3   A one-to-one relationship

Entities may also be related by the key of one entity constituting a subset of the key of another entity. Such a relationship is given in Figure 7–4. The PRODSUPP entity contains the standard order quantities of each product for each supplier. This example shows two intersecting one-to-many relationships since each supplier supplies many products and each product is supplied by many suppliers. But each PRODSUPP occurrence (i.e. a single record) is uniquely owned by one supplier and one product. In a similar way as was observed for the one-to-many relationship, the SUPPNO, PRODNO (here the key field) data items may be omitted from the

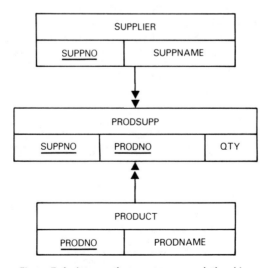

Figure 7–4   Intersecting one-to-many relationships

PRODSUPP entity with no loss of information, as these data are contained in the logical relationship links connecting PRODSUPP to PRODUCT and SUPPLIER.

The most general relationship links many entities of one type to many entities of another type, and is called a many-to-many relationship. For an entity SKILL containing a skill code SKILLCODE and description SKILDESC, each employee can possess one or more skills and naturally each skill can be possessed by one or more employees. This presents a many-to-many relationship between SKILL and EMPLOYEE, as shown in Figure 7-5.

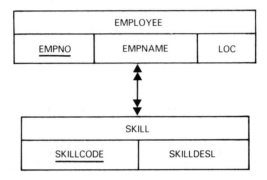

Figure 7-5   A many-to-many relationship

One of the difficulties in designing data entities and identifying their relationship is that it is not always clear whether a data item should be included as an attribute of an entity or constitute an entity in its own right. A simple example to illustrate this point is the data item LOC (location) which is included as an attribute in the EMPLOYEE entity. This could equally be set up as an entity, in which case it would have a one-to-many relationship with EMPLOYEE, as is shown in Figure 7-6. The LOCATION entity may be just a key field, or it may contain attribute data fields. In a like manner the employee address field could also be set up as an entity.

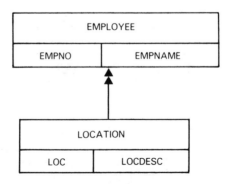

Figure 7-6   Creation of an entity from an attribute

No hard and fast rules can be laid down concerning the identification of entities in a database. Section 7.9 examines one methodology which provides substantial assistance but leaves some aspects up to the designer's judgment.

All the currently used DBMSs physically store the attribute data of an entity contiguously as a record. Thus, accessing an entity makes all its attribute data available. However, the methods used to store and manipulate entity relationships fall into a number of distinct categories. At the logical level, DBMSs fall into three general classes based on the nature of the model used to convey the entity relationships. Section 7.7 examines these model alternatives.

7.7   DATA MODEL ALTERNATIVES ON COMMERCIAL DBMSs

Although there are many competing DBMSs available in the marketplace, they fall naturally into three categories based on the data model each one supports. By *data model* is meant the possible database schema structure that is implied by the architecture of the system, its data-description language (DDL), and its data-manipulation language (DML). The three data models are hierarchical, network, and relational, although some authors view the hierarchical as merely a restricted network.

To facilitate the description of the three models, a simple database is defined which consists of three entities: CUST, PROD, and ORDER (see Figure 7–7). This constitutes two intersecting one-to-many relationships since each customer may order many products and each product may be ordered by many customers. The entity relationship diagram is given in Figure 7–8. In the interests of simplicity no order number is given and all products on order are regarded identically.

CUST   =   CUSTNO, CUSTNAME, ADDR, . . .

PROD   =   PRODNO, PRODNAME, . . .

ORDER   =   CUSTNO, |PRODNO, QTY|

| | designates a repeating group in a record

Figure 7-7   A simple database of three entities

7.7.1   Hierarchical Model

The hierarchical data model has developed from the data-storage and handling techniques commonly used for sequentially organized files. This can be seen by first constructing sequential files containing the given database. This could be done by setting up a customer file containing customers and orders, as shown in Figure 7–9. This record layout provides for an arbitrary number of order subrecords (PRODNO, QTY) in each record. A second file containing the product data (PRODNO, PRODNAME, . . .) would also be required. The hierarchical data model requires, as

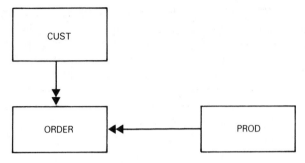

Figure 7-8 The example database

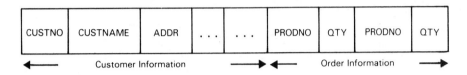

Figure 7-9 Customer file

its name suggests, each member record to have one owner record. In the sequential customer file each ORDER occurrence is owned by a customer record, and access to an order is through a customer. This scheme can be illustrated as shown in Figure 7-10. An alternative would be to have the ORDER entity owned by PROD in place of CUST. This would require ORDER to contain the CUSTNO data item instead of the PRODNO. This is illustrated by the dotted lines in Figure 7-10.

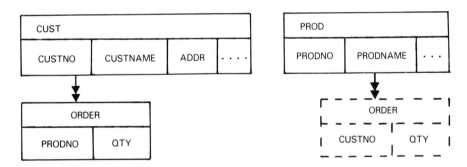

Figure 7-10 Hierarchical schema

Note that the sequential file links orders to customers by physically storing the orders in the customer data record, while the hierarchical DBMS typically uses pointers for the linkages. However, as regards logically accessing the data, the sequential file and the hierarchical database are quite similar.

The hierarchical schema can be made a little easier to understand by using some data to represent a few occurrences (records) in the database. Figure 7-11 gives a representation of the database when Bloggs Pty Ltd (CUSTNO = C1) has ordered 15 units of part P5 and 12 units of part P7. Sam Repairs has ordered 8 units of P5 and 5 units of P6. In the hierarchical representation shown in Figure 7–11, customers are superior to orders. To access an order record it is necessary to specify the customer to which it belongs. Thus, preparing a list of the products on order to a particular customer is a simple task when customers are the 'owner'. However, listing all the customers who have ordered a particular product requires a more complicated procedure of searching each customer to locate the wanted product. Note here that, had products been chosen to be superior to parts, the opposite situation would apply for the two listings. This asymmetry is at the root of the problem of using the hierarchical model for intersecting one-to-many or many-to-many related data. For genuine hierarchically related data (one-to-many) the model is obviously well suited.

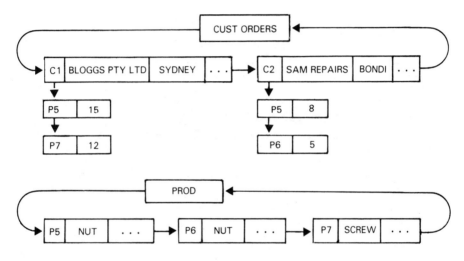

Figure 7-11   Details of hierarchical database

The hierarchical model is popular due to its simplicity and also because IBM's DBMS Information Management Systems (IMS and DL1) use this data model.

7.7.2 Network Model

The asymmetry of the hierarchical model is overcome in the network model, which specifically caters for intersecting one-to-many relationships such as that shown in Figure 7–4. It allows the modelling of many-to-many relationships by the device of introducing a link record to convert a many-to-many relationship to two intersecting one-to-many relationships as shown in Figure 7–13. The network model is the approach embodied in the CODASYL Data Base Task Group (DBTG) proposal, which has fallen short of its objective of being a DBMS standard but has provided a guiding framework for the development of many DBMSs on the market today.

Since the network model allows intersecting one-to-many relationships, the database schema of Figure 7–8 can be modelled directly without further change. The network model links the member records of each owner in a ring structure connected back to the owner. Thus in the example each order is a member of two rings, or 'sets' in DBTG terminology: a customer-order set and a product-order set. Figure 7–12 presents the network database for the record occurrences described in Subsection 7.7.1. Each customer record and each product record is the starting point and finishing point of a ring structure of pointers which includes all the orders belonging to the owner record. Thus customer C1 owns two orders: C1, P5, 15 and C1, P7, 12. Product record P5 owns two orders: C1, P5, 15 and C2, P5, 8. Now the order record C1, P5, 15 belongs to two ring structures or sets. It belongs to the customer-order set which has C1 as owner and to the product-order set which has P5 as owner.

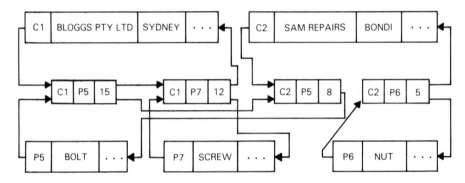

Figure 7-12   Network database

The customer number and product number on the order record occurrences are included to make this exposition a little clearer. They are redundant information as the owner record of each set can always be found by following the respective ring structure of pointers back to the owner record. Whether or not this data is included in practice depends on the trade-off between performance efficiency and data-storage cost.

Entry to the database may be to the product record, or to the customer record, or direct to the order record if it has been specified as a keyed record with its address generated from its key. Now, let the same question as raised for the hierarchical model be posed. To prepare a list of the products ordered by Customer C1, the program requests entry to customer C1 and then follows its customer-order set of pointers. As each order record is encountered, the program needs to access its owner record in the product-order set to obtain the product name information for the product on order, before returning and traversing the C1 customer-order set to the next order record. A symmetrical procedure is followed to prepare a list of customers ordering a particular product. Thus the network approach permits symmetrical procedures to answer symmetrical questions. The price paid for the flexibility of the network model is the complexity of traversing links or 'navigating' in the database to access the data.

Since the links represent physical pointers in the database, the network data model contains some of the major aspects of the physical model. This transparency is a real benefit, enabling the application programmer to anticipate what will happen at the storage level when issuing database commands. This permits efficient use of the database.

To model many-to-many relationships, such as that between the SKILLS and EMPLOYEE entities, it is necessary to introduce a link entity to convert the many-to-many into two intersecting one-to-many relationships. This replacement is shown in Figure 7–13. Each link record occurrence corresponds to one employee and one skill. To show the actual database, assume there are two employees EMP1 and EMP2 and three skill codes SK1, SK2, and SK3, and the employees and skills are related in the following way:

> EMP1 has skills SK1 and SK2
>
> EMP2 has skills SK1, SK2 and SK3

Figure 7–14 diagrams the network database structure for this many-to-many situation. In this database diagram there are no data in the link records. The link records exist merely to permit each employee to be linked to a number of skills and each skill to be linked to a number of employees.

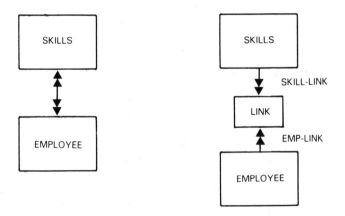

Figure 7-13   Handling a many-to-many relationship

Link records are also used to accommodate the CODASYL DBTG rule that no entity can participate as both owner and member in the one set. Assume that a database is being designed for modelling an organization chart. Figure 7–15 presents the typical stylized view of a responsibility chart. Each box would contain an employee's name and position. It is important to notice that all supervisory employees act in two capacities: as a supervisor, and as a supervised employee. Thus, without using a link record, it is not possible to model this one-to-many hierarchy

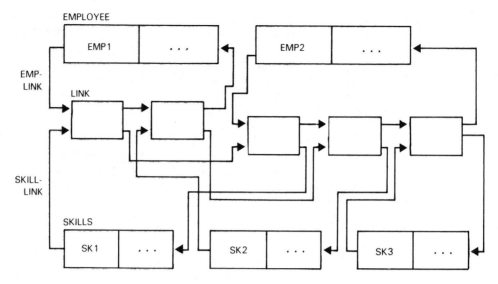

Figure 7-14 Network structure for many-to-many relationships

and observe the condition that the employee entity cannot participate as both owner and member in the one set. The link entity permits two sets to be established, an employee-link set (EMP-LINK) and a link-employee set (LINK-EMP), as shown in Figure 7–16.

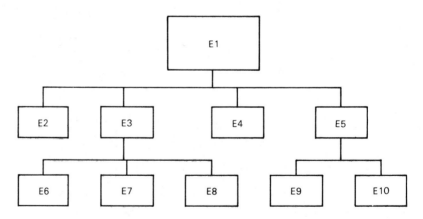

Figure 7-15 Responsibility chart

A single-headed arrow is used for the EMP-LINK, as one employee is assumed to supervise one department, while a double-headed arrow is used for the LINK-EMP set, as a number of employees can be supervised by the one employee. The database for Figure 7–15 is illustrated in Figure 7–17.

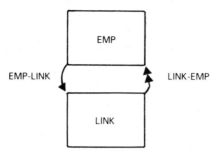

Figure 7-16   Structure for the organization chart database

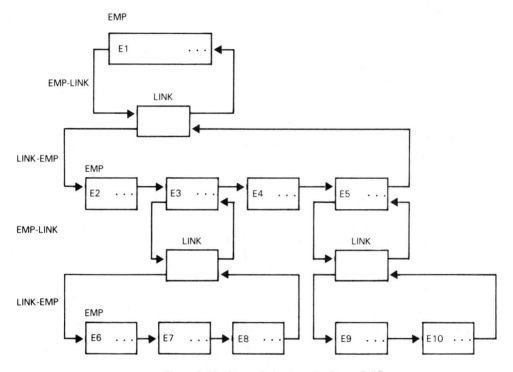

Figure 7-17   Network database for Figure 7-15

7.7.3   Relational Model

The relational data model has its origins in the realm of mathematics. It springs from an attempt to define a fundamental theory for the structure of data that will enable data manipulations and indeed data-processing systems to be expressed with the same rigour and ease that a mathematician enjoys when using, say, matrix algebra. The matrix product $A \times B$ or the matrix inverse A^{-1} can be simply defined and are widely understood, even though the physical calculation for a large matrix may be quite complex. Most mathematicians or engineers needing to perform such a calculation can utilize the computer quite unaware of the physical procedure used by the machine to arrive at the result. On the other hand, commercial application systems developers, not being armed with a suitable theory and vocabulary, need to specify, at a low level, the physical procedure to be carried out on their data on a record-by-record basis.

The relational model is based on tables — or relations — containing a fixed-length record and a unique key for each entity. For the example there are three relations or tables: a customer relation, a product relation, and an order relation, with their contents as shown in Figure 7–18. All data, both attribute and relationship, are conveyed by means of data items in the tables. There are no pointers and no owner or member records. This means only one type of data is dealt with. The fixed nature of the relation means that an algebra of operations can be defined on the whole relation in much the same way that matrix operations are defined on a matrix.

Customer relation

CUSTNO	CUSTNAME	CUSTADDR
C1	BLOGGS PTY LTD	SYDNEY
C2	SAM	BONDI

Product relation

PRODNO	PRODNAME
P5	BOLT
P6	NUT
P7	SCREW

Order relation

CUSTNO	PRODNO	QTY
C1	P5	15
C1	P7	12
C2	P5	8
C2	P6	5

Figure 7–18   Relational database

There is a one-to-one correspondence between the network model and the relational model. Figure 7–12 illustrates a network database which contains redundant information in the order entity, where customer number and product number are redundant as they are also contained in the linkage sets. Thus, should the links be removed, there would be no redundant information and the result, with a little reorganization, is the relational database of Figure 7–18. It is always a relatively simple matter to translate from a network database to a relational one and vice versa, provided a unique key can be identified for each record occurrence in each relation. Readers may satisfy themselves that the relational database corresponding to Figure 7–17 is given in Figure 7–19. The employee relation holds all the attribute information for each employee, while the organization relation contains the data specifically related to the organization chart.

Organization relation

SUPERVISOR	SUPERVISED
E1	E2
E1	E3
E1	E4
E1	E5
E2	E6
E2	E7
E2	E8
E5	E9
E5	E10

Employee relation

EMPNO	EMPNAME
E1	
E2	
E3	
E4	
E5	
E6	
E7	
E8	
E9	
E10	

Figure 7-19   Relational database for Figure 7-17

The relational model is a purely logical model, and provides no clues as to how the database would be physically implemented. Since the physical view of the data is hidden, the programmer using a relational database employs a data-management language which specifies what needs to be done but cannot incorporate any information about how to do the job. This naturally increases the data independence but may have a detrimental effect on operating efficiency.

Databases which use the relational model have been employed for some years in universities and research establishments, and there are a number of commercial packages available. There is a growing body of opinion which holds that widespread use of relational databases will have to wait for the availability of hardware which permits a transparent implementation; i.e. an implementation in which the physical model is identical with the logical model in much the same way as the CODASYL physical and logical models are fused together. Current relational DBMS implementations use pointers, indexes, and other physical devices to implement the database. A transparent implementation would be one where these techniques would not need to be used. One way in which the relational logical model could also become the physical model would be to use storage devices which can be accessed by their contents (content-addressable memory). See Kim (1979) for a survey of relational database systems.

7.8   DESIGNING THE DATABASE

7.8.1   Design Errors

The overall objective of database design is to enable all users to obtain the data they require in an efficient and timely manner. This objective breaks down into two areas:

- The database design should embrace the complete data needs of the organization and be sufficiently flexible to continue to meet those needs in the future.
- The design needs to perform efficiently, i.e. allowing data to be accessed fast enough for application systems to meet their objectives while using a minimum of machine resources.

Two common errors made when designing a database are related to these subobjectives. The first error is designing the database to use the existing file and record formats which have grown up with the EDP applications. Many of these formats were specifically set up to meet particular application needs, or to satisfy certain equipment restrictions, or to improve operational efficiency on equipment long gone. This approach to designing the database has the advantage of easy design and easy conversion of existing applications; but it has the significant liability of a tendency to freeze future development into what is likely to be a poorly structured database which is probably illogical as well as inefficient, and almost certainly bears little relationship to the data needs of the organization.

The other error, probably the more common, is to go overboard linking and relating every conceivable entity relationship on the offchance that it may be needed in the future. The problem here is that present DBMSs use a considerable amount of memory and processing time to maintain linkages in the database and, if these linkages are never used, this overhead cost has been for naught. It is possible that in the future databases will be a lot more effficient in this regard, links being set up only when needed for processing. However, with current DBMSs the overhead cost is too high to be ignored even though computer hardware is now comparatively cheap.

7.8.2   Methodology

The methodology of database design presented in this section adopts a framework of logical design followed by physical design similar to that proposed for systems design in Chapter 5. Figure 7–20 illustrates the steps proposed for the design of a database. The starting point in the design of a database is modelling the real-world situation of the organization's data. The database model design adopted is an abstraction of this reality which suits the information needs of the organization, the constraints of the DBMS, and the computing resources that are to be used.

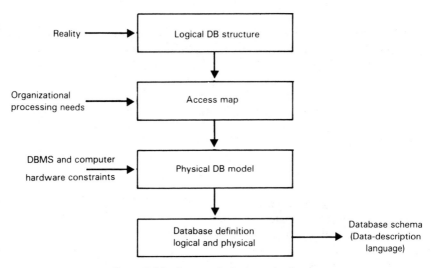

Figure 7-20   Steps in designing a database

The access map shows the frequency of logical access within the database for the projected application systems. The access map can, if needed, assist in selecting the most appropriate DBMS, and is the basis for developing the physical model which optimizes the use of the target DBMS. Due to the features and operating cost structure of the chosen DBMS some defined data relationships may not be designated for linkage in the database. In other instances data redundancy may be incorporated to eliminate the need for links and so improve performance. By allowing costs to be estimated in terms of record accesses for alternative physical models, the access map represents a significant input in the final choice of physical model.

The methodology presented here structures the database in terms of the relational model. The reasons for this choice include:

- Experience with teaching database design indicates that students grasp logical design using the relational model more easily than when using the network or a general entity relationship model.
- Codd's normalization theory (Date, 1981) provides a sound basis for designing relations which exhibit desirable properties when records are amended, added, or deleted. This theory is briefly discussed in Subsection 7.8.3.
- The relational model may, if needed, be redrawn as a network model with no essential change in its basic structure.

Teory & Fry (1980) present a detailed account of a slightly different methodology together with a worked example. They also present a complete bibliography of published work in the database design field.

7.8.3 Normalized Relations

The theory of levels of normalized relations provides a basis for subdividing an organization's data items into entities and attributes. First the concept of normalization is introduced, and then the various levels are presented and discussed.

A *normalized relation* is one in which each of the domains or data fields is a single non-decomposable entity. Thus, repeating fields cannot be permitted in a normalized relation, nor can variable-length fields. It is easy to develop an equivalent normalized relation for any un-normalized data structure as can be seen in the following example.

Assume that a normalized relation for an employee history file is wanted. The data to be contained in the file are:

- Employee number
- Employee name
- Employee address
- Promotion job code ⎫
- Year of promotion ⎭ repeating fields

As indicated, promotion job code and year of promotion are repeating fields; they will occur as many times as the employee has had job promotions. To normalize this data two relations are developed: an employee relation and a job history relation. These are:

EMPLOYEE (*Employee number*, employee name, employee address)

JOB HISTORY (*Employee number, promotion job code*, year)

The fields in italics represent the (unique) key for the relations. In the job history relation the key is a composite one involving two data fields. Note that it is not possible to use employee number and year as the composite key because an employee could have more than one promotion in any one year and so the key would not be unique. It is assumed here that employees are not demoted to jobs previously held. Were this so the key would need to be employee number and date, to ensure uniqueness.

The first three levels of normalized relations are called first, second, and third normal forms. All relations which are normalized are in first normal form (1NF), some are in second normal form (2NF), and some 2NF relations are also in the third normal form (3NF). This can be represented as in Figure 7-21. A *2NF relation* is defined as a normalized relation in which the non-key data fields (if any) depend functionally on the key. By *functional dependence* is meant that each value of the key determines a single value of each data field. For example, employee address is functionally dependent on the key: employee number. Where the key is composite, consisting of two or more data fields, functional dependence on the key means that the whole key, and no subset of it, determines a single value of each data field. For example, in the job history relation, year is functionally dependent on employee number and promotion job code, and both parts of the key are needed to uniquely determine a single value of the year field. Figure 7–22 illustrates the functional dependence of the employee and job history relations.

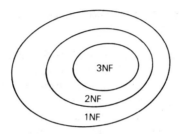

Figure 7-21   Levels of normalization

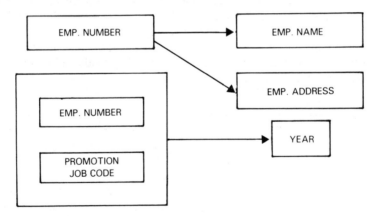

Figure 7-22   Functional dependencies of employee and job history relations

To illustrate the difference between 1NF and 2NF relations consider a normalized relation in which employee name is added to the job history relation:

JOB HISTORY 2   (*Employee number, promotion job code,* year, employee name)

This is *not* in 2NF as the non-key fields are not fully functionally dependent on the key and on no subset of it. Employee name functionally depends on the key subset: employee number. This relation is 1NF but not 2NF. The difficulty that a 1NF relation would present can be seen immediately. To update, say, for change of name

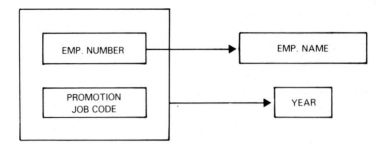

Figure 7-23   Functional dependencies of job history 2 relation

it would be necessary to search for all occurrences of the subkey:employee number, and update the name in it. And also, there is considerable data redundancy here as employee name may be stored many times for the one employee.

A 3NF relation is defined as a normalized relation in which the non-key fields are (1) mutually functionally independent, and (2) functionally dependent on the key. The job history and employee relations defined earlier are in 3NF. The difference between 3NF and 2NF relations can be illustrated by adding the employee's office location and phone number to the employee relation. Assume for this example that the office location depends on the telephone number only. That is, the phone and its number are fixed to a particular office. Now the data structure for the employee relation is as shown in Figure 7–24. In this example office location functionally depends on both the employee number and on the phone number. As office location and phone number are non-key fields and functionally dependent, this relation is 2NF but *not* 3NF.

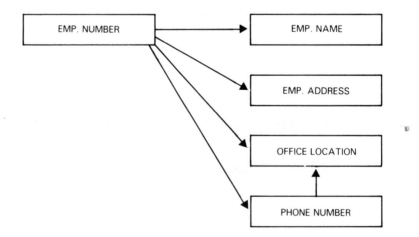

Figure 7-24   Functional dependencies in 2NF relation

Consider some of the problems which can arise when manipulating a 2NF relation, using the example situation:

- *Amending:* Should a telephone number in an office be changed, the record of each occupant of the office may need to be updated (there may be more than one person sharing the telephone) as there are redundant data in this relation.
- *Adding:* On this file it is not possible to add a telephone to a new office until it has an occupant. A possible but not entirely satisfactory way around this would be to use a dummy occupant.
- *Deleting:* Should an employee, being the sole occupant of an office, quit, then deleting that employee's record would lose the telephone number/office location data.

It is preferable to convert this 2NF relation to its 3NF equivalent by removing the office location from the employee relation to give two relations:

EMPLOYEE   (*Employee number*, employee name, employee address, telephone number)

TELEPHONE (*telephone number*, office location)

Hence 3NF relations possess desirable properties for adding, deleting, and amending. Note that data can be structured in 3NF relations by knowing only their functional dependencies without any reference to the way they are processed. It is assumed that these functional dependencies rely on basic methods of operation and procedures within the organization and, as such, are not likely to change much over time. Thus data modelled in 3NF relations should be relatively invariant and require little structural modification in the course of time. This property is not possessed by data structured to a particular application running on a particular set of hardware. A 3NF relation can be developed by following the steps:

1. Normalize the relation by removing all repeating fields and variable-length records.
2. Convert to 2NF by removing dependencies on subfields of the key.
3. Convert to 3NF by removing all transitive dependencies to separate relations.

For another example, which builds on the previous illustration and is used again in the next subsection, suppose that a consulting firm wishes to keep the following data for an employee and costing database:

- Employee number
- Employee name
- Employee address
- Salary
- Current job code
- Job history (job promotion code
                    (year
- Office location

- Telephone number
- Project number
- Project name
- Task number
- Task name
- Project budget
- Task expenditure to date
- Department number
- Department name

There are none, one, or more job promotion code/year entries per employee. The office location uniquely depends on the telephone number, and there may be more than one employee using the same telephone and more than one telephone in the one office. Tasks are uniquely numbered only within each project. An employee may be concurrently assigned to more than one project and task, but belongs to one department.

Readers may satisfy themselves that the 3NF relations for this data are:

EMPLOYEE   (*Employee number*, employee name, employee address, salary, current job code, telephone number, department number)

DEPARTMENT   (*Department number*, department name)

JOB HISTORY   (*Employee number*, *job promotion code*, year)

TELEPHONE   (*Telephone number*, office location)

EMPLOYEE-TASK   (*Employee number*, *project number*, *task number*)

PROJECT   (*Project number*, project name, budget)

TASK   (*Project number*, *task number*, task name, task estimate, expenditure to date)

Figure 7–25 represents the possible interconnections between these relations. The lines between the relations indicate the presence of data in one relation which match the same data in another relation. Thus DEPARTMENT and EMPLOYEE are joined through the field department number which is an attribute of EMPLOYEE and the key field of DEPARTMENT. It is these common data which enable the database to logically form a connected model of the organization's data structure.

7.8.4 Access Map

The access map superimposes, on the relational model, the number of logical accesses on each path required to satisfy the defined and projected information requirements of the organization. It bridges the gap between the data that exist in the organization and the information that is needed. To illustrate how the access rate is developed from an information requirement, suppose that a report is required which relates all the employees to their tasks on a particular project. It is necessary to first access PROJECT to get project name, then TASK for task number, then EMPLOYEE-TASK for the employee numbers and finally EMPLOYEE for the employee's name.

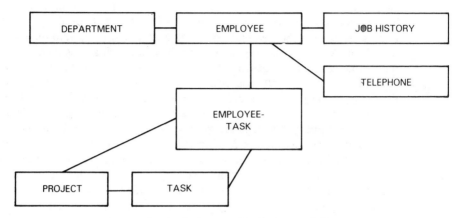

Figure 7-25   Logical connections between relations

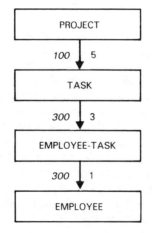

Figure 7-26   Access map to report employees by task on a given project

Figure 7-26 illustrates the access sequence and direction. The numbers to the right of the access path denote the average relative frequency of record occurrence. Hence each project has on average five tasks, and each task has an average of three employees assigned, and each employee-task has one employee. Assume there are on average 20 of these queries per month, which includes both ad hoc and routine reporting. Then the path access loads per month are:

Project/task	20×5	=	100
Task/employee-task	$20 \times 5 \times 3$	=	300
Employee-task/employee		=	300

These monthly loads are denoted on Figure 7–26 by the italic figures to the left of the path arrows.

The access load could be similarly calculated for each information requirement which the system has to satisfy. The total path access load would be the sum of the loads arising on that path from each of the information requirements. This calculation, carried out for each path in the relational map, gives the access map, which shows the frequency of use of each potential path in the relational data model. Since the access map shows the loads on each access path, it allows those paths which are heavily used and those which are little used to be identified. If, in the subsequent physical database design, the access rate on some paths is felt to be excessive, it can be reduced either by modifying the design, such as incorporating redundant data, or by using special DBMS features to improve performance. Another possibility for reducing accesses is to consolidate relations. Obviously, jeopardizing the advantages conferred by 3NF relations in redesigning the data structure should be approached with some reluctance. But at times it may be felt that such a step is warranted by performance and design considerations. Also, data and relations that are never accessed may be identified. In this case the designer may choose to eliminate these segments with no loss of information to the organization.

7.8.5 Physical Database Model

The physical database model reflects the constraints imposed by the particular DBMS adopted. Modifications to the relational model, to provide satisfactory performance, may need to be considered in the construction of the physical model and, further, may be needed if a hierarchical model DBMS is selected. The access map enables a rapid estimation of the relative advantages and disadvantages of the alternative competing DBMS implementations to be made. However, the access map is not sufficient by itself to guide physical database model selection, as certain important factors like the extent of sequential reporting, the activity and volatility of the data, the volume of on-line inquiries and their required response time are not part of the access map, but have a strong bearing on physical model selection and necessary DBMS performance. Additional information is required to give a rounded picture of the database needs for the most appropriate physical model to be selected. Some of these needed facts are:

- The kind of access required for each transaction — retrieval or update, sequential or direct
- The volatility of the data
- The processing priority of each transaction
- Which transactions are on-line
- The need for concurrent update activity
- The time schedule for updating the database and producing reports
- The security requirements by data item
- The integrity constraints
- Those portions of the database which are critical for the operation of the organization

Some of these data can be superimposed on the access map, or else a number of access maps drawn. For example, one access map can be drawn for retrieval and reporting accesses, one for update accesses, and another for time-critical on-line accesses.

The activities undertaken in the physical design stage include:

- Designing the physical access paths — choosing the appropriate means to access each relation or data set (i.e. whether indexed, random, or located via a parent record), the physical ordering of records, pointer options (two-way or one-way), and overflow techniques
- Physical clustering of records — choosing which records or data sets to locate in the same database area and on the same physical storage unit
- Integrity and security constraints
- Selection of block size and buffer size

Appraising the strengths and weaknesses of each competing physical model is a creative and demanding task which cannot be easily tied down to a formula. But critical to the job is a thorough analysis assisted by good display tools. This aids the process of communication and encourages the creative talent of the EDP department to be focused on the vital task of logical and physical design.

7.9 DATA-DESCRIPTION LANGUAGE AND DATA-MANAGEMENT LANGUAGE

7.9.1 Data-description Language (DDL)

The data-description language communicates the schema design to the DBMS. While it is beyond the scope of this book to present details of any individual DDL, a simplified example of a CODASYL DBTG DDL is given to communicate the style of the language and some of its features. The illustrative example chosen is a variant of that given in Section 7.8, and is repeated in Figure 7–27 in a network formulation.

The DDL must be able to define record types and set types. A simplified DDL is:

```
1  SCHEMA NAME IS SALES-DATABASE.
2
3  RECORD NAME IS CUST.
4        02  CUSTNO;TYPE IS CHAR 5.
5        02  CUSTNAME;TYPE IS CHAR 30.
6        02  ADDR;TYPE IS CHAR 50.
7  LOCATION MODE IS CALC USING CUSTNO.
8
9  RECORD NAME IS PROD.
```

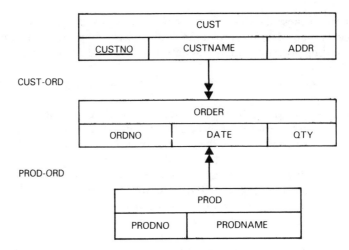

CUST-ORD

PROD-ORD

Figure 7-27   Example schema

```
10        02   PRODNO;TYPE IS NUMERIC 7.
11        02   PRODNAME;TYPE IS CHAR 30.
12   LOCATION MODE IS CALC USING PRODNO.
13
14   RECORD NAME IS ORDER.
15        02   ORDNO;TYPE IS NUMERIC 8.
16        02   DATE;TYPE IS NUMERIC 6.
17        02   QTY;TYPE IS NUMERIC 9.
18   LOCATION MODE IS CHAIN.
19
20   SET NAME IS PROD-ORD.
21   OWNER IS PROD.
22   MEMBER IS ORDER.
23   SET SELECTION IS THRU LOCATION MODE OF OWNER.
24   ORDER IS SORTED USING DATE.
25
26   SET NAME IS CUST-ORD.
27   OWNER IS CUST.
28   MEMBER IS ORDER.
29   SET SELECTION IS THRU LOCATION MODE OF OWNER.
```

Much of the DDL is obvious, particularly to a COBOL programmer. Lines 3 through 19 declare the CUST, PROD, and ORDER record types. For each record type declared, a location mode is specified in addition to the data items. In this example, CUST and PROD are stored randomly using an address-generating algorithm on their key fields, as shown in lines 7 and 12: LOCATION MODE IS CALC USING ..... The ORDER record is specified in line 18 as LOCATION MODE IS CHAIN, signifying that access is gained to an order record by first accessing an owner record and searching along the chain to locate the wanted record. Alternatively location mode could have been CALC USING ORDNO with an extra statement added, DUPLICATES ARE ALLOWED, as a number of line items may be present on an order, thus presenting duplicate ORDNO keys. This would have permitted either a chain search or a direct access.

The sets CUST-ORD and PROD-ORD are specified by indicating owner and member records and the means of establishing set selection. Line 24 indicates that the PROD-ORD set is ordered in DATE sequence to enable the oldest outstanding order to be accessed first.

7.9.2   Data-management Language (DML) — Low Level

The DML is the means of manipulating data items in the database. It may be either a COBOL-like language suitable for embedding in an application program or a high-level query language suitable for a non-programmer. To illustrate the low-level DML, suppose the simple database given in Figure 7–19 is to be implemented in a database using the DDL just described. The DBTG DML for listing product names and quantities for products on order to customer C2 is (in a slightly simplified version):

> FIND CUST WHERE CUSTNO = 'C2'.
> A   FIND NEXT ORDER WITHIN CUST-ORD. If none exit.
> FIND OWNER WITHIN PROD-ORD.
> GET PRODUCT.
> GET ORDER.
> List product name and quantity
> go to A.

The FIND instruction locates records by traversing (navigating) chains or using a hashing algorithm (CALC), but does not transfer data from the database to the program buffer. This is done by the GET instruction, which transfers the fields specified in the subschema from the named record. The most recently located record (using a FIND) is the object of the GET instruction.

Application programs communicate with the DBMS in terms of six types of information:

- The action to be performed, e.g. OPEN, FIND, GET, WRITE, CLOSE
- Selection criteria in the form of positional information, e.g. FIRST, NEXT, OWNER, or a Boolean selection expression
- Names of the data attributes or groups to be read
- User schema definition and the buffer location
- Response on detection of an error or exception condition
- Access authorization to controlled or confidential data

Examples of the first two types may be seen in the example just given. Information for the other four types would be contained in the subschema and in the programs.

Another example of a DML is given, using the DBMS TOTAL. TOTAL's DML is executed by a CALL statement passing a parameter string which contains data necessary for communicating each of the types of DML information given in the preceding list except a security password. The structure of a TOTAL CALL instruction for a simple read or write operation is:

CALL DATBAS USING (FUNCTION, STATUS, DATA-SET, KEY,
DATA-ITEMS, BUFFER, END)

FUNCTION:	the function to be performed which denotes both action and selection criteria
STATUS:	where the status code is to be put — this indicates exceptions or errors
DATA-SET:	the data set (file to be accessed)
KEY:	the location of the key of the wanted data
DATA-ITEMS:	the particular data item to be read (or written)
BUFFER:	the location in buffer (e.g. the data name) for the data items identified by DATA-ITEMS
END:	the end of the parameter string

7.9.3 DML — Interrogation Level

To illustrate the same query as discussed in Subsection 7.9.2 in a high-level interrogation language, it is assumed that the database is implemented using a relational DBMS which supports the query language SEQUEL. An extract of the code to execute the query is:

```
SELECT      PRODNAME
FROM        PROD
WHERE       PRODNO =

            SELECT      PRODNO
            FROM        ORDER
            WHERE       CUSTNO = 'C2'
```

SEQUEL adopts a top-down statement of what data are wanted, and the logic rules which the selection is to follow. In this case the language says that PRODNAME is to be selected from those PROD records where the key PRODNO satisfies the second set of select conditions. These state that the PRODNO is also contained on an ORDER record which has CUSTNO equal to 'C2'. The physical implementation of the query would normally proceed in a bottom-up direction.

The file-level action and non-procedural nature of the query language can be seen clearly and compared with the record-level procedural character of the low-level DML, which specifies a series of record-level steps which result in the correct data being obtained. The interrogation process consists of the following steps:

- *Select* a record or set of records from a *named* file
- *Read* a set of attribute values
- *Derive* additional values or function values
- *Order* the entries
- *Format* and present the results

To enable queries to be reused there should be a simple way of cataloguing and storing queries, thus permitting users to retrieve query commands, modify if necessary, and rerun. A powerful data-interrogation facility can give users great control over meeting their own information requirements, and relieve much humdrum work from the data-processing department.

7.9.4   Data Independence Implications of the DML

The low-level DML permits the programmer to instruct the DBMS how he wishes to navigate through the database. This feature is necessary to provide a controlled and efficient use of the database and so reduce the run time of the application. However, since such a feature generally involves the programmer taking advantage of the physical structure of the database, it restricts the future ability of the database administrator to restructure the database. It is axiomatic that if advantage is taken of the physical database structure in the application programs, then, if the structure changes, the program logic also needs to be changed. This state of affairs does not occur with a high-level interrogation language since it only tells the system

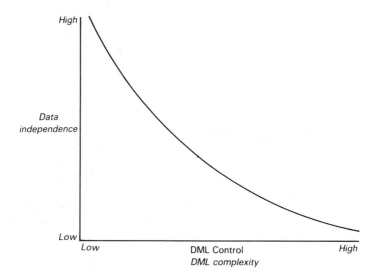

Figure 7–28   Data independence trade-off

what it wants — not how to go about the series of operations which result in the correct data being written to output, as with a low-level DML. The interrogation-level DML is less affected by change to the structure or organization of the database. Thus there is a trade-off between data independence, DML control, and DML complexity, with the more complex DML interface, which allows physical control of execution, providing less data independence. Figure 7–28 illustrates this point.

7.10 DATABASE INTEGRITY

The integrity of a database may be jeopardized by concurrent updates on the same record, hardware faults (e.g. power failure, disk failure), software faults (e.g. bugs in programs, erroneous data) or human errors (e.g. mounting the wrong disk). This section looks at techniques either for preventing these occurrences or for allowing recovery of the database after the detection of an error condition.

7.10.1 Concurrency Control

Concurrent updates to the one data item record will destroy data integrity unless specific preventative action is taken. Concurrent updates are always a possibility in terminal-based systems updating the database in real time. They come about when two users seek to access the same record to modify its contents. A simple example illustrates the problem. Suppose user A enters a transaction to update stock on hand for a sale of 10 units of product 1, and at the same time user B enters a transaction to update the stock of the same product for a sale of 70 units. Table 7–2 gives the sequence of steps followed in both programs carrying out the update. In the illustration it is assumed that user A writes out the record first, followed by user B. In either case the resulting value of quantity on hand for the product is incorrect. To prevent such concurrent updates it is necessary for a transaction, when accessing a record with the purpose of updating it, to lock the record (or the data item in question), thus preventing other access to it until the update has been completed. This ensures that updates to the same record take place sequentially.

While the simple expedient of locking records prevents concurrent updates, it introduces a problem of its own when competing transactions have mutually locked resources required by each other. Thus no one transaction can be completed. This situation is called a *deadlock*. Table 7–3 gives an illustration of two deadlocked transactions, in which each requires a resource held by the other. External action is required to resolve this situation. Actions which can be taken to safeguard against deadlocks include: preventing their occurrence (e.g. by never allowing a transaction to lock a resource unless the way is clear to complete processing); avoiding them (as in serial processing); and recognizing them and rolling back one transaction to permit the other transaction to be completed.

Table 7–2 Illustration of concurrent updates

USER A's PROGRAM		USER B's PROGRAM		
ACTION	QUANTITY ON HAND IN PROGRAM BUFFER	ACTION	QUANTITY ON HAND IN PROGRAM BUFFER	DATABASE CONTENTS OF QUANTITY ON HAND FOR PRODUCT 1
Access Quantity on hand	150	Access Quantity on hand	150	150
Update buffer sale of 10 units	140	Update buffer sale of 70 units	80	150
Write out new value to database				140
		Write out new value to database		80

Table 7–3 Deadlocked transactions

	Transaction A	Transaction B
Locked resources	Customer 1	Product 1
Required resource	Product 1	Customer 1

7.10.2 Recovery

The database needs to be protected against partial or total loss caused by faults or errors. This protection can be given by storing redundant back-up and recovery data, preferably recorded at a site remote from the main database, since a head crash on a disk may destroy not only the database but the recovery data as well if they are stored on the same disk drive. The most commonly used recovery technique involves the storing of a log of transactions updating the database, and a log of the records changed in the database. The latter may consist of a copy of the record before it is changed (the before image) or a copy after it has been changed (the after image), or both. The database and the log files need to be 'checkpointed' at regular intervals to establish consistency of the log files and the physical database. It should be noted that, due to data being stored in database buffers in main memory, updates to the database may not be physically written to the database until a later time. When a checkpoint is taken, the buffers are flushed (either for a database area or for the whole database), and, by physically writing their contents to the database, the log files are marked to indicate that a checkpoint has been taken. When an error or fault is detected (such as loss of power to the computer erasing the database changes held in the main memory buffer), recovery can be carried out by restoring the physical database to the situation prevailing at the last checkpoint, and reprocessing the subsequent transactions.

The procedure normally followed to restore the database to the last checkpoint consists of writing the before images from the log file in reverse order to the database. This leaves the database with the before-image values taken immediately after the last checkpoint, i.e. the values existing at the checkpoint time. An example may make the situation clearer. Table 7–4 gives the values from a log file relating to the quantity-on-hand field for a particular product (product 1). The first two colums give the values held on the log files for the transaction log and the before-image log respectively. The last two columns give the database values for the data item in question. The buffer value is the latest value which is held in main memory and will be written to the physical database (residing on disk) when the buffer space is needed for some other data. The last column gives the value held on the disk. Note that in the example the physical database is written to only once. If disaster strikes after the last transaction is updated, and erases the buffer, recovery is possible by writing the before images successively to the database in reverse sequence. This leaves the database with the value 72 and permits the transactions on the log file to be reprocessed. Should the fault have erased data directly from the database (as in a head crash), recovery presents a more complex task requiring the use of a back-up copy of the database.

Table 7–4   Illustration of log files

Log files		Database Product 1 Quant-on-hand value	
Transaction log Product 1 Quant. on hand Value	Before image Product 1 Quant. on hand Value	Buffer	Physical Database
Checkpoint		—	85
−15	85	70	85
+20	70	—	90
− 7	90	83	90
+10	83	93	90

Back-up copies of the database need to be taken at regular intervals. This can be done by either dumping (copying) the whole database or incrementally copying physically contiguous sections (e.g. whole disk packs) at regular time intervals, or intervals based on update volume. In the event of losing the data on a disk pack, the most recent copy of the database would need to be used, and brought to the current state by reprocessing all the transactions. However, if after images are logged, a copy of the database representing a previous state can be brought to the current state by writing the after images (in a forward order) to the copy. This is generally much faster than reprocessing the transactions.

The amount of logging and the frequency of taking back-up copies have a great effect on the ease and speed of the recovery operation. The optimal recovery strategies chosen depend on such factors as the time-critical nature of the database application, the anticipated fault or error rate, the rate of update transaction, the size of the database, and the hardware facilities available.

7.11   DBMS COSTS AND BENEFITS

Some of the main factors to be considered by an organization which is thinking of adopting the database approach are presented in this section. The decision problem is clouded by the rapidly evolving computer and database software technology, often by a less-than-satisfactory grasp of database concepts on the part of the decision maker, and by the confusion engendered by a lack of consensus among the experts as to the most appropriate data model for the DBMS.

Except in special circumstances, a DBMS should not be considered in isolation from the potential impact of adopting the database approach. This means that the DBMS cannot be viewed as just another piece of software, and its choice left up to the technical specialists — subject to the usual expenditure guidelines. Adopting the database approach or, in popular parlance 'going database', has organization-wide implications for data availability, accessibility, security, integrity, maintainability, and future system costs. Those who have started to implement databases and then decided to retreat have found the pulling back more expensive than the advance. It is a decision of fundamental importance to an organization because of its possible far-reaching strategic impact — both positive and negative.

DBMSs vary considerably in the facilities they offer, the data relationships they can easily handle, their complexity, and in general the user objectives for which they have been chiefly designed. For example TOTAL, one of the more popular DBMSs does not provide the same flexibility and range of options as DMS 1100, but is less complex and easier to use. Selecting the best DBMS alternative starts with understanding the organization's data relationships which the database needs to reflect, and the database facilities required. However, the key decision is whether or not to establish a database, a decision desirably made by upper management after the systems analysts have proposed an initial selection of DBMS alternatives. As with other decisions of this kind, it is essential for success that there is a wide base of commitment, encompassing the EDP and user groups and upper management. Benefits must be widely perceived as significant to generate the necessary level of commitment.

One of the inputs to this decision is the result of a cost/benefit analysis. Subsections 7.11.1 and 7.11.2 examine the areas of benefits and the areas of increased costs. It is argued that, since quantification is difficult and the effect of the decision widespread, senior management needs to participate closely in making the decision. As DBMSs vary considerably in the facilities they offer, the discussions of benefit and cost areas is necessarily kept quite general. It is, however, aimed at the system which offers a fairly full range of database management facilities.

7.11.1 Benefits

The most commonly cited database benefits, many of which are very difficult to quantify, include:

- Improved scope and facility for management control of the data resource
- Increased application-programmer productivity through a standardized high-level data-access language and improved data relatability
- Reduced maintenance of application systems largely arising from improved program–data independence
- Decreased storage requirements from reduced data redundancy
- Standardized and improved data security and integrity
- A faster and cheaper facility for producing answers to ad hoc inquiries

7.11.2 Costs

In the same way that many of the benefits elude easy quantification so, too, do the costs. Some, though, may be easy to quantify; these include training costs, additional new employee orientation costs, system overheads, and system programming overheads. Intangible costs primarily relate to the additional system complexity, which result in: added burdens being thrown onto the systems analyst, a demand for more highly skilled staff, and additional potential problem areas which need to be investigated when an error occurs. An important consideration, if a manufacturer's DBMS software is used, is the potential reduction of future flexibility to change computer manufacturer.

REFERENCES

R.S. BARNHARDT, 'Implementing Relational Data Bases', *Datamation*, October 1980, pp. 161-72.

R.F. BOYCE & D.D. CHAMBERLIN, 'SEQUEL: A structured English query language', *ACM SIGMOD Workshop on Data Description, Access and Control*, May 1974, pp. 249-64.

CODASYL, *CODASYL Data Base Task Group Report*, ACM, New York, 1971.

C.J. DATE, *An Introduction to Database Systems*, 3rd edn, Addison-Wesley, Reading, Mass., 1981.

G.C. EVEREST, 'DBMS: Foundations for MIS', Working paper series MISRC-WP-79-03, University of Minnesota, Minneapolis, Minn., 1979.

J.P. FRY & E.A. SIBLEY, 'Evolution of Database Management Systems', *Computing Surveys*, vol. 1, no. 1, March 1976, pp. 7-42.

J.A. HOFFER, 'Database Design Practice for Inverted Files', *Information and Management*, vol. 3, no. 4, October 1980, pp. 149-61.

S.S. ISLOON & T.A. MARSLAND, 'The Deadlock Problem: An Overview', *Computer*, vol. 13, no. 9, September 1980, pp. 58-78.

W. KIM, 'Relational Database Systems', *Computing Surveys*, vol. 11, no. 3, September 1979, pp. 185-211.

D. KROENKE, *Database Processing*, SRA, Palo Alto, Calif., 1977.

J. MARTIN, *Computer Data-base Organization*, Prentice-Hall Inc., Englewood Cliffs, N.J., 1975.

T.J. TEORY & J.P. FRY, 'The Logical Record Access Approach to Database Design', *Computing Surveys*, vol. 12, no. 2, June 1980, pp. 179-211.

J.S.M. VERHOFSTAD, 'Recovery Techniques for Database Systems', *Association for Computing Machinery Computing Surveys*, vol. 10, no. 2, June 1978, pp. 167-95.

CASE STUDY — STATE RAIL AUTHORITY

The State Rail Authority is interested in developing a database for capturing and maintaining information for the management of goods services. It is desired to use this database to improve goods train management, to analyze trends in goods management, to assist in budgeting and planning, to carry out customer accounting, and for the day-to-day scheduling and control of waggons and trains.

The rail network consists of lines of various types linking goods yards. Goods yards differ in the degree of service facilities provided for shunting, breaking up and assembling trains, loading and unloading, bulk terminals, etc. Waggons are of various sizes and types, e.g. bulk liquid tanker, flat bed. The freight carried belongs to a commodity class which, with the distance hauled, establishes the freight cost. A shipment for a customer may be assigned to one or more waggons. A waggon may carry the goods of one or a number of customers. Trains are made up of waggons and at any point of time are either on a line or in a goods station. The database is to be updated as trains leave and arrive at yards to allow close management of the network.

ASSIGNMENT

In answering the questions, make such additional assumptions as are necessary, or desirable, to arrive at a realistic design. Your design can only be preliminary since it will have to be carefully evaluated in the light of the organization's needs after they have been carefully defined.

1. Prepare a natural data structure design.

2. Prepare a relational design.

3. Prepare a network design which is the analog of the relational design prepared in 2.

In each of the designs, define the entities and their attributes and diagram the entity relationships. Define the key of each entity and document any assumptions you have made.

4. Write interrogation level code to answer the query 'What are the characteristics and customers of waggons arriving in Sydney?'

CASE STUDY — DINGO DENIMS

Background

Dingo Denims Ltd sells jeans and fashion clothing goods through a chain of 60 retail outlets located throughout Australia under the trade names of DINGO and DAG. Their merchandise is imported from a number of manufacturers located mainly in Indonesia and the Philippines. They cater particularly for the fashion-conscious young, and strive to keep abreast of trends by having the latest fashions available in all their shops as soon as they are generally accepted. They also market a range of more traditional items aimed at the mature-age market.

Dingo Denims' sales have increased steadily over a number of years, especially in the fashion items, despite strong competition, a difficult marketing environment, and discriminatory import tariffs and quotas. This increased business volume has thrown a considerable extra burden onto the company's warehouse and the clerical staff who attend to the replenishment orders received by mail or by telephone from the company's retail outlets. An essential factor in the success of the business is quickly replenishing the retail stocks and analyzing sales trends in order to accurately determine the appropriate order quantities to be communicated to the overseas suppliers, the lead time for which is some one to two months. Management considered it desirable that a computer should generate retail outlet replenishment orders on the central warehouse and suggest overseas purchase orders on Dingo Denims' suppliers. A computer system handling the inventory and reorder functions should also be able to report inventory status and provide a variety of sales analyses.

System Description

After discussions with the systems analyst allocated to the project, the objectives of the system have been defined to be:

- Maintaining, on a daily basis, inventory records for all branches and, using appropriately calculated reorder levels and reorder quantities, replenishing branch stocks automatically on a daily basis
- Maintaining warehouse inventory data and creating suggested suppliers' orders
- Producing timely and pertinent sales information reports which can also be used to reconcile branch sales with inventory movements

Since one of the main functions of the system is to control branch inventory levels, each sale must be coded for the exact product sold. This requires the coding of every distinct product and a means of capturing the code at the point of sale. Various alternative systems for accomplishing this function have been investigated and it has been decided to utilize a point-of-sale terminal embodying an OCR wand reader. The OCR wand is able to read a tag attached to the garment, so long as the tag is printed with the style code and size code in OCR-readable characters. The point-of-sale terminal can record, on magnetic tape, the product code and the sales value, keyed by the operator for each garment sold. These data would be transferred daily to the head office for input to the inventory system. Coding the products with the style code and size code is not seen as being a difficulty, as similar requirements have been met for manual systems in the past. The style code can be communicated to the manufacturer on placing the original order, and would remain current for the duration of that style. Size codes are industry standard. The actual task of printing and attaching the OCR-readable tag containing the style code and size code could be done either at the manufacturing

Case Study — Dingo Denims

site or upon receipt of the goods into the main warehouse. In either event the size and style code would need to be also marked on each garment in a way that would enable it to be read should the tag be either accidentally separated from the garment or removed by a purchaser who subsequently wants to return the goods. The question at issue regarding the printing and attaching of the OCR tag is the ability of the overseas suppliers to have the OCR tag accurately printed so that it can be read without error. The point-of-sale terminals provide a back-up facility, allowing the entry of the garment style and size codes through the keyboard.

The next consideration was the best way of communicating each day's sales, recorded on magnetic tape, to the head office. The major alternatives investigated were overnight mailbag and transmission over telecommunications lines. Both alternatives involved the same batch-processing approach at the head office. Management has decided to accept the telecommunications-based alternative as it was felt to be cheaper and more reliable, and would not appreciably involve branch sales personnel in any more work than the overnight mailbag alternative. The information would be transferred to the head office by the branch removing the magnetic tape from the point-of-sale terminal and placing it in a digital tape reader attached to a modem connected to the telephone. After close of trading, the head office computer would dial each branch and activate the tape-read device, which would then transfer the data down the line to be stored as a batch at the head office computer. Limited editing functions are provided on the point-of-sale terminals to verify the check digit on the style code and to accumulate batch control totals on value sold.

The processing schedule envisaged that each day's sales would be communicated to the head office computer in the evening, and be used to update the branch inventory status; then the branch replenishment orders would be produced ready for the warehouse to pick and pack the order the following morning. Any edit rejections would normally be cleared the day after the receipt, and be ready for input the next evening.

Volumes and Codings

- Styles of jeans and other goods — 2000 on average
- Number of sizes within each style — 12 on average
- Number of retail outlets — 60
- Style range volatility — 50% per annum
- Sales tickets — 7000 per day average
- Suppliers — 20
- Style code — 99999+9
- Style description — 40
- Size code — 999
- Commission rates — 9.9% maximum

Case Study — Dingo Denims

Inventory Master File

This is the major file of the system and holds the data from which all the outputs and management information are derived. It has been decided to create variable-length records with one record per style hierarchically split into three levels. The highest level subrecord (level 1), of which there is one per style, holds the data pertaining to the style as a whole. The level 2 subrecord (one per size of the style) holds the data applicable to the style–size combination. Thus, on average, there will be 12 level 2 subrecords in each record. The level 3 subrecord contains the data for each size–store combination within the style. Thus there can be at most 60 level 3 subrecords per level 2 size subrecord. In summary, each record has one level 1 subrecord, up to 12 level 2 subrecords and within each of these level 2 subrecords up to 60 level 3 subrecords giving the details on a store basis. The record contents are:

Level 1 subrecord — style

Style code (excluding the check digit)	99999
Style description	up to 40 characters
Commission rate	9.9%
Product group code	99
Supplier code	999
Sales value month-to-date	9999.99
Sales value year-to-date	99999.99

Level 2 subrecord — size

Size code	999
Selling price	$99.99
Purchase stock	$99.99
Warehouse stock	99999
Forward order quantities for next 6 months	6 × 9999

Level 3 subrecord — store

Store number	99
Store allocation	99
Stock on hand	99
Sales quantities for last 6 weeks	6 × 999
Week/year last updated	999
Sales quantity pointer	9
Sales value month-to-date	9999.99
Sales value year-to-date	99999.99

An analysis of some 3000 records provided the figures in Table 7–5.

Case Study — Dingo Denims

Table 7-5   Master file statistics

		IN EACH RECORD				
		Subrecords		Characters in all subrecords		
Subrecord	Characters	Average	Maximum	Average	Maximum	Standard deviation
Level 1	52	1	1	52	52	0
Level 2	40	12	12	480	480	0
Level 3	28	240	720	6 720	20 692	2 180
Characters per record			7 252	20 692		
Total file size = 7252 × 2000 = 14 504 000 characters						

It was felt the file access should be direct, since this appeared best suited to the requirements of the system. The volatility of the large file has persuaded the designers against sequential organization as this would require frequent and costly reorganization. The remaining file organization alternative is random, that is, placing records on the file in no set sequence. Since a record would be found using the style code, a sequential index for style codes could be maintained to locate any wanted record. This index could be searched by any number of index searching methods, for example setting up secondary indexes, binary chopping, and block searching. However, the highly volatile nature of the style records militate against the efficiency of an index as it would be necessary to re-sort the index quite frequently due to the rate of addition and deletion of records from the file. After further thought it has been decided to use a binary tree index since this would need no reorganization following the addition and deletion of records.

With a style code of 5 characters and the additional binary tree index data (left branch, right branch, record address) occupying a further 12 characters of storage, a total of 17 characters would be required for each index record. Thus the index would occupy around 34 000 characters. For the computer being contemplated this index could not be kept in main memory at one time, so it has been decided to keep only the first three levels of the tree permanently in main memory. If the wanted key is not found in these three levels, which, if the tree is balanced, contains seven records, the last record read acts as a pointer to a branch of the tree stored on disk. This branch is then read into main memory for further searching. With this method care is needed to balance the tree to ensure that each of the eight branches below the third level are approximately the same size to minimize the total search time.

Figure 7-29 shows the system flowchart of the design adopted for Dingo Denims' stock and sales reporting system.

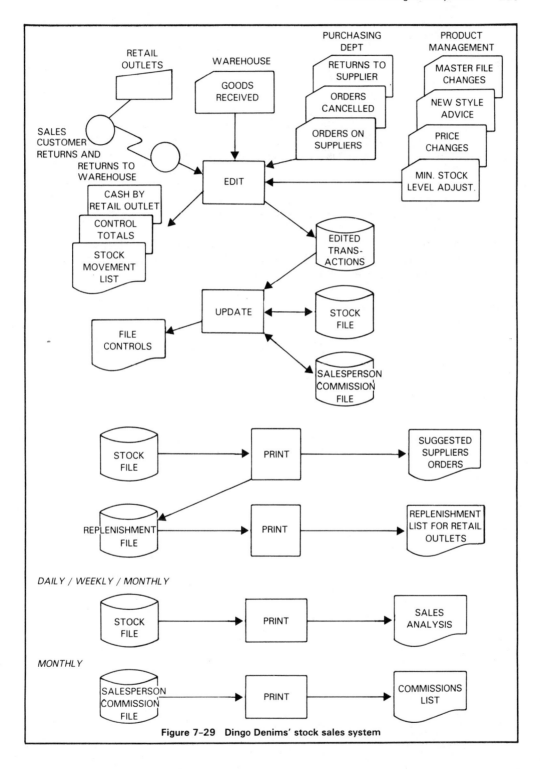

Figure 7–29   Dingo Denims' stock sales system

ASSIGNMENT

1. *Prepare a natural data structure design.* Define each of the entities involved and suggest what other attribute data might need to be stored in addition to that in the case study. Graphically represent this natural data structure.

2. *Prepare a hierarchical data structure design.* Express the natural design by means of a hierarchical data structure. Discuss the advantages and disadvantages of this design and compare with the design in the case study.

3. *Prepare a network data structure design.* What additional advantages does the network model present? What problems, if any, would you have should you choose to use a DBMS like TOTAL, which is limited to a two-level hierarchy?

8 DATA COMMUNICATIONS TECHNOLOGY

8.1 INTRODUCTION TO DATA COMMUNICATIONS

8.1.1 Overview

Data communications may be defined as the transmission, passage, and reception of encoded information, usually by electromagnetic or electronic means. In the information systems environment, the term 'communication' is commonly used for transmissions over some considerable distance, typically between a computing facility and one or more remote data terminals. Nevertheless, communication is an essential component of any computer-based information system, even if the system is merely a traditional 'closed shop' batch-processing operation. The concept of communication and the application of communication theory are involved in the transfer of data, both between the mainframe and its peripherals, and between the modular components constituting the mainframe itself. The efficiency and reliability of the component communication technologies very largely determine the overall effectiveness of the information system as a whole.

There is a growing need worldwide to provide effective data communication facilities. Existing communication technologies (designed primarily for voice communication) have been pressed into service, and newer (specifically digital) communication networks have mushroomed into widespread use.

8.1.2 Application Areas

Some of the forces responsible for the present growth in communications services are:

- Unacceptable time delays in conventional mailing methods
- The need for rapid credit checking
- Electronic transfer of funds
- Interactive/remote programming facilities
- On-line airline reservation systems
- On-line database inquiry networks (such as Tymnet, Arpanet)
- Worldwide defence communication systems
- On-line order entry systems
- On-line insurance proposal systems
- Telemetry (remote measurement methods)
- Growth in business decentralization
- Interprocessor data exchange
- Growth in 'domestic' data retrieval systems (Viewdata, Teletext, Prestel, etc.)
- Electronic mail and facsimile services

While some of these applications can be serviced by traditional spoken communication, the majority demand the efficiency, speed, reliability, and comparatively lower cost of digital communication. There has been significant growth in the size of established networks in terms of the numbers of both processors and pathways over recent years.

8.1.3   Elements of Communication

The two broad categories of communication systems are analog and digital. *Analog* communication involves the transmission of continuous waveforms (represented by a voltage or current), whereas *digital* signals are short, separate pulses. The distinction is illustrated in Figure 8–1.

The most familiar analog system is the telephone network, which is designed to convey spoken information. A microphone in the telephone handset converts the variable air pressure (corresponding to the sound waves) into equivalent voltage levels which are then transmitted (over a distance) to a receiver. The receiver translates the voltage waveform from the line into audible sound signals which are a close approximation to the original speech signal. By the nature of its design, the telephone (or 'switched') network functions on frequencies which lie wholly within the bandwidth 300–3300 Hz. Since frequencies below 300 Hz are lost in this network, the telephone system is not practicable for transmitting unprocessed digital information, which generally contains frequencies well below 300 Hz. These characteristics are further discussed in Subsection 8.3.1.

As Figure 8–1 shows, digital communication involves transmitting short pulses down the line. This type of system is explained in more detail in Subsection 8.2.3, while Subsection 8.3.3 describes how digital systems can be connected to the switched network without losing information by the use of special equipment known as 'modems'.

A second major distinction of communication technology is that between hardware and software. The term *hardware* is used to describe the equipment used in

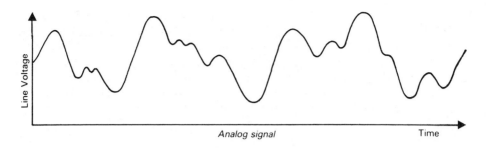

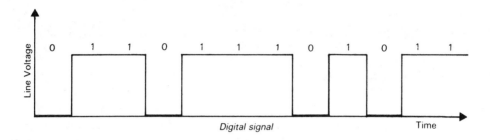

Figure 8–1   Analog and Digital Signals

Analog signals convey continuously varying waveforms such as those generated in speech. Digital signals are 'two-state', the state changes occurring at a synchronous rate.

transmitting, carrying, and receiving information (and to some extent in the processing of that information). *Software* includes special-purpose programs designed to control the processors involved in communication as well as the protocols (the semantics) under which the communications take place. The hardware and software are discussed in more detail in Subsections 8.3.3 and 8.3.4.

8.2 BASIC CONCEPTS

Data transmission systems can be classified in terms of control (on-line or off-line), interaction, mode (analog or digital), volume, speed, and response time.

8.2.1 Control

Whether a data transmission system is on-line or off-line control depends on the involvement of the system's main processor. Generally, the system is *off-line* when a computer is not required to control the transmission of data which it is subsequently required to process. An example of an off-line transmission system is the generation of machine-readable records such as punched cards or paper tape.

Other examples are key-to-disc and key-to-tape data-entry systems. Although this latter group generally involves the use of a small computer, the transaction records are normally processed by a different machine.

On-line systems communicate directly with the main processor, the processor controlling the transmission. The input data enter the computer directly from the point of origin and/or the output data are transmitted directly to the point where they are required. On-line systems may involve a computer communicating with:

- Human users at terminals
- Other computers
- Standard peripherals (tape, cards, disc, plotter, etc.)
- Remote instrumentation (telemetry, process control sensors, etc.)

The on-line system environment is discussed in more detail in Chapter 9.

8.2.2   Interaction Levels

The level of *interaction* in a system is a measure of the system's ability to conduct two-way 'conversations'. The most rudimentary interactive systems simply advise the operator that the transmitted data have been received. Some interactive systems give the impression of machine intelligence, and are capable of engaging the human user in a constructive dialog designed to improve the efficiency and reliability of the data transmitted.

Although off-line systems are generally regarded as non-interactive, some stand-alone key-to-disc systems exhibit levels of interaction which allow the user not only to add new records to a data base, but also to modify existing records in the base, to perform data searches, and to obtain statistics. Such systems are on-line with respect to the data entry processor but are off-line with respect to the computer system which processes that data. On the other hand, some on-line systems are non-interactive. A particular case is that of a batch system which derives its data from a device such as a card reader. Interaction makes sense only when the terminal device gives the operator the possibility of an alternative action resulting from the computer's response. The most frequent application of interactive systems involves human operators at remote two-way terminals. Techniques applicable to these devices are discussed in Chapter 9.

8.2.3   Analog and Digital Systems

The analog mode of data transmission (outlined in Subsection 8.1.3) is inherently suited to conventional communication facilities such as the telephone switched network. Computers (and their peripherals) are complex logical structures built up mainly of elementary two-state devices. Individual components (e.g. switches, flip-flops, indicator lamps) may be in one of two different states. The states may be described as 'on' and 'off' or 'mark' and 'space'. Traditionally, computer engineers work with the binary logical constants zero and one. Data commmunications generally consist of a timed stream of such two-state values. A set of n such binary states can represent up to 2^n separate predefined patterns or codes. In typical communication (asynchronous serial digital), characters are transmitted as a sequence of eight binary digits or 'bits' (zeros and/or ones) sandwiched between one start bit (a zero) and one or two stop bits (ones). The bits are transmitted as individual pulses or square waveforms such as shown in Figure 8–1.

The telephone switched network would degrade a digital signal when that signal contained long unbroken sequences of zeros or ones, since there would be a considerable frequency component well below the cut-off frequency of 300 Hz.

Accordingly steps must be taken to convert digital signals to analog signals (and vice-versa) in order to permit the communication of digital data through an essentially analog channel. This conversion is performed by a device known as a *modem*. Modems are described more fully in Section 8.3.3. The modem therefore allows the communication lines of a public carrier to appear as normal digital communication channels.

The remainder of this chapter is primarily concerned with digital communication.

8.2.4 Volume

Data transmission systems can also be classified according to the quantity of data transmitted. These quantities vary widely. At one extreme, on-line mass storage devices (e.g. drum, disc) may require the transmission of millions of characters per second. Such high-volume links are normally kept as short as possible for reasons of economy. At the other extreme is the communication of data from the keyboard of a terminal. The low-volume use of interactive terminals permits economical communication over long distances. Between these two extremes are intermediate-volume systems such as those involved in telemetry or real-time control systems.

8.2.5 Speed

The *speed* of a transmission system is the maximum rate at which it can carry data. The usual measure for transmission rate is the *baud*. This term is often used loosely to describe the maximum number of data bits which can be transmitted in 1 second on a communication line. More accurately it should be used only when describing a modulation rate, that is, the rate at which changes can be made in the signalling condition of a circuit. To illustrate, a normal voice-grade channel can handle a 300 baud communication when used in conjunction with the standard frequency shift system employed by modems. Since each character is transmitted as a sequence of ten state changes, a 300 baud line can handle up to 30 characters per second. Lines of various speeds are generally available. The switched telephone network is well suited to the low or irregular data rates associated with interactive terminals. This service suits many small installations, since it gives economical operation and provides freedom of operating time and duration with high reliability.

The advantages are related mainly to low operating costs per bit transmitted and the freedom from unused overheads if the computer system is disconnected. The main disadvantage is the speed limitation (although 'conditioned' lines offering higher baud rates are available at correspondingly increased tariffs).

8.2.6   Response Time

Response time must not be confused with transmission time. The *response time* is the time between completing a transmission from a terminal and receiving a reply to that transmission from the computer. As such, response time is a function of the speed with which the computer can process the data received. System designers must consider not only the average response time of an interactive system, but also the maximum response time as a function of loads placed on the computer system. For other types of system, response time may be defined as the interval between an event and the system's response to the event. The term *delivery time* may replace response time (for the round trip) in non-interactive systems. Thus, the delivery time associated with a large batch-processing installation may be measured in anything from minutes to days.

A commercial real-time system would typically involve response times measured in seconds, where the control involves interaction at the inquiry or transaction level. A generally accepted definition of a *real-time system* is: one in which the computer system forms part of the operational 'control loop'. Although batch systems offering weekly or monthly status reports are also involved in the control of the organization, they are not classed as 'real-time' since their control is not related to inquiry or transaction processing.

8.3   COMMUNICATION CHANNELS

8.3.1   Channel Characteristics

This section is concerned with the characteristics of channels used strictly as carriers of digital information. By far the most important characteristic of a communication channel is its capacity. The *capacity* of a line or channel is the maximum amount of data which it can carry in unit time. The value of a channel's capacity is determined by various physical line characteristics. Of particular concern is the phenomenon known as 'electronic noise'. Noise of one type or another is present in all electronic circuits due to the random movement of electrons. This effect is aggravated at higher temperatures. If an operator attempts to transmit data over a channel at speeds higher than its rated capacity, the data become subject to increasing distortion. Put another way, the reliability of the channel decreases sharply as the transmission rate increases beyond a particular threshold. Other physical factors contributing to the performance of a channel include the length of the line, its electrical characteristics, and the power of the transmitter.

The different practical implementations of communication channels vary widely in their transmission capacities. At one extreme is the coaxial cable which can transmit data in excess of millions of bits per second. A simple twisted pair of wires, on the other hand, may have a limit of thousands of bits per second.

When data are to be transmitted over a distance greater than a few hundred metres, it is normal engineering practice to terminate both ends of the line with modems (see Subsection 8.3.3), thus using the line as a carrier for an analog signal. The range of frequencies which make up such an analog signal is called *signal bandwidth*. Bandwidth is normally measured in Hertz, Hz (cycles per second). A kilohertz, kHz, is 1000 cycles per second, while a megahertz, MHz, is 1 000 000 cycles per second. The bandwidth of a typical telephone line is approximately 3 kHz, i.e. it carries frequencies from approximately 300 Hz to 3300 Hz. It is important to note that bandwidth refers not to a particular frequency of transmission, but rather to a range of frequencies. The information-carrying capacity of a channel is directly proportional to its bandwidth. Thus a channel with a bandwidth of 30 kHz can carry ten times as much data per second as the telephone line with its 3 kHz bandwidth. It may be noted that, depending upon the technique chosen for modulation/ demodulation, the achievable data rate measured in bits per second is normally higher than the channel bandwidth (expressed in Hertz). According to Shannon's law, the maximum capacity of a channel of bandwidth W is given by:

$$W \log_2 (1 + S/N) \text{ bits/second}$$

where S is the power of the signal and N is the power of the electronic noise inherent in the channel. To illustrate, a typical telephone line may have a signal-to-noise ratio of 600 (i.e. $S/N = 600$). Since $W = 3000$ Hz, Shannon's law shows that the maximum data-carrying capacity of the line is $3000 \times \log_2 601$, or about 27 700 bits per second. This is a theoretical ideal. In practice, a telephone line rarely achieves better than 9600 bits per second (an efficiency of 35 per cent). Beyond 9600 bits per second, the probability of transmission (reception) errors increases sharply, although the use of redundancy-encoding systems permits the recovery of much lost data.

Digital data are frequently transmitted over long distances by modulating an appropriate carrier signal. The higher the frequency of the modulated carrier, the greater the degree of possible frequency deviation due to modulation. The maximum extent of this frequency deviation is the bandwidth. Since the maximum data-transmission rate is proportional to the bandwidth, higher transmission rates are made available by the application of higher frequency carriers. Normal radio frequency carrier signals are restricted to bandwidths determined by regulation. Typical data links may be limited to bandwidths comparable to the switched network, however very high frequency (VHF) or ultra high frequency (UHF) carriers may offer bandwidths measured in megahertz. UHF communication has the further advantage in that it may be 'beamed' from point to point (line of sight). The recent application of high-transmission fibre optics to the transmission of data has brought two main advantages: extremely high bandwidth, and strict point-to-point communication. The high bandwidth follows from the very high frequency of light itself. Further, there is a considerable boost to the signal-to-noise ratio since fibre optics are virtually unaffected by external electromagnetic interference.

8.3.2 Communication Techniques

Communication lines are classed as simplex, half-duplex, or full duplex:

Simplex   Information may be transmitted in only one direction
Half-duplex   Information may be transmitted in either direction, but only
                   in one direction at once
Full duplex   Information may be transmitted in both directions at the
                   same time; the full duplex line is sometimes referred to
                   simply as duplex

Half-duplex lines normally have a disadvantage known as 'line turnaround time', which is the time required for both modems to switch from one mode (send or receive) to the other. In a more formal terminology, the term *circuit* would be used to describe each of these transmission links. In particular, a circuit is a form of two-way communication between two data terminals. The terms *channel, link,* and *line* are used interchangeably to describe a path for electronic or electromagnetic signals. Whether a channel corresponds to one or more circuits can generally be inferred from the context. The distinction is of signficance when discussing multiplex methods (see Subsection 8.3.3). Some writers use 'channel' to describe the link carrying a large number of individual circuits (or 'subchannels') while others use the same term (channel) to refer to the individual circuits themselves.

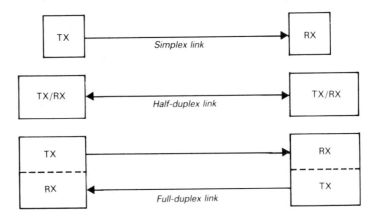

Figure 8-2   Simplex, half-duplex, and full-duplex lines

Schematic representation of the three basic transmission classes. TX and RX denote transmitter and receiver respectively.

8.3.3 Communication Hardware

The communication of data is a combined function of hardware and software. Rapid development in both areas is seen by some writers as a cause of potential conflict. A number of computer vendors have attempted to introduce their own standards for data transmission which would make it difficult for data to be communicated between that manufacturer's equipment and any other. At the same time, agreements are being sought by worldwide standards organizations on how such incompatibilities may be avoided. Because of the implications, it is imperative that users are informed about the alternatives. The urgency is underlined by an estimated growth of total data communications in Australia to 200 000 megabits per working day by 1985 (a growth rate of approximately 25 per cent per year) according to a Telecom-commissioned study by W. D. Scott & Co. (1975).

Channels

The variation in hardware representations of communication channels is discussed in Subsection 8.3.1. Irrespective of the individual line characteristics, channels may be configured in arrangements ranging from simple point-to-point links to complex hierarchical distributed networks. The use of interfaces to the channel, and the communication protocols to be used are subjects which clearly concern standards committees. Communication protocols are discussed in Subsection 8.3.4.

Modems and interface standards

The modem (modulator/demodulator) interfaces digital signals to the analog requirements of the common carrier-provided communication lines. It is clearly essential for this interface to be well standardized to guarantee interchangeability of modems, terminals, and transmission control units. A particular standard has been specified by the Electronics Industries Association; known as the EIA RS-232-C standard, it is closely followed by most manufacturers. It is a detailed specification concerning all aspects of the interface, ranging from the type of plug to be used, the pin allocations, and voltage/current levels, to the sequencing of the various control signals and data items. The signals are briefly outlined in Table 8-1.

In principle, of the two units being interfaced, one is a logical 'data terminal' while the other is a logical 'data set' or 'modem'. Normally the logical data terminal is a physical terminal. Similarly the logical data set is normally a physical modem. On the other hand, a physical modem may be configured to 'look like' a physical terminal so it can be connected to a transmission control unit which normally interfaces directly with a terminal. Similarly, two terminals may communicate over a common RS-232 interface, however one must be configured to look like a standard modem. The signals specified for the RS-232 interface fall into four groups:

- *Data signals.* Two data signal lines are provided: one for received data, one for transmitted data. The data are transmitted serially, synchronous by bit, and either synchronous or asynchronous by character. The particular code is user-specified.
- *Timing signals.* These signals are used only when the logical modem has no provision for START-STOP transmission. Two connections are prescribed for both transmitted and received data.
- *Control signals.* RQ2S (request-to-send), CL2S (clear-to-send), and DSR

Table 8-1   Summary of representative RS–232 signals

SIGNAL (RS-232)	Comments*
Transmit data (TD)	Serial data from DTE to modem
Receive data (RD)	Serial data from modem to DTE
Request to send (RQ2S)	Set by DTE when it is ready to send
Clear to send (CL2S)	Set by modem to advise DTE OK to transmit
Data set ready (DSR)	Set by modem when it is powered and ready to transfer data in response to DTR signal from DTE
Carrier detect (CF)	Set by modem when carrier signal is received
Ring indicator (CE)	Set by modem when incoming call received
Data terminal ready (DTR)	Set by DTE to enable modem to answer call

*DTE is Data Transmission Equipment (possibly a terminal or computer interface).

(data-set-ready) are the normally provided control signals. For example, a computer raises the RQ2S signal to a modem when it is ready to transmit data. The modem replies with CL2S to the computer when it has established its carrier and is ready to transmit. The DSR signal is generated by the modem to the computer to indicate that it is powered up. The optional control signals include DTR (data-terminal-ready), CE (ring-indicator), and CF (carrier-detect).

- *Ground signals.* Two reference levels are provided: protective ground and signal ground.

As an illustration, consider the case where the operator of a remote terminal wishes to send a message to the central site over the switched network. The operator's terminal is interfaced to an 'originating' modem, and the computer is interfaced to an 'answering' modem.

1. Operator dials computer on terminal's phone.
2. Answering modem detects ringing (CE).
3. Computer responds with DTR to answering modem.
4. Answering modem transmits carrier tone which operator hears. Operator presses button on modem.

5. Originating modem sends DSR to terminal and answering modem sends DSR to computer.
6. Both computer and terminal initially raise RQ2S (assuming full-duplex mode). Each modem responds with CL2S whereupon full-duplex communication is then established between the terminal and the computer.
7. Termination is achieved by both parties dropping RQ2S causing the carriers to cease.

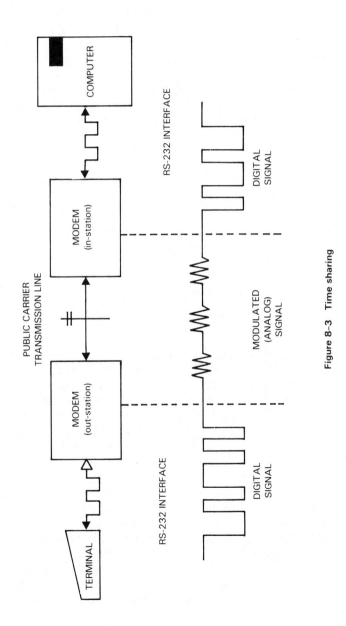

Figure 8-3   Time sharing

In a typical timesharing environment a remote user may use a data terminal via the switched network. The user receives the same service as if using a terminal which is 'hard-wired' to the processor. The digital signals generated and required by both the terminal and the computer are transformed into analog signals (tones) by the modems for transmission through the network. The modems interface with the terminal and computer through standard RS-232 connections. The transmission procedures are invisible to the user. This process is illustrated in Figure 8–3.

Apart from the functional differences between the 'originating' (or 'out-station') modem and the 'answering' (or 'in-station') modem, their analog frequencies (tones) must be alternately assigned. If the out-station modem transmits a 'one' as a tone of frequency f_{01} and a 'zero' as f_{00}, the in-station must receive f_{01} and f_{00} as one and zero respectively. Similarly, if the in-station transmits the frequency pair f_{11} and f_{10}, these frequencies must be received by the out-station. The use of these four frequencies permits simultaneous (full-duplex) communication between both stations (Figure 8–4). The values of f_{00}, f_{01}, f_{10}, and f_{11}, and of their permitted tolerances are specified as an international standard.

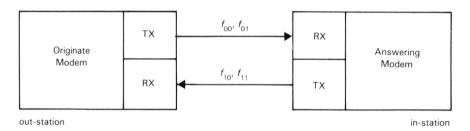

out-station   in-station

Figure 8–4   Analog frequencies

Four frequencies f_{00}, f_{01}, f_{10} and f_{11} carry information between communicating modems.

There are three principal categories of modems: those used in transmission over voice-grade lines; those used for very high speed transmission over wide-band communication channels; and short-haul hard-wired modems. Voice-grade modems are either low speed or medium speed. The low-speed modem operates at up to 300 bps. Medium-speed modems operate at up to 9600 bps. High-speed modems are employed for higher bit rates. Each modem type uses a different modulation technique such as frequency modulation, phase modulation, and amplitude modulation. Low-speed modems are suitable for interfacing low-speed asynchronous terminals (e.g. Teletypes) to the switched network. Medium-speed modems can be used with terminal controllers and with faster terminals such as those employed by airline reservation systems. High-speed modems are used for transmissions between computers and high-speed batch terminals.

The coupling of a modem to the switched network may be either by means of hard-wiring or by acoustic coupling. Acoustic couplers are convenient in situations which require the data terminals to be used at variable locations. Although the acoustic coupler still offers the RS-232 interface to the data terminal, it communicates through the standard handset of the user's telephone.

Parallel and serial transmission

The transmission of data over long distances (e.g. using a common carrier) is normally conducted over a single line, bits being transmitted in strict time sequence. Short-haul communications (e.g. between a computer mainframe and a nearby peripheral) may however take place using multi-line, or 'parallel', methods.

In a parallel communication system, each bit of a transmitted character has its own line. A bundle of eight lines can be used to transmit 8-bit characters eight times faster than a corresponding binary synchronous serial line running at the same bit rate. In practice, parallel channels carry additional lines for specialized protocol purposes. A 'strobe' line may be included to mark the time that the receiver should 'sample' the signals on the parallel data lines. The character codes used may be specialized (since this is local communication) or may correspond to one of the more usual serial communication codes. The essence of parallel communication is that all the bits of a character are sent simultaneously. One character is transmitted each bit time.

Figure 8-5   The Texas Instruments Model 745 portable data terminal

This terminal features an integral acoustic coupler. In use, the handset of a standard telephone is positioned over the coupler's microphone and speaker. Carrier tones are transmitted to and from the handset by sound.

Multiplexers and concentrators

A *multiplexer* is a device which transmits and receives data on several communication links at the same time. The device may be hard-wired or it may be a specially programmed mini- or microcomputer. To illustrate, a minicomputer with up to 32 RS-232 interfaces, each configured to 300 bps, could effectively multiplex

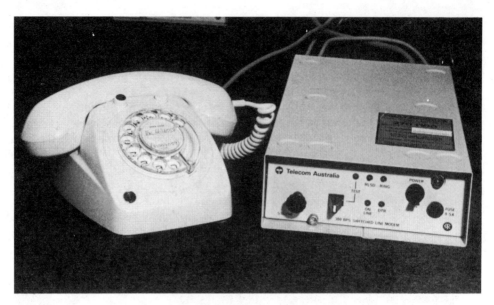

Figure 8-6   Standard Telecom hard-wired modem and associated Datel handset

This equipment connects directly to the switched network. It offers a standard RS-232 interface to an attached DTE.

the communications of 32 data terminals connected to those interfaces, with the multiplexed line connected to a single 9600 bps RS-232 interface. Acting in this role, such a minicomputer may also be described as a concentrator. In general, *concentrators* are used to interface clusters of terminals with the long line to the host computer. The concentrator combines many low-speed lines into a single high-speed line. Unlike the multiplexer the concentrator may make use of internal buffers, allowing it to concentrate the data from high-speed terminals which, through periods of idleness, have a low net data-transmission rate.

As data communications grow, the costs of lines and other hardware facilities escalate. Techniques for combining data streams on independent lines have evolved which allow, through the facility of multiplexing, transmission along multiple data paths as one signal. *Multiplexing* means the use of one facility to handle in parallel several similar but separate functions. Multiplexing is possible, and economically valuable, because the operations that are multiplexed may take place at a considerably slower speed than the optimum operating speed of the host facility. Should two different speed channels be needed in a common office, multiplexing could be considered as a cost-saving method. As the hardware to provide this feature is costly and complex, the network may require design optimization to ensure true cost benefits. Detailed techniques may require clarification with public-carrier engineers.

Multiplexing should not be considered early in network planning as much valuable effort may be expended for low net results. It is only after on-line testing and observation that multiplexing could emerge as a realistic communications alternative. Two multiplexing techniques are in common use: frequency-division multiplex and time-division multiplex.

Frequency-division multiplex. This technique subdivides the available transmission bandwidth into narrower bands (not necessarily equal), each used as a separate subchannel (also known as a 'frequency-derived' channel). Thus a single broad band UHF channel having a bandwidth of 1 megahertz could be subdivided into 300 independent frequency-derived channels of voice-grade quality (3.33 kilohertz bandwidth each).

Time-division multiplex. This multiplexing technique provides 'time-derived' subchannels by the sequential, repetitive allocation of time slots of the host channel. The number of time slots is equal to the number of subchannels. The method is analogous to the timesharing of a CPU. Elementary time-division multiplexers allocate short time slots of equal duration. In such a system, the use of the line is equally apportioned among all the users, even if some actually require far less than their allotted time. An 'intelligent' or statistical multiplexer can vary the lengths of the various time slots to optimize the line usage. Time allocations may be set up as constraints for a given shift or may be dynamically adjusted in response to the measured use on each subchannel.

Front-ending

The term *front-ending* refers to the process of interfacing multiple communication lines to a single host computer facility. This is roughly the reverse process of concentration. Again, this role may be carried out by a hard-wired front-end device, or by a suitably programmed minicomputer or microcomputer. Some minicomputers (e.g. Perkin Elmer model 74) are specifically designed with instruction sets suitable for the rapid transfer and analysis of large blocks of data. The use of mini- and microcomputers to perform this function offers the user a degree of flexibility in the face of possible changes in communication protocols.

Automatic callers

The interfacing of automatic equipment to the regular signalling and switching components of the switched network is facilitated by automatic calling units. Whereas an answering modem may respond to an incoming call it may not originate a call. The automatic caller is driven by a suitably programmed processor. It enables the processor to call automatically on the switched network and then to communicate via an associated modem.

Data terminal devices

With some exceptions, the term *data terminal* refers to devices which communicate in serial mode. Thus, parallel devices such as printers and disk drives are not normally considered to be data terminals. Some display screens, however, may be driven in parallel mode to provide rapid and continuous updating of information. While such displays are sometimes referred to as data terminals it is not possible (without the use of special-purpose interface equipment) to conduct such communications over extended distances.

Data terminal devices cover a broad range of peripheral devices which may be grouped into three classes:

- Receive only
- Send only
- Send/receive

'Receive only' devices include hard-copy printers, display screens, LED (light-emitting diode) readout panels, and the like. 'Send only' devices encompass equipment such as badge readers, data-collection terminals (which read single punched cards), and digital telemetry devices. The 'send/receive' group of devices enables the operator and the system to interact; however it should be borne in mind that many send/receive devices are in fact peripheral computing facilities. Thus intelligent nodes would be included in a computing network, as well as interactive terminals such as 'glass teletypes' (or VDUs), hard-copy terminals (the ASR-33 and more recent and faster equivalents, etc.), and terminals containing integral communications equipment (such as the TI 475 portable hard-copy terminal shown in Figure 8–5).

The most recent tendency in the design of interactive terminals is to use microprogrammed, rather than hard-wired, logic. The use of such firmware to control the characteristics of the terminal allows major design modifications without hardware changes. Such design methods are predicated on the widespread use of microprocessors. A direct consequence of microprogrammed logic is the 'intelligent terminal'. This term covers a spectrum of devices ranging from VDUs with a wide range of selectable display and communication modes to terminals which the user can program to perform quite sophisticated exercises. Such devices can pre-edit data before transmission, compress/expand data to optimize line usage, and even provide complex prompting of the operator together with a wide range of diagnostic/error messages.

The term *dumb terminal* (coined by Lear Siegler to describe their ADM-3A VDU) has been used widely to describe VDUs which offer the basic facilities but no user-programmability. Its facilities however are generally still quite extensive. A dumb terminal usually offers most of the following features:

- Switch selectable baud rates
- Upper and lower case ASCII display
- Graphics
- Direct cursor positioning
- Blinking fields
- Protected fields
- Inverse video fields
- Half intensity fields
- Selectable parity
- Number of 'stop' bits
- Number of data bits

- Synchronous or asynchronous communication
- Separate numeric keypad
- Audible 'bell' signal
- Auto self-test
- Special user-defined function keys
- Block or character transmission modes

An intelligent terminal may well be difficult to distinguish from a packaged microcomputer system. It generally features software tools such as a text editor, BASIC interpreter, and a floppy disk operating system. One such system, the Intecolor 8035, offers medium-resolution colour graphics, two built-in minifloppy disk drives and facilities for two serial and one parallel communications lines. Data may be captured, edited, and batch controlled interactively off-line on floppy disk for subsequent transmission to a remote host computer.

Systems designers are becoming increasingly aware of the importance of carefully designed interactive sequences (such as might be implemented for an intelligent VDU) as well as the need for well-engineered terminal designs to meet the needs of operators who may spend many hours each day keying in data and reading the screen or printout. The 'in' word is *ergonomics*. Desirable features include non-glare screen coatings, flicker-free displays, well-formed characters, convenient keyboard layouts, numeric keypads, tactile response to keystrokes, and so on. As the level of sophistication or training of the user increases, the number of interface interactions drops. For the less trained or infrequent user, the system may need to supply many 'prompts' and edit checks. The end result of a well-defined interface is well-formed and edited data being passed to the processor.

The display of a prompting question (such as NAME?) cues the user to type in the data required next. The prompt may also be the display of a blank form, with the implication that the user complete the required entries. In this case, the system might position a blinking cursor at the location of the next required entry. Prompts may also have an educational element, the intention being to reduce the level of prompting as the session proceeds. Prompt messages may be highlighted by display systems capable of intensified or coloured fields. A prompt message may also be made to blink on and off. Some terminals allow the display of different fonts to highlight the message. The availability of low-cost colour graphics terminals has increased the range of options available for prompting and coding. If a user fails to respond to a prompt message within a given time, the terminal may alert the user audibly, and/or it may display a more forceful prompt. Security may dictate that the intelligent system disconnect itself from the system should there be no user-response within, say, five minutes. The design of good, clear, meaningful prompts greatly affects the user's view of the system as a whole.

The responses supplied by a user at a remote intelligent terminal are normally checked before being passed to the system. In particular, it may be necessary for the user to be validated before further access to the system is permitted: many systems require the user to supply identification information as well as a password. Where a dumb terminal is used for this latter purpose, it is common to suppress the echoing of the password on full-duplex lines, thus ensuring that what is typed on the keyboard is not displayed on the screen. An intelligent terminal may perform a similar function without reference to the remote processor. Once the user is approved by the system, the terminal normally edit-checks the subsequent entries in terms of range, format, etc. This function is most appropriate to the intelligent terminal in view of the net reduction in channel use. Edit-checks might verify that non-numeric responses are drawn from an appropriate dictionary and follow a predetermined syntax. Numeric responses may be subject to reasonableness checks (range, precision) and to internal consistency checks (e.g. modulus 11). Only edited data (possibly compacted/ encrypted) would be sent to the remote processor.

Errors detected by the editing routines normally result in the display of a diagnostic message pointing out the nature of the problem and requesting a new data entry by the user. An acoustic signal should accompany a diagnostic message since most operators tend to be looking at the source documents rather than at the screen.

8.3.4   Communications Protocols and Software

Here the term *software* is used, not in its normal generic sense of computer programming, but rather to encompass the protocols, data structures and architecture of communication systems. A *protocol* is a set of conventions for the transmission of data and control information. These conventions may provide facilities for the handling of errors and for the hand-shaking and coordination procedures used in originating calls and/or recovery from failures.

Error handling implies the possible correction as well as the detection of errors. Detection is based on the presence of redundant information in the transmitted message. Correction is generally achieved by retransmission of a section of the message. Character redundancy may be achieved by adding an extra parity bit to each set of bits defining the character. Other methods involve LRC (longitudinal redundancy checking) and CRC (cyclic redundancy check).

The remainder of this chapter is concerned with serial communication since this is the only form of transmission appropriate over distance. The two major categories of serial transmission are synchronous and asynchronous. A third, hybrid, form (isynchronous) is also described.

Asynchronous transmission

Asynchronous transmission of data is character oriented. Individual characters are transmitted within an elementary envelope with strict internal bit timing. By contrast, no time constraints are placed upon the spacing between separate characters. Asynchronous transmission is appropriate to low-volume applications typified by the link between an interactive terminal and a remote computing facility, particularly where the terminal is not responsible for local processing. For each keystroke originating at the terminal, a single character is transmitted to the host. If the line has full-duplex protocol, the host echoes the character back to the terminal for display. The timing of characters is determined primarily by the rate at which the operator keys the data at the keyboard. The *enveloping* protocol for each character consists of a pre-fixed start bit and a post-fixed one or two stop bits. The stop bits have opposite polarity to the start bit, thus forcing a voltage transition at the start of each new envelope. This is important since the receiving hardware uses this transition to synchronize its internal clock, which is used to strobe the individual bits within the enclosed character. The enclosed character, although usually eight bits in most timesharing applications, may be more or less depending upon the agreed protocol. In addition, the communicating devices must use the same bit rate to define the spacing within the packaged characters. An example is given in Figure 8–7.

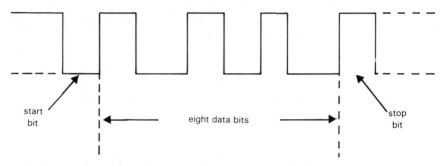

Figure 8-7   Asynchronous data transmission

An eight-bit character (10010100) is shown here framed between a leading start bit (logical zero) and a terminal stop bit (logical one). At 300 baud the individual pulses have lengths which are multiples of 1/300th seconds. The entire frame is 10 bits long (lasting 1/30th second).

The popularity of asynchronous communication has allowed the production of low-cost special-purpose chips (integrated circuits) capable of converting between the asynchronous line protocol and the internal (parallel) form of the data required by the host computer. These devices are variously described as ACIAs (Asynchronous Communication Interface Adapters), UARTs (Universal Asynchronous Receiver/Transmitter), and so on. These chips are usually supported by separate crystal-controlled clock pulse generators, which define the bit speed. The clocking needs sufficient accuracy to ensure that the trailing stop bit is strobed within its pulse range. Most UARTs check this condition. Since only ten bits are transmitted in a typical frame, the relative clock rates between the receiver and transmitter may be out by up to 5 per cent (half a bit in ten) without causing a framing error. ACIAs and UARTs generally produce (and receive) voltage levels unsuitable for direct transmission. Accordingly additional chips are used to 'buffer' the line to the communication chip. There are two principal line levels in use, RS-232-C and current loop.

Synchronous transmission

While asynchronous communication requires framing information to be added to each character, synchronous systems add framing information to blocks of data, or messages. Since the synchronous format is the more efficient but requires more complex decoding, it is usually found on high-speed data links. The message (record) to be transmitted in synchronous form is usually framed between two or more SYN characters which are used by the receiver to determine character boundaries within a bit string. As synchronization must be held over fairly long bit strings, clocking information is usually extracted from the data stream by the modem or is supplied by an external source. The relative efficiency of synchronous transmission is apparent only when the message length exceeds eight ten-bit characters.

Modems for synchronous applications are somewhat more complex than those designed for asynchronous transmission. Asynchronous modems generally employ FSK (frequency shift keying) which translates specific audio tones into MARK or SPACE. They may therefore run at any baud rate up to the maximum for the line. By contrast, synchronous modems supply timing information to the data terminal and require data to be presented at the same speed as that information. The synchronous modem may operate only at certain preset baud rates. To preserve synchronism between messages, SYN characters may be used to fill idle time.

Isynchronous transmission

This a hybrid mode which involves the asynchronous format with synchronous modems. It may be used to increase the net line speed without changing the basic system protocol. Individual characters are framed as if for asynchronous transmission, but the time between characters is held at a multiple of character times.

The Intel 8251 chip is designed to handle all three transmission methods. It is described as a USART (Universal Synchronous/Asynchronous Receiver/Transmitter) (see Smith, 1976).

Communication codes

In any data communication system the communicating parties must agree on the character set to be used and the bit representations of each of those characters. The set of representations forms the 'communication code'. The growth of inter-connected digital communication systems has resulted in a high degree of code standardization. In serial transmission the character codes may be sent in 'unwrapped bundles' (synchronous) or as individually packaged characters (asynchronous). The 'code' applies only to the contents of the character — not its packaging. The packaging (i.e. start bits, stop bits, etc.) is a question of protocol (see earlier in this subsection).

The codes most commonly used are: ASCII (or USASCII), Baudot, Data Interchange Code, and EBCDIC.

The ASCII (American Standard Code for Information Interchange) is given in Figure 8–8. It is a seven-bit code with a 128-element character set ($2^7 = 128$). The eighth bit position carries an optional parity bit for validation purposes. The character set includes the letters of the English alphabet (upper and lower case), the numerals 0–9, 32 special symbols (e.g. \$, #), the blank (or space), and 32 control characters (e.g. line feed, horizontal tab). Referring to Figure 8–8, readers may verify that the character B is a binary 1000010 (most significant bit first) and that the SYN character is 0010110.

bits 4 3 2 1	Col / Row	bit 7 — 0 bit 6 — 0 bit 5 — 0 / 0	0 0 1 / 1	0 1 0 / 2	0 1 1 / 3	1 0 0 / 4	1 0 1 / 5	1 1 0 / 6	1 1 1 / 7
0 0 0 0	0	NUL	DLE	SP	0	@	P		p
0 0 0 1	1	SOH	DC1	!	1	A	Q	a	q
0 0 1 0	2	STX	DC2	,,	2	B	R	b	r
0 0 1 1	3	ETX	DC3	#	3	C	S	c	s
0 1 0 0	4	EOT	DC4	$	4	D	T	d	t
0 1 0 1	5	ENQ	NAK	%	5	E	U	e	u
0 1 1 0	6	ACK	SYN	&	6	F	V	f	v
0 1 1 1	7	BEL	ETB	'	7	G	W	g	w
1 0 0 0	8	BS	CAN	(	8	H	X	h	x
1 0 0 1	9	HT	EM	)	9	I	Y	i	y
1 0 1 0	10	LF	SUB	*	:	J	Z	j	z
1 0 1 1	11	VT	ESC	+	;	K	[	k	{
1 1 0 0	12	FF	FS	,	<	L	\	l		
1 1 0 1	13	CR	GS	-	=	M	]	m	}
1 1 1 0	14	SO	RS	.	>	N	^	n	~
1 1 1 1	15	SI	US	/	?	O	—	o	del

Figure 8-8   The ASCII code

The Baudot code is a long-established five-bit code used on older teletype equipment. Although five bits can support only 32 characters, the Baudot code includes a letter-shift and figure-shift allowing a total of 62 graphics. There is no provision for parity check. The Data Interchange Code is similar to USASCII and is used on subvoice-grade lines which use teletype equipment made since the early 1960s. In asynchronous transmission it uses eleven bits per character (one start, seven data, one parity, two stop). EBCDIC (Extended Binary Coded Decimal Interchange Code) is IBM's 360/370 code. It is an eight-bit code, relating its bit patterns to the (very old) Hollerith card code.

Transmission reliability

According to Shannon's law (see Subsection 8.3.1), the reliability of transmission improves with increase in signal-to-noise ratio. Sporadic noise however can corrupt a signal. Unless there is some means for detecting such noise, corrupt data may be accepted by the receiver as valid data.

Clearly, thorough systems design must incorporate appropriate checks, edits, and validation procedures on operational information before using it to update working and/or master files. There are however, methods for detecting data corruption at the point of reception. Such detection techniques rely heavily on the introduction of redundant information into the transmitted data stream.

In the case of asynchronous transmission, the eighth bit position (not used in the ASCII code) is often set by the hardware to force the parity of the transmitted character to odd or even (according to an agreed protocol). A character has 'odd' parity when the number of '1' bits in its makeup is an odd value. Thus the string 11011010 is odd while 110000101 is even. Most UARTs, etc., are capable of placing a correct parity bit immediately following the start bit. Similarly, the same chip can detect incorrect parity on a received character and report this error to the attached hardware. In the case of a terminal 'wired' to detect parity errors, an error may cause the screen to display a special symbol to indicate corrupt data.

In synchronous transmission, redundancy may be included within a message as a short 'check-sum' which can be verified by a receiver. Such methods are error-detection systems only. They cannot indicate where the corruption is, nor the corrections to make. Indeed, there is a small chance of mutually cancelling errors which together act to set (falsely) the redundancy to its correct value. For example, two bits in error in a single asynchronous character do not affect the overall character parity. Error-detecting/correcting systems use additional redundancy so that a receiver system can either regenerate the correct data or request retransmission of the faulty message. It may be noted that including redundant information effectively reduces the throughput of a channel, although this is generally regarded as being offset by the gain in reliability.

Compacting/expanding

If the traffic between a remote terminal and the processor follows a limited range of groups (e.g. replies of Yes, No, or common entries such as 'part number'), each common group may be replaced by a suitable abbreviated code. The resulting compacted transmission may be used directly by the system software. Similarly, the processor may transmit compacted messages to the remote terminal which performs the necessary substitutions to expand the transmission for display purposes.

Security

In this context, *security* means preventing data falling into unauthorized hands, although the term is sometimes applied to providing the system with failsafe features.

Security is a combined function of the hardware and the system software. Both individual users and specific terminals must be authorized to access and/or modify sections of a system's database. This is particularly necessary when the absence of such controls is liable to invite interference ranging from the unauthorized exploration of personnel files to outright sabotage. Security systems commonly employed use techniques such as automatic terminal authorization, user validation, terminal locks, cryptography, and surveillance. Cryptographic techniques, in particular, employ intelligent terminals to encrypt and decrypt transmitted data to defeat wire-tapping. The substitution code used for data compacting serves only to reduce the communication load on the channel; it offers very little security. More sophisticated techniques are required to effectively encrypt a message for security reasons. The methods employed are similar in structure to those used in military applications. Clearly, as with compacting, encrypting is feasible only when the remote terminal is intelligent. See the appendix to Chapter 10 for a discussion of cryptographic systems.

8.4 CONFIGURATION METHODS

Communications systems are typically configured for transmission from:

- One-to-one (point to point)
- One-to-many (broadcast)
- One-to-one-of-many (multidrop)

Maintaining terminal discipline is obviously more complex on multidrop lines. When several devices or terminals all share a common communication line/computer port, only one terminal can input traffic at a time, but several devices could receive data simultaneously. Each device therefore has an address, of one or more characters, and an ability to recognize messages or commands sent to that address. Certainly if a broadcast facility is available in the control program, all terminals would need to have decode facilities incorporated. For transmission towards the computer, multidrop services must be able to 'invite' each terminal to transmit in its turn. The technique known as 'polling' must then be provided.

There are broadly two systems by which terminals may communicate with the processor. These may be classified as 'conditional' and 'unconditional' transmission systems, according to the manner in which the terminals send data to the processor. In an unconditional transmission system (a form of 'contention communication'), the sending of single characters or blocks of characters (messages) is initiated by the terminal operator without regard for the 'readiness' of the receiving processor. Conditional transmission systems require the terminal to hold a completed message until the processor is ready to receive it.

8.4.1   Unconditional Transmission Systems

To cope with characters or messages received in an unconditional transmission system, the processor must make frequent line checks, or it must possess some form of interrupt-handling facility. Under these circumstances careful watch must be kept on the maximum data rate handled by the processor. If for instance, the processor is required to handle 20 lines each capable of 9600 baud, it must have the capacity to handle a situation in which all 20 lines are sending at the same time. The maximum data rate would then be $20 \times 9600 = 192\,000$ bps; assuming one interrupt per eight bits, this amounts to an average interrupt interval of 42 microseconds. Such a setup would need to be serviced by a processor capable not only of analyzing, reformatting, and transmitting the received signals, but also of servicing each interrupt in well under the 42 microseconds available. A typical minicomputer requires 10 microseconds simply to detect each interrupt, quite apart from the time needed to service the interrupt.

Multidropping is not normally performed with this type of transmission, since each terminal requires its own cable connection to the processor, and each cable needs an appropriate electronic interface within the processor. The exception is when a number of terminals 'contend' for a single line to the processor by means of a line splitter or similar equipment.

8.4.2   Polling Systems

Although more complex than unconditional transmission systems, the conditional approach provides a number of potential cost-saving benefits. In particular, the method is appropriate to clusters of VDUs linked to a local processor. The processor might be a mini- or microcomputer acting in the role of a data concentrator for remote parts of the network. In many applications the terminals interface with the processor by use of full-duplex lines, possibly with the aid of a concentrator.

Polling protocols

Each polling terminal connected to the processor is allocated a unique address or call sign. This address may be hard wired, switch selected, or be set in internal software. Depending upon traffic volume, a given number of terminals may be connected to a single interface in the processor. Thus, since the interface may communicate with only one terminal at a time, only one may be on-line at any given time. With higher traffic volumes, additional processor interfaces may be installed to handle additional terminal clusters. A typical interface might handle more than 64 separate terminals, the actual maximum being determined by line speed, traffic volume, processor speed, and maximum acceptable response time. A small mini-computer with 20 terminals could provide response times of one to five seconds in an environment using 2400 baud polling protocols, an average message length of 100 characters, and each terminal originating five messages per minute. The multidrop line would be used to about 65 per cent of its maximum capacity. It is usual to determine response times by simulating the proposed system using a mathematical model.

A polling protocol requires the processor to selectively invite responses from the individual terminals, usually in a round-robin fashion. If an addressed terminal has no message pending, the processor inquires of the next terminal and so on until one with a pending message is polled. That terminal then transmits its entire message back to the processor. When the processor has serviced the message the next terminal in its polling list is polled. The term *protocol* here defines the set of rules governing the communication between the processor and its terminals. The specific protocol chosen for a particular application depends largely upon the characteristics of the terminals themselves.

A particular example is afforded by the TEC 425 series of message-oriented polling terminals. The 425 is a desk-top VDU with a normal ASCII code and two RS-232 serial interfaces. One interface receives the line from its predecessor in the daisy chain (or the processor). The other interface relays the line signals to its successor in the chain. To operate, the user constructs a message on the screen using the normal keys plus a number of special editing keys (cursor movement, selective erase, delete and/or insert character or line, etc.). On completing the message (as assembled in the VDU's internal memory), the operator presses the XMIT (transmit) key which signals readiness to transmit when next polled. The VDU must wait (with locked keyboard) until a transmission has been invited by the processor.

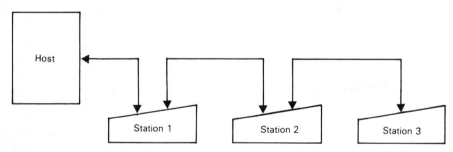

Figure 8-9   Polling

Three local stations connected in multidrop mode to a processor. A serial RS-232 full-duplex line is daisy-chained from station to station.

Each 425 in the chain has a hard-wired address which is used by the processor when polling. For example, to poll the terminal with hexadecimal address 5F, the polling sequence would be SOH, 5F, ENQ (ASCII codes). The message is received by all terminals. The SOH turns off-line any terminal which may have been on-line, and readies all terminals to listen for their call sign. Only terminal 5F responds to this sequence — on hearing its address, that terminal 'comes on-line'. That same terminal responds to the ENQ (inquiry symbol) either with an EOT (if it has no pending message to transmit) or with the entire message if one is waiting. In the latter case the 425 appends an ETX symbol to the end of the message to tell the processor that the message has ended and that it may continue polling the other terminals.

Polling protocols may be enhanced by the inclusion of error detecting/correcting components as well as time-out provisions for terminals which become inactive as a result of hardware malfunction.

Benefits of polling systems

Provided that the proposed polling system meets the demands of traffic volume and operator service times, polling can offer the following advantages:

- There is only one interface required at the processor to handle the complete cluster of terminals.
- Additional terminals may be added to the cluster without extensive recabling or hardware modifications to the processor.
- The processor determines the maximum volume of traffic which it is required to process. Accordingly, the operating system software should be simpler and be less liable to the effects of transient traffic overload.
- A single cable may service an entire cluster in a multidrop fashion. Some terminals allow for daisy chaining.

Disadvantages of polling

The primary disadvantage is the extra cost of each terminal. The terminal must contain additional logic to deal with the polling protocol and the terminal's responses to polling messages. A lesser problem is that the associated processor software must contend with noisy lines and unresponsive or missing terminals.

8.5 COMMUNICATION NETWORKS

A *communications network* is a system comprising a number of terminal points which are able to communicate with each other through a series of lines and switching facilities. The switching may be 'hard' or 'soft'. The switched network is hard switched in the sense that the exchange responds to dialled information by establishing a direct one-to-one link between the caller and the called party. Soft switching refers to the establishment of logical or 'virtual' circuits within a network designed to carry digital messages. The terminals within a network can be user display terminals, intelligent terminals, unattended data acquisition devices, mass storage devices, printers, or full computer systems. Indeed any hardware capable of interacting with the network may be described as a terminal. A terminal is not normally concerned with the routing of messages through the network on behalf of other terminals. This latter function is the responsibility of 'nodes'. Nodes may however have their own local terminals.

Interaction with a network presupposes a common language or protocol. In view of the propensity for networks to grow and to be linked to other networks, considerable effort has been directed towards the establishment of standard network protocols. The early popularity of small-scale or local networks gave birth to a wide range of network protocols designed to improve communication efficiency and ease of interfacing. A number of manufacturers developed and marketed network packages for use with their own hardware (e.g. Digital's DECNET), but most were at variance with protocols being developed by the International Standards Organization. It may be noted that ISO comprises standards groups from over 20 countries. In particular, data communications standards are developed by ISO Technical Committee 97.

Protocols concern several levels (or 'layers') of communication. At the lowest level is the specification of the electrical/physical interface between the data terminal equipment (DTE) and data circuit-terminating equipment (DCE). Particular standards at this level include CCITT recommendations V24 (telephone networks) and X21 (data networks). These recommendations also define methods for establishing, maintaining, and disconnecting the link between a DTE and another DTE or DCE. The International Consultative Committee for Telegraph and Telephone (CCITT) is a Geneva-based part of the International Telecommunications Union. At the second level are protocols defining the data structures used in communicating over a single link between two points. Examples of such standards are the Advanced Data Communication Control Procedures (ADCCP), the ISO High Level Data Link Control (HDLC), and IBM's Synchronous Data Link Control (SDLC). These standards generally define the packaging of messages for transmission in synchronous mode. HDLC and SDLC are described in more detail in Subsection 8.5.5.

The nodes in a network are generally processors capable of rerouting packaged messages to other nodes or terminals. In addition, a node may provide computing or information-processing services in response to packaged requests. Third level protocols relate to communication procedures between adjacent nodes or DTEs, while the fourth level concerns mechanisms for linking end user/node to user/node across a network. This requires addressing, verification, and routing control.

The CCITT recommendation X25 for packet-switched services is an example of an implementation of the first three levels.

8.5.1 Systems Network Architecture (SNA)

SNA is a network protocol developed and marketed by IBM and is described in IBM document GA27-3102. A useful comparison of SNA and X25 may be found in Corr & Neal (1979). An excellent overview of SNA is provided in Fitzgerald & Eason (1978). SNA protocols encompass the four levels already described and another three levels:

- Level 5 — Transmission and data flow control
- Level 6 — Presentation services
- Level 7 — End user

Level 5 activates and deactivates SNA sessions between end users. Data flow control enforces dialog between end users. The presentation services level (6) provides data formats (e.g. code translation, VDU display functions, printer control functions). The end user level (7) is a person or process requiring the SNA network. External end users may be human operators; internal end users may be node-resident application programs.

In general, end users request functions or services which may be provided by a named element within the network. A network name is associated with each physical unit, logical unit, and link within the system. Describing SNA as an 'overall system solution', IBM claims the following benefits:

- Improved response time
- Decreased communication line costs
- Decreased main processor load
- Attachment independence
- Device independence
- Configuration flexibility

A key concept of SNA is the division of the communication system functions into a set of well-defined logical layers corresponding closely to those just described. This layer structure (or macro-modularization) allows changes to be made in one layer without implications for other layers. It also allows interactions between functionally paired layers in different units. The transmission of information from one addressable unit in the network to another proceeds along the following lines:

- The unit creates a request unit (RU) which is passed to the transmission layer.
- Transmission control prefixes a request header (RH) to form a basic information unit (BIU).
- Path control prefixes a transmission header (TH) to the BIU forming a single basic transmission unit (BTU).
- Data-link control prefixes a link header and appends a link trailer to form the basic link unit (BLU) which is transmitted over a line to the first node in the transmission route.
- The node data-link control strips off the line header and trailer and replaces the TH in readiness for the next transmission. The link header and trailer are then restored and the BLU is transmitted to the next node, and so on.
- The final (target) node strips the headers and the trailer, passing the original RU to the target element.

The higher levels of SNA allow for complete user-to-user communication. X21, SDLC, and X25 encompass only the lower levels of SNA, and of themselves do not assure full communications ability between end users.

8.5.2 AUSTPAC

An example of a public packet-switching network is Australia's AUSTPAC system. Packet switching is the routing of data in discrete quantities called packets. Each packet has a controlled format and a maximum size. The AUSTPAC specifications support soft switching of packets, allowing high-speed links to be shared between multiple users through the use of multiplexing methods. Broadly, each packet consists of a formatted header (containing addresses, control information, etc.), a block of data (up to 1024 bits), followed by an error-checking 16-bit sum.

DTEs access AUSTPAC through locally called nodes. DTEs may be special packet-mode terminals (conforming to X25) connecting to the node via the Datel (switched network) or the Digital Data Network link. More conventional asynchronous terminals may also access the network provided they are connected to the node's PAD (Packet Assembly/Disassembly) facility in accordance with CCITT recommendation X3 and conventions X28. Present Datel services support this connection. Certain synchronous-mode DTEs may also access the network although they are not compatible with X25. The network is illustrated in Figure 8–10. Telecom (Australia) anticipates likely uses in areas where:

- A large number of users transmit small volumes of data over long distances
- A large number of widely dispersed terminals access a common host computer in interactive mode with long pauses between accesses
- There is a requirement for communication between terminals with incompatible characteristics (speed, code, protocol, etc.)
- Terminals need to access more than one host

Telecom (Aust.) expects that AUSTPAC will be found more suitable for current and/or developing requirements of those who presently use the following data communications applications:

- Timesharing and other types of resource sharing
- Access to databases and information services
- Credit checking
- Remote job entry
- Travel reservation
- Order entry, stock control, goods handling
- Management information systems

8.5.3 The Australian MIDAS Service

In 1979, Australia's Overseas Telecommunications Commission (OTC) established a multiplexed wide-band trans-Pacific satellite link so that Australian users could make low-cost connection to a wide range of computing networks such as Tymnet and Lockheed's Dialog database. These networks carry large database

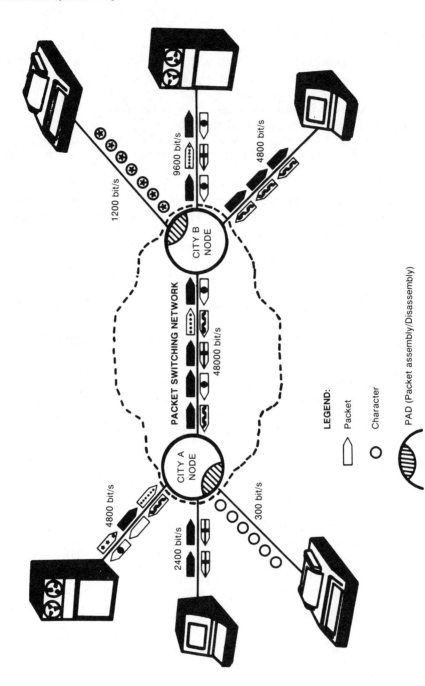

Figure 8–10 AUSTPAC network illustrating potential DTEs

facilities to assist research workers and librarians in literature surveys, etc. Users are charged the standard US fee by the network host plus a connection fee set by OTC based on connection time and the amount of data transmitted. The service is reviewed briefly in MIDAS (1980).

8.5.4 The ARPA Network

ARPANET was the world's first major communications network and provided the groundwork for many subsequent systems. It is a large-scale distributed computer network employing a packet-switching technique developed for the Advanced Research Projects Agency (ARPA) of the US Department of Defence. By 1976 the ARPANET had grown to a 57-node network spanning the continental United States from its beginnings as a 4-node system in 1969. In 1978 the network included 73 trunk lines, more than 100 host computers and about 800 terminals.

In spite of frequent software and hardware developments, including major changes in protocols, the ARPANET users report excellent system uptime and reliability. Users include Xerox, UCLA, Rand, Stanford University, and SDC on the west coast; MIT, MITRE Corp., the Lincoln Lab., Harvard, and the Pentagon on the east coast. Satellite circuits link Hawaii and London into the network. Additional information may be found in McQuillan (1976).

8.5.5 Some Synchronous Protocols

At level two of SNA is a requirement for a specific link control, SDLC. Other link control systems may be employed by non-SNA systems. The most elementary of these is Binary Synchronous (Bisync), an IBM protocol for half-duplex links. Bisync provides a set of rules for the synchronous transmission of binary-coded data. It can be used to communicate a variety of transmission codes on a wide range of medium-speed and high-speed equipment. Bisync employs common control characters for formatting text, indicating status, synchronizing functions, and error control. Interframe timing is provided by filler SYN characters.

SDLC (Synchronous Data Link Control) is a more recent protocol also developed by IBM (see IBM document GA27-3093). Unlike Bisync, which is character oriented, SDLC is bit-string oriented. It is more efficient than Bisync, and is more suitable for computer-based data communications. It supports both full-duplex and half-duplex loads. HDLC (High-level Data Link Control) is also a full-duplex protocol. Like SDLC it is bit oriented. The concepts of HDLC are built on the experience of SDLC and support the routing of data through complex networks.

Synchronous data link control (SDLC)

SDLC is an IBM protocol designed for point-to-point communication over half-duplex or full-duplex links although multipoint or loop links may also be used. The basic level of communication is the 'frame' within which all data are transmitted in binary synchronous form. Bit synchronism is the responsibility of either the modem or the data terminal. SDLC has a basic structure which governs the function and use of control procedures. This basic structure includes:

- Definitions of primary and secondary station responsibilities
- Definitions of the transmission states affecting information transfer
- Designs for information grouping for control and checking
- Formats for the transfer of information and control data

Once established, the data communication channel may be idling or active. A full-duplex link may be idle in one direction but active in the other. A channel is active when carrying data link control or data signals. All information in SDLC is transmitted in groups of one or more frames. Each frame is checked for transmission errors. At the group level the frame sequence is checked for missing or duplicated frames. Each transmitted frame carries a three-bit sequence number. This number starts at zero, advances by one and 'wraps' from seven back to zero. The receiving station checks this sequence. The receiver holds the sequence number of the last correctly received frame and reports this value regularly (at least every seven frames) back to the transmitter. In this manner the sender unit may retransmit those frames missing or in error.

Each frame has a basic bit sequence structure:

- A flag (hexadecimal 7E)
- An eight-bit address
- An eight-bit control byte
- An optional variable-length information field
- A 16-bit CRC checkfield
- A terminating flag (hexadecimal 7E)

Although the information field may be any number of bits in length, most applications of SDLC use multiples of eight bits. The hexadecimal 7E flag sequence cannot appear by chance between the flags since the protocol requires an additional zero bit to be inserted after the transmission of five consecutive ones. This device not only avoids creating false flags, but also assists the maintenance of bit-synchronism. The receiver deletes the excess zeros.

Before discussing the address field it should be noted that SDLC specifies two types of station: primary and secondary. The primary is the control station for the data link and thus has responsibility for the overall network. There is only one predetermined primary. All other stations assume secondary status and 'speak only when spoken to'. The primary polls the secondaries for responses. The message from the primary contains the required secondary's eight-bit address in the address field. When responding, the secondary uses its own address in that field. The primary needs no identification. This ensures that the primary knows which of many secondaries is responding since the primary may have many messages outstanding at various secondary stations.

The control byte defines the format of the frame. There are three basic formats: supervisory, information transfer, and non-sequenced. The supervisory format conveys 'ready', 'busy', or sequence error conditions; it has no information field. The non-sequenced format is used for data link management (activating/initializing secondary stations, procedural error reporting). The CRC field is used to validate all the fields lying between the flags of a frame.

SDLC specifies procedures for the handling of timeouts (non-responsive terminals), unrecoverable errors, aborts, and recoveries from half-duplex data links.

High-level data link control (HDLC)

HDLC is a protocol built on SDLC concepts. HDLC views a network as a more-or-less homogeneous structure to which computers and terminals may be interfaced. HDLC is more general than SDLC, and consists of a set of permissible standards, rather than defining a single standard: SDLC is a true subset of HDLC.

As with SDLC, HDLC can require a primary/secondary network structure in which one DTE is assigned the role of primary. HDLC also supports primary/primary structures, which are essentially two-point symmetrical systems. This structure permits the interconnection of two networks since neither is required to be 'in control'. The frames of HDLC are very similar to those of SDLC. Two flags enclose the frame; however an HDLC frame contains a packet header situated between the control byte and the information field. The 16-bit packet header contains a 4-bit ID (specifying type of destination) and a 12-bit 'logical channel number' or 'virtual circuit number'. Logical channel numbers are assigned to permanent (as distinct from switched) virtual circuits. HDLC enables the user of a computing network to regard that network as a resource in its own right. There is less emphasis on the whereabouts of a required file or resource.

The Intel 8273 SDLC/HDLC Protocol Controller is a single-chip controller designed to handle both protocols, enabling relatively simple DTEs to participate in a network structure (see Beaston, 1978).

8.5.6 Timesharing Operating Systems

Computing resources sited at network nodes may handle both batch and interactive user applications. Timesharing operating systems allow a single processor to service the needs of multiple interactive users. The essence of timesharing is the successive allocation of small units of computer time (time slices) to each interactive user. The software module responsible for these time allocations is a 'scheduler'.

In a typical timesharing environment, tens of users may be logged individually into the system, some at local DTEs, others at remote DTEs. The timesharing operating system is not concerned with user proximity. Provided the user is validated, that DTE is accepted for service.

Timesharing schedulers vary widely in the choice of scheduling algorithms. A simple algorithm known as 'round-robin' dedicates a standard time slice to each user. That time slice is short enough to permit a complete cycle of all users in at least two seconds, yet is long enough to reduce the portion of computer time lost through the overheads of switching from one user to the next. A hardware clock is frequently used to control this switching operation. Should a user program initiate an input-output operation, the scheduler terminates the time slice at that point since the remainder of the allocation would normally be unproductive. Some scheduler designs rely entirely on input-output operations to define user switch points. More sophisticated algorithms employ priority systems which give preference to particular users or tasks (e.g. those with heavy input-output loads).

The timesharing of a single user's application program across more than one processor in a network is not practicable unless those processors are close enough to be able to share common on-line mass storage.

8.6 COMMON CARRIER SERVICES

In the United States, common information carriers are licensed and regulated by the US Federal Communications Commission (FCC); these organizations provide communications services across the country.

8.6.1 Telecom (Australia) Lines

In Australia, Telecom is the sole common carrier. Telecom also acts as a regulatory body, determining and enforcing communications practices using its facilities. Along with corresponding organizations throughout the world, Telecom aims at ensuring compatability and ease of interfacing between different national systems.

Several line types are available from Telecom, which can be conveniently grouped into four operating styles.

Telex. Telex is an Australia-wide public system of communication, providing point-to-point teleprinter connection. It operates at 50 baud, and uses the Baudot code. Telex is generally an unattended service — it gives automatic connection facilities. Each machine has an individual line and number, and subscribers may make and receive direct international calls via OTC facilities. Telex is ideally suited to low-volume traffic. Direct computer connection and handshaking using an approved interface is permitted by Telecom, and such operations are ideally suited to low data rate collection and inquiry systems.

Private telegraph. Point-to-point and, to some extent, multidrop, telegraph systems are available on a private rental basis. Remote control equipment and receive/transmit facilities are all provided for direct connection to this network. The two speeds available are 50 baud and 75 baud (Baudot code) with asynchronous transmission. Very successful computer-controlled data and message-switching systems have been established on this network.

Switched network. Although the public Telex service works over switched networks, the switched telephone network refers to data services which are accessed by phone-dialling techniques and (generally) operator intervention. Data equipment is attached to the switched telephone network by modems as described in Sub-section 8.3.3.

Private leased lines. Signalling speeds of 2400 baud and higher require better line fidelity than can be assured in the switched telephone network. This is usually achieved by using private (dedicated) lines. Private lines are also preferable when large volumes of traffic requiring long periods of connection are needed. Added to this, some computer-signalling techniques cannot be satisfactorily operated with the setup/signalling delays which occur on switched lines.

Whenever line-connect time approaches or exceeds 40 hours per week, private line connection should be investigated. Telecom provides traffic officers at the line exchange to switch or patch part-time services. However, part-time users run the risk of time extensions not being available, and possibly being difficult to arrange at short notice.

Data rates in excess of 1200 baud or multidrop operations between local and distant offices generally require private lines.

8.6.2 Australian Datel Services

Datel services provided by Telecom (Aust.) include the connecting link (private line or switched network) and modem. A range of Datel services is available according to particular applications, speed of transmission and response, and the volume of traffic. In general, DTEs must be connected to the Telecom network through Telecom modems. A Permit-to-Connect is required for each DTE. Common carrying and message switching on behalf of other organizations is not permitted.

Datel services conform to international specifications (V24 for speeds up to 9600 baud, and V35 for the 48 kilobit/second service). If the standard switched telephone network is used, facilities are available for the following options:

- 300 baud — asynchronous transmission, full-duplex or half-duplex
- 600/1200 baud — synchronous or asynchronous, full-duplex or half-duplex; half-duplex supports an additional backwards channel at 75 baud
- 2400 and 4800 baud — synchronous transmission and half-duplex

A specially designed telephone handset (Datelphone) provides control functions and status lamps for use in conjunction with the 300 and 600/1200 baud services. If private lines are used, Datel services also include full-duplex at the 600/1200 and 2400 baud rates as well as a 9600 baud and 48 000 baud synchronous full-duplex service.

REFERENCES

ANON., 'MIDAS in Retrospect — the First Eighteen Months', *Australian Computer Bulletin*, November 1980, p. 12.

J. BEASTON, *Using the 8273 SDLC/HDLC Protocol Controller*, Intel Corp., Santa Clara, Calif., 1978.

F.P. CORR & D.H. NEAL, 'SNA and Emerging International Standards', *IBM Systems Journal*, vol. 18, no. 2, 1979, pp. 244-62.

J. FITZGERALD & T.S. EASON, *Fundamentals of Data Communications*, Wiley/Hamilton, New York, 1978.

T. HOUSLEY, *Data Communications and Teleprocessing Systems*, Prentice-Hall Inc., Englewood Cliffs, N.J., 1979.

J. MARTIN, *Introduction to Teleprocessing*, Prentice-Hall Inc., Englewood Cliffs, N.J., 1972.

J.M. McQUILLAN, 'A Status Report on the ARPANET', *Proc. ACS Joint International Symposium on Data Communications Technology and Practice*, 1976, pp. 61-8.

W.D. SCOTT, 'Telecom 2000 — An Exploration of the Long Term Development of Telecommunications in Australia', *Aust. Telecommunications Commission*, 1975, p. 179.

L. SMITH, *Using the 8251 Universal Synchronous/Asynchronous Receiver/Transmitter*, Intel Corp., Santa Clara, Calif., 1976.

9 ON-LINE AND DISTRIBUTED SYSTEMS

PART A — ON-LINE SYSTEMS DESIGN

9.1 INTRODUCTION

Not so long ago the high cost of network hardware and the lack of reliable, comprehensive, and easy-to-use network software meant that on-line systems were found only in those applications in which the level of expenditure was justified because of the need for one or more of the following characteristics:

- Remote access to a central database (e.g. airlines reservation, banking, betting systems)
- High-speed response for transactions, calculations, and/or inquiries (e.g. a quotation system to assist selling insurance policies, a sales inquiry system, plus the previous examples)
- An ability to verify the accuracy of data and to make corrections before either the originator or the subject of the data became unavailable (e.g. data collection in a complex production environment, plus the previous examples)

However, reductions in the cost of hardware and extensive systems software developments have encouraged a trend towards the use of communications-based systems for almost all types of application — apart from routine batch-oriented tasks such as envelope label printing and payroll processing. Thus, the benefits of access, speed, and prompt validation are now available to a much larger number of problem areas.

After a definition of terms, this chapter mainly deals with the question of on-line systems design techniques, network specification, and the distribution of data and processing within a network. Attention is focused on the differences between the design of batch-based systems and the design of communications-based systems.

A typical on-line system is sketched in Figure 9–1. It comprises:

- Terminals or other remote input-output devices
- Communications lines and associated equipment (the network)
- Processor and its usual peripherals
- Disk storage devices

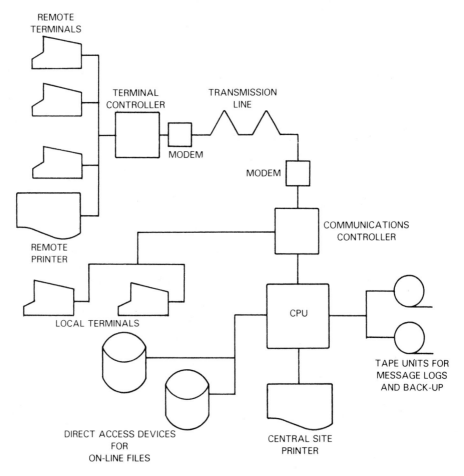

Figure 9–1   Components of an on-line system

The scale of these systems varies widely, from one or two terminals connected to a microprocessor to 1000 or more terminals linked to a network comprising several processors and databases. In this book, the term *on-line processing* implies:

- A direct connection (at least in a logical sense) between a user (a person or machine) and a computer system
- Almost immediate processing of a message or transaction
- A reply being generated which in some respect depends on the input message content — even if final processing may not occur until a later batch run

Real-time processing requires (in addition) that the reply is received within a time frame which is satisfactory for the application.

Frequently, communications systems are designated as employing 'off-line' processing when the application does not require the second or third of the on-line characteristics. An example of this would be data collection for subsequent batch processing (e.g. input via a badge reader of employee number, start or stop time for a payroll system which is processed weekly).

The major differences between batch and on-line systems, as far as they affect the systems design tasks, are:

- Direct access. The user is directly responsible for input and output of transactions in an on-line system — therefore no data clerks, or keypunch or computer operators need to be involved in data flow, as in a batch system.
- Control. Many of the controls normally relied on for data-input integrity, accuracy, and completeness in a batch system are not available in an on-line system since transactions are usually processed one by one. Therefore, it is necessary to give special attention to editing, validating, and the detection of input transactions lost or overlooked in an on-line system, since the system logic is frequently the only integrity-checking barrier between the user and the 'live' data files.
- Equipment and special software. Hardware and systems software characteristics are more important factors in the design of an on-line system and need to be considered at an earlier stage in the lifecycle of the project. This is because the characteristics of terminals, communication lines, communication interfaces, main memory and direct access storage, the CPU, communications software for message handling, and file access software all play a role in determining response times, throughput rates, and allowable operator/system dialogs.
- Human behaviour. Behavioural factors relating to operator satisfaction with the interface design and overall system logic are more important in an on-line system than in a batch system due to the close interaction and direct penetration of the on-line system into the workplace.

9.2 ON-LINE SYSTEMS DESIGN

This section presents some overall issues which are critical factors in determining the adequacy of an on-line systems design. After briefly introducing the factors which affect the system structure, the rest of the section deals with those aspects of the design which are different from those used for batch systems.

9.2.1 Overall Systems Structure

Before work on detailed aspects of either the logical or the physical systems design can commence, a number of architecture-related questions need consideration. This phase of work in an on-line application is more significant than the corresponding task in a batch environment because of the enhanced flexibility offered by the on-line approach. Usually the objectives set for the system performance can be met in a wide variety of ways, and so this determination of the overall system structure is important in narrowing the project scope to manageable proportions. Of course, as detailed design proceeds and new factors emerge, it may become desirable, or even essential, to review the earlier architecture decisions. Once the network layout and the hardware and software environment are broadly specified, work on logical and physical design can proceed as for a batch system project.

The location of input-output devices

The selection of terminal locations affects the network configuration (and therefore cost and complexity), the choice of operators' dialog, the frequency and type of messages for both input and output, and the choice of terminal hardware. Terminal numbers are most critical for those likely to be employed to input transactions (i.e. messages which result in changes to stored data) or complex inquiries. Terminals used for simple inquiries can often be added at will, since the number of them is unlikely to affect any system variable seriously (except the direct cost of the terminals and lines, of course).

The location of processing and data storage units

The systems design complexity and its ability to provide management with information reports may depend on the degree to which processing capacity and data are decentralized. The specific issues surrounding this choice are discussed more fully in Part B of this chapter, where emphasis is placed on the difficulties which can arise from distributed databases.

Choice of systems software

The technical performance of an on-line system can be measured in terms of response time, message throughput rates, and security/integrity. All of these factors are probably affected as much by the software employed for terminal driving, message routing, queue handling, database organization and access, and recovery, as by any feature of the applications software designed and written specially for the project. Consequently, the selection of these software products is critical to the ultimate success of the project.

9.2.2 Message Types

Inputs

On-line systems are normally designed to process terminal inputs or messages in the form of transactions and inquiries. Transaction messages result from an event such as a telephone call from a customer who wants to place an order, or the receipt of a payment, or the completion of a workshop task. They involve both the access and the updating of database or file records — for example, the entry and processing of a customer order or an account payment. Inquiries also require access to filed data but there is no updating of the stored record.

As well, inputs for control purposes associated with the application are required; for example:

- Logging on or off a terminal to a particular program
- Status inquiries to obtain progress reports on a job or message
- Supervisors' inquiries to check the performance of the system or specific operational aspects

These control message types are additional to those required by the systems software for network supervision.

Outputs

It is virtually standard practice in on-line systems design to require an output message for every input message. Most volume statistics are quoted in 'message-pair' units. Usually the terminal remains 'locked-up' — i.e. no further input is possible — until the reply is received. This is the case even if the input causes a 'background' or deferred-processing type of job to be initiated, for in this situation a suitable interim reply would be generated to indicate that processing had been scheduled. Therefore output messages are of the same types as inputs, i.e:

- Transaction replies — which may include edit, validate, or control information; in trivial cases an 'input received and processed OK' response is suitable — it may involve only a single-character message
- Inquiry replies — occasionally with edit, validate, or even control content if the inquiry is invalid or unauthorized
- Control/unsolicited messages — required so that the applications system can respond on a unilateral basis; examples of these messages include: the results of deferred processing jobs, system status responses, and supervisory messages dealing with incomplete input or editing operations

As for inputs, some messages originate within the communications systems software; for example, network status information (*system is going down in 5 minutes!*), or messages switched from other terminals.

9.2.3 Dialog Specification

Specification of the conversation exchange between operator and system is obviously an important factor in determining successful project outcome. Creative design of message content by the systems analyst can often improve operator acceptance of the system, the efficiency of processing, and the accuracy of input data. Factors which are important in the selection of these conversation formats include the operator characteristics, software development aids, any restrictions on terminal type or processor resources, and security and authorization.

The operator characteristics. Two attributes are important here. The first is related to the operator's familiarity with the system; and the second is the match of the operator's skill/knowledge level with the system complexity and its data flow. Obviously a full-time operator working on simple data input (e.g. entering receipt amount and relevant invoice number in an accounts-receivable application) requires less prompting and support than a part-timer entering messages with a complex structure (e.g. an accountant entering budget details at the annual financial planning period).

Software development aids. A major factor in dialog choice can be the software provided to support terminal handling. Most types of computer system now have available 'screen management' software aids which facilitate the programming of display terminals. Examples of such packages are DMS from IBM, and ITC from Perkin-Elmer. Without such aids, coding programs to handle complex display panels, and linking various display fields with data element names in programs, are difficult and time consuming. Therefore the systems development costs — and the future maintenance/enhancement costs — can depend heavily on how adequate these software tools are.

Restrictions on terminal type or processor resources. Clearly the complexity of the terminal device affects the allowable dialogs. Facilities such as variable-intensity display, 'block-mode' data input, two-screen buffers, automatic terminal identifiers, the ability to suppress transmission of certain fields, internal format checks, etc., enhance flexibility — at increased unit cost. Since portable terminals are normally of the printer variety, complex panels are not possible with them — nor for any typewriter terminal which is to be used interactively. Transmission line congestion, cost, or CPU buffer size restrictions may require messages to make extensive use of codes and mnemonics rather than full text entries with associated prompts.

Security and authorization. The need to keep data secure while being entered may enforce the use of special codes or encryption procedures — whereas including a password or other identifier within the dialog may be important to inhibit unauthorized file access or updating.

There are many options available to the systems analyst for dialog design (see Martin, 1973). The more common of these options are:

- Unrestricted natural language
- Restricted language
- Menus
- Question and answer

- Form filling
- Mnemonics

Unrestricted natural language

With this approach the operator is free to use any words to express the message content. It requires very sophisticated software to process the keywords in the text and transform them into an identifiable instruction or data-entry transaction.

Probably the best known example of unrestricted English language dialog is that used by 'Eliza' (Weizenbaum, 1966). This system is designed to appear as if it is responding in an intelligent way to ordinary English statements. A short analysis of a section of Eliza conversation demonstrates that the program identifies keywords and particular sentence structures and generates replies accordingly. Here is a short example of a dialog with Eliza. The user's entries are in lower case, the computer's responses in upper case.

> i don't like computers
> WHY NOT?
> because they are threatening my job
> WHAT KIND OF WORK DO YOU DO?
> i am a lecturer
> WHY ARE YOU A LECTURER?
> because i like to talk
> YOU LIKE TO TALK??? THAT IS INCREDIBLE
> is it?
> WHY ARE YOU ASKING ME QUESTIONS, I AM THE ONE WHO IS
> SUPPOSED TO ASK QUESTIONS
> sorry, but computers are a worry
> DO COMPUTERS WORRY YOU?
> yes
> I WISH I WERE AS SURE OF MYSELF AS YOU SEEM TO BE
> but the computer is able to replace lecturers' work
> DO YOU LIKE COMPUTERS?
> they are ok i guess. it's the programmers that are the difficulty
> WHAT DO YOU THINK ABOUT PROGRAMMERS?
> they are only interested in their own little lives
> WHAT ARE YOU MOST INTERESTED IN LIFE?
> i want to be able to develop my courses to improve the standard of education
> WHY DO YOU WANT TO BE ABLE TO DEVELOP YOUR COURSES TO
> IMPROVE THE STANDARD OF EDUCATION?
> there is a real need for this
> HOW DO YOU KNOW THERE IS A REAL NEED FOR THIS?
> everyone i talk to says that education is the key to a stable future
> EVERYONE?
> well, those i talk to
> SURELY YOU CAN THINK OF AN EXCEPTION
> my brother is one, he's a farmer
> TELL ME ABOUT YOUR SIBLINGS
> i am very happy with my son

DOES YOUR MOTHER KNOW YOU ARE VERY HAPPY WITH YOUR SON?
yes but what does that have to do with computers?
YOU ARE ALWAYS MAKING EXCUSES
computers are my main worry
DO YOU THINK THAT A COMPUTER IS AFTER YOUR JOB?
how did you know?
SURELY YOU KNOW HOW
i was just checking
YOU ACT LIKE A COMPUTER

A system designed to understand unrestricted imprecise dialog would need to respond, when the message is unclear, with a request for further details. Frequently it is necessary to reformat the request in a standard form and ask for confirmation. An example is this conversation between a supervisor (lower case) and a computer (upper case):

i'd like to know how many bolts are in stock which fit part number AD-3679
I INTERPRET YOUR REQUEST AS PRINT STOCK HOLDING FOR BOLTS OF PART AD-3679
yes
PART NUMBER AD-3679 USES 3 BOLTS: 50 mm, 112 mm, AND 130 mm. WHICH IS REQUIRED?
50 mm
THERE ARE 1725 50 mm BOLTS IN STOCK

Normally the effort required to program such a system, as well as high processing overhead, makes such an approach infeasible.

Research in the fields of artificial intelligence, automatic translation, and other related topics may yet provide solutions to syntactic analysis which are feasible in terms of coding complexity and hardware cost. For the present, the on-line designer must look to more structured approaches for practical systems.

Restricted language

A much more common approach is to permit a restricted language subset to be input, usually in a defined format. An inquiry conversation frequently comprises two parts:

- The qualifier, with the format:
  OPERATOR : DATA ELEMENT NAME : VALUE
  Examples:
  FIND : EMPLOYEE NUMBER = 5694
  WHERE : SALESMAN = JONES OR SMITH

- The instruction, with the format:
  VERB : DATA ELEMENTS OR VARIABLES

Examples:

PRINT : EMPLOYEE NAME, SALARY, POSITION

SUM : SALES AND PRINT 'TOTAL SALES =' , SUM

These types of dialog find considerable use within self-contained inquiry packages which work with DBMS systems. The qualifier segment defines the database elements which 'qualify' for further processing, while the instruction segment determines what is to be done with those elements.

For transaction input purposes a similar approach can be used which defines the variable to be input and then gives details of value, quantity, etc. As an example:

Operator: Receipt, valves type 5941, quantity 500, cost $158.72

Computer: TRANSACTION COMPLETE

In practice, although the restricted language approach is common in inquiry situations, its use for data acquisition/transactions processing is relatively rare. This is because the relatively free format causes programming complexity and introduces data control problems. Simple format errors or field omissions made by the operator can be difficult to detect. This difficulty is not critical in an inquiry mode, since the problem is normally apparent to the operator when examining the response — or when no response at all is obtained! In file-update mode, however, an error may not be detected for some time — and the integrity of the database may be compromised.

Anyone who has worked with these types of dialog is aware that it can be a frustrating experience unless the dialog is 'user friendly'. Points to watch are:

- Format flexibility. Ensure that embedded blanks, capital letters, etc. can be tolerated even if they are not part of the actual data-element name or record content.
- Spelling tolerance. Attempt to 'forgive' simple spelling and punctuation errors, for example, by proposing a 'correct' inquiry and asking for acceptance by the operator.
- Major errors. Where an irrecoverable error is introduced by the operator, make correcting easy by not requiring the full query to be re-entered.
- Help. Provide a help facility which describes allowable formats, qualifiers, and instructions — and also data-element details.

Menus

The menu is a basic tool in the dialog design kit. Its great virtue is that it allows simplified access to the complex logic which often surrounds a real-time on-line system. It is used in two basic situations:

- Subsystem selection
- Category or option selection

Subsystems of an on-line applications environment are collections of programs/ routines designed to handle specific types of transactions and/or inquiry. For example, an inventory/warehousing application may include the following sub- systems:

- Goods receipt
- Stock adjustment/customer returns
- Order processing
- Warehouse despatch/invoicing
- Order inquiry
- Stock inquiry
- Order history analysis
- Customer-detail file create/maintenance
- Product file create/maintenance

In a typical application an operator would be invited to nominate one of these subsystems via a 'master menu' after logging on with a valid ID code to the system. Usually selection is performed by entering the appropriate line number at the bottom of the menu list. Frequently, a second menu is displayed to allow selection at a second level of detail. Once the desired transaction/inquiry environment has been nominated, the dialog usually takes on a second format to handle the actual processing.

Category or option selection is a valuable technique for cutting down on operator-input keystrokes and improving accuracy. It can be utilized when a particular field or data element, to be included in a transaction, is to be selected from a list. For example, in entering new customer data the system may need an industry classification. Rather than force the operator to consult a code book or decide on an appropriate value, the menu technique could be invoked:

        Computer: Industry Classification
                        1. Manufacturing — light
                        2. Manufacturing — heavy
                        3. Retail
                        4. Transport
                        5. Service
                        6. Education
                        7. Construction
                        8. Government (Federal)
                        9. Government (State or local)
                        10. Other
        Operator: 7

The menu approach can rapidly achieve great depth of classification, through the use of multiple levels of a tree-structured logic such as in Figure 9–2, which shows how a succession of menus might be employed to identify the agent closest to a new customer's location. The operator's entries are underlined, and the symbol ▲ indicates that the transmission key has been depressed at that position.

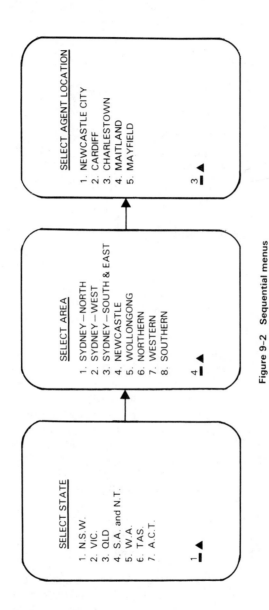

Figure 9-2 Sequential menus

The menu approach can be developed to a high level of complexity, especially by using multiple menus, with the operator requested to select an option from each in order to specify a transaction — Figure 9–3 shows an example of this. One advantage of this technique for simple terminals is the lack of complex formats — so it is easily employed on a teletype or similar printing device.

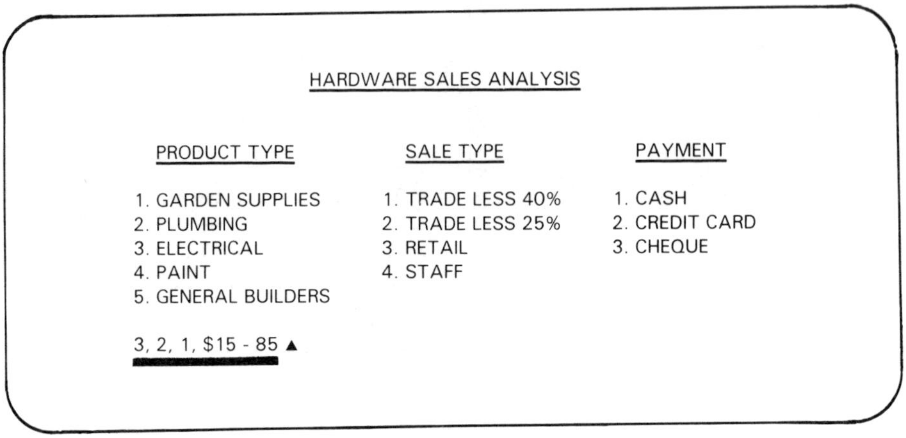

HARDWARE SALES ANALYSIS

PRODUCT TYPE	SALE TYPE	PAYMENT
1. GARDEN SUPPLIES	1. TRADE LESS 40%	1. CASH
2. PLUMBING	2. TRADE LESS 25%	2. CREDIT CARD
3. ELECTRICAL	3. RETAIL	3. CHEQUE
4. PAINT	4. STAFF	
5. GENERAL BUILDERS		

3, 2, 1, $15 - 85 ▲

Figure 9-3   Multiple menus

Question and answer

The Q–A dialog technique is particularly useful when operators are unskilled or unfamiliar with the application. The technique simply involves the computer controlling the sequencing of transaction or inquiry formulation by a series of questions or prompts. Often the particular sequence (and the amount of detail included in the questions) is predetermined using a menu before the Q–A session commences. Thus an operator may speed up the process by requesting the 'experienced' user's dialog rather than the 'novice'. As an example, drawn from the accounts-payable system environment:

COMPUTER: Select subsystem
    1. Accounts receivable
    2. Accounts payable
    3. Costing
    4. General ledger
OPERATOR: 2
COMPUTER: Accounts-payable subsystem
    Select function required:
    1. Enter new supplier fixed details
    2. Inquire on supplier fixed details
    3. Enter account/payment data
    4. Inquire account history
OPERATOR: 1

```
COMPUTER:    Enter supplier name — number allocated is 15897
OPERATOR:    John Smith Pty Limited
COMPUTER:    1st address line
OPERATOR:    15 Maple Drive
COMPUTER:    2nd address line
OPERATOR:    Campbelltown
COMPUTER:    State
OPERATOR:    N.S.W.
COMPUTER:    Postcode
OPERATOR:    2560
```

Clearly this is tedious for all but the most casual, inexperienced operator. Equally, the dialog can be speeded up by seeking responses on the same line, using abbreviations, and allowing multiple field responses.

As with all other dialog designs it is necessary to pay close attention to accuracy and the maintenance of operator goodwill. Frequently changing dialog format to and from Q–A and menu a number of times can be effective — especially where a specific format of reply is desired for subsequent processing. For example, state may be obtained using a menu to be certain that the formats N.S.W., Qld, Vic., etc. are obtained rather than other representations such as Victoria, Q'land, etc., which may make subsequent searching difficult. For typewriter terminals or other non-buffered devices, the Q–A dialog is virtually mandatory where significant prompting is needed. However, video display terminals with buffers provide an alternative which is usually preferred by both designers and operators: form filling.

Form filling

Most of the terminals now used for commercial applications are of the video display type, with a buffer which can store at least one screen of characters — located either within the terminal or in a cluster controller which services a number of remote devices. The form-filling capabilities of a system depend both on the terminal's characteristics and the programs used to perform message handling.

This dialog technique involves displaying a 'form' on the screen; this form is often called a screen format or a panel. The operator is required to 'fill in the blanks' with transaction details. The format of each panel's field is usually specified in terms of alpha/numeric type characters and length, together with allowable range limits if appropriate. These characteristics are checked by the terminal microprocessor, cluster controller, or communications software depending on the type of network system installed. Checking may take place immediately a field is entered, or when processing the whole panel is initiated. To avoid excessive use of the space bar, the tab facility is usually employed to jump from the end of one field to the beginning of the next until the TRANSMIT function is required. Often, an exchange between an operator and a computer requires several message pairs, with each successive pair gradually building up the complete panel. The example dialog, shown in Figures 9–4 to 9–7, is drawn from an inventory application. The operator's entries are underlined; ▲ indicates TRANSMIT, and ⭡ indicates the cursor position.

WAREHOUSE SUBSYSTEMS

1. STOCK INQUIRY
2. GOODS RECEIPT
3. DESPATCH
4. STOCK ADJUSTMENTS

2 ▲

Figure 9-4   Warehouse master menu

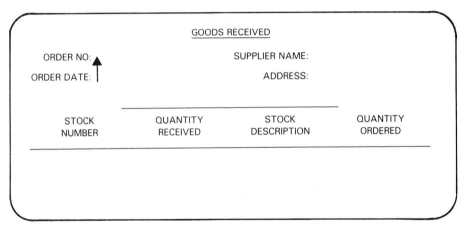

GOODS RECEIVED

ORDER NO: ▲   SUPPLIER NAME:
ORDER DATE: | ADDRESS:

STOCK NUMBER	QUANTITY RECEIVED	STOCK DESCRIPTION	QUANTITY ORDERED

Figure 9-5   Blank panel

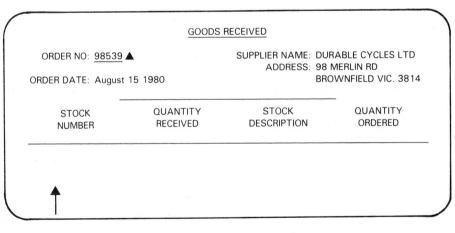

GOODS RECEIVED

ORDER NO: 98539 ▲   SUPPLIER NAME: DURABLE CYCLES LTD
                                                                    ADDRESS: 98 MERLIN RD
ORDER DATE: August 15 1980   BROWNFIELD VIC. 3814

STOCK NUMBER	QUANTITY RECEIVED	STOCK DESCRIPTION	QUANTITY ORDERED

▲

Figure 9-6   First message pair

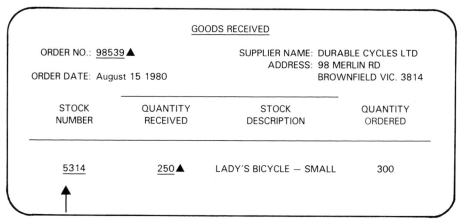

GOODS RECEIVED

ORDER NO.: 98539 ▲

SUPPLIER NAME: DURABLE CYCLES LTD
ADDRESS: 98 MERLIN RD

ORDER DATE: August 15 1980

BROWNFIELD VIC. 3814

STOCK NUMBER	QUANTITY RECEIVED	STOCK DESCRIPTION	QUANTITY ORDERED
5314	250 ▲	LADY'S BICYCLE — SMALL	300

Figure 9–7   Second message pair

Initially the master menu is displayed and, subsequently, a warehouse goods receipt panel is completed with two message pairs involved. Alternatively, a complete panel may be created by the operator before being transmitted as a block of data entry. See Figure 9–8 for an example involving the input batch of goods received. Note that with this approach a control total may be called for to assist in detecting errors.

As with the Q–A dialog, it can be beneficial to include a menu as part of the dialog when the operator has several options open, but is unclear which to take. For example, consider the part-description search covered in Figures 9–9 and 9–10 which could take place when the operator does not know the item number to complete the panel in Figure 9–7 and so enters part of the description field with 'cycle' (a field normally completed by the computer). This abnormal entry would trigger a file search followed by a menu output to facilitate selection of the correct item. Similarly, a new panel could be displayed if needed; for example, after the stage reached with the panel in Figure 9–7, a new panel might be used to determine what should be done about the discrepancy of 50 units between receipt and order quantities. This could be a useful input error detection and correction procedure.

Error conditions, when detected, can be handled in many ways. One of the most popular approaches is to write a message — possibly blinking on and off — at the bottom of the screen, while returning the cursor to the start of the field in error. The operator should not have to re-enter any correct fields. Some systems display a menu of possible corrections when an invalid field is found.

Mnemonics

Although form filling can be quite efficient as an input technique when full use is made of the tab facility and transmission of 'constant' fields is suppressed, the dialog approach most often favoured for high-volume and structured transactions makes extensive use of mnemonic abbreviations. This shorthand form is normally used for both operator and computer sides of the conversation. The airlines reservation application is typical of the environment which can employ this approach with benefit:

GOODS RECEIVED

ORDER NO: 81417

STOCK NUMBER	QUANTITY RECEIVED
1581	210
2471	100
3549	10
7854	96
9514	5

TOTAL UNITS RECEIVED: 421 ▲

Figure 9-8   Multiple line entry

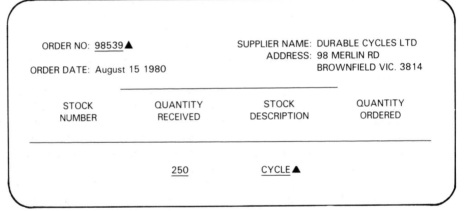

ORDER NO: 98539 ▲   SUPPLIER NAME: DURABLE CYCLES LTD
                                    ADDRESS: 98 MERLIN RD
ORDER DATE: August 15 1980   BROWNFIELD VIC. 3814

STOCK NUMBER	QUANTITY RECEIVED	STOCK DESCRIPTION	QUANTITY ORDERED
	250	CYCLE ▲	

Figure 9-9   Stock number not known

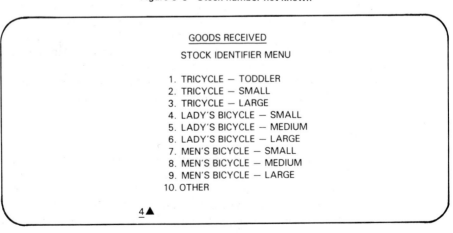

GOODS RECEIVED

STOCK IDENTIFIER MENU

1. TRICYCLE — TODDLER
2. TRICYCLE — SMALL
3. TRICYCLE — LARGE
4. LADY'S BICYCLE — SMALL
5. LADY'S BICYCLE — MEDIUM
6. LADY'S BICYCLE — LARGE
7. MEN'S BICYCLE — SMALL
8. MEN'S BICYCLE — MEDIUM
9. MEN'S BICYCLE — LARGE
10. OTHER

4 ▲

Figure 9-10   Menu for operator assistance (leads to Figure 9-7)

- The operators are experienced, full-time staff who have been trained in the full use of the system
- The application itself is well-structured, involving a limited range of possible input and response types
- Message frequencies are high with a consequent need to minimize data-transmission volumes

Examples of panels used in this application, with explanatory notes, are shown in Figures 9–11 and 9–12; they were provided by Qantas Airways. Because of the brevity of the messages, the mnemonic technique is quite applicable to all types of terminals.

9.2.4   Response Characteristics

The most visible performance indicator for an on-line system is the response time — that is, the time between the TRANSMIT key depression and the arrival of the system's reply. It is affected by transmission delays, internal system queueing, message-processing time, and database access. Consequently any form of congestion or contention for resources shows up as an extended response delay. Tests on the relationship between response time, operator accuracy, and operation satisfaction have shown the following pattern:

Response Delay (seconds)	Comments
0–2	Good performance
2–4	Adequate performance
4–15	Operator concentration wavers and the delay is annoying
over 15	The on-line character is lost; when the reply does arrive the operator must ask 'what was the question?'

A further factor discovered by research is the apparent desire for a relatively constant (but short!) response time — so it may be desirable to actually 'slow down' a system with an artificial delay during its initial phase of operation, when volumes are low, and so avoid a drop in response time once load builds up to maximum levels.

9.2.5   Edit/Validate/Control

The nature of these three functions in systems design for the on-line environment frequently requires a different approach from that which would be

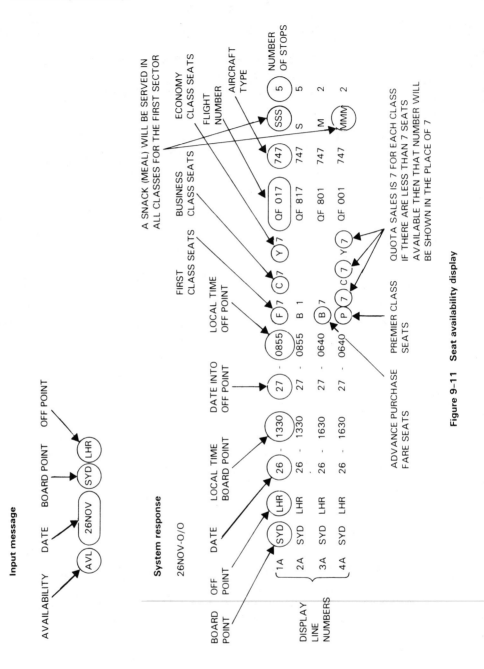

Figure 9-11   Seat availability display

adopted if the same system was being implemented using batch-type input and printed output. Techniques used for editing and validating in an on-line system are much the same as those used for batch. They include format, range, check digit, edit

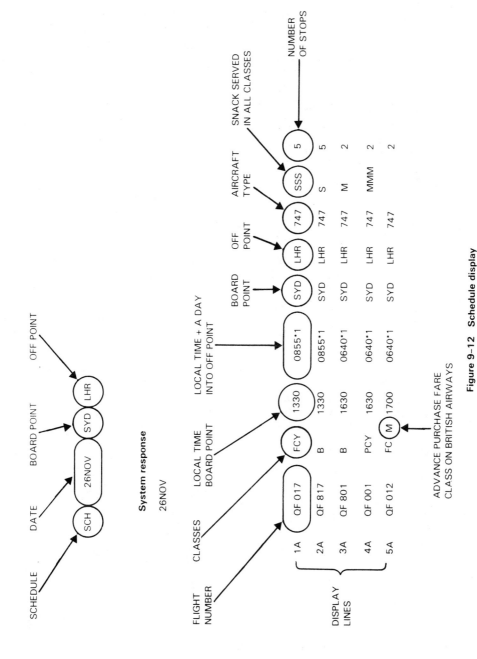

Figure 9–12 Schedule display

checks, and the normal validation against file contents (e.g. to establish that a particular customer does exist on the customer file). The difference lies in the manner by which corrections are made. Normally a data clerk, or other trained person, handles edit and validate rejects in batch mode; but for an on-line system the terminal operators must be able to correct their own data. Therefore, the procedures must be simple, comprehensive, well documented, and reliable.

The validation operation can be more difficult to control in situations where the on-line file does not contain all the details which are stored in the database. This occurs when the relevant file or database section is so voluminous that major updates are carried out in batch mode although preliminary edits and balance computations are performed on-line, with a scaled-down version of the file. An example of this situation would be a savings bank which updates the master files associated with customers' accounts on overnight batch runs, but provides an on-line service which can record current balances without maintaining a full history of transactions. The problem arises because errors, which were not apparent at the time the on-line transaction was completed, may be detected during the subsequent batch update run. Special procedures are needed to handle these types of late-detected errors (e.g. the use of a supervisor's terminal as discussed later in this sub-section).

Batch-processing controls are built around transaction counts, hash totals, and similar techniques. While these techniques can be used in some on-line input environments, for example that shown in Figure 9–8, normally a transaction involves only a single input record and therefore batch controls have no meaning. It is possible, of course, to institute controls over, say, a day's transactions — but this always causes difficulties since the files are likely to have been updated and possibly some form of action taken as a result of the input transaction. To make up for deficiencies in the controls aspect for on-line input, the designer must usually fall back on extended editing techniques, especially for those fields which constitute independent data, i.e. data which cannot be checked against file contents. Order quantities, dimensions, weights, are all examples of this variable type. A particularly valuable technique is checking the relationship between various fields — often with some of these fields intentionally added for checking purposes — i.e. they need not be present to serve the basic function of the system. An example of this technique is given in Figure 9–13, which is drawn from a warehouse despatch environment. In this case all the system is likely to require for identification of the particular transaction is the picking ticket number. The picking ticket will have been issued by

WAREHOUSE DESPATCH

ORDER NO: 8514   PICKING TICKET NO: 51489

STOCK ITEM NO: 15185   QUANTITY   58

VALUE: 1276.00 ▲

Figure 9–13   Use of redundant fields for editing

the system previously, following the ordering of the goods. By requiring input of both order number and picking ticket number it is possible to cross-check the accuracy of each. Similarly, the quantity 58 is cross-checked by requiring the operator to compute the value of the order, and to input this as well. Thus the value field and the order number field are probably redundant in this particular example. Naturally, the addition of such fields adds to the time required for data entry and may also introduce operator dissatisfaction with the system. Consequently these checks should not be introduced until a thorough evaluation is made of the advantages and disadvantages.

A useful technique for enhancing control of the on-line environment is the use of a supervisor's terminal. Frequently the designer can have difficult situations, which arise during transactions processing, brought to the attention of a supervisor with a terminal that has special system privileges. Thus, edit rejects might be overridden by a supervisor although not by an ordinary operator. Similarly, the supervisor could be regularly given a list of outstanding edit/validate errors which have not been corrected by operators — for example, an operator could walk away from a terminal with an input transaction partly complete. The supervisor's terminal can also be used to correct validate-type error rejects which arise during batch processing some time after the original input transaction has taken place.

9.2.6 Message Processing

Because most on-line systems involve either transactions or inquiry processing, the structure of the program sequence necessary to process messages is very similar for all message types. This sequence can be broken into three sections:

1. Message-checking program. A program designed to receive the message from the communications system, check any status information returned with it from the communications software, perform preliminary checks on field existence, and determine whether special facilities such as HELP have been requested at some part in the message. This program may also do some logging for audit purposes if it is felt desirable at this point.
2. The main message-processing program. The program which performs the edit, validate, and control functions, and the file read and processing operations. The reply message is likely to be generated in this program/s and further audit activity may take place.
3. File and database update. This program performs all database or file updates and completes the auditing process.

By structuring the programs in this way it is possible to achieve a good measure of standardization and commonality, particularly for program types 1 and 3. In addition, the collection of type 3 programs can be useful for back-up, auditing, and recovery from log files since these are the only programs which alter the database status.

9.2.7   File or Database Design Issues

File design techniques are covered in Chapter 3. It is intended here to high-light only the important issues likely to be encountered by the designer. The characteristics which require particular emphasis are:

- *File organization.* Speed-of-response needs must be matched against storage size limitations and the need for batch-processing subsystems which make use of the same file. This need for sequential-type batch processing often dictates an indexed sequential approach.
- *Access keys or paths.* Careful thought must be given to the design of access methods and keys. If the systems designer has not allowed for appropriate entry points into the file or database, providing new inquiry or update modes may require extensive redesign and file reorganization.
- *File control fields.* To assist in overall system control it is advisable to maintain control fields for each major file used. These fields contain control totals which are updated each time the file is changed. Routine file-integrity checks can then be carried out regularly, for example at the time back-up copies are taken.
- *Recovery.* The recovery procedure for a file or database must be effective and efficient. While most database systems provide recovery routines, they may not be suitable for the application. Use of a file-update log (including time identifiers) together with the type 3 programs discussed in Section 9.2.6 usually give a worthwhile recovery approach.
- *Batch interface.* Most often the files or database are open for read or write by the on-line system while it is operating. If this operating period is restricted to daytime shifts then batch runs on the same data — for example, summaries or long print jobs — may be performed overnight. When the on-line environment works three shifts/seven days there is a problem in obtaining a stable version of the data which can be used for batch reporting or printing.

  One solution to this difficulty is called the 'lagged transactions file system'. It is shown diagrammatically in Figure 9–14. The main file is used for batch-reporting purposes (read only) and for on-line read-only access. File updates are performed on either of two transactions files. Periodically the switch is changed so transactions accrue on the second file and a file-update routine is initiated which runs the transactions in the previously connected transactions file against the main file, thereby bringing it up-to-date at the time of the switch. With this system the main file is only out of balance for batch jobs during the short time the update routine is active.

9.3   NETWORK DESIGN ISSUES

The technical aspects of communications networks are covered in Chapter 8. This section considers the major issues faced by the systems designer in matching the network hardware to the application environment.

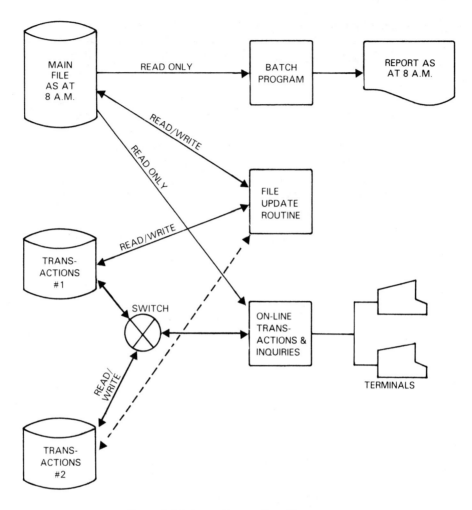

Figure 9-14   Lagged transactions file system

9.3.1   Performance Considerations

Foremost in the designer's mind when considering the options for network specification is the performance obtainable from a given hardware/software configuration. To use the vernacular, the question which must be asked is: 'Will the system hack the load?'

System performance centres around the number of message pairs which can be processed in a given time and the response characteristics. Discussion earlier in this chapter indicates that performance is governed by message frequency, transmission time, queues which form in the systems software and application program, processing time, and file access delays. Another factor, not yet considered, is the effect of message arrival rate. The pattern of message arrival has a very marked effect on the length of queues which form in the system. Even though operators may be handling message transactions at fairly evenly-spaced intervals, the cumulative effect of different processing times by different operators invariably causes a bunching of message arrivals at the communications interface. This is shown diagrammatically in Figure 9–15. This bunching is important because of the well-known effect that a random arrival time has on queue length. When the average arrival time of messages starts to approach the processing time of a given queue service point, a queue of infinite length builds up if the arrival pattern is random rather than evenly spaced. This well-known characteristic of queue formation is a common reason for on-line systems failing to meet performance expectations. Too often, systems designers rely on throughput calculations based on average message-arrival rates and processing delays, with catastrophic effects. Queue length build-up is sketched diagrammatically in Figure 9–16.

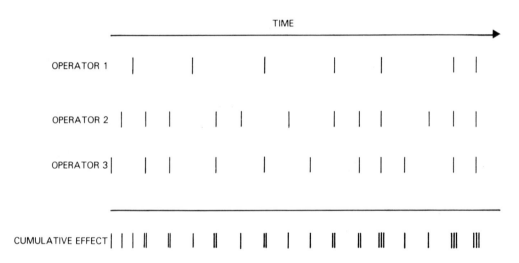

Figure 9-15   Message arrival pattern showing bunching effect

Thus, in attempting to estimate the performance characteristics likely to result from a given network installation, the calculations become inordinately complex as soon as the network becomes non-trivial. However, the investment of a large amount of money is usually at stake and consequently some attempt must be made to ensure adequate performance. The techniques available, other than using broad rules of thumb — which so often end in disaster — are:

- Comparisons of the new application with performances obtained from similar communications system environments
- Experimenting with a network similar in scale to the one proposed — using the same systems software environment and simulating the delays of applications programs and file accesses with appropriate delay programs, incorporating some statistical variability

Simulating the network environment using computer programs which generate messages, create queues, perform dummy processing, etc.; most computer companies provide simulation tools which can be used to test a wide range of proposed network configurations

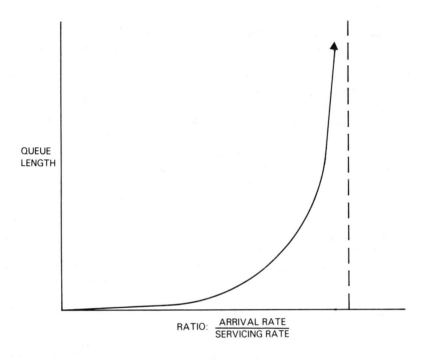

RATIO: $\dfrac{\text{ARRIVAL RATE}}{\text{SERVICING RATE}}$

Figure 9-16   Effect of random arrival pattern on queue length

All of these techniques can be used with good effect, and circumstances dictate which one is the most appropriate. In practice, a number of deficiencies always exist with these techniques. They include:

• The systems software environment is critical, and some small changes in the packages used for transactions processing and database storage and update can, in practice, cause wide variations from the experimental or simulated performances.
• The database or file access environment may be very different from that simulated when the actual file sizes and access patterns are established.
• Performance in the processing area is very dependent upon the amount of main storage available for buffers, etc. In practice, other systems tend to impinge on the physical main storage availability, and this can cause wide deviations of actual performance from that anticipated.

9.3.2   Terminal Hardware Considerations

The choice of terminal has already been identified as a major issue for the systems designer. To demonstrate the range of choice available and the impact of flexibility on the design, a list of some terminal hardware variables is given in Table 9–1.

Table 9–1   Terminal capabilities evaluation

Terminal characteristics	Potential impact on design
Input facilities e.g. keyboard, light pen, special keys to reduce keystrokes, card readers, tab key	Operator satisfaction, accuracy, and performance
Back-up capability — cassette, internal storage	Can improve recovery situation after a failure
Output modes — print, video, voice, display and panels, character size and stability, scrolling	Operator satisfaction and performance
Security aids — keys, badge readers, automatic identifier transmission	Security and integrity — reduces reliance on passwords
Character set — special characters/displays	Can allow for more design options in dialog
Buffer size and transmit mode flexibility — block transmission, multiple-panel storage	Dialog design flexibility, systems software choice flexibility
Edit and control features — range and format checks	Reduces load on CPU and applications software
Alarm and unsolicited messages — bell/whistle, separate message area for unexpected messages	Ability to permit system/operator communication without affecting routine work
Line interface — polling response, interfaces with different data transportation standards, transmission speeds, retransmit function	Systems software interface, ability to upgrade network performance without redesign or new equipment
Remote on/off switch	Introduces design flexibility for unattended operation
Slave device connection — local printer, cassette storage	Provides for hard copy or bulk data transfer function
Reliability — sensitivity to dust and vibration: Can it survive the hot sweet tea test?	Introduces location and environmental insensitivity
Maintainability	Cost and down-time effects

9.3.3   Systems Software Considerations

The fact that the choice of system software has a marked effect on both the designer's flexibility and system performance has already been highlighted. Set out in this subsection are some of the areas which need particular attention from the designer when considering either the selection of system software, or the effect that a particular system software environment could have on the design.

Overheads

The overheads introduced by the system software affect the efficiency of message processing. Areas of particular importance are the efficiency with which applications programs are called, and the path length (i.e., the number of instructions to be obeyed) introduced at the interface with both the screen-handling software and the database management system. Experience with a range of systems has shown that a complex systems software environment may limit throughput performance to the range 2–6 message pairs per second for each million instructions per second that the CPU is capable of performing, depending on the complexity of processing. With less complex systems software, oriented towards the particular application, throughput can be between 35 and 50 message pairs per second for each million instructions per second of processor power. Although these results are not necessarily applicable for all processors across all applications, they are indicative of the effect of software overheads.

Security/Integrity

Some of the more advanced network software provides end-to-end control, thus virtually ensuring that a message will be delivered to an applications program once the terminal transmit key has been depressed. Other software provides control on message integrity between the terminal controller and the communications controller — refer to Figure 9-1 — but the links between terminal and its controller and between the communications controller and the processor are not so well protected. In this event, operating procedures and specially designed applications software may be necessary to provide the desired degree of control.

Recovery/Restart

This is probably the area in which systems software exhibits greatest variability between manufacturers, and even different offerings from the same manufacturer. The designer needs to work through all the possible types of event which may occur in the network and which would effect the recovery/restart situation. This includes considering the effect of a failure in any hardware box or any software module. Particular points of importance are the effects on messages at the following stages of progression through the system:

- Those which have left the terminal but have not yet been received completely at the CPU or logged
- Those which have been received and logged but not yet passed to the application program
- Those messages which were in the process of being handled by the applications program, which may have resulted in complete or partial updates to the database
- Messages for which processing has been completed but the response has not yet been transmitted back to the terminal

In each case the designer must be sure that the integrity of the system is maintained and that there is some standard procedure which can be followed to ensure that data are not lost and also that double updating of the database does not result from retransmitted and reprocessed messages.

PART B — SYSTEMS DESIGN IN A DISTRIBUTED PROCESSING AND DATABASE ENVIRONMENT

9.4 FACTORS LEADING TO DISTRIBUTED PROCESSING AND DATABASES

A distributed processing configuration is one containing:

- Multiple processors each with its own local systems software
- A communications network linking the processors

If, in addition, the network has multiple independent databases, it is a distributed database configuration.

Of all the technical developments in the information systems field, the move towards multiple computer systems and distributed databases probably represents the most significant challenge to information systems managers and systems analysts. This is because the control of the data-processing and data-management environment is passing from a centralized situation to one of distributed control and responsibility. While benefits can be expected from users becoming more involved as their responsibility increases, very real problems arise from the complexity of maintaining a corporate database in a number of processing locations, especially when it is felt necessary to interconnect these processing systems so that data resources can be shared. For the systems analyst the problems which emanate from a move towards distributed databases mostly concern the distributed database itself rather than the systems design and implementation techniques, for these latter are similar to those used in a conventional system. Consequently this section deals almost totally with the design and specification of the distributed database environment and with the implications for the systems designer of the various configurations possible for distributed databases.

A combination of technical and attitudinal factors is causing the move towards distributed processing and database systems. Five of these factors are now discussed.

First-time users of computer systems. It is certain that a very large number of new computer applications will emerge as the cost of hardware is reduced and a wider range of standard systems/programs becomes available. Most of these new applications will involve first-time computer users, and they will occur in large, medium, and small enterprises. For organizations which currently use computers, even if a centralized computer equipment/project management policy is in effect, this trend must result in a number of stand-alone systems being installed. Thus the corporate computerized database, comprising all data held in machine-readable form within the organization, will start to become distributed — even if this is a slow trend at first.

Extension of existing applications. The ease with which low-cost 'front-end' processors, with communications capability, can be added to existing systems has already caused many enterprises to develop data collection/preprocessing systems to interface the sources of data with existing computer applications. Often, these data collection systems are complex — for example an order-entry/inventory-control/sales-analysis application may be installed as a front-end to an invoicing/accounts-receivable system.

There is a high probability that these new sections of the corporate computerized database will be stored on devices controlled by the front-end machines rather than by the central computer — because this will be a simpler and less expensive approach than adding new files and functions to the existing computer and its database.

Office automation. Although word-processing systems in their simplest form do not appear to be of interest to information systems specialists, the concept of an 'automated office' — with electronic mail, text processing, and the storage of text data about the enterprise's activities — is totally different (Morgan, 1976; Ness, 1974). Partly, this is because several of the automated-office systems may require access to the normal files created and maintained by data-processing systems. In addition, office systems could well provide a convenient input source for some data-processing systems; for example, account balance adjustments, name-and-address changes, etc. However, the main reason for interest is the scope for providing information to all levels of management by processing the text which is captured and stored by office-automation systems. Text-based information systems will probably involve data storage on separate computers rather than a centralized EDP system.

Archives. As the volume of data increases there will be a tendency to use data archive systems, which are able to hold higher volumes of data at reasonable cost although with the penalty of slow access. Because of the specialized nature and low access priority it is again likely that a separate computer system would take over this task.

The attitude of users. The rapid rate at which computer information systems have penetrated into all areas of data and word processing must bring about a rapid change in the attitudes and involvement of users. As users gain more experience with these systems their knowledge of 'good' and 'bad' systems design increases. This knowledge leads to users being able to take an active part in systems design and eventually to take over project management. Such a trend is already apparent in a number of enterprises which have been using computers for a number of years.

The emerging technology has also provided the user group with the opportunity of installing dedicated systems of high capability with little or no participation from a central data-processing group, especially if a standard applications package is employed. This ability and opportunity for independent action reinforces the latent desire felt by many managers to be in control of their own data processing. Thus the pressure for user autonomy becomes continually more intense.

These five factors illustrate the pressures within organizations which are forcing the pace towards distributed processing. It should be realized, however, that it is the distribution of the database which is by far the more important issue in the debate on distributed processing and distributed databases. By and large, it does not matter where or how a particular processing job has been triggered. The location of data is a most important question within the overall information systems policy of an organization, since this restricts the processing options greatly. It certainly is not now, and may never be, economic to transport large quantities of data from one place to another merely for the purpose of processing it. In addition, the location of the data is significant to the security, integrity, and reliability questions. These points are discussed more fully in subsequent sections of this chapter.

9.5 NETWORK OPTIONS

9.5.1 Introduction

A good deal of the research work undertaken in the distributed database area has concentrated on the different network options which are available and the resulting implications that choice of a particular network has for the distributed database design problem. Among the articles which cover the distributed database field well are those by Kunii & Kunii (1977), Ramamoorthy (1978), Bray (1978), and Smith (1979). The standardization of database models in the distributed environment has also been discussed by the CODASYL Committee (CODASYL, 1978) and by Bachman (1978). The discussion in this section deals with three possibilities:

- A general distributed database network
- A star network
- A ring or data highway network

9.5.2 The General Network

A graphical representation of the general network is given in Figure 9–17, which shows that it consists of a communications network linking one or more of:

- Local processing nodes
- Data storage nodes
- Terminal controller nodes

The local processing node comprises a stand-alone computer system which has its own processor, a local database with DBMS and a facility whereby user

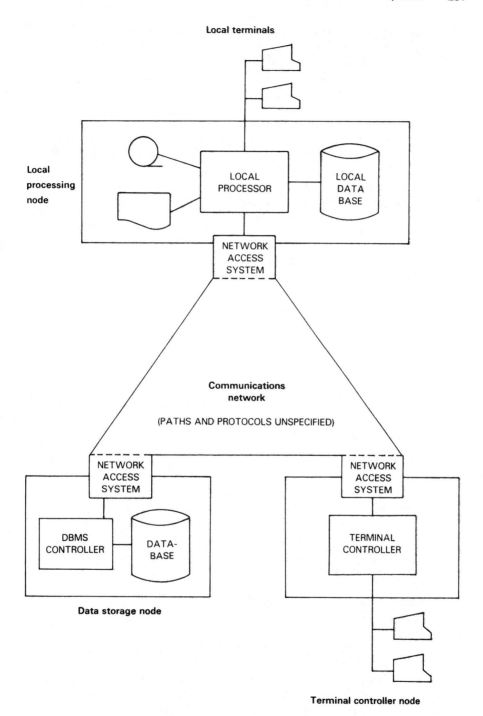

Figure 9-17   General distributed network

application programs can be initiated and controlled through a 'user process'. Thus any conventional computer system could be one of these nodes. If it is to work within a coordinated network DBMS environment it must also contain 'network DBMS' software of some form. The data storage node also has a processor, but this controls only a database management system with an attached database. However, there is no user attached directly to this system. An example of such a node might be an archive system which stores rarely used information of a historical nature gathered over a period of years from conventional data-processing systems, or a back-end database machine shared by several processors. The third type of node is simply a user access facility with sufficient intelligence to be able to connect terminals to the network — being able to handle the protocols and other processing requirements of the communications facility which links all the nodes together.

In this representation there is no restriction on the number of paths between the nodes nor is there any restriction on the number of possible routes which might be taken between a particular node and another node with which communication is required. There is also no requirement that the database management system or the hardware — in fact any aspects of the system — are common or similar. It is within this environment that the CODASYL Committee is attempting to build a series of guidelines and specifications to form the basis of the design of network DBMS.

9.5.3   The Star Network

Normally, reference to a star network implies that all data are held in a central system and the nodes merely perform data acquisition, job initiation, time-sharing or distributed-processing functions. The trends mentioned in Section 9.4 are leading to the storage of 'temporary' and even of 'local' databases, as indicated in Figure 9–18.

In this type of network the same three kinds of node as in the general network can be used, although a data-storage node is uncommon as yet. The essential difference to the general network is the control over the communications system exercised by the central processing installation (CPI). Most traffic is CPI-to-node or vice versa. Since the greatest proportion of data is stored in the corporate database attached to this processor, it also runs most programs. This leaves the node systems with relatively trivial applications, restricted data availability, and restricted network access. There is normally no significant node-to-node communication (apart from message switching) since operations nodes tend to be unaware of the database contents of other nodes — the CPI is the centre of activity. Where a node requires local storage of a file — say, for a protracted data-validation session — it is often 'down-loaded' from the CPI for the purpose. Programs as well as data may be treated in this way. In all instances where two or more copies of a file or part of a database exist, the one held at the CPI is the 'truth'.

Because the star network is the most natural path for growth from a fully centralized system (the most common commercial EDP configuration) it is the most common distributed processing/database network. The IBM System Network Architecture (SNA) is a prime example of a system which supports a central 'host' approach, although it also supports multiple-host configurations as well. SNA is a

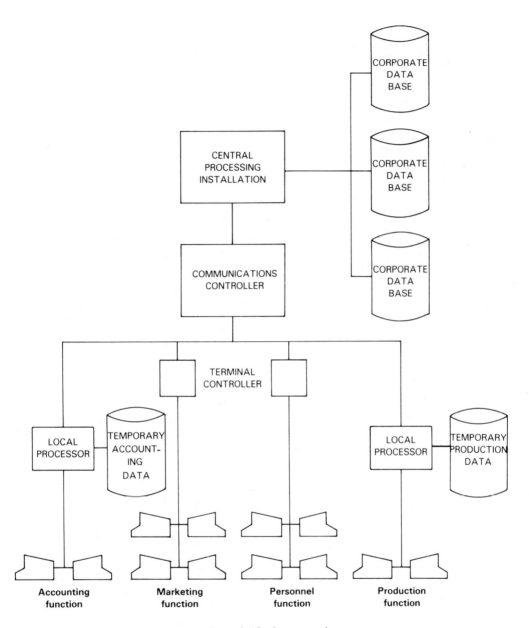

Figure 9–18   Star network

combination of systems software products which provide a software environment for receiving, transporting, and interfacing messages with files and application programs — see Chapter 8.

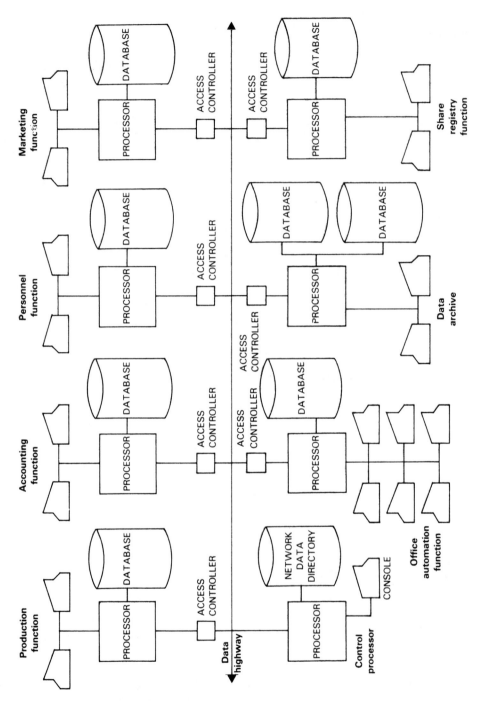

Figure 9-19   Ring or data highway network

9.5.4   The Ring or Data Highway Network

An alternative to using a large CPI as the centre or junction point of a network communications system is to utilize a ring or data highway approach as indicated in Figure 9–19. The distributed network shown in Figure 9–19 has a number of notable features which affect its ease of implementation. Three of these features are:

- The network configuration implies multiple (and therefore possibly different) processors, operating systems, databases, and database software. Therefore existing systems can be incorporated into a unified network without the need to rewrite applications. Clearly, similar or identical units and/or software would facilitate implementation and operation.
- The unifying aspect is the 'data highway' and its associated controller processor. The major cost is the requirement that each processor connected to the highway should either be compatible with the highway logic and software protocols, or be linked by means of an interface 'box' which performs the necessary transformations. Design of this box can be complex if the processors/software are very different in nature.
- To keep the volume of data transfer at a practical level the selection of database contents at each processor should depend on the data requirements of the systems using the processor. This implies that most accesses to data from programs running under the control of a processor should be satisfied by the local database. Kunii & Kunii (1978) refer to this concept as 'the principle of maximum locality'.

The 'data highway' within a network is envisaged as providing a very high speed data communication path which links all processing units. One possible implementation already being used for similar purposes can operate at 50 Mbytes/s (Thornton, 1975). This high-speed channel, in fact, becomes the standard link within the system and all processors need to be connected through interface units as indicated in Figure 9–19. The highway may operate on a broadcast basis, that is a processor wanting to send a message finds an unused path (the highway can comprise a number of parallel paths) and sends its messages with an address inserted at the beginning. All units receive the message but only those addressed will respond.

A controller system is probably required if the highway is to be used for database access among more than two or three processors. Many ways of organizing such a system are possible, with the critical factor being the location of the data dictionary/directory files. If this set of files is held in a data-highway control processor, then it is not necessary for each system to have a record of the location of data elements other than those within its local database. An access request for a data element or array not held locally would first require a message to the controller. The controller would then consult the directory, and issue a directive to the processor which holds that data to send them to the processor which generated the request. Although design of a controller and software able to perform these functions is not trivial, it appears to be well within current (1981) hardware/software capability. It is, of course, a special case of the interim software proposals for distributed databases as outlined by the CODASYL committee (CODASYL, 1978; Bachman, 1978).

9.6 NETWORK DATABASE MANAGEMENT SOFTWARE

The design of a general network DBMS for a configuration comprising different processors, operating systems, DBMSs, and applications software is obviously a complex one. Even when the node components are identical the task is formidable. There are three basic options for an architecture for network database management systems. They are outlined by Bachman (1978) and more details are given by Smith (1979). The three options are:

- Cooperating user workstations
- Cooperating storage management of workstations
- Cooperating database management workstations

The data flow involved in each of these options is shown diagrammatically in Figures 9–20, 9–21, and 9–22 respectively.

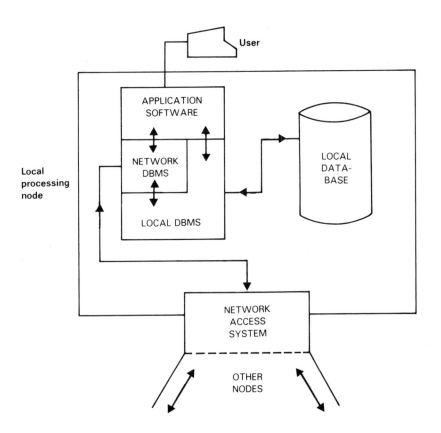

Figure 9–20 Cooperating user workstations — data flow

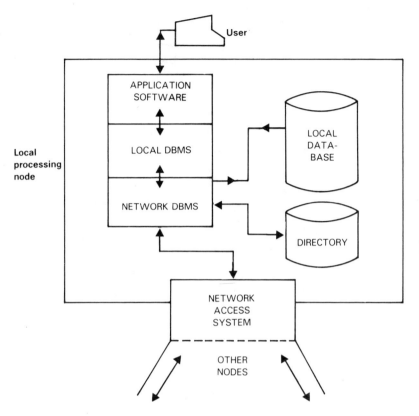

Figure 9-21 Cooperating storage management workstations — data flow

The cooperating user workstation approach envisages three separate layers of software existing within a local processing node. Terminals initiate applications programs and these programs make normal calls on the local DBMS, which accesses the local database, as required. If the data needs cannot be satisfied from the local database, another node must be accessed, and a request for this data would have to be passed to the network database management system, which then communicates with the relevant node. On receipt of the data back at the local node it is passed to the application program. In cases where requests for data are received from other nodes, then the network DBMS requests these data from the local DBMS software and they are then returned through the network. This approach to distributed databases can handle a wide variety of processor types, operating systems, and local DBMS. It is able to do this by placing responsibility for determining whether data are held locally or not — and possibly the path to be followed in accessing the remote node — in the hands of the user. In simple implementations the user also needs to know the format and access rules of the data as they are stored at the remote location, so that the appropriate request can be formulated and the reply can be interpreted. Clearly, however, it is desirable that the network DBMS perform message routing and data format mapping to and from the individual node database environments.

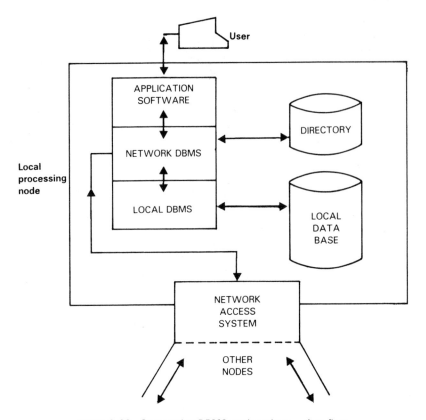

Figure 9-22   Cooperating DBMS workstations — data flow

The cooperating storage management workstations approach is at the other end of the complexity spectrum. As shown in Figure 9–21, it is the network DBMS which handles access to and from the local database at each node, as well as providing for communication between nodes. The local DBMS (if it exists at all as a separate software entity) merely serves as an interface between the applications software and the network DBMS. In this environment the data-access and data-storage mechanisms are totally transparent to the user. Thus, the same procedures are followed by the user whether the data are stored locally or remotely. In fact the user is not aware of the location of the data — apart possibly from slower response when data have to be obtained from other locations. Clearly, to implement this concept it is necessary for the network DBMS to have detailed knowledge of both logical and physical storage information at each node. Given the complexity of this design it is difficult to imagine how it could be implemented on other than completely identical processing nodes.

The third approach, cooperating DBMS workstations, appears to be the one favoured by the CODASYL Systems Committee which is working on distributed database specifications. It also envisages three separate software entities, an application program, and local and network DBMS. The data flow sketch in Figure

9–22 shows that the local database access is controlled by the local DBMS. However, the network DBMS software is interposed between the applications program and the local DBMS. All applications software data requests are passed through the network DBMS software which calls for data either from the local node or from the remote nodes as required. This approach also provides transparency from the user's viewpoint but does not require the network DBMS to have a complete picture of the physical storage information within the network. For this configuration the CODASYL Systems Committee summarizes the tasks to be undertaken by the network DBMS as:

- Intercept a user request and determine where to send it for processing, or what nodes must be accessed to satisfy the request
- Access the network directory or at least know how to request and use the information in it
- Coordinate the processing and response to a user request if it spans nodes, that is, the target data exist at more than one node
- Function as the communication interface between the user process, the local DBMS, and DBMSs at other nodes
- Provide data and process translation support in a heterogeneous distributed database environment

9.7   ISSUES IN DISTRIBUTED DATABASE DESIGN

9.7.1   Introduction

In considering the distributed database design problem, it is appropriate that the systems analyst considers the important issues likely to arise in any such project. The points which are included in this discussion have been a subject of analysis and research by a number of workers including Ramamoorthy (1978), Kunii & Kunii (1977), and Bray (1978). Discussion of these issues often raises the various alternatives which are available to the designer and considers the merits and demerits of each.

9.7.2   Distribution of the Database

Foremost in the mind of the designer is the manner in which the organization's data are to be distributed over the various computer systems which either already exist or are to be established as a result of this project. The three components to be considered when addressing the distribution question are:

- The schema
- The data
- The control/security programs

Essentially, the design problem is finding a solution for the location of these three elements.

Schema considerations

Probably the most important aspect with the practical design of distributed systems using current technology is the question as to where file directory type information is to be stored. There appear to be two basic alternatives:

- Centralize the directory but distribute the data (as proposed for the operation of the data highway network)
- Distribute both the directory and the data among the nodes

In considering the database questions, normally the word *schema* is used to describe the logical and physical structure of the entire database, and the term *subschema* is used to describe data structure related to a specific application. Therefore, in a distributed system, the schema and subschema may be either centralized at a central node or distributed over many nodes, and the data they describe may or may not be located at the same node or nodes. In simple applications, a less complex 'switching' schema can be used which describes the node location for each file or data element and possibly a path directory indicating how that particular node can be located.

Most current implementations of distributed databases require the location of schema-type information, as well as control facilities, at the node where the data are stored, as well as at the processing nodes. They are, therefore, functioning as cooperating user workstations. The various nodes in a network may include different hardware and database management systems, or even conventional file systems, and it is necessary for user programs or inquirers to have a knowledge of the schema and control protocols before access is attempted. If a switching schema is available, a communications link can be established with the remote node, without the user having to know how it is done.

Data distribution

The question of storing data in a distributed database is normally viewed from two angles:

- Minimizing communications requirements
- Maintaining adequate control and security within the network

The requirement to minimize communications is often described as the criterion of maximum locality. This concept specifies that the major design criterion of a distributed database system is to physically and/or logically distribute the sub-systems so that the database transactions (search, create, delete, update, etc.) are kept as local as possible. It follows that there is a natural accumulation of data types that form the nucleus of distributed databases; i.e. the distributed databases centre around transactions and applications subsystems which utilize these accumulations of data. For example, the distributed database system shown in Figure 9–19 separates the operational functions of a manufacturing organization in such a way that the individual processing subsystems have access to local databases which satisfy a high proportion of the data calls from programs and user inquiries. A procedure for determining the distribution pattern is discussed by Baker (1980).

Control and security

The answers to the control, security, and integrity questions naturally depend on the organization for which the distributed system has been designed. However, one important issue concerns the decision of whether or not to replicate data within the network. Replicated data have the distinct advantage that greater local data access is possible even when certain categories of data are in strong demand throughout the network. It also improves reliability since there is less likelihood of essential data items being inaccessible due to failure of hardware or software at a particular node. The major drawback of having multiple copies of data is the updating problem of having to keep all copies identical.

To finalize the schema data and control specifications, five specific issues need to be addressed. They are:

- How will a request for data be routed through the network?
- How will the response or responses be routed back to the originating node?
- Where will the data, in its stored form, be mapped to the form required by the user as specified in the user program's own subschema?
- When sufficient information to perform this mapping process is not available, what information should be transferred, and to which node, so that the mapping required by the user function can be carried out?
- At what point will security against unauthorized access be provided?

9.7.3 Updating and Retrieval

When several users share data there is always the problem of how the designer should handle the multiple access requests so that deadlock does not occur and an efficient queueing system is established. This problem is exacerbated in the distributed environment because of the logical and physical separation of the databases and the control programs. There is also the problem of consistency when duplicate copies of the same data are stored in different parts of the network, any one of which may be subject to update at any time.

It has been established that simple locking systems, whereby files or data elements are reserved either when a program is begun or at the time of the acknowledged request, introduce very long delays whenever activity within the system is high. However, it is desirable that the efficiency of local processing should not be degraded by having additional safeguards because other processing nodes are in the network. One possible solution is to insist that only the home node can update a data element although any node can read any element.

Note that deadlock is possible in distributed systems when two or more nodes are each waiting on a message from another, as well as when each is waiting on access to data reserved by another. Detecting a deadlock situation is more complex in a distributed system. Roll-back of a database may not be easy if transactions occurred at remote workstations, especially under the cooperating user workstation option.

9.7.4 Standards

In a centralized system, many standards tend to be set and enforced automatically — the hardware/software interconnection protocols do not allow incompatible enhancements. However, the cooperative nature of distributed systems requires the introduction of a set of standards which cover the following areas:

- Hardware procurement needs to be restricted to systems which can be interconnected and with which the network software can interface.
- Systems software must be similarly compatible at interface points.
- Internode communications protocols must be established.
- Data structure mapping protocols are necessary.
- The maintenance of timeliness, accuracy, and security of local databases must be monitored — at least for those data elements of interest to other nodes.

9.8 SYSTEMS DESIGN CONSIDERATIONS

9.8.1 Evolution is the Key

Once it has been decided to install multiple computer systems, each with its own database, it is necessary to determine the approach of the organization towards distributed database management. This can take place in the following steps:

1. Nomination of the applications systems to be run on each processor, and determination of the data resources which are required by each of these applications systems.
2. Specification of the database contents at each local processing node — bearing in mind the advantages and disadvantages of data replication as discussed in Section 9.7.
3. Specification of hardware, network communications software, local DBMS, and network DBMS components which will provide the processing and interconnection facilities necessary. Note that there is no real requirement that all aspects of the system be implemented from the outset of the project. For example, an evolving systems software and network schema environment is possible in which early applications require more complete knowledge of the database by users, with the level of knowledge

required dropping off as more sophisticated network software becomes available.

9.8.2 Program Execution and Data Exchange Requests

When working on an application at one of the local processing nodes, there are two basic approaches a systems designer can take to the access of remotely held data:

- A program execution request involves initiating an applications program at the remote site where the relevant data are stored, and allowing for the transmission back to the local processing node with the results of that processing. Thus, in a distributed banking environment, any transactions which involve accounts not held at a local branch would be sent to the branch at which the customer's data are held for processing.
- The data exchange request involves the transfer of the relevant data from the remote node to the local processing node so that a program can carry out the required operation. This is the approach followed by those designing the more sophisticated network DBMS software systems such as the co-operating DBMS workstations, because it is envisaged that the data-storage environment will be transparent to the user in such cases.

The choice in any particular case depends on many factors, including the network software support, the compatibility of the data management software in the different nodes, security standards, and the volume of data involved.

9.8.3 Benefits of the Distributed Database

The cost/benefit evaluation surrounding distributed database projects is difficult since many of the benefits are intangible. Champine (1977) has discussed the advantages of distributed systems compared with those of centralized database systems.

Advantages of the centralized system

- Lower cost of operations — operators, systems programming staff, etc.
- Economies of scale in hardware purchases
- Compatibility of hardware and software
- Relatively easy intrafile communication since all data are held under the control of one system

Advantages of the distributed database system

- The communications subsystem is less critical since there is a higher degree of local processing capability

- A central site fail-soft capability, since operations do not depend on any one particular computer system
- A lower data rate on the communications network and thus communications costs are lower
- Greater flexibility with respect to the development of the network — in particular it is possible for the upgrading of systems and the implementation of new applications to be carried out in a modular fashion
- The possibility of achieving high system performance (through the provision of fast response and high transaction rates) because specific applications can be matched with hardware and software

Summary

Since the economies of scale are decreasing in absolute terms as costs fall, the main points of comparison are those relating to performance, modularity, and flexibility. In the end, the choice is frequently determined by the management style of the organization. If it tends towards decentralization and local responsibility then the distributed approach is clearly more appropriate, and the opposite is true for more autocratic organizations.

REFERENCES

C. BACHMAN, 'Commentary on CODASYL Systems Committee's Interim Report on Distributed Database Technology', *AFIPS National Computer Conference*, June 1978, pp. 919-21.

C.T. BAKER, 'Logical Distribution of Application and Data', *IBM Systems Journal*, vol. 19, no. 2, 1980, pp. 171-91.

O.H. BRAY, 'Distributed Database Design Considerations', *Proc. Fourth International Conference on Very Large Data Bases*, 1978, pp. 121-7.

G.A. CHAMPINE, 'Six Approaches to Distributed Data Bases', *Datamation*, May 1977, pp. 69-72.

CODASYL SYSTEMS COMMITTEE, 'Distributed Data Base Technology — An interim report', *AFIPS National Computer Conference*, June 1978, pp. 909-17.

T.L. KUNII & H.S. KUNII, 'Design Criteria for Distributed Data Base Systems', *Proc. Third International Conference on Very Large Data Bases*, 1977, pp. 93-104.

J. MARTIN, *Design of Man-Computer Dialogues*, Prentice-Hall Inc., Englewood Cliffs, N.J., 1973.

H.L. MORGAN, 'Office Automation Project — A Research Perspective', *AFIPS National Computer Conference*, June 1976, pp. 605-10.

D. NESS, 'Office Automation System: Overview', *Decision Sciences Working Paper no. 74-08-03*, The Wharton School, University of Pennsylvania, Philadelphia, Pa., 1974.

C.V. RAMAMOORTHY ET AL., 'Architectural issues in Distributed Database Systems', *Proc. Third International Conference on Very Large Data Bases*, 1977, pp. 121-6.

J.L. SMITH, 'Alternatives in the Architecture and Design of Distributed Databases, *The Australian Computer Journal*, vol. 11, no. 1, February 1979, pp. 5-12.

J.E. THORNTON, G.S. CHRISTIENSEN & P.D. JONES, 'A New Approach to Network Storage Management', *Computer Design*, November 1975, pp. 81-5.

J. WEIZENBAUM, 'ELIZA — A computer program for the Study of Natural Language Communication between Man and Machine', *Communications of the ACM*, vol. 9, no. 1, January 1966, p. 26.

CASE STUDY — CHILDPLAY TOY COMPANY

Background

Childplay Toy Company (CTC) is a wholesaler of locally produced children's toys. With a product line of 2600 toys and an annual turnover of about $50 million, CTC enjoys a profitable and growing share of an expanding market. It serves about 4000 customers, many of whom have a number of branch outlets.

Inventory control and the associated order-entry/despatch/invoicing areas have been recognized in a feasibility study as the most significant problem area at CTC. Current procedures are manual. It has been decided by management that these will be the first applications to be implemented on the JAM 86325 computer to be purchased. Design work has commenced already on these applications.

The Manual System

Order entry

The sequence of events followed in handling customers' sales orders is:

1. Receipt of Order — Confirmation. Customer's mail or telephone order is taken and entered onto standard CTC order forms. For a telephone order (75 per cent of orders), preliminary confirmation is given after checking an out-of-stock listing and the credit go/no go status of the customer.

2. Shipping Documents. A despatch docket, which also serves as a picking list, is manually written out in triplicate by the order entry clerk and sent to the warehouse in batches every two hours during the period 8 A.M. to 4 P.M.
3. Picking and Despatch. The warehouse staff assemble the order, and manually enter the quantities shipped on the shipping documents. Often these differ from the quantity ordered when insufficient stock is available. The warehouse staff manually update inventory cards. The order is despatched with one copy of the despatch docket. One copy is sent to accounts for billing and the third copy is sent to order entry, who advise the customers by telephone if all the order has not been shipped. Back orders are not accepted since management believes that the procedures required would be too complex.

Reordering goods

Once each month every product stock card is reviewed and stock is replenished, based on the sales manager's sales forecast and the rule:

- Reorder up to four month's supply when stock-on-hand + on-order falls below two month's supply.

In the case of an out-of-stock item, the sales manager reviews the position and may take expediting action on outstanding purchase orders or issue further purchase orders. The sales manager makes a sales forecast by month by product once a year and amends them when circumstances warrant, usually either by scaling all forecasts up or down by a given percentage or by amending a single product's forecasts.

Proposed Order and Inventory System

It has been decided that the new system will be an on-line design using VDU plus printer terminals located at the order entry and warehouse offices. Broadly, the system will maintain an inventory file sequenced by product code and containing product description, product group to which the item belongs, stock on hand (actual less orders accepted), stock on order, sales forecast by month, average cost of stock in store, date of last movement, and price. Order-entry data will update the product master file and also the order file. The warehouse will be able to initiate the printing of picking tickets for an order or group of orders. Warehouse input data will update the order file after picking and cause an invoice and despatch docket to be printed, for despatch with the goods — resulting in changes to the accounts-receivable file.

Case Study — Childplay Toy Company

Customer master
Code	9(5) The rightmost digit is used for the check digit
Name	X(20)
Address (invoice)	X(40)
Postcode	9(4)
Current credit limit	99999.99

Customer delivery address
Code	9(5)
Del. address 1	X(44)
Del. address 2	X(44)
Del. address 3	X(44)
. . . .	
. . . .	
Del. address N	X(44)

Product master
Code	9(4)
Name	X(30)
Product group	9(3)
Inventory	9(4)
Outstanding order quantity	9(4)
Average cost	99.99
Date last movement	99/99/99
Sales forecast	9(4)
Price	999.99

Order details
	CTC Order No.	9(4)
	Customer Order No.	X(10)
	Customer No.	9(4) + 9
	Delivery address	X(44)
	Date entered	99/99/99
	Date invoiced/shipped	99/99/99
Repeating	Product no.	9(4)
Group	Quantity	9(4)
	. . . .	
	. . . .	

Accounts receivable
	Customer No.	9(5)
	Oustanding balance	99999.99
	Date last payment	99/99/99
Repeating	Invoice no.	9(5)
Group	Date	99/99/99
	Amount	9999.99
	. . . .	
	. . . .	
	. . . .	

Figure 9-23   The five data sets of the order/inventory system

Each transaction will be entered on the terminal as it arises. Edit rejects should be corrected immediately. Once a week the system will be required to product a list of recommended product reorders based on the same policy as used in the manual system. The reorders will not be automatically added to the stock-on-order field in the inventory file, but will be input through warehouse terminals after review and approval.

The design process to date has identified five files, or data sets, associated with the order/inventory system. These have been specified in broad detail and are outlined in Figure 9–23. The delivery address, order details, and accounts receivable have variable-length records.

ASSIGNMENT

1. Design screen layouts and system/operator dialog for the order-entry input subsystem, assuming a VDU with an 80-character per line and 24-line specification. The terminal also has variable intensity display capability, a tab facility for automatic cursor control, 12 function keys, and a buffer which can store up to two screen formats if required. Discuss the design principles underlying your choice of dialog.

2. Perform a similar design exercise on the warehouse subsystem covering picking, despatch, and invoicing.

3. Describe the principles you would use to ensure adequate editing procedures and other controls on data.

4. What master file maintenance subsystems will be necessary to cater for stock level adjustments, new products, etc.? How might use of these be controlled?

5. What additional complexity would be created for the user/system dialog design if back orders were to be accepted?

6. What areas of benefit should the completed on-line system have over the manual procedures? Are there any disadvantages?

CASE STUDY — CONSOLIDATED ENTERPRISES

The Consolidated Enterprises Group is a diversified organization comprising three operating divisions with a head office. The divisions are:

- Hi Eng Pty Ltd — an engineering manufacturing company which produces a range of fabricated steel and non-ferrous products, bearings, and similar consumable items. The division has three production plants, in Sydney, Melbourne and Adelaide. Total turnover is $100 million. The head office of the division is in Melbourne.
- Chemical Compounds Pty Ltd — a chemical company producing a range of plastic and fertilizer products for sale through a limited number of wholesalers. It has two plants located in Sydney and Melbourne. Turnover is $189 million. The head office is in Sydney.
- Mineral Investments Pty Ltd — a mining company with joint venture interests in coal and base-metal mining. One of its subsidiaries also operates a small coalmine. Its proportion of the joint ventures turnover plus the subsidiary is $160 million. There is one office location — in Sydney — but the coalmine is located 95 km west of Sydney.

Each division is operated on a profit centre basis with independence over all operational and control matters. Only the approval of budgets and control of capital expenditure above $100 000 is retained by Head Office. However, Head Office does conduct general periodic reviews of performance against budget of all divisions.

Head Office has a PDP 11/34 with three terminals, 50 Mbyte disk, 128K memory, and a printer system used for financial planning and corporate accounts consolidation. All three divisions make use of computer equipment.

Hi Eng

Hi Eng has three medium-sized computers, one at each plant, with the following capabilities: dual HP3000 machines with 1 megabyte central memory, 200 megabytes of disk, three tapes, printers, etc. Some spare capacity exists, especially at nights and weekends. The operational systems are:

Production subsystem

Customers' orders entry
Back orders (items not supplied)

Warehouse inventory orders
Work-in-process reporting and inventory
Factory scheduling
Raw materials inventory
Daily labour variance report
Finished goods inventory

Sales subsystem

Customer order statistics (including budget figures)
Sales analysis by product or product group, territories,
        salespeople etc. as required
Invoicing and despatch

Accounting subsystem

Accounts receivable
Accounts payable
Works payroll
Staff salaries
Labour distribution
Costing
Purchasing
Sales analysis (for accounting purposes)
General ledger

Administration subsystem

Personnel statistics

Engineering subsystem

Engineering spares inventory
Consumable items inventory
Workshop scheduling
Plant register (machines, vehicles, etc.)
Capital projects progress
Maintenance costs reporting
Maintenance schedules
Various technical computations

Data entry for the order entry is on-line via four terminals, but all other systems are batch operated. Files for production control are held on-line, whereas accounting system files are normally held on tape and are run up to disk when needed. Conventional COBOL-type files are used — mostly index sequential or sequential in organization.

Chemical Compounds

Chemical Compounds has two computer systems, one system being located at each plant. They are from the Qantel range each with 150 megabytes of disk, floppy disk input, a printer, and four terminals. These systems could be expanded to twice their processing capacity. Systems implemented include inventory control, order entry, and there is partial implementation of accounting procedures including payroll and production costing.

Mineral Investments

Mineral Investments has a simple computer system — an IBM 4341 which is used solely for accounting on a batch basis associated with the joint venture activities. All the accounts of the coalmine are kept manually. The machine is lightly loaded.

General Comments on the DP Environment

Since the various systems were developed by different design teams at different periods, the chart of accounts is significantly different for each division, although they are common within divisions. Customer, product, and supplier codes are all different between divisions.

Financial Information System

The Managing Director has directed that a computer-based financial information system be implemented within the company, which would allow frequent and rapid upstream financial reporting and also allow Head Office executives and auditors (internal and external) to have access to detailed accounting figures of the divisions. A task force has been set up to consider the issues involved. Guidelines provided by the Managing Director are:

- All monthly (i.e. figures up to the end of last month) general ledger, costing, and revenue details should be available for terminal access by authorized Head Office executives, and internal and external auditors.

Divisional figures should also be available for access by officers of that division. Figures for like variables, e.g. salaries, should be recorded in the same way.

- Divisional officers should approve the release of month-end figures for general access.
- In line with the decentralized policy of the company, the divisional data should be located in computers under the control of divisions.
- The figures available for the financial information system should be based on those used to prepare all other accounting reports and statements.
- The system should allow for expansion at both corporate and divisional level, without affecting the design of other projects or the financial information system.
- Where possible and economically feasible, the system should make use of existing systems.
- If information is not currently available in computer-processed form, manual input of summary figures should be used.
- A terminal operator should be able to use the same procedures to communicate with any of the divisions' databases.
- Head Office planners may wish to run financial planning models using the data files and, therefore, the facility to transfer large amounts of data must be available. It may be acceptable to run models developed at Head Office on local computers — provided the jobs are under the control of Head Office.

ASSIGNMENT

1. Identify and discuss the distributed database and systems design issues raised by the Managing Director's order.

2. Outline the options available for configuring the network to provide the Financial Information System and for organizing the databases.

3. Discuss the merits/demerits of each option.

4. Describe how data requests and responses would be routed through your most favoured network configuration.

10   CONTROLS, AUDIT AND SECURITY

10.1   INTRODUCTION

This chapter introduces the related topics of controls, audit, and security from the point of view of the systems designer. It gives the systems designer and manager a framework for the design of secure systems and for their future interaction with the EDP audit function.

10.2   THE EDP AUDIT FUNCTION

The objectives of an audit are not changed by using a computer-based information system, but the tools and techniques used by auditors are. The overriding objective of the auditor is to attest to the 'truth and fairness' of the published financial statements. The auditor is therefore concerned with (1) the system of internal controls, (2) the validity of the going-concern assumption (the assumption that the organization will continue to operate, which means that the values placed on assets in the financial statements are operating ones — they are not liquidation values), and (3) the fraud potential of the organization's systems. In making assessments of these areas, computer systems may complicate the task of the auditor in the following ways:
- Computer systems are usually more complex than conventional manual accounting systems, with several traditionally separate operations often being combined
- A large part of the data-processing activity is concentrated in a single department — the EDP department

- Steps in processing are combined and the records are kept in a form which means they are not visible without a printing process
- Real-time processing significantly alters many of the traditional control methods employed in batch-based systems

10.3 CONTROLS

Controls in a computer environment can be subdivided into three different categories:

- Administrative controls
- System development controls
- Processing controls

This is not the only way that controls could be classified, and many others can be found in the literature as a result of the difficulty of clearly differentiating many of the controls. It is however, only a matter of definition; the important consideration is the complete set of controls, and their interactions, which apply to the computer environment. It is important to realize that controls are interrelated and, therefore, a control weakness in one area may well be compensated by a control strength in another. It should also be noted that not having a particular control does not necessarily result in a material error occurring in the organization's records and, therefore, the control weakness may not be sufficient to warrant concern by the auditor. Thus the establishment of controls in any particular situation should be approached from the perspective of potential risk. In other words, the cost of implementing specific controls must be balanced against the possibility of loss or inaccuracy that the organization would face if that control did not exist.

10.4 ADMINISTRATIVE CONTROLS

Administrative controls are those which encompass the day-to-day running of the computer environment. Thus they are concerned with the areas of:

- Physical asset security
- Back-up facilities
- Stand-by facilities
- Control over personnel
- Division of responsibility
- File control
- On-line security

Physical asset security

Physical asset security concerns the system of protection and insurance not only for the hardware, but also for the software which makes up the computing capability. Thus consideration should be given to the security of, and access to: application programs; data files; system software, including utilities; and hardware. Examples of these controls are:

- Authorization for access to application programs and files
- Access restrictions on the computer room
- Control over general system software usage related to the degree of loss or corruption of data possible through misuse
- Fire-detection facilities

The purposes of physical asset controls are to ensure that:

- The files and programs are secure from unauthorized access and alteration when on-line
- Utilities are used for legitimate purposes only
- The going-concern assumption is not endangered by destruction or modification of either hardware or software

Back-up facilities

Back-up facilities are provided for both data files and programs to ensure that:

- Data files can be reconstructed in the event of master file loss or corruption
- Application and system software can be reinstated in the event of loss or corruption

These objectives are achieved by keeping copies of data files and programs in a safe place and in such a way that they can be reconstructed if necessary. Reconstruction of data files is simplified if magnetic tape is used because the update process involves writing to a new physical file (tape). Therefore prior copies of the master files are retained. When the three most recent copies are kept this back-up system is known as a grandfather-father-son system.

Where disks are used, back-up is not a by-product of the update, and consequently the file must be copied to a back-up medium on a regular basis, and transaction files must be kept. The back-up might occur, for example, each morning before regular processing starts. Consideration should be given to including edit logic in the file dump software to check the integrity of the data being copied.

A further aspect of back-up to be considered is the possibility of storing file copies at an alternative site, to ensure recovery if the processing site is affected by a natural disaster or sabotage. Since magnetic media is adversely affected when exposed to heat, a fireproof cabinet may be advisable for the local storage of operational files. In this area as well, a trade-off is involved; this time, between the cost of backing-up files and the cost of reconstruction in the event of corruption or loss.

Stand-by facilities

These controls are closely related to back-up, but cover the hardware. Consideration should be given to the need for, and the availability of, an alternative facility which could carry out critical processing for a period of time, in the event of an extended breakdown of any part of the computer machinery.

File control

File control is to ensure suitable storage and to limit access to the files. Thus files are normally labelled externally and internally, and stored in a library when not in use. Entry to this library is controlled so that unauthorized persons cannot gain access to the files held.

On-line security

In any configuration involving terminals, procedures are needed to ensure that access to the system is gained for legitimate purposes only. Passwords or some equivalent should be used to restrict access to the system or parts of it. Dedicated terminals may be used where only certain facilities are needed by the persons who use those terminals. Further control is provided by logging all terminal usage. Possible attempts to use the system illegally can be highlighted by a review of the log together with an exception report on invalid use (such as failed access attempts). At the data file level, write-protect facilities provide yet another layer of control.

Control over personnel

Leaving aside the question of division of responsibility (see below), control over the activities of personnel is achieved through:

- Logging all transactions with time stamp, terminal number, and employee number
- Scheduling operations so that unusual runs are noticeable
- Authorization, where possible, of transactions
- Controlling output distribution
- Defining personnel duties, responsibilities, and access restrictions
- Enforcing vacations and, where posssible, rotating duties
- Setting standard procedures for activities

Division of responsibility

To provide a cross-check on the accuracy and propriety of systems, the separation of the planning, design, and operations activities of the computer department is a normal control requirement. With the advent of in-house computer use by small organizations, however, this is not always possible. In this case the organization runs the risk of, for example, unauthorized changes being made to software or of modifications being made while systems are running. Ideally, DP management, the user, operations, system design and programming, librarian, and the software assurance functions should all be separated.

10.5   SYSTEM DEVELOPMENT CONTROLS

The environment in which systems are developed has a large effect on the quality of the systems produced, and consequently adequate control over the development process is of concern to all the organization's participants, including the auditor. The areas of concern include:

- Documentation
- Project management
- Testing

Documentation

Controls over the documentation aim at providing a secure record of the system design, programming, and maintenance activities, as well as of user procedures and recovery procedures for each system. This involves setting adequate standards for record keeping in these areas and ensuring that access to that documentation is controlled. One of the major problems faced in this area is maintaining the accuracy of the documentation as systems are modified over the years.

Project management

The project management environment does much to determine the quality of systems and the efficiency of their development. Sometimes the audit objectives embrace efficiency requirements and then the auditor is concerned that adequate feasibility studies are carried out, and that there is enough user participation to be certain that developments are in line with user needs. Further mechanisms should exist to allow resource budgeting, allocation, and review.

Testing

The procedures for testing new and modified systems should aim to minimize the likelihood of system faults in the operating environment. This means that standards for testing procedures should be established, and that the aim of the tests should be to uncover any improper functioning in the system.

10.6   PROCESSING CONTROLS

Processing controls ensure the completeness, accuracy, and authorization of the data processed, and can be subdivided into four aspects of a system:

- Input controls
- Programmed controls
- Output controls
- File controls

Input controls

Input controls include sequence checks, encoding verification, batch control totals, and authorization of input. Of these, the design of adequate control totals is the most complex. In principle, a set of control totals should accompany the data all the way through a system. The precise steps to be built into a system's control and security arrangements obviously depend on the nature of the system, the degree of protection required, the system's external environment, and the nature of the organization. But the following points are generally desirable:

- The level of control for input documents (in a batch system) is a batch of less than about 50 documents. This depends, of course, on the nature of the input. The objective is to facilitate the tracing of input errors, and large batch sizes only make this task more difficult. After the edit stage the input batches in a computer run are, for control purposes, merged into one batch.
- All documents sent for punching need to be accompanied by a batch header slip which contains (1) a count of all documents in the batch, and (2) hash totals of quantities and values of key fields which should be carefully controlled (examples are the quantity field of an order and the cash received field for accounts receivable system).
- With advanced data-entry equipment, the control totals can be checked after the keying of each batch. But more generally they must wait until being input to the edit program to be checked.
- At the end of each batch in the computer input run, the counts and totals are printed; alternatively they may be stored and printed as a table after reading all the batches. As an additional security measure the control counts and totals themselves may also be input and checked automatically against the figures accumulated by the computer. The details of any discrepancy are then not only printed but, if desired, the computer can be programmed to 'lock' so that special operator action is necessary before the run can proceed. There is then less chance of a discrepancy being ignored — deliberately or unintentionally.
- After each program run the control counts and totals are again printed, including any new figures resulting from the processing. These latter are especially important if they relate to data that is used in the subsequent runs.
- Amendments to or updating of a master file should be accompanied by a simple analysis (control account) of the master file before and after the run. This includes the numbers of records and any suitable field totals. The analyses are dated and retained on hard copy as a visible history of the file, and they are also held in the file itself.

- Console log — as printed by the console typewriter or written manually. This is preserved for reference purposes so that the auditor can query the reasons for reruns and be assured that no unauthorized computing has occurred. This log also gives the tape or disk numbers so a person can check that the right files and programs have been used in the correct sequence.
- All computer-printed output must be clearly identifiable in terms of its exact particularity. This entails the precise labelling of every sheet of print with appropriate captions, date, page number and, in certain instances, line numbers also.

EDP and the user department which submits the data need to share the responsibility for data controls, but ultimately it must rest with the user department. Sufficient information must be manually maintained by the user department so they can satisfy themselves that all data submitted for processing have indeed been processed. The biggest source of weakness in many installations is the handling of reject documents from the edit program. When only a few transactions from a batch are rejected by the edit program, the normal procedure is for the batch total to be adjusted for the rejected transactions, and the processing run continued. (If too many transactions are rejected the whole batch is rejected and returned.) The rejected transactions are married to the source documents and returned to the originating department to be corrected. The potential source of weakness here is that as far as the EDP department is concerned their data controls indicate balance and the returned documents are no longer their responsibility. For the originating department there is a temptation not to control these rejections effectively as they are already included in a previous day's totals. Cases have been known where a search through the desk of a clerk following his or her quitting has unearthed many rejected unprocessed documents lying at the back of the bottom drawer and dated months previously. One of the most compelling reasons for organizations to go on-line for data entry and editing is to avoid the costly delays and problems due to correcting and controlling rejected transactions.

Programmed controls

All data first entering a computer system need to be edited. The objective is to detect by means of logic checks every conceivable form of error. Hence every check that can be applied to the data should be. A rich source of ideas on editing data frequently can be tapped by talking to the clerks and supervisors responsible for manually creating and processing the data (if the previous system was manual) to find what checks they applied to determine if the data looked acceptable. Some of the typical edit checks applied to data include:

- *Limit checks* — predetermined limits that all data must fall between. In a real-time system the limit checks may be set more tightly, with a supervisor or operator over-ride.
- *Combination check* — a test applied to a number of fields simultaneously. For instance a transaction may have a price field and a quantity field, and a combination check may be set up on the product of price and quantity.

- *Restricted value check* — a test applied to a field which may be known to legitimately take on only a certain number of values. For example a field indicating sex may be only M or F or 1 or 2.
- *Format check* — all input documents have a defined format which needs to be checked. For example, numerics in numeric fields, alphas in alpha fields, and field sizes correct and in the right location.
- *Relationship checks* — frequently a certain code in one field may require a certain range of codes in another field. For example, the code F under 'sex' will limit the range of codes under 'title' to exclude the titles MR and MASTER.
- *Check digit* — this is the name given to a digit in a code which is mathematically derivable from the other digits by a formula. Application of the check digit formula and comparison with the check digit can indicate whether the code is legitimate or not. This can prevent the further processing of a transaction where the code is meaningless due to miscoding, transposition of two digits, misreading the input document, etc. A number of formulae are used for calculating a check digit.

One of the most common schemes is called 'the modulus 11 check digit". The method of computing it is:

1. Multiply each digit in the code number by its weight. The weight for the least significant digit is 2, the next least significant digit's weight is 3, and so on.
2. Add together the above products.
3. Divide this sum by 11.
4. If the remainder is 0, the check digit is also 0. If the remainder is not 0, subtract it from 11 to give the check digit. A check digit of 10 is usually written as 'x'.

These edit checks refer to internal checks of the data by recourse to predefined logic rules. Validation checks, on the other hand, refer to checks based on external references to file information. For example, a transaction to delete a customer from the master file may be validated, before attempting to process the transaction, by checking to make sure that the customer is actually on the file. Information which may be validated includes codes, names (in a real-time system the name displayed on the VDU allows manual validation in response to a code being input) and status condition.

Whereas the edit checks are compulsory on all systems, the validation check needs to be judged for each individual situation. If no validation program or module is included, any errors become apparent at update time. However, dealing with the problem then is a little more difficult than clearing all the data prior to update. In this case, the cost of both the development and the operation of the validation process have to be weighed against the problems caused by occasional (?) errors being detected and rejected at update time.

Output controls

The major concerns in this area are dissemination of output and the verification of the necessary relationships between input and output. Systems should exist, therefore, to ensure that output is distributed to authorized persons only, and that the data contained in that output have been reconciled with the various controls established over input and files.

File controls

As the whole file is passed in each processing run in sequential-file processing, it is comparatively simple to compute file controls by counting the number of records on the file and summing key fields. These totals can then be compared against totals calculated from the total of transactions input plus the total of the file at the end of the previous processing run. These 'run-to-run' controls afford a very high degree of file integrity, particularly when used in conjunction with a grandfather-father-son method of file version retention.

As an example, consider a simple accounts receivable file which has information on invoices, cash received, and balance due. After each update run the data could be printed as in Figure 10–1. The data marked with an asterisk would normally be held on the file, and the control reports checked to ensure the C/F figure of one run equalled the B/F figure of the next run.

```
              CONTROL REPORT XYZ 99/99/99        Page 1
                  CALCULATED TOTALS

   B/F   Balance Due*                            21 000.00
         add invoices              8 000.00
         deduct cash received     10 000.00

   C/F   Balance Due*                            19 000.00

                  SUMMED TOTALS

   B/F   Balance Due                             21 000.00
   C/F   Balance Due                             19 000.00
```

Figure 10–1   File controls

With direct access files it is uneconomical to read through the entire file after each updating run to sum the key fields. So only the records updated are included in the addition, and the assumption is made that the other records have not changed. Every so often the file must be checked by a complete pass through it to ensure the actual sum of the fields equals the calculated sum. This is normally done each time the file is backed up, when it must be read in its entirety.

An example of integrity controls for an inventory database is now given. The database contains five files:

- Inventory master file
- Inventory detail file

- Purchase order file
- Bill of materials file
- Inventory statistics file

Since these files are controlled independently, the inventory master file only is treated in this example. The inventory master file contains a header record which contains control totals for all five files in the database. Version control information is also kept in this record and consists of update version number, date, and time. The control totals to be kept for the file are:

- Record count
- Current standard price hash
- Last invoice price hash
- Ordering details quantities hash (ROP, EOQ)
- Revaluation amount
- Initial month's variance value
- Monthly increment value
- Anticipated delivery quantity hash
- YTD actual purchasing price variance

Updating and printing of the control totals and the version control information is performed in each update run by means of specially written copy routines, described in steps 1 and 2 and illustrated on the printer layout in Figure 10–2.

1. As each record to be updated is read (i.e. before any update process is performed), the relevant fields are *subtracted* from a standard set of accumulators in memory (initial condition zero). The standard set consists of one accumulator for each total kept in the header record. After each updated record is written back to the file, and also after each newly created record is written to the file, the relevant fields are *added* to the set of accumulators.

   Thus at the end of the program run the accumulators contain the 'net effect' which the update run has actually had on the data files.

2. At the end of the run the inventory update controls are printed as on Figure 10–2.

   (a) First, the header record containing input controls is read and printed.

   (b) Next, the accumulators containing the net effect of the update run are added to the control total fields read from the header record, and the new control totals are written back to the header record and printed as the output controls.

   (c) Then the differences between the output controls and the input controls are calculated, printed as calculated difference, and retained in memory for comparison with the transaction controls (see step 3).

3. Transaction controls for relevant corresponding fields are also accumulated during the program run into another standard set of accumulators, to reflect

PROGRAM:

INVENTORY UPDATE CONTROLS

RUN DATE: 99/99/99 RUN TIME: 99.99

FILE CODE		CONTROL DESCRIPTION	INPUT CONTROLS	OUTPUT CONTROLS	CALC. DIFF.	TRANS. CONTROLS	
(A)							
	(A)	Record Count	ZZZZZ9-	ZZZZZ9-	ZZZZZ9-	ZZZZZ9-	DISCREPANCY
	(B)	Curr. Std Price Hash	Z--Z9.99-	Z--Z9.99-	Z--Z9.99-	Z--Z9.99-	DISCREPANCY
	(C)	Last Invoice Price Hash	Z--Z9.99-	Z--Z9.99-	Z--Z9.99-	Z--Z9.99-	DISCREPANCY
	(D)	ROP. & EOQ Hash	Z---Z9-	Z---Z9-	Z---Z9-	Z---Z9-	DISCREPANCY
	(E)	Revaluation Amount Hash	Z--Z9.99-	Z--Z9.99-	Z--Z9.99-	Z--Z9.99-	DISCREPANCY
	(F)	Init. Month Var. Value	Z--Z9.99-	Z--Z9.99-	Z--Z9.99-	Z--Z9.99-	DISCREPANCY
	(G)	Mthly Increment Value	Z--Z9.99-	Z--Z9.99-	Z--Z9.99-	Z--Z9.99-	DISCREPANCY
	(H)	Antic. Deliv. Qty Hash	Z---Z9-	Z---Z9-	Z---Z9-	Z---Z9-	DISCREPANCY
	(I)	YTD Act. Pur. Price Var.	Z--Z9.99-	Z--Z9.99-	Z--Z9.99-	Z--Z9.99-	DISCREPANCY

Figure 10-2   Printer layout — control totals

the effect on the controls which the transactions processed were intended to have.

At the end of the run then these transaction controls are printed as part of the inventory update controls and compared with the calculated differences stored in memory (see step 2(c)). Where an individual transaction control is different from the corresponding calculated difference a discrepancy message is printed on the relevant line, as illustrated in Figure 10–2.

10.7 AUDIT TECHNIQUES

The changes in methods of data processing which have been brought about by the use of computers have not altered many of the techniques used by auditors to carry out their task. The internal control questionnaire still plays a large part in the audit process, as do physical verification of assets and general review of the organization's results, among others. However, the techniques for verifying the existence and correct functioning of controls within the processing activities have changed considerably.

In the early stages of computer use, auditing 'around the computer' was commonly employed because the systems largely matched earlier manual procedures. They provided clear audit trails, narrow application boundaries, and complete hard-copy reporting of all system activities. Thus the computer was largely ignored in the audit process. Then came the introduction of systems using exception reporting (where complete master-file listings are seldom produced), high levels of integration (where input to one system triggers automatic action in other application areas), and remote-terminal data entry (where traditional batch checking may not be carried out). System integrity became much more dependent on programmed controls. Consequently, new techniques for auditing 'through the computer' were developed to verify these controls. In this section a few of these techniques are examined in order to gain an insight into the current audit technology. The example techniques are:

- Test data method
- Tracing
- Integrated test facility
- Parallel simulation
- Transaction selection
- Generalized audit software

Test data method

Anyone who has written a computer program is familiar with the use of test data to verify the correct functioning of that program, and should also be aware that the most difficult task is designing adequate test data so that it reveals not only that the program can process correct data in the manner intended, but also that it can react correctly to the full range of data input in the operating environment. When using test data the auditor can verify edit routines, batch controls, processing logic, computations, or file update validity. Thus the technique is used to verify that some part of an application program is functioning in the correct fashion. It obviously does not verify any production data. The advantages of this technique include:

- It requires small EDP knowledge on the part of the auditor
- It allows repeated testing which can be enlarged incrementally at a low cost
- It provides objective evidence that certain very important programmed controls are functioning as required

Tracing

The trace module is used by programmers to debug programs, as with test data, but in this case the auditor may apply the tool for a different purpose: that of uncovering 'unusual' code or code which was not executed in processing the test data. Thus it can be used to assess the comprehensiveness of the test data.

A trace module is a set of code which tracks and records the program statements executed in a run and, by comparing this list with a program listing, the unexecuted statements can be found. An auditor might use this facility when running test data through, say, a debtors system, to see if there is any code in the program which is not in accord with the program specifications. The benefits of using this facility, however, must be weighed against the programming knowledge requirement placed on the auditor.

Integrated test facility (ITF)

This technique involves the creation of a fictitious entity (department, customer, etc.) so that test data can be run through a live system during the normal operation. This enables comprehensive system testing (unlike simple test data) at a relatively low cost and on a regular but unscheduled basis. Of course, a major requirement of this approach is that the test data do not carry into the organization's records and reports. This can be achieved by reversing the test data by appropriate accounting entries, or by modifying the system so that the test data are separated and not incorporated in the organization's records.

Parallel simulation

Rather than process test data through a live system (as in ITF) it is possible to process live data through a 'test' system. In parallel simulation, system aspects which concern an audit are programmed by the auditor to simulate the live system, so that the simulated output can be compared with the output of the live system. This provides a very effective audit tool, the major drawbacks being the development time and cost of the simulation software.

Transaction selection

By processing an organization's transactions using specially written software, the auditor can monitor transaction activity, error types and rates, and use the computer to sample transactions for subsequent analysis. This allows more thorough auditing of transactions, but at the cost of developing and running the selection software. An alternative is to code the data-collection modules into the production system (embedded audit data collection) so that separate runs are not required for the collection process.

Generalized audit software

This is perhaps one of the most widely used computer audit techniques, in which parameter-driven software is used to inquire against data files and perform many of the functions that would have been done by hand in a manual system. These packages provide facilities to:

- Balance files
- Select and report data from files
- Statistically sample
- Check data integrity
- Compare file generations

10.8 CONCLUSION

The importance of adequate controls over the EDP environment is evidenced by statistics which compare different types of fraud loss in the United States of America. For example, the average loss through a non-EDP fraud up to 1975 was approximately $19 000, whereas in EDP it was $450 000. The types of manipulation carried out involved the addition, deletion, and alteration of input transactions, changes to master files, changes to programs, and improper computer operations. Furthermore, the perpetrators involved people from data entry personnel to office managers.

Because of the importance of adequate controls it is becoming common for the internal EDP auditor to act in an advisory capacity on all new system development, and for the system designer to view this person as a valuable adjunct to the development team.

REFERENCES

J.G. BURCH & J.L. SARDINAS, *Computer Control and Audit*, John Wiley and Sons, Santa Barbara, Calif., 1978.

N.L. ENGER & P.W. HOWERTON, *Computer Security*, Amacom, New York, 1980.

L.I. KRAUSS & A. MACGAHAN, *Computer Fraud and Countermeasures*, Prentice-Hall Inc., Englewood Cliffs, N.J., 1979.

R.W. LOTT, *Auditing the Data Processing Function*, Amacom, New York, 1980.

THE INSTITUTE OF INTERNAL AUDITORS, *Systems Auditability and Control Study*, The Institute of Internal Auditors, Inc., Florida, 1977.

APPENDIX TO CHAPTER 10 — CRYPTOGRAPHIC SYSTEMS

A10.1 THE ROLE OF CRYPTOGRAPHY

Cryptography (lit. secret writing) is an ancient art. Julius Caesar employed a simple substitution cipher in which each letter is displaced a constant (cyclic) number of places. The growing interest in secure digital communication has sparked a renewed interest in cryptography. Military and diplomatic cryptographic methods have been specially refined to resist the efforts of computer-aided cryptanalysts, at least until the secret communication has lost its intelligence value.

Particularly sensitive information is usually enciphered using the 'one-time pad' method in which both parties use an identical series of random one-time letters to act as a continuous key for both encryption and decryption. The one-time pad must be used once only, otherwise the cipher is liable to subsequent cryptanalytic efforts. As a result, the communicants must have a supply of one-time pad material at least as large as the amount of text to be transmitted. In many practical situations, the sheer volume of data precludes the use of one-time pad systems.

In general, a cryptographic privacy system uses a pair of transformation functions E and D to encrypt or decrypt respectively. If M is the plain text message, then $C = E(M)$ is the cipher text. The inverse function recovers the plain text, i.e. $M = D(C)$. In some systems $E = D$. In others, knowledge of E (or D) allows the simple derivation of D (or E). In such systems the E,D pair must be securely guarded. The weakness lies in the fact that one of E or D must be supplied to one of the communicants, usually over an insecure channel. However, many systems of this category are resistant to cryptanalysis (provided the transforms are themselves securely delivered and protected).

A10.2 THE NBS DATA ENCRYPTION STANDARD (DES)

In the late 1960s IBM launched a research project into non-linear 'block ciphers' (a block cipher is a cryptographic system that divides the plain text message into equal-sized blocks, which are then transformed as independent entities to form blocks of cipher text). In January 1977 the US National Bureau of Standards (1977) adopted one of these as the National Data Encryption Standard.

The DES uses a standard (public knowledge) algorithm which generates cipher text blocks of 64 bits from a 64-bit plain text block and a 56-bit (secret) key. In other words the actual encryption transforms E may be written

$$E = \xi\,(K)$$

where ξ is the public algorithm and K is the secret key. As a result there are a total of $2^{56} = 7.2058 \times 10^{16}$ possible E transforms. The complexity of this E led to an initial estimate that it would take 2500 years of analysis on a CDC 7600 to break the DES (Menshaw, 1979).

However, following a detailed study (Diffie & Hellman, 1977), an approach has been described which, using a specially constructed machine, might find a solution in about one day. The researchers anticipate that by 1987 such a machine could be built for $20 000 and that the cost of a single solution would be around $5. For these reasons, the NBS DES has received some criticism and is likely to be superseded by a more robust algorithm. In the meanwhile, the DES is being used for the transmission of sensitive, but unclassified, messages. An LSI chip (the Intel 8294) was the first practical hardware implementation of the algorithm.

A10.3   PUBLIC KEY CRYPTOSYSTEMS

In secret key cryptosystems, the encrypt/decrypt transformation pair E,D is essentially defined by a single key or finite key sequence K which must be secure. There may be a public algorithm pair ξ and ∇ such that the secret pair E,D are supplied by:

$$E = \xi (K)$$
$$\text{and } D = \nabla (K)$$

In such systems, compromising K necessarily compromises E and D.

By contrast a public key cryptosystem is not compromised by public knowledge of the encryption algorithm E. More particularly, the derivation of any D from a given E (or vice versa) must be 'computationally infeasible' (i.e. the practical derivation would take millions of computer years). This concept, introduced in 1976, is regarded as a breakthrough. The authors show how to create virtually unbreakable ciphers that do not require the advance transmission of a key (Diffie & Hellman, 1976). The associated transforms E and D are efficient. There is, furthermore, an unexpected bonus: messages can be 'signed' or authenticated.

The principles of public key cryptosystems are:

- For each secure (one-way) channel there is a pair of related transforms E (public) and D (secret). D must be physically secured by its owner.
- The determination of D, given E, is computationally infeasible.
- Messages encrypted with E can only be decrypted with D.
- A message encrypted with D can be decrypted by E. (i.e. E and D are 'commutative' transformations.)
- Simple methods must exist for the efficient generation of D,E pairs. The generator is a 'trapdoor function'.

The consequences of these principles imply the following properties:

- Two communicants may engage in secure communication over an insecure channel (e.g. via a public computer message-switching utility)
- Communicants can 'sign' messages

A10.4   THE MIT ALGORITHM

A practical system embodying the five principles of public key cryptosystems was suggested by a team of MIT computer scientists (Rivest, Shamir & Adleman, 1978). The MIT system is (like the DES) a block cipher system. Groups of plain text are treated as large binary integers (at least 200 decimal digits long). The number is transformed by E to create another large integer (the cipher) which is then transmitted. The essence of the MIT public key cryptosystem is in following the steps:

1. Select two large (secret) primes P and Q (each with at least 100 decimal digits).
2. The product $N = PQ$ is part one of the public key (over 200 digits!).
3. Select a large (secret) decryption key D which has no common factors with the product $(P-1)(Q-1)$.
4. Select a large (public) encryption key E such that the product ED has a remainder of 1 when divided by $(P-1)(Q-1)$,

   i.e. $ED = 1$ modulo $[(P-1)(Q-1)]$.

The pair N,E is the 'public key'. D is the secret key. Rivest *et al.* show how steps 1–4 (the key-generating trapdoor) can be achieved using normal digital techniques. Clearly, they are beyond manual — or even calculator — methods.

Before the processes of encryption and decryption are described, readers may care to verify the following 'toy' example. If P and Q are chosen as 7 and 11, N is 77 (public) and D could be 13 (no factors common with 60). The first value of E to satisfy the equation in 4 above is 37 (since $13 \times 37 = 8 \times 60 + 1$). Thus the public key could be (77,37) with a secret key of 13. Other values of D and E exist for the same N (e.g. $D = 11$ and $E = 11$).

The difficulty of the MIT system lies in the computational difficulty of factoring large values of N. In the toy example, N can be factored immediately, hence revealing the product $(P-1)(Q-1) = 60$ from which it is a simple step to derive E (given $D = 13$).

The encryption process then proceeds:

5. Convert each block of plain text to a large integer M $(M < N)$.
6. Compute cypher C as the remainder of M^E after dividing by N.
7. Transmit C (C will be less than N and will have the same block size as the plain text block).

Decryption is similar:

8. Compute plain text M as the remainder of C^D after dividing by N.

Clearly the values of M^E and C^D will be very large indeed, so large that they could not be held in main storage! Rivest *et al.* demonstrate a neat algorithm for computing the remainder using an iterative process which involves values no larger than 10^{400}. In spite of the size of the values required, integer calculations are well within the computational capacities of most 'normal' digital computers — even micro-computers such as the INTEL 8080.

A10.5 PKC IMPLEMENTATION

As with other block ciphers (e.g. the DES) it is preferable that the encryption/decryption processes take place in hardware (or firmware equivalent) to provide maximum security and speed of translation. Denning (1979) proposes a hardware encryption/decryption machine which interfaces a secure computing facility or data station to public (insecure) communications facilities. This machine has separate channels for encryption and decryption using the MIT PKC algorithm. Denning proposes 'hard' (ROM-based) keys for encryption and decryption, with an alternative switch-selectable 'soft' public key for alternative communication paths. If two communicating parties (A and B) share their public keys (P_A and P_B) but secure their secret keys (S_A and S_B) then secure communication proceeds as follows:

1. If A wishes to send message X to B, then message X is passed through A's encryption section (under P_B) to emerge as $P_B(X)$ on the insecure channel. Only B can decipher this message.
2. B receives $P_B(X)$ via B's decryption channel (under S_B), generating $S_B(P_B(X))$ which is the original transmitted message X.

The process is reversed when B transmits to A (using keys P_A and S_A). Clearly, for each party with whom A wishes to communicate, A must have a copy of that party's public key. Alternatively, a central computing facility (CF) might be used as a message-switching centre. In that case, each communicant would use the CF's public key, relying on the CF to decrypt the message, determine the addressee, then encrypt the message for forwarding using the addressee's public key (taken from a stored table of communicants). The danger here is that the message is 'exposed' within the CF. On the other hand, the CF contains no records of 'secret' keys.

The purpose of Denning's 'hard' key (i.e. the station's own public key) is to strictly limit the termination of each receiving line at the decipher box. Thus, if the CF transmits 'plain' text, the pathway must be as shown in Figure 10–3.

A10.6 DIGITAL SIGNATURES

The concept of a 'digital signature' is of concern to those involved with authorization and transfer of electronic funds (or equivalents). The recipient must be able to receive proof that a particular message received did in fact originate under authorization. The PKC system supplies this requirement by allowing senders to encipher their authorized messages using their own secret keys. The message is then deciphered using the sender's public key. This, however, means that any party having access to the sender's public key can read the authorized document. Furthermore, the system violates the principle of Denning's 'hard' key i.e. that the transmission must always terminate at a decipher box.

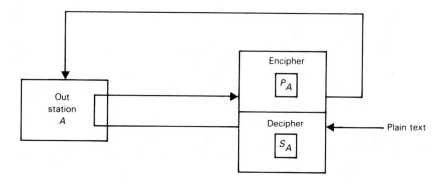

Figure 10-3 Use of 'hard' P-key to decipher plain text message from communication channel

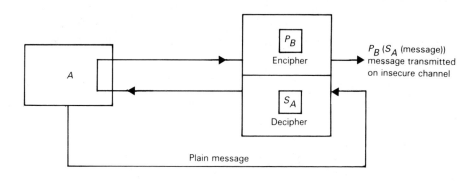

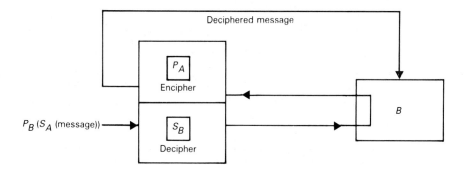

Figure 10-4 Message securely signed by *A* and transmitted to *B*

Denning's solution (see Figure 10–4) retains this principle and adds security to the transmitted authorized message. Clearly, only the (authorized) sender has access to the secret key used to encipher the message.

A10.7 CONCLUSION

The Rivest *et al.* PKC is one example of practical security available both for direct transmission and for the storing of database material of a sensitive nature. Advances in numerical methods, cryptanalysis, and special purposes VLSI devices may in the future drastically reduce the 'breaking time' for these systems. Variations have been suggested by some writers which may extend this breaking time even further. The suggestions are primarily concerned with combining various approaches, but most fall down on the full public key requirements.

Readers interested in pursuing this topic further are referred to the article by Diffie & Hellman (1979), which is an excellent tutorial paper with a large bibliography.

REFERENCES

D.E. DENNING, 'Secure Personal Computing in an Insecure Network', *Communications of the ACM*, vol. 22, no. 8, August 1979, pp. 476-82.

W. DIFFIE & M.E. HELLMAN, 'New Directions in Cryptography', *IEEE Trans. Inform. Theory*, vol. IT-22, November 1976, pp. 644-54.

W. DIFFIE & M.E. HELLMAN, 'Exhaustive Cryptanalysis of the NBS Data Encryption Standard', *Computer*, vol. 10, no. 6, 1977, pp. 74-84.

W. DIFFIE & M.E. HELLMAN, 'Privacy and Authentication: An Introduction to Cryptography', *Proceedings of the IEEE*, vol. 67, no. 3, March 1979, pp. 397-427.

R.V. MEUSHAW, 'The Standard Data Encryption Algorithm', *Byte*, vol. 14, no. 3, March 1979, p. 66.

NATIONAL BUREAU OF STANDARDS, *Data Encryption Standard*, Federal Information Processing Standard (FIPS) Publication no. 46, January 1977.

R.L. RIVEST, A. SHAMIR & L. ADLEMAN, 'A Method for Obtaining Digital Signatures and Public Key Cryptosystems', *Communications of the ACM*, vol. 21, no. 2, February 1978, pp. 120-6.

CASE STUDY — UNION RECIPE SYSTEM
BATCH CONTROL

Refer to the Union Recipe System in the Case Studies to Chapters 3 and 4.

Case Study — Union Recipe System Batch Control

ASSIGNMENT

1. Design control sheets for the Ingredient Transactions and the Recipe Transactions which will enable batch control to be established.

2. List the file integrity controls you feel should be accumulated and prepare the format of the edit and update control listing that could be produced as a result of your design.

3. You may have noticed that the systems flowcharts for this case contained no facility for file back-up. Determine the back-up you consider would be necessary and explain when and how the back-up runs would be carried out.

CASE STUDY — KOOL-KAT LTD ADMINISTRATIVE AND PROCESSING CONTROLS

Kool-Kat Ltd installs air-conditioning systems in buildings throughout Sydney. They pay their employees on a straight time-work basis and, consequently, each employee completes a weekly time sheet showing details of regular and overtime hours spent on a particular job. Overtime is paid at either time-and-a-half or double-time.

Management has decided to implement the payroll procedure on computer and use the system for job costing as well as payroll processing. The main outputs required are:

- Payroll
- Payslips
- Work-in-process totals for each job classified by trade categories
- Coinage analysis

The operation of the system is shown in Figure 10–5. To simplify the system, it is assumed that each employee allocated to a job stays on that job for a full week. Thus staff are allocated to jobs on Friday for the following week.

Case Study — Kool-Kat Ltd Administrative and Processing Controls

ASSIGNMENT

Evaluate the administrative and processing controls of this system as evident in Figure 10–5. In your answer, list suggestions as to how these controls might be improved.

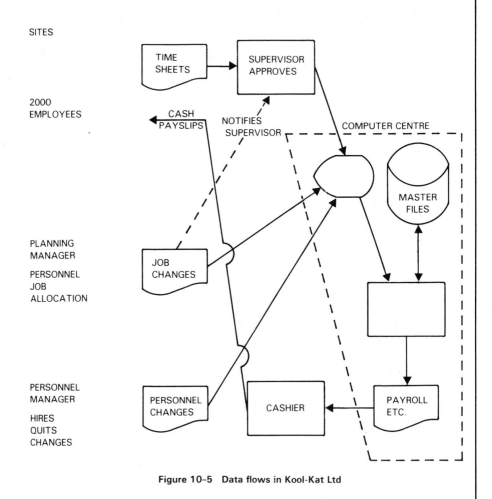

SITES

2000
EMPLOYEES

PLANNING
MANAGER

PERSONNEL
JOB
ALLOCATION

PERSONNEL
MANAGER

HIRES
QUITS
CHANGES

TIME
SHEETS

SUPERVISOR
APPROVES

CASH
PAYSLIPS

NOTIFIES
SUPERVISOR

COMPUTER CENTRE

MASTER
FILES

JOB
CHANGES

PERSONNEL
CHANGES

CASHIER

PAYROLL
ETC.

Figure 10-5   Data flows in Kool-Kat Ltd

11 IMPLEMENTATION AND TESTING

11.1 INTRODUCTION

11.1.1 Typical Activities

Implementation and testing are those phases which follow the approval of the system specification. Once a system specification has been divided into a set of discrete program specifications (see Subsection 5.6.3), each such specification is converted into a program design. The *program design* is a graphical representation which defines the logical procedures needed to meet the program specification. The program design is in turn converted into actual source code. The terms 'program design' and 'program design specification' may be used interchangeably.

Traditionally, the implementation and testing of software have been two distinct developmental phases. More recent approaches have tended to redistribute the bulk of testing across the implementation phase and so emphasize and demarcate particular activities proper to implementation. Implementation is not simply 'writing programs'. While some especially skilled programmers may be able to write a working program directly from a program specification without an intermediate program design, issues related to software reliability, correctness, and maintainability demand an approach which relies on staged development with identifiable milestones. Following such an approach, the individual milestones represent the approved completion of specific activities, accompanied by approved testing procedures which affirm the correctness and suitability of the phases concerned.

The use of phased testing highlights certain activities proper to implementation, and can lighten the workload of testing the finished modules and subsystems. 'Final phase' testing is discussed in a later section of this chapter (Section 11.7).

Although the individual activities may be divided according to the modularization which results from top-down development, there is a clear division between the activities of program design and 'coding'. While a program specification describes *what* actions are to be performed on required sets of data, it does not attempt to specify the *how* of those actions. Each procedure required by a program specification is accompanied by functional specifications which explain what the procedure is to do, not the internal logic of the procedure. A program design specification provides the internal logic for a procedure. By presenting that specification in a form which is independent of the constraints of a particular programming language, designers are able to confine their attention to matters of logic and the requirements of the program specifications. Furthermore, language-independent program designs may be rigorously tested for consistency and correctness before a single line of code is written. The approval of a set of program design specifications is a key milestone in the implementation exercise.

11.1.2   Personnel Responsibilities

The activity of converting documented program design specifications into code requires the conventional skills of a programmer. The testing procedures which are applied during the development of the program design are also appropriate to the verification of the logical equivalence of the source program and the supplied program design. Testing procedures include desk checking and group walkthroughs. The testing of a completed system is an activity which may be assigned to a distinct group such as quality assurance or representatives of the user group. This group's stamp of approval generally signals the start of the (possibly phased) introduction of the new software into the operating environment.

While separation of the testing group from the group responsible for implementation is easily argued, such may not be the case for the group which develops the program design specifications and the group responsible for coding those specifications. The precise demarcation of responsibilities depends on the internal organization chosen for the implementation. In some instances it may be preferable for one individual to generate the program design for a particular group of modules, and then to code those modules. Alternatively, program design may be the sole province of a team quite distinct from the 'programmers'. It should be remembered that most professional programmers would understand that their expertise rests in both camps, with greater emphasis given to the design specification process as the programmer's experience increases. Some organizations employ trainee programmers as 'coders' whose chief function is to 'cut code' with possible brief excursions into the specification of clearly specified modules.

11.1.3   Typical Problems

Various standards of documentation apply to all phases of implementation and testing. Some of these are discussed in Sections 11.2 and 11.5. Apart from supplying clear input to subsequent stages, one of the main reasons for insisting on correct documentation is that it supports the inevitable exercise of maintenance programming.

No matter how careful the implementation or detailed the checking, systems generally expose their hidden bugs over a period of time. Although the techniques of structured systems design and structured program development have significantly reduced the frequency of such malfunctions, there still remains the problem of changed functional specifications. As the needs of a system change, so must the associated programs be amended. These changes are generally the responsibility of a maintenance programming group, for whom the availability of proper documentation is mandatory. A majority of organizations report that maintenance programming consumes more resources than does the development of new systems.

The problem of excessive run timing occurs when system hardware resources are not capable of providing the necessary throughput. Final determination of actual run times is an aspect of testing which must clearly wait until all the required (and tested) software modules are available. Not all timing over-runs are a result of hardware limitations. More efficient processing algorithms or the use of Assembler language for critical areas may solve the problem.

11.1.4   Implementation Planning

Planning the implementation of a new or revised system is linked to the organizational structure chosen. Some specific structures and approaches are given in Chapter 12. They include the chief programmer team approach and egoless team structures. Planning involves the distribution of responsibilities, determination of required resources, and the budgeting of time and money. The budgeting of time (and consequently of resources and money) is a notoriously difficult exercise when the system being implemented carries unfamiliar components. Although the construction of a new program is similar to the construction of a new bridge, usually the bridge engineers would have constructed many similar bridges previously during their careers. The same is not necessarily true for 'software engineers'.

11.1.5   Software Engineering

Parallels between software and the products of conventional engineering abound. In electrical and mechanical engineering formal and informal techniques are applied to the creation of physical products designed to meet certain specifications. These products are tested and documented before being released to users. Standards are applied and construction methodologies are chosen to best suit the product. The term 'software engineering' acknowledges that close similarities exist between the practices in conventional engineering and those appropriate to the creation of computer software, in spite of the less tangible nature of the product.

Software engineering is by far the younger discipline. Accordingly it has seemed appropriate for the software engineer to draw heavily upon the established corpus of methodologies developed in those parallel but more senior fields. Both

methodologies follow the essential sequence of requirements (or functional) specification, detailed (or design) specification, construction, testing, user documentation, and distribution. Added to these phases are matters concerning product
reliability, maintainability, robustness, and legal protection against unauthorized
use. The principal difference is at the level of construction (or implementation). The
conventional engineer frequently constructs a physical prototype from (generally)
graphical specifications, refines that prototype, then develops a production procedure. The software engineer is not as concerned with mass production. There is
rarely a corresponding emphasis on prototype development since there are no
economies of scale in the mass-distribution process. The software product is
therefore designed more with an eye to a parallel validation of the design — as is
generally the case with large and expensive physical developments.

A particular advantage for software engineers is the essentially logical nature of
their products. It is possible, at least in principle, to prove that a given system or
subsystem will meet a requirements specification before the process of implementation is actually commenced. By contrast, normal engineering products are
subject to the variable characteristics of metals, lubricants, and semiconductors as
well as their response to a particular physical environment. On the other hand, where
software requirements attempt to define the performance of a particular
machine–person interface, or where the software must interact with the real (analog)
world, logical design considerations are often less significant than those concerning
the performance of the interface itself.

Both software and conventional engineers apply appropriate tools to the
particular phases of a project. The term *software tools* is generally applied to software
utilities used mainly in the process of implementation. These include text editors,
assemblers, compilers, linking loaders, and debugging packages. Other software
tools may be used to manage the development of application programs, or to assist in
the automatic production of certain sequences of source code. The construction of
new (non-trivial) software would be almost unthinkable without such computer-
based aids. Accordingly considerable attention has been given to software tools since
the days of the earliest stored-program machines. Compilers, in particular, are highly
sophisticated and refined pieces of software in their own right. Newer and more
effective languages have also appeared and matured as particular construction
means.

By contrast, methodologies appropriate to the earlier stages of specification are
of much more recent origin, and are usually less formal in nature. Some of these are
discussed in Chapters 2, 4, and 6. Most, like their counterparts, are graphical in
nature. The oldest of these, the flowchart, has been in popular use since the late
1950s, although the format stabilized only in the mid-1960s.

Examples of currently used specification tools are SRI's Hierarchical
Development Methodology (HDM), TRW's Software Requirement Engineering
Methodology (SREM), Computer Aided Design and Specification Analysis Tool
(CADSAT), and SofTech's Structured Analysis and Design Technique (SADT).

This chapter is concerned with the techniques appropriate to the implementation phase of software engineering. The scope ranges from the program design
specifications through documentation techniques and system testing to
installation.

11.2 PROGRAM DESIGN METHODS

The implementation of a new or revised system is the stage which usually follows on the formal approval of a detailed system specification. It is commonly assumed that this stage demands less creative thinking than that associated with the overall system design. Most programmers would hotly contest that assertion. The process of creating a suite of functioning, interrelated programs to meet set specifications requires not only special technical skills, experience, and expertise, but also problem-solving abilities geared to an ever-changing hardware technology. Slightly less demanding is the role of the maintenance programmer, whose task is generally that of building upon someone else's foundations.

Apart from the normal processes of graphical logic specification and coding, the implementation stage requires appropriate management skills and techniques to bring about that implementation within the required guidelines. Implementation is an expensive operation and is properly subject to the usual practices of cost control and scheduling. The costing, for example, must take into account the various support facilities required by the programming staff. These include computer time, keypunching services and consumables, and secretarial assistance. Other issues include selecting the program specification technique, programming language(s), in-house standards to apply to the chosen techniques, and the form of documentation to be generated during implementation.

11.2.1 Program Specifications

Previous chapters show that in practice, the precise form of a detailed system specification varies widely. It may range from a highly detailed New System Design document, as defined by IBM's SOP, to a broad requirements document which leaves ample scope for creative design at the hands of the implementation team. An example of a program specification format which allows the system designer considerable liberty in the selection of appropriate techniques (graphical or textual) is the skeletal specification shown in Figure 11-1. This skeleton is used internally by software engineering staff in a computer company engaged in the development of interactive data capture equipment. Users of the format are required to include all headings within any particular specification, even if certain headings are inappropriate. The purpose of this requirement is that the essential skeleton is available in any specific application document. Irrespective of the specifications structure, there generally are systems flowcharts, file specifications, data structures, performance requirements, and detailed annotations. Whatever form is selected for documenting the program specification, the end product must serve as an effective and definitive input for creating the program design specifications. Ideally, there should now be no need for members of the programming team to engage in more interviews with potential users of the system (although, in practice, variations to specifications may well require such activities).

<pre>
1   GENERAL INFORMATION

    1.1   Cover Page
            1.1.1   Date of Issue
            1.1.2   Approvals
    1.2   Revision Page(s)
            1.2.1   Date of Issue
            1.2.2   Revision Number
            1.2.3   Approvals
            1.2.4   Description
    1.3   Applicable Documents

2   SYSTEM DESCRIPTION

    2.1   Introduction
            2.1.1   Scope
            2.1.2   Basic Concepts
            2.1.3   System Definitions
    2.2   Functional Requirements
            2.2.1   Capabilities
            2.2.2   Limitations
            2.2.3   System Restrictions
            2.2.4   Assumptions
    2.3   Database Requirements
            2.3.1   Content
            2.3.2   Structure
            2.3.3   Layout
    2.4   Performance Requirements

3   OPERATOR INTERFACE

    3.1   Input
            3.1.1   Command Description
            3.1.2   Command Execution
    3.2   Output
            3.2.1   System Responses
            3.2.2   Error Messages
            3.2.3   Status
</pre>

Figure 11-1   Skeletal program specification

A specification used internally by an organization developing interactive data capture and retrieval systems.

11.2.2 Program Design Specifications

The programs which make up the complete implementation of a system usually fall into a natural set of software modules, each having its own design specification. The techniques of top-down structured programming are appropriate to the development of the individual program specifications for each module. Top-down analysis requires the specification of the overall logic of a module in terms of elementary operations performed by secondary modules. The initial analysis necessarily specifies the requirements of each of the secondary modules. This means that the process of program specification for the complete program becomes a recursive operation which continues until all secondary modules have been expressed in terms of elementary operations. This process naturally enforces a logical development of the entire program specification documentation as a tree structure. Traditionally, the specification for each individual module is in terms of a program (or logic) flowchart with associated narrative supporting the design by explanations and appropriate justifications. In Section 11.4, a number of alternative procedural specification methods are discussed.

The completion of a first draft for a program design should be marked by one or more stages of formal justification. This is to ensure that the proposed logical framework will indeed fulfil the program specifications. Various justification techniques are available, the most common of which involve private desk checking and public walkthrough. Once the programming team is satisfied with a given set of specifications, management authorization is normally required before the coding phase is begun.

It may be noted that, in the context of the foregoing, the term *programming* applies most appropriately to the process of creating formal program design specifications. The conversion of these specifications into actual program source code, as an isolated exercise, is *coding*. However, the one term 'programming' is commonly used to encompass both activities, since both are usually performed by the same individual. The actual distribution of duties depends on the team structure chosen for the implementation.

11.3   MANAGING THE PROGRAMMING FUNCTION

The question of programming-team structure is dealt with in Chapter 12. Typical structures include the conventional approach with an internal hierarchy and well-defined roles. Alternative structures, such as the egoless team and the chief programmer team are also described.

This section is concerned with the selection and application of standards and with the selection of programming languages.

11.3.1   In-house Standards

Global standards generally concern issues such as programming languages, flowcharting symbols, and certain design methodologies such as HIPO and data flow diagrams. Some have been subjected to formal standardization procedures through international bodies such as ISO. *In-house* standards are set locally for internal application. They may relate to forms of documentation, procedures for approving design stages, subsets of programming languages, and syntax conventions. They may define approved design methodologies and local variations.

Consider an organization with a number of small machines running under the CP/M® operating system. A clear requirement is the use of software tools which are designed to function under CP/M. The organization may elect to limit its programming languages to COBOL, PL/I-80®, and Digital Research's Macro-assembler. It would be necessary to further define which COBOL is to be used in the light of possible later applications in which some modules will be written in COBOL,

®CP/M and PL/I-80 are registered trade marks of Digital Research

others in PL/I, and others in Assembler. Unless the translators generate compatible object code, such mixtures would not be possible.

Broad directives are commonly supplemented by more specific guidelines governing such matters as the choice of identifiers, rules for program indentation, the use of lower case in source code, the maximum module size, the use of recursive procedures, the use of non-standard language extensions, rules governing in-line source documentation formats and internal program identification, the use of multistatement lines and multiline statements, conventions for naming files and disk volumes, rules for the maintenance of back-up files, etc. The point of such restrictions is to enhance continued and effective interaction within the programming team. If programming styles are limited, others within the team are more readily able to engage in useful walkthrough procedures. Where teams are very small, the setting of in-house standards may be less formal, very often growing naturally out of shared experience.

A technical writer or librarian is sometimes given the responsibility of ensuring that in-house standards are maintained. This can be done by requiring that all source programs and related documents are authorized by the librarian, say, before final acceptance.

11.3.2 Language Selection

Although programming languages abound, most courses in commercial programming offer only three or four, usually selected from COBOL, RPG-II, BASIC, IBM Assembler, FORTRAN, and PL/I. Other languages, not so commonly used, include Pascal, Algol, Forth, Lisp, and Snobol.

Without doubt, COBOL is by far the most widely used high-level language in the commercial environment. Its development in the early 1960s came about through the observed need for a language more suited to the handling of files and complex data structures as distinct from the 'number-crunching' types of application for which FORTRAN was designed. The name COBOL stands for **CO**mmercial **B**usiness **O**riented **L**anguage, while FORTRAN derives from **FOR**mula **TRAN**slator. COBOL is offered as the main programming language in almost all courses in commercial data processing.

The widespread acceptance of COBOL stems from the ready availability of COBOL-trained programmers, and the considerable body of existing application programs already written in that language. COBOL has been subjected to standardization at various levels. Organizations using COBOL as their sole language are not 'locked' into a particular manufacturer's hardware, since virtually all commercial machines have available excellent COBOL compilers. COBOL nevertheless has its drawbacks. Programmers complain about its 'wordiness' and unforgiving demand for precise syntax. The large list of reserved words requires considerable knowledge of the language before the simplest of programs may be written. More important is the difficulty of writing programs which are required to perform considerable string handling or number-crunching operations.

FORTRAN is a little older than COBOL. Its design derived from the need to generate efficient code capable of performing the extensive and complex numerical calculations which are common in scientific and engineering applications. FORTRAN's input–output facilities are generally primitive (being record oriented) and it does not support the data structures found in COBOL and PL/I. Surprisingly, FORTRAN is still used in a number of organizations for commercial data processing. This would have been understandable in the mid-1960s in view of the relative novelty of business-oriented languages, but it is less arguable today. FORTRAN lacks the elegant string-manipulation facilities of PL/I, and the input–output facilities of PL/I and COBOL. Its syntax is sometimes obscure and lacks some of the constructs beloved of the structured programmer. On the other hand, most FORTRAN compilers are capable of generating extremely efficient object code.

FORTRAN has been upgraded as a language a number of times, the principle versions being FORTRAN II, FORTRAN IV, and FORTRAN 77. In 1964 IBM announced NPL (New Programming Language), a compiler designed to meet, in one language, the needs of both COBOL and FORTRAN programmers. The language was to be at least as powerful in input–output as COBOL, with extensive data types and structures, plus computational facilities rivalling those of FORTRAN. In addition the new language would support list processing by using based variables. Shortly after the announcement, NPL was renamed PL/I (Programming Language One) and was seen by some as the death of both COBOL and FORTRAN and the birth of a new era in programming. As the years have attested, however, old programming languages, like old soldiers, never die. They won't even fade away. The arrival of PL/I simply added one more weapon to the programmer's arsenal.

Although PL/I has a wide scope, and lacks many of the obvious drawbacks of COBOL and FORTRAN, it is a very large language — much larger than either COBOL or FORTRAN. IBM's F-level PL/I compiler was also designed to be particularly forgiving (in response to complaints about COBOL). As a result, that compiler attempts to 'understand' almost anything supplied to it — and often can! Unfortunately, the compiler's understanding of a particular PL/I statement may not coincide with the programmer's understanding. Nevertheless, programmers initially trained in PL/I are quick to proclaim the virtues of that language, extolling its free format, elegant control structures, and ease of use. By the same token, however, it is generally found that programmers normally view their 'first language' through rose-coloured glasses.

IBM's hopes of a clean sweep for PL/I were not to be fulfilled. Few other manufacturers chose to support the language, with the result that to use PL/I was to become wedded to an IBM installation. During the late 1970s this situation changed. A number of large machine companies began to provide quite reasonable PL/I compilers. In 1980, Digital Equipment Corp. (DEC) announced a G-level compiler for its new 'supermini' — the VAX 11/780, a 32-bit machine in wide use in a broad spectrum of applications. The G-level subset included all the desirable attributes of the F-level language, reducing the size of the compiler by judicious pruning.

Shortly following DEC's PL/I announcement, Digital Research (the authors of CP/M) announced PL/I-80, a full G-level compiler (compatible with DEC's compiler) for small business computers based on the 8080-type microprocessor. PL/I-80 runs under the immensely popular operating system CP/M. Within a few months of its release, numerous software houses began offering new application packages written in PL/I-80. The market for these packages is considerable, and is expected to enhance PL/I's place as a popular software tool.

Although the object code generated by a compiler may be optimized automatically, there is little comparison with a machine-language program written in an assembler language for speed and compactness of code. While many commercial applications do not require such efficiencies, those which do frequently make use of modules written in assembler code designed to optimize critical sections or deeply nested loops. Programming at the assembler level is a highly specialized and exacting task. Each type of machine has a unique assembly language reflecting the architecture of the particular CPU. Accordingly, few application programmers are attracted to this form of work since it tends to tie them to a specific manufacturer's hardware. Those who have the aptitude and skills required are in great demand.

Another popular language is BASIC. Having graduated from its early days in educational applications, BASIC is now supported on almost all mainframes, mini- and microcomputers.

The choice of a language clearly depends on available compilers/assemblers, on the skills of available staff, and on attitudes concerning the portability of software, ease of future maintenance and programmer productivity.

11.4 PROGRAM DESIGN

11.4.1 Design Objectives

The purpose of a formal program design is to provide a specification suitable for generating actual programs. The program design therefore embodies the logical or algorithmic statement of each procedure, as well as the hierarchical relationship between those procedures.

Earlier design objectives were quite elementary. For each run (in a batched system), the main program would be subdivided into a number of routines suitable for distribution among the available programming staff. The preferred specification tool was the flowchart (as described in Section 2.4.1) or occasionally the decision table (Section 2.4.2). Neither technique is particularly useful in the determination and specification of the intermediate and internal data structures which might be used by the programs. Nor do they encourage structured programming practices (see Subsection 11.4.2).

Flowcharts and decision tables alike tend to encourage the use of low-level terms in the design specification, to the point where individual boxes or entries each represent a single line of source code. The use of the newer programming languages with extensive control structures has often made such detailed flowcharting redundant. As a result, many systems are developed without a distinct intermediate step of program design, the programs being written directly from the program specification. In such cases the stages of design and coding are virtually identical.

Although the omission of an identifiable stage of program design may have short-term benefits in terms of speed of implementation, these savings may be outweighed by other long-term considerations. The availability of clear program design specifications is essential for effective testing and debugging, as well as for the inescapable task of maintenance programming. Further, a well-presented design specification can permit the early elimination of most logical bugs before they are committed to actual code. Revising a program design specification after locating logical faults is generally much easier (and safer) than rewriting sections of code. This commendation for the use of a clearly defined stage of program design is not made simply for low-level specifications which are scarcely removed from the final code. To be valuable in the analysis of logical correctness and in subsequent maintenance, program design specifications need a generally higher level of statement. Thus, in many cases, a single carefully phrased English statement can express the same logical connotations as are embodied in an equivalent set of source statements. A programmer should have little difficulty translating a clear English expression into whatever language she or he happens to be using. It helps of course if the writer of the design specification has a mind for the ensuing task of the final programmer.

The use of program design techniques also encourages the development of programs with 'clean lines', as described in the section on structured design (Section 6.4). Unfortunately, flowcharts and decision tables, while having a general utility, do not inherently encourage the use of 'good program design' methods. Issues relating to the partitioning of modules and cohesion between modules can be addressed more appropriately by using design-specification methods geared to the methods of structured programming. Indeed, the arguments for structured programming are similar to those which encourage structured program design methodologies.

11.4.2 Structured Programming

The term 'structured programming' was coined by Dijkstra (1969). He, and other early proponents, intended the term to describe a particular programming style. In more recent years, structured programming has been the subject of considerable debate and the target of many definitions. It is not particularly profitable to adopt a strictly formal approach to the topic, in spite of the formal nature of some aspects. The approach taken here is tempered by the need to discuss those elements of programming style now regarded as promoting 'good' practice. Commonly accepted notions of *structured programming* include:

- Programming by stepwise refinement
- Avoiding the GOTO statement
- Placing limits on the size of source code for modules
- Avoiding global variables
- Proving module correctness by formal means

Perhaps the most hotly debated notion has been the second item — the avoidance of the GOTO statement. In many programming languages it is quite impossible to code meaningful programs without the GOTO or its equivalent.

Examples include BASIC, FORTRAN, and assembler languages. This, however, is not the essence of GOTO avoidance (Dijkstra, 1968). The real issue is one of 'control structures', i.e. methods of controlling the selection and repetition of particular blocks of code. This is discussed later in this section.

'Stepwise refinement' presupposes that all programs may be developed as a top-down tree structure. Little is said about the actual order of development other than that a particular module is designed only after a higher-level module (a 'calling' or 'predecessor' module) has been designed. Some low-level modules may have sufficient generality of purpose to be callable from more than one point in the tree.

The third item, limiting the source-code size, discourages complex modules. Dijkstra insists on the concept of modules which may be comprehended by 'brains of limited degree'. It is important for programmers (even super-programmers) to accept the natural finitude of their own intellects. Indeed, acknowledgment of this limitation is an essential part of 'super-programming'. 'Clever' coding is discouraged since subtleties become obscurities with the passage of time.

Global variables are data items known both within the scope of a module, and within modules calling it and called by it. A *local variable* is limited to being known by the module or block in which it is defined. The use of local variables reduces the connectivity between modules and improves the internal cohesion of code within the module. Communication between modules may be better achieved by passing parameters at the point of module invocation. The use of local variables can be illustrated by a simple example. Consider a module (subroutine or procedure) designed to return a random number to the calling routine. The module would require a number of internal variables for use by the algorithm which generates the random number. After returning the single result to the calling module, the internal variables used would have no further significance. The memory space used by those variables and the names used to refer to them are no longer required once the result has been returned. If those variables are inaccessible to the calling module, then they are properly local in nature. If, on the other hand, the random-number routine happened to change a global value called, say, N, then an inadvertent use of the same variable name by another routine could have unpredictable results.

Most of the concepts associated with the control structures of structured programming arose out of considerations of formal 'proofs of correctness'. Unfortunately many modules designed for programs in the real, commercial world are not particularly amenable to formal proof techniques. On the other hand, the programmer should be able to justify a module's logic both in a desk check and in public walkthrough.

The use of preferred control structures, the use of local variables, and top-down decomposition are the key elements of structured programming. The generally accepted set of control structures, originally proposed by Bohm & Jacopini (1966), are:

- Sequential blocks
- IF-THEN-ELSE
- WHILE
- UNTIL

A commonly used convenient extension of the IF-THEN-ELSE is the CASE construct.

Each of these control structures has an elementary flowchart equivalent as shown in Figure 11–2. A sequential operation is represented by a block of instructions with one entry point and one exit point. For purposes of definition, the internal structure of the block is irrelevant. Thus a complete program is a single sequential block. Internally, it may consist of a sequence of smaller sequential blocks as well as others selected from the forgoing list. This is possible since all block types have only one entry point and one exit point, as may be seen from their equivalent flowcharts.

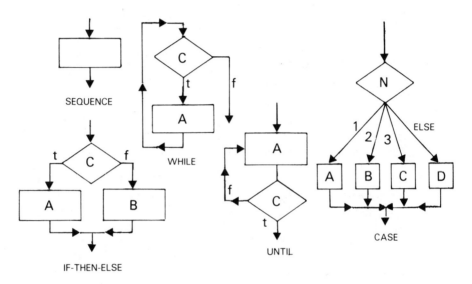

Figure 11–2   Control structures

The commonly accepted set of control constructs expressed as flowcharts.

All the rectangles used in Figure 11–2 represent sequential blocks; further, since each of the diagrams has only one entry and one exit each may be regarded as a sequential block by simply ignoring the operations between those points. Accordingly, these diagrams represent a primitive set of structures which may grow in complexity by progressively expressing each sequential block in terms of other structures until no further break down is possible. This is what is meant by 'progressive decomposition' or 'top-down analysis' of a program.

The IF-THEN-ELSE construct is a familiar selection operation. If, in Figure 11–2, the condition C is tested and found to be true, then the block labelled A is performed, otherwise block B is performed. There is a special case — sometimes called the IF-THEN construct — wherein the alternative B is omitted.

The CASE construct is a more general selection operation. The example shown in Figure 11–2 selects one of the blocks A, B, or C, if N is found to be 1, 2, or 3. If N is none of these, the 'default' or ELSE block D is performed. In some cases D is a null

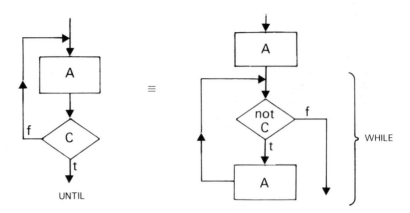

Figure 11-3   Construct synthesis

The UNTIL construct may be alternatively expressed in terms of the WHILE construct by repeating the loop body as shown here.

block. Where the programming language does not have the equivalent of a CASE statement, it is normal practice to code it as a series of IF-THEN-ELSE operations. Nevertheless, although it is technically not a necessary part of the required basic constructs, CASE is a most valuable tool.

The remaining two constructs shown in Figure 11-2 are controlled loops. The only difference between them lies in the positioning of the test. The WHILE block shown tests condition C. If C is true, block A (the body of the loop) is performed and control returns to the test point. Accordingly it is possible for a WHILE block to never execute the loop body (if the condition is false on the first entry). By contrast, the UNTIL block always executes the loop body at least once, since the test for completion is made after the loop body is performed.

The more recent programming languages include most of these control structures, some using the words CASE, WHILE, and UNTIL, in the senses just described. These languages have been designed (or upgraded in some cases) to allow the programmer to pass easily from a structured program design to an actual program. Few languages support all five forms explicitly. Provided that a language supports sequential blocks (and all do!), IF-THEN-ELSE, and WHILE, then the missing structures (CASE and UNTIL) can be synthesized from the others. Figure 11-3 shows how an UNTIL block may be built by performing the loop body unconditionally followed by a WHILE block which tests the opposite condition.

COBOL programmers should be aware of the conflict in the use of the UNTIL keyword. COBOL's UNTIL is in fact a WHILE block which tests the opposite condition.

By developing a program through the progressive decomposition of sequential blocks, at no point is there any need to apply the GOTO, or unconditional transfer of control. GOTO was omitted from the list of preferred constructs, not because it is now redundant, but because its use is downright unproductive. Unfortunately, even languages with a wealth of control constructs continue to support the GOTO (although some 'scold' the programmer for using it). The essence of the problem is that the GOTO is far too powerful a construct. It makes possible the coding of fiercely intricate and complex programs which effectively defy understanding by others — not only a subsequent maintenance programmer, but the same programmer a few months later!

'Avoidance of the GOTO' is not really an issue of programming syntax at all. It concerns the sole use of the preferred constructs, and this relates primarily to the structure of a program's design specifications rather than the actual code itself. All this may be summarized in one sentence: *Structure is properly imposed upon a program not at the coding language level, but at the program design specification stage.* In other words, program structure is independent of the language used to write the program. Structured programs can be written in the most unstructured languages — even assembler language — provided that the program design specifications are properly structured. The process of translating structured specifications into actual machine code is in many respects a purely clerical (although skilled) activity. This is not to deny the value of languages designed for structured programming. As already noted, program complexity permitting, the processes of design and coding may coalesce, the program listing itself being the definitive specification.

The remainder of this section is concerned with representative methods of program design specification. All are graphical in nature, with the exception of pseudocode.

Conventional flowcharts

Although the conventional logic flowchart described in Chapter 2 is capable of expressing an unlimited range of control constructs, disciplined restriction to the forms shown in Figure 11–2 allows the standard flowchart to be a valid means of structuring program design specifications. Most programmers are thoroughly familiar with conventional flowcharting practices, having their own established formats. Restriction to the preferred forms may seem unduly limiting by some, but it is readily accepted if applied as part of top-down decomposition procedures. Predrawn flowcharting forms allow ready identification of and access to individual charts by using page references and row/column coordinates.

Pseudocode

Pseudocode is a non-graphical, somewhat loosely defined means for expressing program logic. It bears a strong resemblance to many high-level programming languages, featuring block indentation and formal English-style statements. Keywords, reflecting preferred control constructs, include IF (with THEN and ELSE), WHILE, UNTIL, and CASE. The primary difference between pseudocode and formal programming languages is the use of informal, but explicit, English expressions where appropriate for describing operations which would otherwise be obscured by more formal statements.

Forms of pseudocode vary widely. A programming team may develop its own pseudocode 'language' by adapting a suitable structured language known to the team through the addition of desirable control statements and means for embedding

English sentences, or by using published versions such as PDL (Caine & Gordon, 1976; Sacks, 1977).

Nassi Shneiderman diagrams

The concept of the linear flowchart appeared first in 1973 with the publication of Nassi & Shneiderman's innovative article on flowcharting for structured programming (Nassi & Shneiderman, 1973). This is a graphical technique, developed for the design of structured specifications, and it is intended to be a substitute for conventional logic flowcharts.

Since its introduction, the Nassi Shneiderman Structured Flowchart technique (NSSF) has become widely accepted, but with local variations. Using this method, the logic of a program is expressed as a group of named rectangular blocks, linked implicitly as a tree structure with the main module as the root. Each rectangle has single entry and exit points (the top and bottom respectively). The preferred control constructs described earlier in this Subsection are individually depicted by specific graphical forms within each rectangle.

Representative NSSF shapes are shown in Figure 11–4. The forms relate directly to their corresponding constructs and are self-explanatory. The unmarked 'internal' rectangles are themselves expressed as specific control shapes. Complete modules may be assembled by this expansion procedure, and by 'stacking' modules vertically. Figure 11–5 shows a simple program expressed as a main module, and separate modules called by the main module. The method used for module identification may be augmented by including page and grid references for large specifications. One clear advantage of the NSSF technique is that diagrams can be constructed without needing special flowcharting templates; a straight-edge is all that is required.

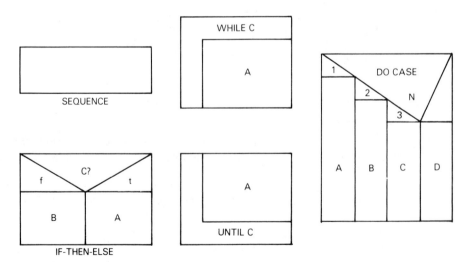

Figure 11–4   Representative Nassi Shneiderman control structures

The forms shown correspond to those in Figure 11–2.

The Chapin chart is a means of combining NSSF diagrams with more conventional flowcharting symbols (Chapin, 1974). It uses arrows to interconnect NSSF diagrams, and so improves the visibility of control flow. Terminal symbols are used to label subsidiary NSSF modules.

A slightly modified form of the NSSF, designed to assist in the implementation of structured programs in COBOL, has been described by Van Gelder (1977). At about the same time Roy & St-Denis (1976) announced a software package designed to generate linear flowcharts, similar to NSSF diagrams, from well-formed Pascal programs. Roy & St-Denis have adjusted the graphic forms to facilitate output on a printer or display screen.

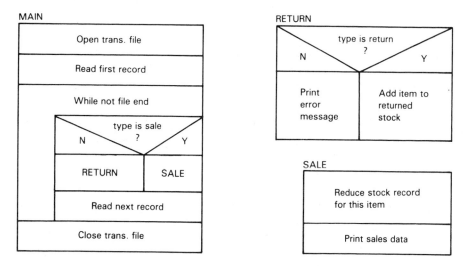

Figure 11–5 NSSF specification for a simple transaction file-processing program

Note the inclusion of simple English as well as more formal specification syntax.

NSSF diagrams and their variants have occasionally been criticized for the way in which they encourage low-level specifications. In common with flowcharts, it is all too easy to use NSSF shapes as convenient boxes in which to write actual program statements. Such use of a graphical representation can be an exercise in redundancy. The entries in NSSF diagrams should be clear, concise, and understandable to readers unfamiliar with the intended programming language. Programming statements should be descended to only when those statements are themselves clear. Adherence to this rule helps to reduce the size of a program specification, and to increase the visibility of its logic.

In 1979, Marca described a formalized documentation technique which combines the concepts of SofTech's SADT (see Subsection 6.4.4) and NSSF. The method is known as Structured Programming Design Method (SPDM) and is intended to be used in conjunction with SADT as a means for covering the needs of the entire design process (Marca, 1979). Marca claims that SPDM provides the

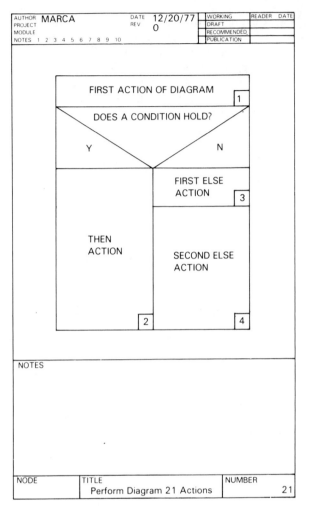

AUTHOR MARCA	DATE 12/20/77	WORKING	READER DATE
PROJECT	REV 0	DRAFT	
MODULE		RECOMMENDED	
NOTES 1 2 3 4 5 6 7 8 9 10		PUBLICATION	

Figure 11-6   An SPDM diagram which decomposes an idea (Marca, 1979, p. 27)

The internal blocks 1 through 4 are detailed by forms numbered 211, 212, 213, and 214 respectively.

formalism necessary for structured walkthroughs, the modularity necessary for CPTs, and the indexing scheme necessary for a program or project library. Modifications to NSSF diagrams made by the SPDM technique include: the redesign of the UNTIL block to have the same form as the WHILE; avoiding the deep 'V' shape of the case block; and including a small tag square in the lower right-hand corner of each internal block. The tag square carries an identifying number designed to indicate the location of the block in the overall tree structure.

A major point of SPDM is the application of a standard form designed to carry individual NSSF diagrams. The form, shown in Figure 11-6, limits the size of individual modules, has space to include written comments as an aid to constructive review, and provides a formal procedure for identifying diagrams and linking them into hierarchies. According to Marca, SPDM inherits the decomposition rules of SADT: no fewer than three boxes (the boring limit) and no more than six boxes (the complexity limit) should appear in a single SPDM diagram.) When a set of SPDM diagrams (each representing a node in the tree) is completed, they are collated into a standard 'tree-walk' order for retrieval.

SPDM still needs supplementary documentation to define the various data structures referenced in the program. This deficiency is not unique to SPDM. None of the documentation tools discussed in this section is particularly adaptable to expressing data hierarchies. While SADT does much for data definition, that technique is less appropriate for program logic specification purposes.

Flowblocks

The flowblock was proposed as a graphical technique for structured program specifications (Grouse, 1978). The method is similar in purpose and form to Nassi Shneiderman diagrams, and was suggested as a rationalized form of the NSSF. Marca's improvements to the NSSF formats still leave two problems unresolved.

The first of these problems is the difficulty of presenting the NSSF diagram on a VDU screen or as a printout, due to the free use of diagonal dividing lines in the IF and CASE formats (see Figure 11–4). Removing these lines allows the diagram to be easily stored and retrieved for display. The linear flowcharts of Roy & St-Denis require inelegant compromises to cope with sloping lines. The second problem concerns the NSSF CASE format. As may be seen from the example given in Figure 11–4 there must be one explicit internal block for each possibility. If the number of possibilities exceeds four or five, the resulting diagram requires unreasonable compression of the individual alternative blocks. Although Marca's revised CASE format is an improvement, it still requires one column for each alternative. The design of the flowblock format addresses these problems, and provides mechanisms for identifying each block as a node in the tree structure in a manner similar to that used by SPDM.

The general forms of the flowblock are shown in Figure 11–7. These three forms correspond to the natural divisions into which all control constructs fall. The sequential form remains as a simple rectangle. The selective form represents a way of choosing alternative actions and can be used for the IF-THEN-ELSE construct as

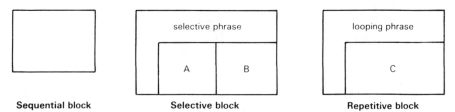

Sequential block   Selective block   Repetitive block

Figure 11–7   The three general flowblock forms

Blocks corresponding to particular constructs are based on these.

well as for the CASE block. The loop construct allows the definition of a block which is repeated according to the condition specified in the control phrase at the head of the block.

Figure 11-8 shows how the selective form can be used to build the IF-THEN-ELSE and CASE constructs. The vertical block divider is absent when the ELSE alternative is null (a non-action). The use of sloping lines is avoided by adopting a graphical notation similar to that used for the loop format. This commonality of form places greater stress on the textual content of the block rather than its shape. The format of the IF-THEN-ELSE block requires that the THEN (or 'true') and the ELSE (or 'false') blocks be placed in the left and right positions respectively. There is no need for an explicit column header to indicate which is which, as is the case with the corresponding NSSF diagram.

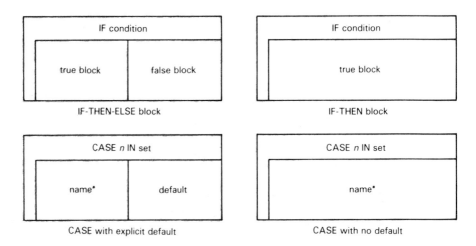

Figure 11-8   The selective flowblocks

The right-hand optional block is used when there is an explicit 'ELSE' action or a default case. The CASE syntax is discussed in the text.

The CASE block requires some explanation. Flowblock syntax requires that the n in the selective phrase be an expression, the value of which can be found in the 'set'. The *set* is the name of a previously defined set of values, or is written as a literal set. To illustrate, the control phrase 'CASE X IN |1,2,3,4|' implies that X should be one of the values 1, 2, 3, or 4. The name of the module to be performed is found by substituting the appropriate value of X for the asterisk used in the skeletal name given in the left-hand block. If X is not found in the specified set then the default block (if there is one) is executed. Specific illustrations are given in the example in the appendix to this chapter.

The looping phrase may be any appropriate repetitive control construct such as WHILE and UNTIL. Unlike the NSSF form of UNTIL, the flowblock version requires that the UNTIL phrase be placed at the head of the controlled block or 'loop body'.

Figure 11–9 is a complete flowblock (written at a very low level) for the Shell sorting algorithm (Shell, 1959). It contains examples of the WHILE, UNTIL, and IF-THEN-ELSE constructs. A flowchart equivalent of this algorithm is given in Figure 2–5. The algorithm is designed to sort an array A of COUNT items (numbered 1 to COUNT) in ascending order. This is a particularly fast sorting method for arrays which are originally in near-random order. All the variables (SPAN, LIM, etc.) are assumed to be integers.

```
SHELL SORT
 ,---------------------------,
| SPAN = COUNT                |
| WHILE SPAN > 1              | B
| ,-------------------------|
| | SPAN = INT(SPAN/2)       | C
| | J = 1                    | D
| | LIM = COUNT - SPAN       | E
| | UNTIL J > LIM            | F
| | ,-----------------------|
| | | LO = J                 | G
| | | UNTIL LO < 1           | H
| | | ,---------------------|
| | | | HI = LO + SPAN       | I
| | | | IF A(LO) > A(HI)     | J
| | | | ,-------------------|
| | | | | Swap A(LO) | LO    | K
| | | | | with A(HI).| = 0   |
| | | | | LO=LO-SPAN |       | L
| | |-----------------------|
| | |      J = J + 1         | M
 '--------------------------'
```

Figure 11-9   The Shell sort algorithm

The algorithm is here expressed as a low-level flowblock. See text for details.

Although normally used for high-level specifications, the flowblock may convey programming language or pseudocode, as in this sorting algorithm. If Marca's technique of combining such diagrams with SADT forms is used, that form would carry information explaining the more cryptic entries by reference to the appropriate lines using the letters shown at the right in Figure 11–9. For example, line C is an instruction to divide SPAN by 2 and to assign the integer part of the result back to SPAN. The 'swapping' operation in the double line K is more pseudocode than programming language. The ELSE block in line K is designed to force an exit from the UNTIL block.

Although there is a superficial resemblance between a low-level flowblock such as this and a pseudocode equivalent, there is one major difference. Pseudocode and high-level languages are written as a vertical sequence of statements. Flowblocks (and NSSF diagrams) are two dimensional; that is, they are written both vertically and horizontally. This follows from the side-by-side placement of alternatives in selective blocks. As a result, the flow of program control is much more visible when drawn as a flowblock. Nevertheless, in principle, entries in graphical design specifications should be written at a more concise level.

A particular use of low-level flowblocks is their potential for automatic code generation. Since the flowblock can be stored in machine-readable form, it may be provided as a data file for a suitable translator, which generates a corresponding high-level language 'vertical' program with the required block control syntax. Such a translator is described in the original flowblock publication (Grouse, 1978).

In common with other linear flowcharting systems, the flowblock notation supports means for identifying individual modules within the overall tree structure. A useful convention is to denote the root of the tree (the main program) as node 0, this number being written at the top of the block as shown in Figure 11–10 (a flowblock equivalent of the NSSF specification in Figure 11–5). The two internal blocks RETURN and SALE become nodes 1 and 2 respectively (following the node-numbering conventions of SADT). A flowblock requiring more than the nine submodules allowed by this scheme would be judged too complex, and should be further simplified. Using these node designators on both the node definition and the point(s) of invocation provides a way of traversing the tree in any direction. Covering documentation can index node designators against module names and page numbers for easy reference.

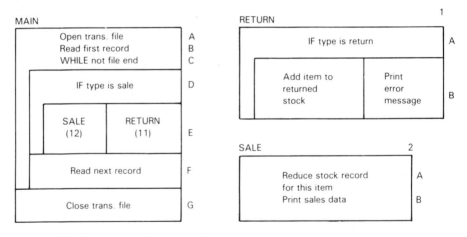

Figure 11–10   Flowblock equivalent of NSSF diagram in Figure 11–5

Note node designators.

There is a particular advantage of machine readability. It is the ability to include graphical specifications within the body of a source program as primary internal documentation. Traditionally flowcharts are relegated to supporting (external) documentation. The frequent result of this dissociation is the eventual obsolesence of the flowcharts as programs are modified without the corresponding modifications being made to the external documentation. If all the documentation is internal there is less tendency for this dislocation to occur.

The simplicity of form of linear flowcharts means that the designer requires nothing more complex than a pencil and a straight-edge: flowchart templates are not required. However, to take advantage of their ability to be displayed on the screen of a VDU, either a carefully preplanned hand-drawn version is required for direct transcription, or a specially designed interactive 'flowblock editor' is needed to look after the optimal placement of margins. One flowblock editor in particular is available as a software tool to run under CP/M. Known as FDL-80, it supports page-oriented full-screen interactive flowblock composition and modification. The package recognizes and provides correct graphics for the specific (initial) keywords IF, IF-ELSE, CASE, CASE-ELSE, WHILE, UNTIL, and REPEAT. Vertical margins are constantly corrected as lines of different length are entered. The editor prompts the user by locating the cursor at the most appropriate point for data entry. Each flowblock (complete or partly constructed) is held as a named subfile on disk. The internal form of each subfile is geared to the input needs of a translator package. An associated 'configurator' program allows the users of different types of VDU to tailor the editor to suit their particular hardware characteristics.

11.5   PROGRAM DOCUMENTATION

11.5.1   Internal Documentation

Narrative included as an integral part of a source program listing is generally termed *internal documentation.* Although it is of value primarily to the programming staff, non-programmers may refer to internal documentation for program identification, general specifications, detailed specifications, file specifications, and current level of revision. In view of the possible reference by non-programmers, it is usual to provide this type of internal narrative material at the head of the program itself.

Some languages force a minimum degree of internal documentation. COBOL, in particular, requires an 'identification division', defining such matters as program name, author name, date written, etc. COBOL also provides for a NOTE statement, allowing free use of narrative throughout the body of the source text. Notes, remarks, or comments are permitted in virtually all the popular programming languages. Programmers, however, tend not to spend too much time in writing internal comments since their primary objective is simply to get the program to work. Programming discipline here is vital. Inadequate internal documentation jeopardizes the subsequent debugging and maintenance of a program. A well-documented program should include the prefacing comments as well as descriptive material scattered throughout the text. The aim of internal documentation should be to allow another programmer to follow the logical processes involved without the need for analyzing subtle coding segments. By the same token, the programmer should avoid redundant comments in which obvious code is accompanied by a comment restating the obvious. An example would be:

A = 0; /* Set A equal to zero */

(The example is in PL/I where comments are always enclosed between the /* and */ pairs.)

The role of maintenance programming includes the parallel upgrading of all internal documentation affected by any changes to the code. All too often this aspect is ignored in the face of the pressing need to get the program operational. Clearly, a program can work correctly even if all the comments are incorrect, or even absent. The problem occurs at the next stage of program modification. Programming management must establish check procedures designed to ensure parallel upgrading of both code and comments.

One objection voiced by programmers is that the inclusion of internal documentation adds considerably to the size of source-program files. While this may be relevant to certain small systems with low-capacity disk drives, such an argument is specious since most systems can adequately support the increased text sizes. Further, after compilation, the object code size is independent of the amount of internal documentation since the compiler (or assembler) ignores all internal comments. The operating disks generally contain only current operational object files and relevant data files, and are therefore unaffected.

The flowblock editor FDL-80 provides a way of generating disk files corresponding to descriptive flowblocks in a form acceptable to the selected compiler as a sequence of comments. Such files may be 'edited into' the source code at appropriate points.

11.5.2 External Documentation

External documentation refers to literature which is relevant to the implementation phase but which is separate from the internal documentation. Although not necessarily machine readable, much external documentation consists of computer-generated or typed listings. The widespread use of word processors may mean that much of the external documentation is available on a medium such as floppy disk. The external documentation most relevant to the programming task is the functional specification from which the graphical program specifications are prepared. Supporting documentation includes schedules, planned staffing and resource usage, interview reports, required report layouts, operations manuals, screen layouts, and so on.

If a formal system such as SADT or SPDM (see Subsection 11.4.2) is used, there is a degree of repetition if the linear flowcharts (NSSF diagrams or flowblocks) are also part of the internal documentation. Potential problems associated with duplicate representations can be avoided if the origin of both the internal and the external flowblock diagrams is the graphical database used by the flowblock editor. Updates to flowblock modules must be made to this database alone, the editor being used to provide the hard copy for the external documentation as well as the 'comments' file for inclusion in the source program.

11.6   FILE CONVERSION

In the implementation stage it is most unusual to be in a position where the master files have no previous equivalent, in either a manual or a computer-based form. A major task of implementation is therefore the conversion of existing files to the form required by the new system. At the simplest level, this conversion may mean creating new files on a different medium although unchanged in format or content. It may mean taking data previously stored in different files and changing the format, medium, and possibily the timing of the data stored.

The following tales illustrate the difference in effort that can be required in different circumstances. The two cases demonstrate that file conversion may range from a trivial exercise (Company A) to a major task within the implementation phase (Company B). Company A was converting a system from one manufacturer's computer to another's. In this case the file conversion was achieved by writing a program to read the old master file, converting it to a form suitable for the new hardware, and writing it to magnetic tape. Thus the file conversion could be carried out any number of times at little cost. In consequence, if the first-level run of the new system was unsuccessful, the old system still existed and conversion could be tried again later without the risk of not having a current revision of the master files. Company B was converting from punched-card files to magnetic disk. The old master files (a history file and a billing file) contained duplicate data and were to be combined in one new disk file. Each old file consisted of approximately 20 000 records with an average of three punched cards for each record, and thus consisted of 60 000 cards. The first task in file conversion was to check the accuracy of the two files, as it was known that some data was erroneous. This exercise revealed that 25 per cent of the records contained discrepancies between the two card files which should not have existed. Correcting these errors took six months to investigate and rectify. This effort did not, however, reveal cases where both files agreed but were incorrect. Detecting these cases continued for a further two years after the file had been converted to disk.

The size of the task of file conversion varies according to factors which can be summarized as:

- Hardware change
- File format and access mechanism change
- Media change

These categories are not mutually exclusive.

The simplest conversion is one involving a hardware change alone. Thus media and file formats are unchanged. In this case it may be possible for the two computers to communicate and thus to transfer data files from the old to the new hardware via a communications link. Another alternative is to write the data files to a mutually compatible magnetic medium. Again, a service bureau could facilitate the transfer if common magnetic media are unavailable. In any of these situations, however, it is desirable to edit or check the data to increase the likelihood of the new files containing only 'correct' information.

Where there is a file format change, some programming is necessary. Once-off programs must be written to accept the old files, and to restructure them in a format suitable for the new system. This also requires validation of the data contents, and can involve programs, perhaps first to write the old files to a mutually compatible medium, and then to accept this as input to a restructuring program on new hardware.

The third case (that of media change) is unlikely to occur in isolation, but if it does it is a relatively simple task to validate and copy the data to a new medium on the same equipment configuration.

11.7 SYSTEM TESTING

11.7.1 Introduction

During the formative years of business data processing, 'bringing up' a new system was regarded as being an essentially iterative process of debugging. Programming students were taught to expect errors in their programs as a fact of life. The development of structured programming techniques and of associated management techniques has largely given the lie to those early fatalistic attitudes. Today's programmer is much more optimistic. There has been a trade-off of time between the stages of program design and debugging. The use of structured walk-through methods has been a major step towards producing systems which are correct, reliable, and robust.

Achieving such systems is a carefully staged matter. The 'correctness' of the system is established at certain key points during the development cycle. This may be achieved by periodic presentations and peer-group critical analyses (walk-throughs). Essential checkpoints occur on completion of the system's functional specifications, the system design specifications, the program specifications, the program design, and the final code. Additional checkpoints may be set at the completion of the definitions of each identifiable module.

11.7.2 Top-down Testing

If a system can be regarded as a tree structure of successively called programs, then there are two possible methods of system checkout. One is to validate the performance of each program by traversing the tree from the top down, and the other is by traversing from the bottom up.

Top-down testing suffers from the disadvantage that modules high in the tree rely on lower-level modules for their performance. Accordingly it might seem that such an approach can only be adopted when all the lower tree levels are 'populated' by complete programs. It is, nevertheless, possible to analyze the program performance of a module even if certain callable routines are not yet available. Missing routines may be replaced temporarily with dummy modules designed to fulfil minimal requirements for test purposes only. The cost of this approach is in the design and coding of the necessary dummies.

The advantage of top-down testing is that the system can be tested in parallel with its implementation, since programs are generally (although not always) developed in a top-down sequence. As further modules become available, they may replace their surrogates, allowing more intensive testing of the higher level modules. Only when all modules are coded is it possible to run full test operations with meaningful timing figures.

11.7.3   Bottom-up Testing

Whereas top-down testing requires dummy modules to replace yet-to-be-coded lower modules, bottom-up testing requires specially written 'test beds' designed to validate the performance of modules which are logically complete. Provided that the program design stages have fully specified the logic of a number of lowest-level modules, these modules may be examined by an appropriate test bed for their adherence to specifications. As the number of validated lower-level modules grows, modules using them may also be validated by additional test beds.

Bottom-up testing provides a more rigorous test environment than top-down testing, since test beds can be developed which thoroughly examine the module's performance for conformity to specification. Dummy modules, by their nature, are generally less exacting and the test procedures correspondingly less critical. This follows from the fact that the code for a dummy module should represent only a small fraction of that required by its 'real' counterpart.

It should be appreciated that neither method can 'prove' a system. Test beds generally provide selected sequences of critical operations, and monitor the results. If the module under test contains a hidden bug whose nature was totally unanticipated by the test-bed designer, it is likely that specific tests to flush it out may be missing. There is certainly no warranty that any test bed will detect all the bugs in a given module. It is for this reason that the emphasis on validation is preferably located in the program design stage, where the notion of 'proof' is more at home.

11.7.4   Program Validation Methods

Validation of logic at the level of the program design is an effective procedure in the assurance of error-free code. During walkthroughs involving selected programming-team members, individual logic specification diagrams may be displayed by the author using an overhead projector. Detected errors in logic may be written directly to the projection transparency for subsequent detailed desk checking. The author of the logic, or a technical librarian (as in the CPT), may be responsible for collating and recording logic changes and for redrafting and filing affected diagrams.

Walkthroughs are often a trial for passive participants, who tend to drift off unless the presentation is interactive. Good presentation techniques involve isolating specific logic problems, questioning, asking the participants to try the displayed logic using a small set of their own (invented) data, and so on. Can participants express the displayed logic in a more elegant manner? Can they detect limitations in performance not realized by the author? It nevertheless remains true that the person most likely to pick up an error is the presenter, since the activity is an attempt to justify his or her thinking before peers.

With the group's approval of an entire set of design specifications, the process of coding commences. Since the specifications are usually at a 'high' level, being written in broader terms than are acceptable to a compiler, the coding exercise requires the intelligent, and sometimes inventive, use of programming techniques. The result may be expressed directly in any one of a number of high-level programming languages, from which point the procedure becomes essentially one of clerical operations involving standard computer software. If the program specifications were supplied as high-level flowblocks, these may be subsequently refined into detailed flowblocks in which all entries are syntactically correct with respect to the target programming language. The low-level flowblocks are effectively the self-documenting source program, since the generation of a source-program file is performed by an appropriate software package. The high-level flowblocks, being in machine-readable form, should be included with the source program as part of the internal documentation. Walkthroughs may be used to verify the correct derivation of source code from specifications, although this tends to be performed by the programmer as a desk check.

Manually generated source code can contain a variety of errors. Examples include:

- Misspelled keywords and variable names
- Invalid punctuation
- Form layout errors (esp. COBOL)
- Uninitialized variables
- Invalid data types
- Use of unsupported features

If the code has been keypunched by someone other than the programmer who wrote it, it is likely to contain transcription errors. These include the transposition of adjacent symbols, confusion of the characters 1 and I, 2 and Z, 0 and O, etc. Although a program may be reported as clean by a compiler or assembler, it is still wise to proofread each line of code before attempting to test or debug.

11.7.5 Modular Testing

Since each module in a program is individually specified it should be a straightforward exercise to test whether or not a compiled module meets its specifications in practice. If the module makes no calls to other as yet untested or unwritten modules, then it should be fully functional and can be placed in a specially prepared test bed as described in Subsection 11.7.3. Two points should be noted concerning this test procedure: first, someone other than the originating programmer should prepare the test bed and run the tests. Second, an allowance must be made in the implementation schedule for creating and running the test beds. Similar remarks apply to top-down testing with dummy modules.

The higher the level of a module (in terms of its place in the tree structure), the more difficult it is to establish adequate testing procedures, since the specifications tend to grow in complexity. However, if the subordinate modules have been thoroughly tested, it should be possible to bypass particular variations in the testing sequences. Coupled with a careful scrutiny of the program as described in Subsection 11.7.4, this approach is normally more effective than attempting an exhaustive check of all possible data combinations — usually a completely impractical goal. Nevertheless, some time should be spent in running selected data sequences since these are the quickest means for detecting gross errors in logic and general performance.

11.7.6 Cost of Testing

Apart from the exercises of designing and writing test beds and/or dummy modules, other costs are incurred by the actual running of tests and the time taken to track down and correct bugs. Allowance must also be made for the costs of revising the documentation, which frequently follows the discovery of errors.

Although the process of testing individual test beds and dummy modules must also consume resources, the design of these programs is properly validated at the program design specification level. In some cases, a dummy may be developed to test a test bed, or conversely a test bed may be developed to test a dummy. Clearly, the line must be drawn well before the cost of developing these temporary programs grows to an unacceptable proportion of the whole.

Where the emphasis on testing is shifted to the earlier design phase, the costs of personnel involved can become more significant than, say, the cost of computer time for test-bed runs. A strong opinion exists, however, that the former approach is cost effective in the long term.

11.7.7 Responsibility for Testing

The validation of a conventional engineering product is commonly the responsibility of a group set apart for that function. The hardware developed by a computer company must be checked at two stages. At the first stage a prototype may be checked and benchmarked to test the principles of the design. In the second stage, individual units from the production line are each put through a rigorous testing regime, usually involving tests conducted at higher than normal temperatures and under adverse vibration. The group responsible for the initial checkout may be an ad hoc arrangement, since its responsibilities are often short lived. The testing of production hardware is, however, a continuing exercise and is generally the responsibility of a quality assurance department.

The reasons for dissociating development and testing are twofold. The skills and practices required for development are not necessarily the same as those needed for testing, nor is the hardware the same. Secondly, dissociating the two exercises separates the designers (with their preconceived notions of performance, etc.) and the testers (whose sole concern is with product conformity to specifications). The split is similar in concept to that which divides responsibilities in accounting departments.

In similar spirit, it is common to dissociate the groups responsible for software development and for testing, although in the case of software engineering the skills required for system testing are little different from those needed for design. There nevertheless is pressure to use the design group, either in part or in whole, to undertake the exercise of system testing. This follows since the design group not only has a keen interest in seeing the product through to completion, but has a natural desire to keep to itself any glaring faults which may lurk beneath the software. Further, the testing phase usually occurs when the workload on the design team has diminished. This pressure is almost irresistible in the case of relatively small organizations where the development is in the hands of a few specialists.

11.7.8   Time Considerations

The requirement that a system conform to the logical system specifications is clear. Frequently, however, problems in timing emerge which can seriously degrade the performance of the system in its operating role.

On-line real-time systems are particularly sensitive to timing shortfalls. System response times in, say, an inquiry system for a public utility, must satisfy the needs of customers as well as the operators of the terminal equipment. Excessive run times in batched operations can result in management reports becoming untimely and therefore of no value.

It is rarely justifiable to use inspired guesswork when attempting to determine operating run times. In many applications, the timing may be accurately determined by knowing the performance of the storage systems being used. This is because the input–output access times are generally well in excess of CPU times. Again, common applications sometimes involve standard utilities (such as a sort/merge) for which run times can be determined from tables supplied with the utility.

In instances of timing over-runs due to CPU sluggishness, two solutions are available. The more expensive answer is to move to a somewhat faster model of the same CPU. A better solution is to identify the component(s) of the software which are 'CPU-bound' and to rework them using more efficient algorithms and/or optimized assembly language routines.

Over a period of time, and as file sizes grow, system run times may rise dangerously. Early warning signs may be noted before too late if run times and response times are regularly monitored during the operating phase. In many cases the designer may be able to provide a mathematical model describing run times against file sizes. Since file growth is somewhat easier to predict, such models may supply the necessary warnings of timing deficiencies.

11.7.9   Test Data Development

The design of test files for final system testing requires more than an understanding of file layouts and record structures. Things usually go wrong when a file contains something 'funny'. Test files, such as masters and transaction files, should contain a mixture of valid records and records which hold all conceivable forms of invalid data. The philosophy of the test file designer should be to deliberately knock the system out of action. The armoury includes null (empty) files, excessively large files, sequential files with internal sequence violations, duplicate records, invalid formats within records, range violations, and the like. Direct access files may be provided with 'glitches' — pointers to other records deliberately garbled.

Along with these deliberate errors, the test file designer must provide a list of those errors which the system should not only detect, but which it should survive.

11.8   TRAINING AND SYSTEM INSTALLATION

Training the operating staff must be begun early enough to support the phasing in of the new system by the target date. Users also need training, in various degrees according to their level of interaction with the system.

Since training programs require trainers, time (and resources) must be allocated for familiarizing the training staff with the operational characteristics of the new system. They need run manuals and access to the system design documentation. In many cases, the system design staff undertake the role of training the trainers.

The phasing in of the new system concludes the implementation phase, and has been covered elsewhere (e.g. Section 5.3).

REFERENCES

C. BOHM & G. JACOPINI, 'Flow Diagrams, Turning Machines and Languages with only Two Formation Rules', *Communications of the ACM*, vol. 9, no. 5, May 1966, pp. 366-71.

S.H. CAINE & E.K. GORDON, 'PDL — A Tool for Software Design', *Software Design Techniques Tutorial*, IEEE, October 1976, pp. 172-7.

N. CHAPIN, 'New Format for Flowcharts', *Software-Practice and Experiences*, vol. 4, no. 4, February 1974, pp. 341-57.

E.W. DIJKSTRA, *Notes on Structured Programming*, Technological University, Eindhoven, The Netherlands, 1969.

P.J. GROUSE, 'Flowblocks — A Technique for Structured Programming', *ACM SIGPLAN Notices*, vol. 13, no. 2, February 1978, pp. 46-56.

D. MARCA, 'A Method for Specifying Structured Programs', *ACM Software Engineering Notes*, vol. 4, no. 3, July 1979, pp. 22-31.

I. NASSI & B. SHNEIDERMAN, 'Flowchart Techniques for Structured Programming', *ACM SIGPLAN Notices*, vol. 8, no. 8, August 1973, p. 12.

P. ROY & R. ST-DENIS, 'Linear Flowchart Generator for a Structured Language', *ACM SIGPLAN Notices*, vol. 11, no. 11, November 1976, pp. 58-64.

J. SACKS, 'Program Design Language as a Documentation Tool: A Case History', *ACM SIGDOC*, vol. 3, no. 10, April 1977, pp. 11-14.

D.L. SHELL, 'A High Speed Sorting Procedure', *Communications of the ACM*, vol. 2, 1959, pp. 30-2.

A. VAN GELDER, 'Structured Programming in COBOL: An Approach for Application Programmers', *Communications of the ACM*, vol. 20, no. 1, January 1977, pp. 2-12.

NOTES

Other articles joining in the controversy generated by Dijkstra's letter (1968) include the following:

E. ASHCROFT & Z. MANNA, 'The Translation of "GOTO" Programs to "WHILE" Programs', *Proc. IFIP Congress*, Ljubljana, August, 1971.

H.W. BESEL, 'After the GOTO Debate', *ACM SIGPLAN Notices*, vol. 9, no. 6, June 1974, p. 13.

M.E. HOPKINS, 'A Case for the GOTO', *ACM SIGPLAN Notices*, vol. 7, no. 11, November 1972, pp. 59-62.

D. KNUTH, 'Structured Programming with GOTO Statements', *Report STAN-CS-74-216*, Computer Science Department, Stanford University, Calif., 1974.

D. KNUTH & R.W. FLOYD, 'Notes on Avoiding GOTO Statements', *Information Processing Letters 1*, North-Holland, Amsterdam, 1971, pp. 23-31.

B.M. LEAVENWORTH, 'Programming Without the GOTO', *ACM SIGPLAN Notices*, vol. 7, no. 11, November 1972, pp. 54-8.

W.A. WULF, 'Programming Without the GOTO', *Proc. IFIP Congress*, Ljubljana, August 1971.

W.A. WULF, 'A Case Against the GOTO', *ACM SIGPLAN Notices*, vol. 7, no. 11, November 1972, pp. 63-9.

APPENDIX — A STRUCTURED
FILE-UPDATING ALGORITHM

In spite of the ready availability of packages for updating sequential files, programmers frequently need to reinvent this particular wheel for specific applications. In spite of the simplicity of the concept, the logic required is surprisingly complex if tackled by conventional flowcharting methods. Accordingly, the following analysis and algorithm is offered both as an exercise in structured programming and as a useful contribution to the programmer's repertoire. The technique adopted is quite recent (Grouse, 1978), demonstrating a particular application of 'state-switching' methods frequently applied within computer science, but rarely used in data processing. This is surprising since the technique permits the isolation of small, discrete modules with clear functions.

The specification for this program is essentially the same as that given for the update analyzed in Section 2.4. That section provides both a decision table (Figure 2-9) and a flowchart (Figure 2-10), but neither are developed using structured programming principles.

The functional specification of the sequential file update involves three files: the old master file (M), a variations file (V), and the new master file (M') which is created by this algorithm. It is assumed (for the purposes of the exercise) that all three files are guaranteed to be in monotonic increasing order of key. In other words, each file consists of a sequence of records, each with a single key, the keys of successive records always increasing in value as the file is traversed towards the end. Within any file no two records may share the same key (hence monotonic). The algorithm is not required to check this assertion, but presumes it to be correct. The algorithm does, however, guarantee that the output file M' is also monotonic increasing.

The variation file V is allowed to contain three types of record. The types are A (for addition), D (for deletion), and C (for change). Accordingly, variation file records must have a reserved one-byte field in which to locate the type. The detail of the algorithm remains broad enough to allow detailed record layouts to be included as required by the application. 'Dud' variation records are also permitted in the V file — records with type values which are not A, or D, or C. These are to be flagged as errors by the program.

The potential error messages which the algorithm may print are:

1. Invalid variation type (not A, D, or C)
2. The input master file M has been closed and a variation (not being an addition) has been read
3. An attempt has been made to add a record with a key which already exists in the old master file
4. An attempt has been made to change a non-existent record in the master file
5. An attempt has been made to delete a non-existent record from the master file

The flowblocks refer to the messages by number. To understand this approach it helps to view the computer to be controlled by the algorithm as a 'finite-state machine', i.e. as a black box which has a small number of states. By knowing what state the machine is currently in, things about what it is actually now doing, and about what it should be doing next can be inferred. The success of this approach depends upon the choice of state definitions.

A good set of states may be obtained by considering the possible states of the various input files. Both of the input files (M or V) can be in only one of three possible states at any one time. These states relate to how the files are read by the computer. For each file there is a section of main memory into which the successive records are placed (by the input hardware) to allow the program to process the data they contain. This area is a buffer. Initially the buffer is notionally empty. After a READ operation is executed by the computer, the buffer should contain one complete record. The program then processes that record, at which time the buffer is notionally empty again, or is waiting for another READ operation to refill the buffer. There is one such buffer for each of the input files. After a number of READ and process cycles, the input file eventually reaches its end (marked by a machine-detectable end-of-file mark). At this time the file enters the 'finished' state. Accordingly, the three possible file states are:

P Buffer empty, waiting for next record
Q Buffer contains record awaiting processing
R Buffer empty because last READ hit the end of file

Since there are two input files, the number of possible machine states is nine (3^2). These nine states are defined as 0 through 8 in accordance with the state table in Table 11–1. The solution may then be approached by considering what action is wanted in each of the separate machine states. It can be seen that this approach really allows a view of the problem with true tunnel vision, untroubled about what is going on in the other states.

Table 11-1   Update-algorithm state table

ALGORITHM STATE	INPUT FILE STATES	
	M	V
0	P	P
1	P	Q
2	P	R
3	Q	P
4	Q	Q
5	Q	R
6	R	P
7	R	Q
8	R	R

To illustrate, state 7, as defined in Table 11–1, says that the old master file M has finished (the last READ hit the end-of-file mark) but that there is a record waiting in the variation file buffer. It is most likely an addition, but this would have to be checked before acting accordingly. Before trying to solve the problems associated with individual algorithm states, it is necessary to begin at the beginning. This is, after all, top-down structured programming. Begin at the top!

When starting with the top module (or any module for that matter), it's a good time to pause and reflect on the question: 'What is really wanted?'. In plain English, it is opening the necessary files, setting up the correct initial state of the machine, then performing selected modules according to the machine's current state. After each module has done its job it will change the state to reflect the new conditions which apply. This continues until both input files are at an end, after which the three files are closed and the run is stopped. All this activity is summarized in the main flowblock in Figure 11–11. It leaves eight implied modules to be defined (UPDATE0, UPDATE1, and so on), but this is exactly the process of top-down decomposition. Note, by the way, that an UPDATE8 module is not needed. When one of the other modules eventually sets the state to 8 (indicating the update is over), the WHILE clause will terminate the loop and allow the files to be closed.

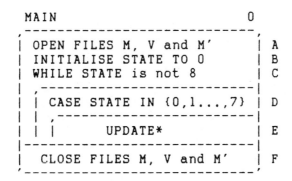

Figure 11-11   Main module for sequential update

Since each of the modules UPDATE* are required to take some action appropriate to the current state, and are then to change the state so that the next module may be selected, it would be prudent to limit the number of file-reading operations within any one module to one. The reason is that a single file read must necessarily change the state, allowing the rest of the action to be performed by a different module. Unless this point is appreciated it is very easy to start designing modules which do far more work than is actually necessary.

Let's begin with an obvious choice — UPDATE0. This corresponds to a STATE of 0, meaning that both buffers are empty. The most obvious action is to select one of the files (it doesn't matter which) and to try to read it. The word 'try' is used advisedly since any read operation may well encounter the end of the file. Accordingly, whenever an attempt to read a record is made, it is also essential to test immediately for the end-of-file condition. In Figure 11–12, the M file has been chosen as the first to read. Following the read (line A), the end condition is tested (line B). If the end has been reached, the M file is now in state R while the V file remains as it was — state P. The state table (Table 11–1) shows that this corresponds to STATE = 6, hence the entry in the 'true' block of line C. If the READ operation had been successful then the M file would be in state Q. Table 11–1 says that this is STATE 3, as set in the 'false' block of line C. This effectively completes all that need be done for STATE 0, since the module contains its maximum of one READ operation. The subsequent actions are left for UPDATE6 and UPDATE3.

```
UPDATE0                               1
  _____
|                                 |
| READ record from M file  |  A
| IF file M is at end       |  B
|                           |
| |_____|  |
| | STATE = 6 | STATE = 3 |  C
|_____ |
```

Figure 11–12 Preliminary design for **UPDATE0**

In the analysis for UPDATE0 the current state of the V file is not used. This can be used to advantage, looking at the way in which the state table has been organized. Modules UPDATE1 and UPDATE2 can also follow the logic of UPDATE0 with an allowance being made in line C for the (unchanged) condition of the V file. These three modules all share in the common initial condition of the M file — state P. Reading the file end in any of these three modules must shift the current state six rows down the state table (this preserves the V file state but takes the M file from P to R). Similarly, if the read is successful the new state is three rows down since the M file has shifted from P to Q. All this is depicted in a single multipurpose flowblock in Figure 11–13. Stacking the module names UPDATE0 etc. on top of the flowblock indicates that they are all aliases for one single logical specification.

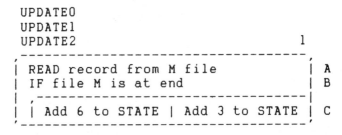

```
UPDATE0
UPDATE1
UPDATE2                                          1
  _____
|                                           |
| READ record from M file            |  A
| IF file M is at end                 |  B
|                                     |
| |_____| |
| | Add 6 to STATE | Add 3 to STATE | C
|_____ |
```

Figure 11–13 A common module for **STATEs** 0, 1, and 2

The design of UPDATE3 is just as easy as that for UPDATE0. STATE 3 means that file M is in state Q (a record is in the buffer) and file V is in state P (buffer empty). There's not much that can be done with the master record in the M buffer until it is known what the next variation happens to be. Therefore, try to read the V file. This is done in Figure 11–14, line A. In line B the mandatory test for end of file is made. If file V has run out, the true block (line C) reflects this with the new STATE of 5 (see Table 11–1). The false block sets STATE to 4, indicating that both file buffers contain a record.

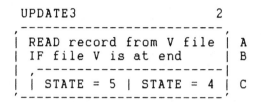

Figure 11-14 Preliminary flowblock for STATE 3

It is clear that the same kind of combined logic can be applied here as in Figure 11–13 since it should be possible to deal with UPDATE6 at the same time. These are the only two modules left in which the V file starts in the empty (P) condition. The combined approach should work since the state of the M file is irrelevant in UPDATE3. Further, it means that this module is the only one charged with the responsibility of reading the V file. Accordingly a check can be added to see if a successfully READ variation record has a valid type. See how this has been done in Figure 11–15. Put simply, when the V buffer is empty, an attempt is made to fill it (line A). If the file has ended, the new state reflects that file V is now in condition R (the STATE has moved two rows down the table). If there is a variation record it is tested for validity (line C, right). A valid record means that it is accepted and the V file is moved to condition Q by adding 1 to the STATE. An invalid type issues error message number 1. Accordingly, in subsequent modules which make use of the variation record there is no further need to test for types other than A, D, or C.

With relatively little work five of the required eight modules have been completed.

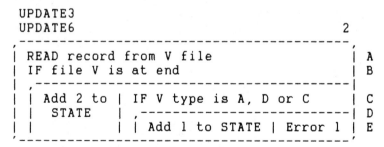

Figure 11-15 Combined logic for modules which read V file

The module for STATE 4 is not quite as simple. With two records available (a master and a variation) it's time to do some real work. Clearly, what is done now depends on the relative values of the two respective keys. For example, if the master record has a key lower than that of the variation record it is only necessary to write out that master record (unchanged) to the new file M′ and to reset the value of

STATE to 1 (why?). If the two keys are identical then the variation must be either a deletion or a change. If the type is A, then error message 3 must be issued, in which case STATE is set to 3 (why?). A deletion means that the two records 'mutually annihilate' each other — nothing is to be written to the new file and the STATE becomes 0 (both buffers are now consumed or empty). With a change, part of the variation record now replaces the current master record. This is done by simply writing the variation record to the new file and then treating both buffers as empty (STATE 0). In the case where the key of the master record is greater than that of the variation, that variation must be an addition (in which case write the variation record to the new file and set STATE to 3). If the variation is a C or D then appropriate error messages (numbers 4 or 5 respectively) must be printed and the bad variation record 'forgotten' by setting STATE to 3.

The two remaining modules reflect cases in which one of the two files is at its end-of-file mark. UPDATE5 has a master record in the buffer, but there are no more variations. As shown in Figure 11–16, this record is written directly to the new file M′ and the STATE is set to 2 indicating that the master buffer is now empty and the variation file is finished.

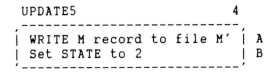

```
UPDATE5                              4
,--------------------------------,
| WRITE M record to file M' | A
| Set STATE to 2            | B
'--------------------------------'
```

Figure 11-16   Flowblock for STATE 5

UPDATE7 is a little more complex. In this case the master file is exhausted but there is a record in the variation buffer. If this record is not an addition, this module must print error message 2. Note how a common setting of STATE to 6 can be used irrespective of the outcome of the test on the type. This follows since, whether the variation record is written to the new file or whether it is rejected with an error message, the effect is the same — the variation file returns to condition P. The logic is shown in Figure 11–17.

```
UPDATE7                          5
,-------------------------------,
| IF type is A            | A
| ,-------------------------|
| | WRITE V    | Error | B
| | to file M' |   2   |
|-------------------------------|
|     Set STATE to 6      | C
'-------------------------------'
```

Figure 11-17   Flowblock for STATE 7

The preceding analysis has made use of the restriction to monotonically increasing files. It has not, for example, supported a change technique which deletes a master record then adds a new record with the same key value. Nor has it allowed a new record to be added, and then be changed by the next variation record. This follows from the fact that a record to the new master file is written out as soon as possible. Subsequent attempts to change the record so written would involve considerable changes to the logic.

The techniques used in these examples may be extended generally to situations in which multiple sequential files are to be read for processing. For each input file there are the three states P, Q, and R. If the number of input files is N, then the total number of discrete machine states is 3^N. When N is greater than 2 this can mean a great many states. However, it is found that many state modules can share common logic, as can be seen in the first example.

ASSIGNMENT

1. The discussion on the module for STATE 4 represents a verbal logical specification for UPDATE4. Draw this logic as a flowblock (node 3).

2. Assume that the variations file V may contain adjacent records with identical keys. Further, the only allowable types are additions and deletions. Changes to the master file are now effected by a deletion followed by an addition for the same key value. Redraw the entire program logic as a set of flowblocks then do a desk check of its performance using two (short) sample input files.

3. Design the logic for a three-way file merge. Assume that there are three (monotonically increasing) input files. The output file is also to be sequential and increasing in key, however it need not be monotonic since a given key value may occur in each of the input files. In such cases, the order in which records with identical keys are written to the output file is immaterial.

12 PROJECT SELECTION AND MANAGEMENT

12.1 IDENTIFYING THE CANDIDATES

Choosing the right information systems applications to be implemented on computers is absolutely vital if an information systems department is to be effective. It is possible, though of course not recommended, for a computing section to be somewhat sloppy in its controls and adherence to standards and yet be tremendously effective in promoting the objectives of the organization — the requirement is that appropriate projects are selected for computerization. Conversely, a data-processing department may be run like a military establishment with absolute adherence to good and efficient implementation standards and yet it may contribute virtually nothing to the organization's overall performance, because inappropriate projects are selected. It follows that the project selection activity must identify those areas of the organization which are important in achieving its objectives. Factors such as the technical interest of an area, the enthusiasm of a departmental manager, and the need to 'gain experience' with a particular technique or type of equipment, ought to be heavily discounted during this process.

The formulation of a project master plan, which comprises an optimal sequence of projects, is therefore one of the most important decisions to be taken by an organization with respect to its computer policy. Before such a plan can be drawn up though, the candidates for inclusion in the plan must be identified. Taking a 'top-down' approach, the steps frequently involved in this phase of the process include:

- Each of the key areas of the organization is analyzed with departmental management being involved, reviewing the decisions made at all levels of each area, and the information required by the decision makers. Emphasis should be placed on those aspects which have the greatest effect on the organization's performance.

- The constraints which limit performance in these key areas are analyzed, e.g. the time needed to search files, insufficient working capital, inability to increase productivity, poor customer relations.
- These constraints are investigated to determine how a computer-based solution can either remove or relieve them. Examples of computer-system attributes which may assist are: processing speed; the ability to centralize files so that all sections of the department are using the same information; the ability to relate data obtained from different sources by common data identifiers; and the ability to monitor inventory levels or queues to allow reduction in lead times.
- A tentative cost/benefit evaluation is made to determine whether a computerized solution is likely to be economically justified. This would include the intangible, or more accurately, unmeasurable, benefits. Evaluations tend to be more reliable for those proposed systems which operate in well-defined or structured situations. As the level of uncertainty increases so does the probability of error.
- A management review is made to decide which of the projects fall within the policy guidelines set by general management (see Chapter 1).

Alternatively, an evolutionary or 'bottom-up' approach may be adopted which identifies deficiencies in current systems. Although easier to follow, this path is likely to result in a plan which concentrates on short-term problems at the expense of meeting overall long-term goals.

12.2 THE PROJECT MASTER PLAN

The preparation of a master plan requires the matching of three different viewpoints:

- General management policy, i.e. overall objectives, limits on expenditure or resources, criteria for project approvals, etc.
- The priorities of different user departments for projects in their areas of interest — often these overlap
- The priorities of the information systems department based on organization-wide considerations and technical criteria

Therefore, a review of the master plan every six or twelve months requires negotiations in which the user-management groups compete for available resources while the computer managers seek endorsement of plans for new equipment and services. The plan formulation includes the steps:

- Identification of systems which should be developed together — evaluating the potential for integration of various systems because they share common data elements and data collection facilities

- Precedence determination — a process in which each of the projects is evaluated in turn to determine what work must be carried out before the project can be implemented; normally, 'natural' strings of projects are identified whereby data collected and processed in one system are used as input for a subsequent system (e.g. the way that an order entry system provides the database entries or files for subsequent production scheduling, despatch, invoicing, and sales analysis systems)
- Evaluation of the intangible, or perhaps more accurately, unmeasurable, benefits likely to be derived from each string of systems — obtaining appropriate endorsement from management where necessary
- Carrying out a study on the effect of the developing plan on the current hardware/software/database/communications/staff environment — determining new hardware/software and staffing needs to implement alternative plans
- Reworking cost/benefit evaluations on each project sequence — seeking to satisfy the precedence requirements and to obtain the benefits from integration, and matching these evaluations against policy guidelines
- Formulating a plan covering (say) three years work which maximizes the expected returns whilst recognizing the value of the intangible benefits

For a more detailed review of information systems planning approaches see Bowman, Davis & Wetherbe (1981).

12.3 CORPORATE DATABASE SPECIFICATION

Specification of the corporate database — i.e. the complete set of computer-based data storage — is a vital part of the project-planning process. This is because the quality of its specification affects:

- The cost of systems design — a well-specified database ensures that the data-handling requirements of systems fit together in a logical manner, without necessitating reworking of data-element formats and relationships as new systems are developed
- The flexibility and therefore the effectiveness of information reporting — this also depends on the adequacy of the logical data model; a flexible reporting structure is needed to allow for changes in organization structure and to provide for decision support when new types of problem situations arise

Therefore the specification of the logical data model for the whole organization should be reviewed at the same time as the master plan is considered. The steps to be followed in this review are those shown diagrammatically in Figure 12-1. This figure illustrates the links between the two independent, but related, top-down paths involved in project selection and database specification. In practice, it is desirable to compare the results of the two sequences at the end of steps 3 and 4. This helps to identify errors and discrepancies. Specification of the master plan sequence of

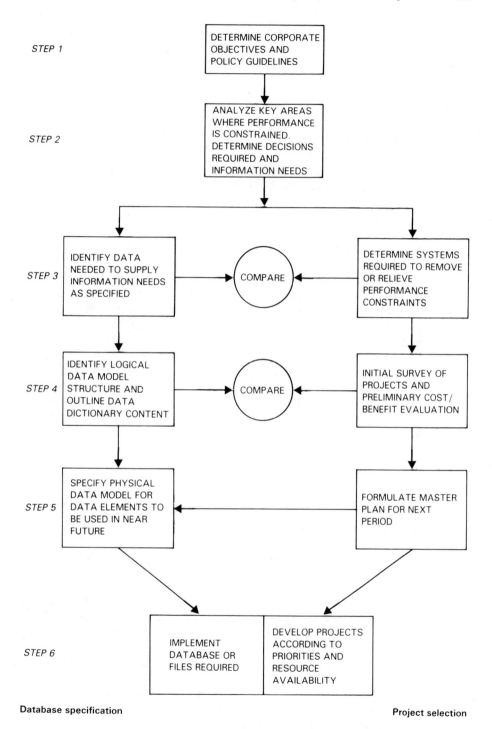

Figure 12-1   Steps in project selection and database specification

projects is a necessary input to the process of designing the physical database, since this sequence determines the database implementation schedule.

Both components of step 6 of Figure 12–1 are frequently carried out by the one group — the project team involved with the application system design.

12.4 PROJECT JUSTIFICATION

When a project is nominated during the selection process, a cost/benefit evaluation is necessary. In fact it is likely that the economics of a project will be considered a number of times throughout its history, with the major evaluation taking place at the end of the feasibility study stage. Less detailed evaluations are also likely at the time the logical and physical designs are completed, to ensure that project costs and benefits are still in line with those anticipated.

Estimation techniques are covered in Section 12.8. Once again it is necessary to stress the fact that uncertainty in the requirements specification introduces potential inaccuracy into any evaluation, both of costs and of benefits. Also, estimates made early in the project lifecycle are less accurate than those made later, since changes in the specification are always likely and it is difficult to foresee pitfalls, at least until the logical specifications are complete.

Often it is desirable to evaluate two or more projects into natural groupings as 'portfolios'. This is because some projects are more 'risky' than others and a department would not normally wish to be developing a number of high-risk projects at about the same time. This also allows the synergy, which frequently arises when two or more projects are implemented together, to be included as a benefit.

12.4.1 Costs

The costs associated with the development of an information system can be separated into the following categories:

- Analysis and design — staff and material resources required
- Program coding and testing (string and systems testing) — staff and computer resources
- Implementation — including extra clerical and operator effort during file conversion, and parallel running of old and new systems
- New equipment and/or systems software needed to run the system
- Training of operators
- Maintenance of hardware, systems software, the applications system, and back-up facilities
- Computing operations/data control/data-entry staff
- Additional staff required by the user to liaise with system development and computer operations people
- Materials costs, e.g. stationery, magnetic tapes, disks

In addition, some consideration should be given to potential intangible costs, including:

- Disruption of the current operation during development and the implementation period — often key user staff need to be reassigned to help with the design, and training is often time consuming
- The impact of system bugs, late delivery, or other implementation delays
- Behavioural problems with user staff associated with the changeover due to the changes in informal reporting relationships, job assignments, etc.
- The inflexibility introduced by the computer system, which is likely to slow down adjustment to changes in the organization or its environment

12.4.2   Benefits

It always appears easier to estimate costs rather than benefits accurately. Benefits are nearly all subject to variability and inaccuracy since the exact nature of the operation, once the computer system is installed, is usually difficult to determine, and it is necessary to estimate the value of benefits that will not be actually realized until some months or years in the future.

The areas of benefit frequently included in an evaluation are:

- Staff reductions
- Reduction in inventory and other working capital areas
- Improved quality control, lower reject rates, etc.
- Improved productivity and resource utilization
- Reduced number of mistakes requiring correction

It should be noted that staff reductions seem to be more significant in terms of the ability of the organization to handle increased throughput without staff increases, rather than an ability to identify redundant positions soon after implementation.

There are a number of intangible areas of benefit which normally form a part of any computer proposal. These intangibles are likely to include:

- Improved service to customers or other users
- Improved working conditions, fewer menial tasks, etc.
- Improved management information — more timely, more accurate, etc.

Very often these intangible benefits can be of great significance and justify the expenditure of large amounts of money. Nevertheless, it is important to keep these claims under control since the enthusiasm of those immediately associated with a project can easily mask either the real difficulties associated with achieving the benefits — for example, providing the required information may not improve decisions because of other factors — or the problem may be a transient one likely to disappear once new products are available or personnel are reorganized.

12.4.3 Evaluation Methods

Once costs and benefits have been established, and values have been assigned, it is possible to carry out a financial evaluation. Normally this follows the procedures established within the organization for project analysis, and so only a brief review of these techniques is given here.

Pay-back or break-even analysis

Pay-back is defined as the period of time required for the project's cash investment to be recovered from the net cash inflows generated as a result of the project. Thus, if the expenditure of $C produces an annual net return of $R, the pay-back period is C/R years. An example illustrates the calculation of pay-back:

Capital expenditure $8000
Expected net annual
   cash inflow $2000

$$\therefore \text{ Pay-back period} \quad = \quad \frac{\$8000}{\$2000} \text{ years}$$

$$= \quad 4 \text{ years}$$

Break-even analysis is a similar approach: it calculates the number of years for the new system to break even with the current system, when all the expenses and

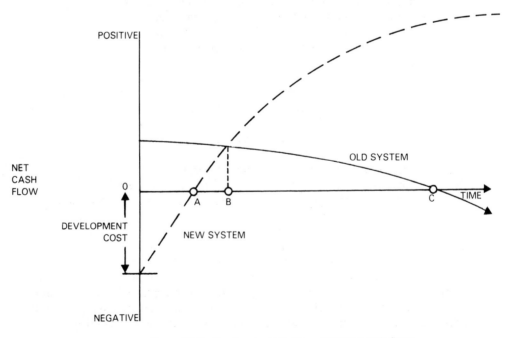

Figure 12-2 Break-even analysis — projected cash-flows

revenues of the new system are included. A result of such break-even analysis might be a graph like that shown in Figure 12-2. The point B gives the time at which the new system is expected to break-even with the current system. The point A shows when the new system is expected to generate positive cash-flow, while C is the time that the old system is expected to yield negative cash-flow.

Discounted cashflow techniques

The pay-back and break-even techniques do not take into account the time factor and depreciating value of money which are integral parts of the capital investment environment. Most organizations use techniques such as the present-value or the internal-rate-of-return methods to assess the profitability of a computer investment, since they include the time value of money.

The *internal rate of return* is defined as that rate of interest which discounts all future net cash flows to an amount equal to the initial outlay. If this rate is greater than the organization's established 'hurdle rate' then the project is acceptable. The *present-value* method involves discounting the future net cash inflows at the hurdle rate to calculate a present value. If this is greater than the initial outlay then the project is acceptable. The following example illustrates the two methods.

Initial outlay	$50 000
Future cash inflows	
Year 1	$10 000
Year 2	$20 000
Year 3	$30 000
Year 4	$21 600
Hurdle rate	10 per cent

Present-value calculation

Year	Net cash inflow	10% discount factor	Present value at 10%
1	10 000	0.9091	9 091
2	20 000	0.8264	16 528
3	30 000	0.7513	22 539
4	21 600	0.6830	14 753
			$62 911

Present value	=	$62 911
Net present value	=	$62 911 − 50 000
	=	$12 911

Thus the net present value of the project at a 10 per cent discount rate is $12 911.

Internal-rate-of-return calculation

Discounting at 20 per cent

Year	Net cash inflow	20% discount factor	Present value at 20%
1	10 000	0.833	8 330
2	20 000	0.694	13 880
3	30 000	0.579	17 370
4	21 600	0.482	10 411
			$49 991

Thus the internal rate of return is approximately 20 per cent, since the sum of the discounted values of the future cash flow is $49 991, which roughly equals the investment of $50 000.

12.5 INFORMATION SYSTEMS DEPARTMENT ORGANIZATION

The organizational structure of an information systems department has significant bearing on the management style applied to project development. There are two basic extremes and these are sketched in Figures 12–3 and 12–4 and described in Subsections 12.5.1 and 12.5.2. In addition, a variety of team structures for covering the programming task are possible, and two examples are discussed in Subsections 12.5.3 and 12.5.4.

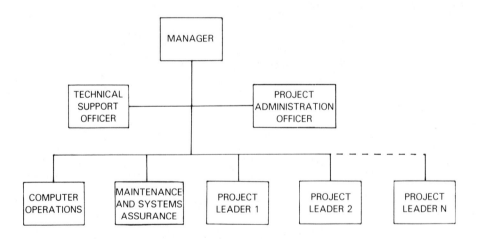

Figure 12–3 Project team structure

12.5.1 Project Team Structure

This concept is illustrated diagrammatically in Figure 12–3, and its essential features are:

- Project leaders are appointed for each project with responsibility for time, cost, and performance factors, at least from an EDP point of view. Sometimes (increasingly so) a user department representative may carry overall project responsibility, but she or he still relies greatly on the expertise of the EDP specialists for estimates and guidance on technical matters. It is of great benefit if the project leaders always concentrate on one application area of the enterprise. This allows them to develop familiarity with the systems within their area, and also improves the communications between EDP and user departments. Note the short communication path between manager and project leader in this organization structure, as illustrated in Figure 12–3.

  Team members are normally drawn from a pool of analysts and programmers who are allocated as needs arise. With this structure there is often little difference between the work of analysts and programmers. Each person does the job at hand irrespective of title.
- Technical support is given by an officer responsible for ensuring that the technology being used on projects is appropriate. This officer can also monitor the adherence to standards. Specialist programming skills and systems programming support would also be located in this section. Much of the technical support officer's time is spent, however, on negotiation for equipment and software procurement, enhancement, and maintenance.
- Since project administration is a time-consuming activity, it is desirable that the manager be relieved of the routine aspects and so be able to devote more time to the creative aspects of project control. The project administration officer's tasks would include staff allocation between projects, computer resource allocation, project costing, staff requirements forecasting, estimate checking, and routine project control.
- Operations include the computer operations, data preparation, and data control activities associated with the ongoing data-processing work. While the basic task is one of production control, there is also a need for close liaison with development staff on the resources and time schedules needed once new projects are completed. Sometimes responsibility for maintenance is given to this officer.
- Maintenance and systems assurance is becoming a more vital function within established EDP departments as more and more systems are being implemented. The need for good systems testing and operations documentation becomes more critical as the tendency for more interaction between systems and the sheer workload on operators both increase. The growing obsolescence of older systems also throws emphasis on control of maintenance requests.

  Systems assurance is a quality control task which involves checking the work of the systems designers, particularly in the testing and documentation areas. The concept requires that a system not be implemented until someone other than a project team member has checked the basic design, the operating manuals, controls, system and program documentation, and the test results. It seems appropriate that those responsible for future maintenance should be allocated the assurance job so that they cannot complain later about the inadequacies of the design (or at least will complain less often!).

Maintenance activity often used to be carried out by those who developed the original system. However, as systems become older as well as their number increasing, it is not always possible to locate one of these analysts and, even if one is found, a delay to a current project will ensue. Some EDP managers still adhere to this technique because they believe that it improves services to the user. It is more common now to find a separate group charged with maintenance responsibilities.

Many programmers dislike the term 'maintenance programmer' and so EDP managers often try to elevate the status of this section by allocating project enhancement duties — or even by paying extra money!

- Enhancement of systems is a more vexed issue. The critical question is: 'At what point does a system modification cease to be a maintenance request and become an enhancement project?'

If maintenance work is defined as the effort necessary to keep a system operational without changing any of the specifications, then there should be relatively little of it once a system has settled down after the implementation series of bugs. All others changes should be treated as enhancements and allocated to a project leader as a new project. This could include even 'simple' changes such as tax-table modifications. Otherwise, the use of the maintenance 'back-door' becomes a convenient way for systems design work to be performed without passing through the normal approval channels.

12.5.2 Functional Structure

In the early days of EDP this type of organization structure predominated. It seemed natural to separate the analysis and design function from the programming, mainly because programming in assembly language required a high degree of skill. The structure is illustrated in Figure 12–4.

The basic differences between this approach and the project team structure can be summarized by reference to the job classifications, which are:

- The chief systems analyst assumes responsibility for all projects — at least while they are in the design stages. Therefore this person's workload comprises much of the project administration officer's and some of that done by the manager in the project team structure. On completing the design phase, program specifications are handed over to the chief programmer for coding. Often there are formal 'sign-offs' associated with this transfer of responsibility. Project leaders work under the control of the chief systems analyst and therefore they are not responsible for the entire project. Sometimes the divided responsibility gives rise to argument over the origin of system defects.
- The chief programmer is in charge of all applications coding. This task combines some of the administrative work of project control (scheduling,

allocation, project control) with managerial functions (techniques, standards, resolving logic problems).

• The technical support role includes most of the technical functions within the department, including supplier liaison, programming standards, and systems programming projects. The interface with the chief programmer is always a difficult aspect in this organization structure. Nevertheless it is usually necessary for the manager of a larger department to be able to obtain a balanced set of views on software-related topics.

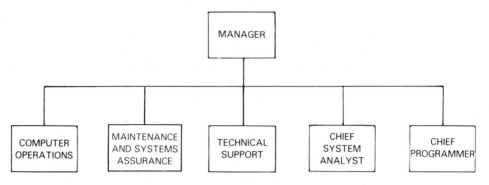

Figure 12-4   Functional structure

12.5.3   The Chief Programmer Team (CPT)

The CPT concept was formulated by Dr Harlan Mills following his involvement with a so-called Super-programmer Project in 1969. This was an attempt to use one highly qualified programmer supported by carefully planned back-up facilities to create a Definitive Orbit Determination system for IBM. Subsequently the same concepts were applied on a somewhat larger scale to IBM's now famous New York Times Project (Baker, 1972). It has been claimed that the CPT approach not only reduces the total programming effort but assists materially in generating almost fault-free code.

There are four key elements in the CPT concept. They are:

• Structured programming
• Top-down design and integration
• The programming production library and its associated machine and human procedures
• The organizational structure of the CPT

The most distinctive feature of the CPT approach is the functional organization of the team. In control of the team is the chief programmer who, like the skilled surgeon in charge of a major operation, technically directs the team effort and performs the most demanding tasks. Thus, key modules or programs are designed, coded, and integrated by the chief programmer, while the less complex or less vital modules are handled by the back-up programmer or support programmers. The back-up programmer both supports the chief programmer and, by staying abreast of the development effort, is prepared to take over at any time.

The Programming Production Library (PPL), together with its associated back-up and procedures, is designed to separate the clerical and intellectual tasks of programming. There are two forms to the PPL. There is an internal library normally maintained on disk, and an external library of catalogued listings. Library maintenance is a job of a librarian, not a programmer. Programmers work only with the external library. They request changes and additions by notes on the current listings and/or additional coding sheets. The librarian performs the required changes using standard catalogued procedures and clerical techniques. This task can be performed by someone with clerical or secretarial skills.

In some small projects the basic team of three people may produce the entire system. With more complex systems, additional programmers may be appointed who are directly responsible to the chief programmer.

12.5.4   Egoless Programming Teams

The CPT approach is, by definition, an egocentric affair. Not only does the chief programmer take the responsibility of the entire overall design, but must also code all the high-level routines and supply detailed functional specifications or even program specifications for the various submodules which are to be invoked. Apart from the back-up programmer, the programmers in a CPT are unlikely to be engaged in conceptual developments; they code relatively small, well-formulated modules which are capable of straightforward, independent testing. Examples of such modules might include routines for:

- Invoice totalling, tax calculation
- An input–output driver for a VDU terminal
- Table look-up

Distinct from the CPT or similar approaches, 'egoless' programming teams spread the overall design responsibility among 'equal' members. Following a democratic subdivision of the programming tasks, all members develop the programming specifications and code for their own divisions (Weinberg, 1971). Overall coordination of such a team may be performed by a manager with little programming expertise but with a sound understanding of the functional specifications.

Enfield & Rodden (1977) have reported on democratic team organizations used by the A.D.P. Implementation Service Group of the N.S.W. Public Service Board. They conclude:

> Our approach has been to create an environment where teams determine for themselves the programming practice and techniques they will employ, rather than have these decisions made for them by way of management directives, organisation standards etc. This approach is based on the premise that

programmers who are mature, well informed and experienced are capable of deciding these matters for themselves.

Whilst, overall, there is a conservative tendency, programmers being inclined to continue doing what they understand well, there is nevertheless a degree of experimentation and innovation. This, combined with the autonomous nature of the teams, has led to a diversity of practices and techniques being employed. Additionally, programmer satisfaction and morale is improved.

We consider that this diversity is healthy and gives the Group a measure of flexibility, and consequently strength, not possible under a traditional form of organisation.

12.6 AN OVERVIEW OF INFORMATION SYSTEMS PROJECT MANAGEMENT

Managing the development of computer systems has always been regarded as a difficult problem. There are many reported cases of projects costing five or even ten times the original estimate, and even more numerous examples of projects where the time to complete the job was underestimated by smaller amounts. Project management is normally considered to consist of the following areas:

- Selecting the systems development methodology to be adopted by the analysts and programmers
- Estimating the resources and the time required to complete individual phases of the project
- Controlling the project development to ensure that the objectives are being met, that standards are being adhered to, that personnel are fully occupied on useful tasks, and finally, that the time and cost schedule for development is being met

Because the design of computer systems requires a high degree of creativity on the part of the systems designer if the end product is to be worthwhile, it is necessary to handle the project management with some care. On the one hand it is essential that adequate control and monitoring be placed on the system's developers to ensure that the budget is not exceeded and that the organizational policy constraints are not breached; but on the other hand it is necessary to allow, or even to encourage, creativity by not restricting the actions of the designer too closely. It is important that the particular project management and control techniques adopted should resolve this dichotomy as it applies to the particular organization.

A principle followed in many organizations is to determine what a project leader or team member should do at any particular phase of the project, without specifying in detail how the task should be carried out. One way of doing this is to specify the 'table of contents' of reports which are to be made when each phase of a project is completed. This approach, often termed 'control via deliverables', is discussed in more detail in Section 12.9.

Because the project management task is virtually the same for all computer projects in all organizations, a uniform approach is possible. A number of packaged products are marketed which provide: a methodology (usually a set of steps with instructions and pro formas to be completed by the analyst/programmer); an estimation guide; and project control aids. Some of these packages are produced in computer program form with the result that the project schedule and current-status information are available either on-line or by computer printout.

12.7 A SYSTEMS DEVELOPMENT METHODOLOGY

A standard approach to the systems design question is usually adopted by an organization to facilitate common ways of handling project management. Standardization also assists in the training, interteam communication, staff interchange, and documentation aspects of development work. While there is growing use of the packaged methodologies mentioned in Section 12.6, many organizations have produced their own standards. In this context, the term 'methodology' embraces the procedures and sequence of tasks to be followed from initiation to completion of a project. Thus it covers 'what' should be done at each point in the lifecycle. The question of 'how' each task is performed is not addressed in this chapter. This material is covered in Chapters 4, 5, and 6.

To illustrate the project management issues, a checklist/guideline approach is introduced here. It also serves to show the detailed steps involved in the progress of a project.

In Chapter 1, the system lifecycle was described as comprising the following steps:

1. Terms of reference statement and requirements specification
2. Feasibility study
3. Systems analysis
4. Logical design
5. Physical design
6. Programming
7. Implementation
8. Post-implementation review

The first part of step 1 normally has been completed once the project commences in earnest, since it is part of the project selection and master plan formulation process. However, subsequent steps in this lifecycle cannot be initiated with confidence when there is uncertainty surrounding the requirements specification. Sources of uncertainty include ill-defined objectives; a complex problem area which is not adequately understood by user groups; and unclear boundaries for the project scope. In most situations a suitable set of requirements can be determined after further analytical work, which may involve simulation studies, interviews, group discussions or even, in extreme cases, pilot studies where a section of the project is implemented on a trial basis.

This step-by-step or top-down lifecycle approach needs a firm starting point, otherwise it becomes necessary to rework earlier stages as deficiencies in the original specification become visible. Some uncertainty in the requirements is almost inevitable, especially due to the changing nature of all organizations, but the probability of major error at this point must be kept low. When the uncertainty cannot be removed by analysis, as often occurs with the design of decision support systems, an evolutionary or 'middle-out' approach is needed. Chapter 13 includes material on this topic.

The methodology described in this section is based on the premise that major checkpoint reviews for project control purposes are conducted at the end of steps 2, 5, and 8, with less rigorous reviews at the end of steps 4, 6, and 7. Reports on progress are therefore included at these points. The systems analysis activities (step 3), which are not subject to review until the end of step 4, are included as part of the logical design phase. This is because the feasibility study includes a systems analysis overview. The level of detail required in each phase depends on the complexity of the application. In particular the scale of feasibility study varies considerably, being much more comprehensive when there is significant uncertainty about the cost, technical feasibility, or effectiveness of the final outcome.

12.7.1 Phase 1 — Feasibility Study

1. Establish feasibility study plan:
   - Define the objective and scope of the system study
   - Establish phase 1 work plans including staff and cost schedules
   - Submit feasibility study plan for approval to information systems management
2. Analyze requirements and prepare recommendations:
   - Collect current systems documentation
   - Analyze current system functional processing
   - Identify business issues which are important in the target area
   - Determine and evaluate alternative options which meet all or part of the objectives
   - Prepare preliminary recommendations for the most effective option and review with user management

The preliminary recommendation is explored further by developing a preliminary design and evaluating relevant costs. If no technical or economic surprises are encountered in this more detailed examination, then the preliminary recommendation becomes the recommendation of the feasibility study. Should major problems be revealed in the preliminary recommendation, another alternative will need to be selected and carried forward.

3. Prepare preliminary design for proposed system:
   - Identify functional requirements
   - Identify output requirements and proposed media
   - Identify input requirements and proposed media
   - Identify database and file requirements
   - Develop general systems flow
   - Identify software and hardware requirements

Note: If the system includes an extensive network of terminals and other remote devices, a good deal of effort is needed to establish factors such as:

- Overall network configuration
- Probable systems software environment
- Terminal type
- Back-up approach
- Feasibility of adequate control and data integrity

4. Establish costs, benefits, and time schedule:
   - Establish development costs and schedules
   - Establish operating costs
   - Prepare benefit analysis

5. Prepare feasibility study report for major checkpoint review

12.7.2 Phase 2 — Logical System Design

The logical system design phase is concerned with specifying user needs to a level of detail which virtually determines the information flow into and out of the system, as well as the data resources required for reporting purposes.

1. Systems analysis:
   - Review current physical system in detail, including data sources, flows, file content, volumes, frequencies, exceptions, report usage, resources used
   - Determine weaknesses in the current system, e.g. bottlenecks, inaccuracies, lost data, out-of-date files, inadequate reports, high cost

2. Prepare output specification:
   - Determine content and general format of reports
   - Determine frequency and distribution pattern of reports, including terminal specifications and location for on-line systems
   - Specify ad hoc reporting procedures

3. Prepare input specification:
   - Determine the mode, content, and general format of the input function
   - Determine the document or message-flow pattern from input data source to the location where input takes place; terminal location and specification are required for on-line systems

4. Prepare edit, validate, security, and control specifications:
   - Specify the rules for edit detection and correction
   - Specify the rules for validating data against the database and correction procedures
   - Specify back-up procedures
   - Specify the controls to be used to ensure complete processing and file/database integrity
   - Specify security procedures consistent with requirements

5. Design the logical data model:
   - Specify the data element descriptions in general terms

- Determine the necessary logical relationships between elements and data sets or files
6. Specify the implementation strategy, training needs
7. With users and team members, complete a logical design walkthrough of data and information flow, output, input, controls, and implementation plans
8. Review costs, benefits and schedules
9. Prepare the logical design report for checkpoint review

12.7.3   Phase 3 — Physical System Design

The physical design phase includes most of the work required to fit the logical design into the target hardware/software environment. Although program specifications are not produced until later in the project, processing sequences are determined as are all aspects of codes, input–output media, database design, communications network specifications, and implementation plans.

1. Design detailed physical system:
   - Specify the output media details completely — formats, frequency of distribution, etc.
   - Specify input media details completely — format, codes, locations
   - Specify communications network requirements
   - Design the physical database — including data model, data dictionary, access modes, etc.
   - Specify back-up requirements
   - Design the physical flow of information through the system, including functional modules and programming definition
   - Complete a physical design walkthrough
2. Plan the system implementation:
   - Devise a conversion approach and timetable for the database
   - Specify a conversion approach and timetable for system implementation
   - Determine training needs and plan necessary instruction courses
3. Determine the test and operating environment:
   - Devise system test and audit specifications
   - Determine the impact of the system on existing facilities, hardware, software, database, and communications
   - Specify new hardware/systems software, if required
4. Revise costs, benefits, and time schedules:
   - Revise development costs
   - Revise operating costs
   - Revise benefit analysis
   - Revise implementation schedule
5. Prepare systems specification report for major checkpoint review

12.7.4 Phase 4 — Programming

This phase is a far more straightforward component of the systems development process and is seen as comprising the following tasks (however, new equipment may need to be installed before program testing can commence):

1. Design, code, and test programs:
   - Prepare systems test procedures from the approved plan
   - Prepare string-test environment — test JCL, database, and file test data
   - Develop program-structure design
   - Design program using a top-down method
   - Code, document, and desk check
   - Walkthrough
   - Compile and include the program in the string test
2. Detailed implementation procedures and pilot training:
   - Prepare detailed procedures from the approved plan
   - Prepare user-procedures manual
   - Prepare conversion procedures
   - Develop training material
   - Conduct pilot training
3. Satisfy operating requirements:
   - Prepare operating documents from the approved plan
   - Confirm the availability of supplies and processing facilities
4. Devise system test data and conduct systems test

12.7.5 Phase 5 — Implementation

Again, the purpose of this phase is self-explanatory.
1. Complete equipment installation
2. Complete procedures manuals and conduct training
3. Establish the database so it reflects the physical situation at the time of implementation
4. Conduct parallel running of old and new procedures
5. Perform acceptance tests and systems assurance evaluation

12.7.6 Phase 6 — Post-implementation Review

The post-implementation review closes the cycle back to the user. Users initiate (or approve the initiation of) systems projects because they have certain expectations that they believe a computer-based system can fulfil. Most of these expectations will have been captured in the requirements specification but some may have been missed. Hence the post-implementation review must judge the system not only on the criterion of the defined systems objective but also on the less concrete expectations of the users. There are thus three bases for evaluating a system after it has been installed for some months:

- Review technical and cost aspects, e.g. timeliness of reports, systems controls, accuracy of data, system response times, development time and costs, operational costs
- Review benefit claims used to justify the project, e.g. staff reduction, improved decision making, better customer relations
- Review user satisfaction with system, e.g. ease of using input and output facilities, adequacy of 'fit' with the manual procedures, impact on job satisfaction

After the system has been evaluated, a review report must be prepared:

- Present the results of the three review aspects
- Recommend changes needed to the system itself or to project management procedures

12.8   ESTIMATING PROJECT TIME AND RESOURCE NEEDS

12.8.1   The Variables

A critical part of the project management technique is estimating the variables surrounding the EDP project to determine time schedules and resource requirements such as staff and money. All those responsible for estimating EDP project variables must realize that there is a definite link between the stability of the task specification and the accuracy of estimates. The accuracy of estimates improves as the project moves through the lifecycle, since each phase reduces the level of uncertainty. The end of the feasibility study is probably the earliest point at which a reliable set of estimates can be made.

Even though the project leader may strenuously attempt to 'freeze' a specification, it is often impossible to do so, for changes can occur in the organization, in the user environment, and in the expectations of operators and managers. In addition, the definition of the problem being addressed by the system's design may alter as the users become more aware of the computer's potential. Therefore, the estimation procedure must allow for these possibilities, either through 'contingencies', or by providing for reviews as soon as a significant change is made. Formal authorization of specification changes is most desirable in a large project.

The variables to be estimated include:

- The time required for completing the individual work tasks
- The time required to complete all of the work tasks — note that it may be possible to perform some tasks simultaneously and independently, and so

the total time is not necessarily the sum of the individual work-task requirements
- Resource requirements for each subtask in terms of personnel and equipment requirements, e.g. computer-testing time
- Costs for staff and equipment

12.8.2   Estimating Techniques

- *Informed guessing* — the situation in which the estimator guesses the size of the variable being examined on the basis of some impression of task difficulty. Because it is not a formal approach, the estimator is often influenced by the amount of resources or time that may be acceptable to those responsible for authorizing the project. Although widely used, this approach is usually inaccurate, especially if there is a fair degree of complexity or uncertainty about the project.
- *Analysis and synthesis* — this technique is frequently used where there is no database of previous project-development parameters, either because the estimator is new to the task, or because the organization does not keep such records. It usually involves breaking down the tasks to be performed into subtasks, and then the estimator makes an assessment, based on experience, of the time and staff required to complete each of the subtasks. Once this breakdown is completed, the time and effort requirements are accumulated to give a total for the overall task. This approach can be quite accurate, if the estimator is experienced, once the feasibility study and logical design phases are complete.
- *Historical analysis* — if a history of other projects is available then the estimator may be able to use the analysis and synthesis technique as a basis for comparing the difficulty of the new task with that of a previously completed task. Therefore the essential difference between this historical analysis technique and the analysis and synthesis is that the actual times involved in previous projects are employed rather than the estimator's own assessment of the time taken for each subtask.
- *Parametric systems* — considerable research has been carried out trying to obtain estimates for the completion times of different types of EDP tasks by using multiple-regression analyses based on variables which ought to be related to the time, cost, or resource requirements.

While none of these parametric methods has been accepted as sufficiently accurate for general use, they often do point out interesting relationships which appear to exist between variables. As an example, results of analyses of data from 20 US army systems were reported by Dorothy Pope (1975). Two resulting equations were:

$$Y_1 = 2.57 X_1 + 5.10 X_2 \, 0.12 X_3$$

$$Y_2 = 0.38 X_4 + 0.19 X_5$$

where Y_1 is the person-months required for systems development
       Y_2 is the number of computer hours required for running the system
       X_1 is the number of output formats
       X_2 is the number of record types in the database or files
       X_3 is the number of input transactions per month (in thousands)
       X_4 is the number of input transaction types
       X_5 is the number of input data fields

Although several other variables were included in the analyses, only those given here were significant in estimating these particular resources.

A detailed analysis of many projects has enabled Larry Putnam (1979) to propose the existence of complex relationships which link system development cost to size, development time, and the level of technology available to the project team to assist design and testing. Specifically, his experiments indicate that cost is proportional to the cube of system size and is inversely proportional to the cube of a technology factor and the fourth power of development time. The implications for project management from these results are obviously very significant. In particular, Putnam's concept of a minimum development time is vital since it imposes strict limits on the ability of a project manager to speed up the rate of development.

12.8.3 Recommendations

It should be clear to readers that there are no failsafe techniques for estimating resources for the various computing projects. However, provided the estimator does not try to do the impossible, i.e. estimate what is not estimatable (e.g. a system cost before a full feasibility study is carried out), reasonably accurate results can be obtained.

A few extra helpful hints — some drawn from Fred Brooks' book *The Mythical Man-Month* — are:

- People and months are not interchangeable. Because of communication and control overheads, six people do not work at twice the rate of three people. Hence Brooks' law: *Adding staff to a late software project makes it later.*
- It is easier to estimate small projects, so subdivide into logical entities and then rebuild the total estimate.
- Keep interactions between modules to a minimum.
- Add time to the 'optimistic' estimate for urgent calls on maintenance work, consulting, machine down-time documentation, reworking of logic with bugs, training, etc. Possibly only 60 per cent of a designer's time will be available for the actual project.

- Assume an 'average' person, and then apply a factor when a particular person is assigned to the task.

  Note that the relative performance of two unequally performing analysts or programmers is a non-linear function of project complexity — see Figure 12–5. Thus while programmer A may be twice as fast as programmer B on relatively simple tasks, programmer B may never finish a complex job such as task X!

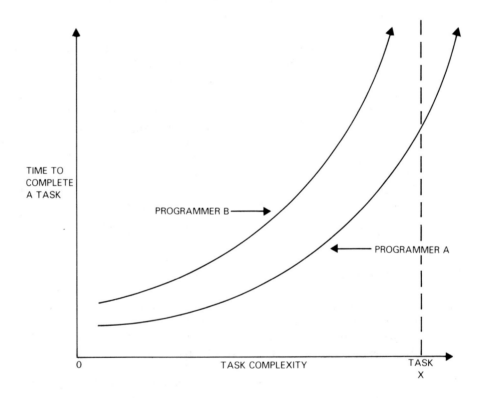

Figure 12-5   Completion time is a non-linear function of task complexity

- Where the project is to be designed and programmed in-house, estimate a time loss due to specification changes and imprecision. This always seems to be less of a problem for projects let to outside contractors, possibly because specification changes then are seen to cost 'real money'.
- Don't forget a component for testing and implementation — 25 per cent of the total.
- In computer project management, things can get worse without limit!

12.9   PROJECT CONTROL

12.9.1   Overview

The objective of the project-control mechanism is to ensure that the performance requirements of the system are met within time and cost budgets, while at the same time the organization's guidelines and standards are conformed with. The critical aspects of project control are therefore:

- A well-defined set of system requirements
- A project plan which sets out anticipated rates of progress and resources utilization
- A reporting from the project team compiled at both detailed and overall levels to inform management about progress and current status
- Reviews of the performance of the project team against the project plan

12.9.2   Detailed Reviews

The purpose of detailed reviews is to allow information systems management and the representatives of the user department to ensure that the project is running smoothly. Thus this level of reporting centres around:

- Activities performed since the last review
- The current status of the project in terms of the methodology adopted
- The validity of current estimates for resource requirements
- A revised schedule to completion
- Constraints which are affecting the rate of progress, for example lack of computer test time, inappropriate or inadequate staff allocations, lack of test data, non-cooperation with user department

Naturally the actual format of reporting depends on standards adopted within the organization.

12.9.3   Checkpoint Reviews

Probably the most important technique available for achieving the overall effectiveness of project development is the checkpoint review. Frequently major reviews are conducted at the end of the feasibility study, physical design, and post-implementation audit phases. In addition, less extensive reviews may be carried out at the end of the logical design, programming, and implementation phases. Of these reviews, those at the ends of the feasibility study and the physical systems design phases probably are the most important. It is common practice in many organizations to actually stop work on the project at the end of these two phases and debar any further work and expenditure until the review is complete and a go-ahead signal given. Naturally, the authority to proceed is given only if cost, performance, and time expectations are in line with the original estimates — or at least still lie within acceptable ranges.

In order for management to be able to evaluate the project team's performance at these reviews in an appropriate manner, it is necessary for comprehensive reports or 'deliverables' to be prepared by the team members. A proposed table of contents for each of these deliverables is now given.

The feasibility study report

This report is best prepared in two sections: part 1, a management report; and part 2, a technical report. Typical tables of contents are given for a management report and for a technical report.

(i) *Management report*
  - Management summary, reviewing briefly: the scope and objectives of project; the constraints and limitations; the alternatives reviewed; and a recommendation
  - Description of the current system including its strengths and weaknesses
  - Major business opportunities and risks arising from the system
  - Limitations and constraints imposed by the business or the system
  - Alternative proposals available for improvement of performance
  - A review of the impact of the recommended system on the organization

(ii) *Technical report*
  - An outline of the proposed system
  - An indication of draft input and output formats
  - A description of file and database requirements
  - A description of the flow of information through the system
  - A review of the impact of the system on the computer-operating environment, including database and communications

The logical system design report

The objective of the logical system design report is to document the user-oriented characteristics of the system's design as it is evolving. After reading the report, the project manager and team members ought to be able to determine:

  - The scope of the system, its objectives, and the basic implementation plan to be followed in achieving the objectives
  - The scope and style of the reporting and data-input function and what will be expected generally of those interacting with the system
  - An appreciation of the controls and back-up procedures to be developed

Consequently the items expected to be contained within the details of the report are:

- A general system description, including discussion of problems with current procedures
- A description of information flow, and the logical data-model design proposals
- Output and input specifications
- Control, back-up, and security specifications
- Implementation plans and training proposals
- Cost, benefit, and time schedule review

The output and input specifications need not be complete but they should be sufficiently detailed so that the user can appreciate what it will be like to work with the system. Included in the input section should be some discussion on the operating procedures which will have to be followed, as well as a discussion on any particular coding systems or other new aspects of system input which will be different from the procedures currently in force.

The emphasis in the section on the database logical model should be on the relationships between data elements which are required to meet reporting and processing needs, rather than a full specification of contents.

The physical system design report

The objective of the physical system design report is to document the details of the proposed system as they are to be implemented on a particular target computer. This report will be written for the project leader and also the persons responsible for carrying out the program design. It may also be used by the programmer to back-up any design specifications. Therefore it is important that all program-related details be included in the report. It is expected that the following aspects would be covered:

- A technical specification covering the information flow through the system and giving design details for all of the design entities, including:

  1. An information flow overview
  2. Design details for outputs and inputs
  3. Design details for files or database including proposed access methods
  4. Security procedures proposed
  5. Back-up and restart proposals

- A discussion of the effect that this system is expected to have on current data-processing operating facilities, particularly related to the target computer system
- An implementation plan, including:

1. A plan for conversion from existing procedures
2. Training of those who are going to use the system
3. A discussion of the procedures to be followed by users in accessing the system, putting data in, and obtaining reports
4. System acceptance schedule and test specification

- A revised — and now presumably more accurate — cost/benefit evaluation

Beyond this point in the project evaluation, all of the deliverables will be in the form of programs, or the completed system documentation.

12.9.4 Project Control Aids

There are a great number of control aids available to help the project manager monitor progress and to plan resource allocation for future activity. They include pro forma report sheets, a vast range of bar-charting techniques and display systems, and the much more sophisticated computer-based PERT (Program Evaluation and Review Technique) systems which prepare reports on current status, schedules, and allocate limited resources.

A simple example of the Gantt bar-charting technique is shown in Figure 12–6. This style of chart can be used to:

- Display the estimated dates for start and completion of each activity — and thereby show the overall project plan
- Provide a visual record of actual progress against the plan by including actual times required for each activity
- Record the tasks assigned to individual team members, thereby facilitating the personnel planning

The basic limitation of this kind of chart is that it cannot portray precedence requirements — for example, the code design task must be complete before the input forms can be designed. The dotted lines in Figure 12–6 indicate that staff will be transferred to another activity when the first one is complete.

Network diagrams have been used for many years in the construction industry to portray the sequences of individual activities to be undertaken from start to completion of a project. The network in Figure 12–7 shows part of the implementation plan for a combined inventory control and order entry/despatch system. It is assumed that preliminary training and systems testing have already been carried out. The activities are:

Activity

1,2   Train data clerks in order-entry data pick-up procedures, i.e. collect details of all current outstanding orders and customer master file records (requires 2 days)

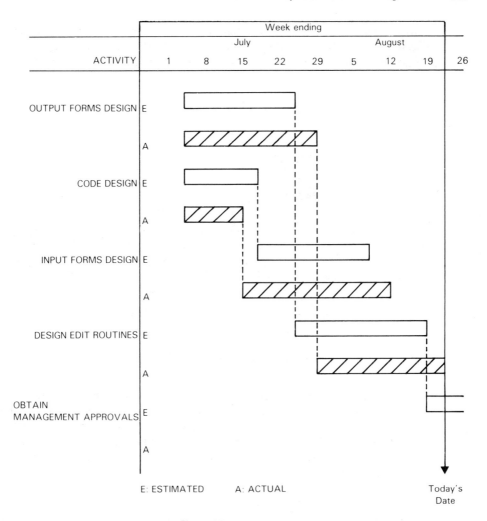

Figure 12-6 A Gantt chart

1,3 Train data clerks in the inventory data pick-up procedures, i.e. collect details of all inventory items (3 days)

2,4 Collect, and enter on the database, data on product pricing (1 day)

2,5 Collect, and enter on the database, data on orders and customers (4 days)

3,5 Collect, and enter on the database, data on inventory (6 days)

5,6 Train operators of the order-entry system on the full-size file (2 days)

5,7 Train operators of inventory system on the full-size file and live data (3 days)

7,8 Parallel run the system (7 days)

Note, in Figure 12–7, that activities 4,5 and 6,7 are dummy entries in that they do not occupy any real time, but they are needed to indicate precedence requirements, e.g. order-entry training must be complete before parallel running commences.

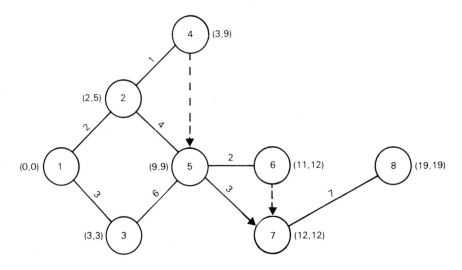

Figure 12–7 A network for system implementation

The table shown in Figure 12–8 gives details of the earliest and latest start and finish times which are possible if the whole project is to be completed in the shortest time of 19 days. The slack is, of course, the delay possible in completion of any activity without affecting the completion date. The path 1, 3, 5, 7, 8 is referred to as the 'critical path' since it comprises activities with zero slack. Any delay here will delay the completion of the entire project.

ACTIVITY	ESTIMATED DURATION (DAYS)	EST	EFT	LST	LFT	SLACK
1,2	2	0	2	3	5	3
1,3	3	0	3	0	3	0
2,4	1	2	3	8	9	6
2,5	4	2	6	5	9	3
3,5	6	3	9	3	9	0
5,6	2	9	11	10	12	1
5,7	3	9	12	9	12	0
7,8	7	12	19	12	19	0

EST: EARLIEST START TIME   LST: LATEST START TIME
EFT: EARLIEST FINISH TIME   LFT: LATEST FINISH TIME

Figure 12–8 Network table

Therefore, in summary, the network diagram can be used to:

- Show the logical order in which tasks must be performed
- Monitor project progress and provide warning when delays will affect the target completion date
- Assist in resource allocation by highlighting critical tasks

Finally, it is worth observing that the project manager should evaluate the 'vulnerable paths' in the network, as well as the critical path. Often the activities on the critical path are structured tasks with little likelihood of excessive estimation error. At the same time, other activities may be far less certain of successful outcome and, therefore, constitute the real threat to meeting deadlines.

One drawback of network diagrams is the absence of a time scale like that found in Gantt charts. Of course, the more complex PERT computer-based systems are able to incorporate timing, critical path, and resource allocation factors into reports.

12.10 USER PARTICIPATION IN PROJECT DESIGN AND MANAGEMENT

12.10.1 Stating the Problem

During the late 1960s it became obvious that participation by user-department representatives in systems design was almost essential if the resulting system was to fit well into the target environment. Since then a number of researchers have studied the impact of information systems on organizations and have attempted to correlate the degree of user, and particularly operator, satisfaction with the degree of user participation in the original design. In this context refer to the publications by Mumford, Land & Hawgood (1978), Bjorn-Andersen (1980), and Lucas (1974).

A number of dissatisfactions have been identified, some of which have resulted in reaction by way of strikes, refusal to work the system, sabotage or more passive expressions of objection through resignations, poor performance, in-accuracy, etc. Users have expressed concern at their loss of control over their database and over the process of change within their information-processing and reporting function when computer systems were installed. Similarly they have objected to their lack of understanding of the processes necessary to obtain change, and to the need for them to interact with computer experts.

Clearly, it is possible to design systems which are empathetic with the users' expectations for control over their work environment. All that is needed is the appropriate stimulus to the design team and control over the evolving design to ensure that all objectives — economic, social, and technical — are achieved. In spite of all the flexibility which exists — at least at the commencement of a project — systems designers are frequently accused of assuming too technical an orientation. In particular, reference is made to:

- The narrow scope of the designer's objectives — these objectives are frequently oriented around high-performance and rule-formulation goals rather than looking at a global framework which includes the satisfaction of the operator and other users (for example customers, suppliers, supervisors). The identity of the real users is often mistaken to be those who authorized the project — the management group — rather than those who interact directly with the system.
- Attitude of the designers to users — frequently, users are considered to be 'machines' in the sense that their needs and actions are likely to be consistent and unaffected by their interaction with the system and other aspects of the work environment. This attitude is reflected in the users perceiving the system to be arrogant, an attitude which sometimes is engendered by apparent technical arrogance on the part of designers during interviews.
- Black-box approach — designers frequently ascribe too much stability and rationality to the target project environment. All complex information-processing situations are in constant flux, and within almost all there is a high degree of informality with information exchange. Attempts to freeze such an information-flow structure and to make explicit all that is implicit usually results in dissatisfaction.
- Technical sophistication — designers usually consider themselves 'agents of change', but their understanding of instruments for bringing about change is restricted to technical tools and concepts. Consequently, there is little consideration given to non-technical solutions, or even to low-technology options either because of ignorance or the lack of job interest which would result.

12.10.2 Possible Solutions

If these difficulties are to be minimized, systems designers must be trained in a range of people-oriented skills, and more active participation by users in design teams should be fostered.

The first option is clearly the responsibility of those in charge of systems development groups, who can sponsor the training and motivate individual persons to incorporate people-oriented objectives into the project. The second is more complex since it requires a change in the organization's approach to the design task itself. Participation can be accomplished at three broad levels:

- Consultation
- Representation
- Consensus

Consultation involves the design team actively consulting with users, or their representatives, about the project — taking a broad view of the word 'user' to incorporate groups outside the system's immediate zone of impact, but who still require access to the system. The representation approach usually encompasses choosing a design team with representatives of a wide range of user interests. These persons include nominees of operators and other users, as well as management. The consensus type of participation clearly envisages all those affected having a role in the design, or at least in accepting the general design principles. There are many different methodologies for the participative design process, and they are being augmented regularly by those engaged in research. Some of these are covered in the reference material. Ultimately the degree of participation has to be determined by the management group. Potential disadvantages of the approach which must be considered when making the decision include:

- The time and cost required to achieve a design may be significantly increased and the level of work disruption may be unacceptable. This depends on the ability of those directing the group — and good group leaders are not necessarily good systems analysts.
- The group design may not be as innovative, or optimal, as that likely to be obtained by a smaller, more cohesive, team.
- There is a chance that some groups may attempt to use the design process for purposes outside the scope originally envisaged, thus creating a politically divisive environment, incompatible with effective design work.

REFERENCES

F.T. BAKER, 'Chief Programmer Team Management of Production Programming', *IBM Systems Journal*, vol. 11, no. 1, 1972, pp. 56-73.

N. BJORN-ANDERSEN (ed.), *The Human Side of Information Processing*, North-Holland, Amsterdam, 1980.

B. BOWMAN, G. DAVIS & J. WETHERBE, 'Modelling for MIS', *Datamation*, July 1981, pp. 155-65.

F.P. BROOKS, *The Mythical Man-Month*, Addison-Wesley, Reading, Mass., 1975.

M. ENFIELD & A. RODDEN, 'Experiences with Software Engineering Techniques in a Large Programming Group', *ACS Computer Bulletin*, vol. 1, no. 5, June 1977, pp. 3-5.

H. LUCAS, *Towards Creative Systems Design*, Columbia University Press, New York, 1975.

E. MUMFORD, F. LAND & J. HAWGOOD, 'A Participative Approach to the Design of Computer Systems', *Impact of Science on Society*, vol. 28, no. 3, 1978, pp. 235-53.

D.J.M. POPE, 'Estimating the Resources Needed for ADP Systems', in A.B. Frielink (ed.), *Economics of Information*, North-Holland, Amsterdam, 1975.

L.H. PUTNAM & A. FITZSIMMONS, 'Estimating Software Costs', *Datamation*, (in three parts) September, October and November, 1979.

G.M. WEINBERG,, *The Psychology of Computer Programming*, Van Nostrand Reinhold, New York, 1971.

CASE STUDY — AVEGO SOCIAL CLUB LIMITED

Background

The Avego Social Club, formed in 1955, now provides a range of catering, recreation, and entertainment services and discount shopping facilities for some 20 000 members. The range of services provided include, principally, catering, bottle shop, stationery shop, sporting-goods shop, recreation facilities, evening craft courses, and entertainment. The club is administered by five departments, each headed by a director responsible for operating the department within budget. These departments and their responsibilities are:

- Catering — cafeteria, restaurants, coffee bars, vending machines, liquor shop, and bars
- Shop services — clothing, stationery, and sporting-goods shops
- Program department — cultural activities, tuition courses, craft area expenses, tutors' fees, recreation facilities, and entertainment
- Administration — general administration of club accounts, payroll, cashier, and management reporting
- Slot machines — the poker machines and other amusement machines

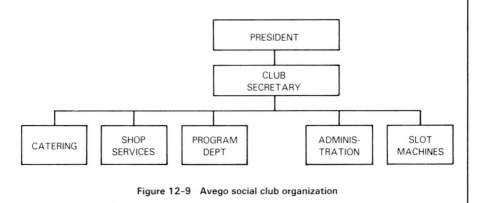

Figure 12-9 Avego social club organization

The office systems operated by Avego Social Club were, in 1976, completely manual using hand-posted ledger cards. Five clerks were responsible for running the system under the direction of the 58 year-old accountant, John Hruska, the director of administration. The allocation of the clerks was: debtors — two clerks; creditors — one clerk; general ledger — one clerk; and payroll — one clerk. The organization of the club is represented in Figure 12–9.

The chief executive officer of the club is the club secretary, Joan Helpmann, who reports to the president, which is a part-time position elected each year by the members.

The Search for a Computer

By 1976 the annual turnover of the club was more than $7 million. Joan Helpmann felt strongly that the manual system was incapable of producing the level of management reports needed to run such a diverse enterprise. This point was reinforced for Helpmann when it was found, late in 1976, that a loss situation would undoubtedly result for the 1976 calendar year. Helpmann believed that better reports would have identified the loss-making areas early enough for her to have taken action.

In November, Helpmann invited a number of small business computer firms to come to the club and discuss the possible computerization of the club's office systems. She followed up these conversations by attending a number of demonstrations of small business computers. In December 1976 she submitted a report to the club committee requesting permission to invite tenders for the supply of a computer and associated application programs to enable the following systems to be automated:

1. A stock-recording system for all the stock kept by the club, including fresh and frozen catering supplies, and shop and liquor supplies
2. A menu-costing system to calculate the cost of each meal based on standard-ingredients cost obtained from the stock-reporting system and standard labour costs
3. A payroll system for the 300 permanent and part-time staff of the club, which should be capable of producing pay cheques and reporting hours worked, sick leave, absenteeism, and a labour-cost dissection
4. General accounting system, including the production of cheques for accounts payable, accounts receivable, and general ledger
5. Budgeting system using the accounting files to project future costs and estimate budgets based on inflation and growth rates

The system should also have the capacity to be able to accept the following additional systems at a later date:

1. A reservation system for the booking of rooms, equipment, and special functions
2. A membership register and club-dues billing system
3. Capacity for running a bureau service to process the data of other clubs in the area

The system tendered should also have the following characteristics:

- Use ordinary language
- Require minimal staff training
- Be interactive
- Use A4 stationery
- The one company should supply both hardware and applications software

The request-for-tender document was three pages long, giving a very brief description of the club and outlining the above requirements and characteristics. Tenders closed on 30 January 1977 and on this date the secretary found that she had received quotes from three manufacturers' representatives and one software house. Brief notes on the four quotes follow.

Quote 1: Datanow Limited

This quote, from the supplier of one of the most widely used small business computers (SBC) in Australia, tendered a small Datanow computer and their standard debtors, creditors, inventory control, payroll, and general ledger applications systems, with no modifications to these packages. As these packages had been principally developed to suit the needs of a manufacturing environment, Helpmann was doubtful that they could be readily used by the club. Datanow Limited stressed the reliability and wide use of their equipment, and their opinion that the club should get 12–18 months operating experience with their, perhaps not optimal but certainly workable, system so that the club would be able to define their requirements accurately. The hardware cost of this quote was $55 000 and the standard software at $15 000, to give a total tendered price of $70 000.

Quote 2: Interactive Computer Resources (ICR)

ICR tendered the Quadrex small business computer and undertook to carry out a detailed study of the club's requirements, submit a systems design report for approval, and make such modifications as necessary to the standard payroll, debtors, creditors, inventory control, and general ledger packages, and develop from scratch a menu-costing system. A number of Quadrex systems are installed in the same city as Avego. Their tender cost was

Case Study — Avego Social Club Limited

Hardware — $46 000
Software packages — $4000
Modifications to software — $5500
Total — $55 500

Quote 3: Exodus Computers Limited

Exodus Computers Limited (motto: 'With us to the Promised Land') is a very small computer company representing the US firm of the same name. As yet it has no machines installed in Australia, although a number are said to be on order. They undertook to supply their club package which is nearing development completion in the USA. However few details are available at present. Their hardware was quoted at $45 000 with the software at $25 000 — the total $70 000.

Quote 4: Software Services Limited

Software Services is a software house supplying software and small business computers on an OEM basis. Their quote was along the lines given in Quote 2 by ICR; that is, carrying out a systems study first before software development. Their quote:

Hardware — $95 000
Software — $36 000
Total — $131 000

The Computer

At the club committee meeting on 10 February 1977 it was decided to accept the secretary's recommendation that the quote of Interactive Computer Resources be accepted, as it was the cheapest received. On 22 February 1977 contracts were signed with ICR. The terms were:

Hardware

(i) The supply of an installation of the Quadrex system with:
  - 8K of user memory expandable to 96K in 8K stages; 6 million bytes of disk storage — 3 million fixed and 3 million on a removable pack
  - 1728-character video terminal display
  - 968-character inquiry video terminal
  - Business-operating system (BOS) with expanded BASIC compiler
  - 100 line per minute matrix printer

(ii) Cost of the hardware $46 000 tax exempt. Cost of maintenance per month $360. Delivery, installation, and testing to be completed by 12 April 1977.

Application software

Supply of the following software:

Inventory recording & purchasing	$4048
Menu costing	1056
Debtors	990
Creditors	550
Product group analysis	880
General ledger	330
Costing system	715
Budgeting system	330
Payroll and labour dissection	550
	9449

The software to be developed, implemented, and running by 18 July 1977.

Conditions of the Tender

1. The full specification of the system to be developed by ICR and provided to the club by 28 March 1977 and agreements to be reached on the specifications by 4 April 1977.
2. There may be a variance of up to 10 per cent in the cost of the software due to clarification of information requirements.
3. Full maintenance of the system to be provided for 6 months following installation.
4. The software to be developed according to proper professional standards and a high level of documentation to be provided.
5. The computer to be paid for when it has been installed and shown to be operating.
6. The applications software to be paid for according to the following schedule: 50 per cent on signing the contract; 30 per cent on approval of the program specifications, and the remaining 20 per cent on successful installation of the software.

Interactive Computer Resources subcontracted the applications software to the software firm ACE Computer Services on the grounds that this would be the most efficient way of ensuring that the software deadlines were met, as ICR had very few programmers on their own staff. ACE Computer Services was a two-person partnership specializing in supplying applications software for the Quadrex system. Shortly after ACE started work on Avego's systems specification, their senior partner, Jan McGrill, sold her 70 per cent partnership equity to her partner Neil Stoat, and left to work for a multinational company. Stoat took over all the current projects which McGrill had been personally involved with, including that for designing, developing, and installing the applications software for the Avego Club. On 28 March 1977 a brief document (around five pages) was signed off by the club as an adequate specification for the requested application software. This document made many references to the standard Quadrex software packages, the 5 centimetre thick documentation of which was supplied as an appendix to the specifications.

On 14 June 1977 the Quadrex system was installed on the club's premises. Hardware testing was completed three weeks later after some initial trouble with the disk drives had been overcome by the installation of a replacement unit. At that time the installation engineers drew attention to the fact that the computer room had no air conditioning and was located in a north-facing office. On 10 June 1977 testing commenced on the applications software, beginning with the payroll and inventory packages.

Systems testing on the payroll and inventory packages continued for the months of June, July, and August, using live files and involving heavy effort by the office clerical staff, who were attempting to run the computer system while using the manual system. Many objections were voiced by the clerical staff on account of the clumsy and poorly designed screen formats, which required duplicate entry of information and had many fields not required by the club which had to be tabbed over. It became obvious that the package was better suited to a manufacturing organization than to Avego Club. In addition, the machine response was very slow, further delaying the testing. The reports produced by the packages contained a large number of errors which could be traced to the modifications that had been made by ACE. In September, Stoat succeeded in getting Avego Club to upgrade their CPU main memory to 24K bytes in an attempt to improve the machine's response.

On 16 November 1977 a letter was written to Interactive Computer Resources by Joan Helpmann, which said, in part, 'The club's computer has been operational for almost 6 months now and the club is completely happy with the hardware aspects of their purchase. Unfortunately, the situation regarding software is nowhere near as happy. Your contractor, Mr Stoat, is proceeding extremely slowly. None of the software packages are operational yet, there is friction between Stoat and the office staff, and office functions are being disrupted. Finally, we do not believe that we are getting the service we are entitled to under the terms of our contract.' ICR responded to the letter by calling a meeting at which Stoat presented a plan for rectifying the problems.

John Hruska, the director of administration, had played no part in the acquisition of the computer. He had given silent opposition to the idea right from the start as he believed the existing systems were satisfactory and that the computer would represent much more work for his department, which was being asked to reduce staff by one clerk on account of the supposed benefits the computer would bring. John was open in his wish that he could delay implementation sufficiently to allow him to retire at age 60 without having to learn about the new system.

Over the 1977–78 summer, a second-year information systems student from a nearby university, Ron Boucher, was hired to work with Stoat. Helpmann took this action as a way of spurring on the work, which was proceeding very slowly with Stoat spending no more than one day a week at Avego on account of servicing ACE contracts with other organizations. Work was frequently delayed during the summer when the computer room, warmed to over 28°C, precipitated random CPU errors, necessitating shutdown of the system. In February, Stoat folded up ACE Computer Services and took a job with an airline company as a programmer. On 24 February 1978 a confidential memo was circulated within the club which said that, although the creditors and debtors ledger and inventory control packages were the only applications implemented so far, only the debtors ledger was working satisfactorily. The creditors ledger and the inventory control systems were faulty, with some fairly major flaws in their operation. The memo ended with 'It is regrettable but true that the computer, which has cost some $70 000 to date, has not produced anything of real value since installation.' At this point ICR had been paid for the hardware, the memory upgrade, and $7000 for software, despite the fact that none of it was operational. In addition, around $5000 had been paid for printing new forms, stationery (e.g. input forms, statement forms, cheque forms) and $4000 spent for casuals hired to code products, customers, and menus.

After some thought Helpmann outlined three options to get the club out of its mess.

1. Sue ICR for non-fulfilment of the contract obligations.
    Although this seemed initially an attractive option, it was realized that since Boucher, an employee of the club, had worked on and altered the computer programs it would be difficult to prove non-fulfilment by ICR of the contract. As well, this would be a complex and long-drawn-out affair during which time development would be further delayed.
2. Demand that ICR fulfil its contract obligations.
    Essentially this had been the policy for the preceding four months and had not yielded much progress. Relations with ICR had continued to slip since May 1977 when Ted Weasley, the salesperson responsible for the

sale to Avego Club, had left ICR. It was felt that pursuit of this option would be fruitless.

3. Pay off ICR and develop a system within the club.

This appeared the most attractive option in that the club would have control over systems development and be able to accelerate their implementation.

Helpmann, long the most ardent and enthusiastic supporter of the club's computer, hired three part-time third-year information systems students from the same university as Boucher and, being now pressed to produce some tangible benefit from the computer, asked the students to select the application which would give the quickest implementation of a working system. The students, Rickie Head, Ho Tong, and Ong Ho, in May 1978 selected the payroll system for immediate implementation. It appeared to be close to working and, being a stand-alone system, would not involve interfaces to any future systems which they were not certain about.

They produced a plan which, with full-time work during the June mid-semester break, was implemented during September 1978. Their plan assumed that the systems design as embodied in the half-working payroll system was satisfactory and their job was to get the programs going.

None of Head, Tong, and Ho had had any prior experience with the Quadrex system or its programming language. In addition, they were not able to base their estimate on a good understanding of the problems in the payroll system. It took until January 1979 before Head, Tong, and Ho were able to demonstrate a working payroll program to the administration staff. During the demonstration, the pay clerk pointed out a number of major problems with the system, and it became clear that changes would have to be made. The clerical staff had by this time adopted the point of view that the computer would never work and so gave the students little cooperation. In October 1979 the modifications requested by the pay clerk had been completed and the system was at last operational having completed a three-month parallel run successfully. This represented the first useful work performed by the club's computer. In October, John Hruska retired.

The club's manual systems had been slowly disintegrating as clerical effort was diverted to assisting with the abortive computer-system implementation and Helpmann had discouraged as pointless any but the most necessary efforts to sustain the manual system. By mid-1979 the club could only produce profit-and-loss statements twice a year to coincide with their stock-takes. At monthly intervals an estimated profit-and-loss statement was produced, based on budgeted gross margin percentages, which were frequently in substantial error due to price rises failing to keep pace with cost increases.

In February 1979 the club hired its first full-time permanent programmer, an 18-year-old trainee, to commence work on programming an inventory control and financial reporting system designed specifically for the club by a consultant.

ASSIGNMENT

1. What were the chief reasons for the problems experienced by the Avego Social Club in implementing their computer?

2. Evaluate (a) the method and approach to calling tenders used by Helpmann and (b) the tender responses received.

3. Was Helpmann's decision to implement the payroll system wise?

4. What human relations problems are evident at Avego? What actions (by whom) might have avoided them?

5. Evaluate Helpmann's role as chief executive officer in the acquisition and implementation of the computer.

CASE STUDY — EXCELSIOR COMPANY PLANNING AND JUSTIFYING SYSTEM DEVELOPMENT

Excelsior is a manufacturer of copper wires with 2500 employees. Up to the present time they have been running some batch systems on their parent company's computer, but the increasing cost of this form of operation led to a study which determined that costs could be reduced by 40 per cent and facilities improved markedly if they were to install their own in-house computing capability.

On completion of this study the Board gave approval for a further project to define the necessary systems and select the appropriate hardware. This study has now been completed and thirteen major systems identified. Some of these will remain batch oriented but many will be on-line.

The projects identified and relevant information are given in Figure 12–10.

Case Study — Excelsior Company Planning and Justifying System Development

The Board has also stated that a hurdle rate of 20 per cent before tax is necessary on all capital projects, which includes these.

The useful life of each project can be assumed to be four years with no residual value. The present value of annuity factor 20 per cent for four years is 2.589.

ASSIGNMENT

On the basis of the estimated costs and benefits:

1. Which projects should be implemented and in what sequence? State the criteria used when determining the sequence.

2. Develop an implementation strategy for the projects selected in 1, under the condition that only five systems personnel are available. Aim to complete the projects selected in minimum total elapsed time using all personnel at all times wherever possible.

3. In response to questions 1 and 2 you have made many simplifying assumptions. List those that you are aware of.

4. Which items listed as 'intangible benefits' do you feel should be able to be quantified? How do you suggest this might be achieved in each case?

Project	Preceding Projects (1)	System	Estimated Man-Month Effort	Minimum Elapsed Time (Mth)	Cost '000	Annual Net Tangible Benefits '000	Intangible Benefits
1	—	On-line Order Entry	50	10	240	100	Better response to customer orders
2	3	Stock control & Purchasing	48	12	230	170	Easier operations, fewer stock-outs, better supplier relations
3	1	Sales Forecasting	9	3	43	15	Better support for management decision-making, improved operation of stock control system
4	1	Invoicing	15	5	72	28	
5	4	Accounts Receivable	24	8	115	120	Once in operation it may be possible to further reduce bad debts
6	2	Accounts Payable	24	8	120	25	
7	1,2	Production Planning Scheduling & Control	72	12	346	300	Reduced management achievement improved response to customer enquiries, improved information for management decisions
8	—	Payroll	8	4	38	15	Faster access to employee data
9	8	Personnel	6	3	29	5	Improved employee relations
10	8,2,7	Costing	18	6	86	36	Improved product line decisions
11	—	Asset Register	12	4	57	12	Improved control over assets
12	5	Sales Analysis	6	3	28	0	The sales Dept is unwilling to quantify the expected benefits, but state that considerable improvement in their effectiveness could be achieved
13	4,5,6,8,11	General Ledger	24	12	116	83	Improved information for management decisions & control

(1) These projects must be implemented before this one can start, i.e. before we do project 7 we must do projects 1 and 2.

Figure 12-10 Excelsior co. project options

13 DESIGNING DECISION SUPPORT SYSTEMS

13.1 INTRODUCTION

The term 'decision support system' (DSS) evolved during the 1970s to replace the more general expression 'management information system' (MIS). MIS was the title frequently used (and, indeed, still is common) to differentiate systems which provide information required by managers from transaction-processing systems. A sales-analysis system which generates exception reports, printed summaries, trend display graphics, and is able to respond interactively to inquiries on order progress, product demand, customer-ordering history, etc. is a typical example of an MIS. Other examples of MIS include personnel systems which service the administrative departments of large organizations, and financial-reporting systems which report and respond to inquiries based on costs, revenues, budgets, assets, and other accounting data.

Most MIS (and, therefore, DSS) are based on databases established and maintained by transaction-processing systems. Thus, in the order-and-despatch processing system of Figure 13–1, the data used as the basis for reports and responses to inquiries are derived from, or may actually be, the files or database used for the order-processing, production-scheduling, despatch, and invoicing procedures. Almost every data-processing system has a reporting/inquiry module and, therefore, part of each system design project is likely to involve consideration of the concepts and guidelines presented in this chapter.

The distinction between the design approaches to an MIS and to a DSS can be rather fine. Most authors who favour the latter title emphasize the 'decision'-oriented characteristic of the DSS against the 'information supply' bias of an MIS. Thus a DSS design should take problem-specific details into account as well as the

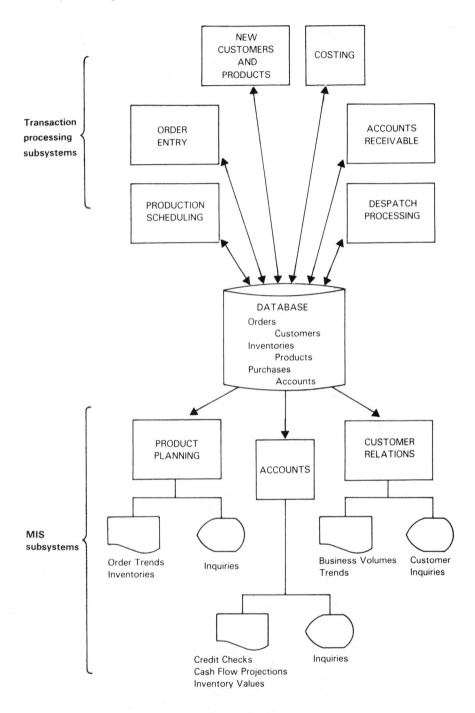

Figure 13-1 Relationship between MIS and transaction-processing systems: an order-processing/despatch system

decision style of the particular decision maker. In the end, the name makes no difference, it is the effectiveness of overall organization performance which should be the objective. In this text the term *decision support system* is used, with the meaning: a management information system designed to support decision making in specific problem areas by a particular individual or class of persons.

In Chapter 1, decision-oriented reporting is emphasized as being an important and desirable attribute of all information systems. Information is also described as having two vital characteristics — surprise value and relevance. It follows that the design of all information systems must be aimed at facilitating effective decision making: the payroll clerk must decide how much to pay each employee, the production supervisor must choose new work for an idle production unit, the credit manager must judge the significance of an outstanding debt, etc. However, each of these situations obviously requires a different DSS design approach.

Because the DSS concept involves problem and decision-maker issues as well as the supply of information, this chapter includes a discussion on the types of problem areas which are the target of DSS design, and on the way that behavioural characteristics influence the decision maker's 'decision style' and hence ability to use information and to interact with a computer-based system. When MIS type applications were first being developed, Ackoff (1967) and Dearden (1964) recognized a fundamental difficulty facing the systems analyst/designer. Ackoff summarized his view with the questions:

- Do managers need the information they want?
- If we give managers the information they need, will their decision making improve?
- If we improve communications between managers, e.g. increase the availability of data, will this result in improved performance of the organization?

Central to the answers to these questions is the relationship between the supply of timely, accurate information and the individual manager's ability to use it in a manner which contributes to the organization's performance. They also point to the fact that many decision makers do not fully understand how they make decisions.

This information-supply/decision-quality relationship is obviously complex, and is likely to be unique for all but the most basic, simple decision environments. Creativity is needed by the designer (and the user, of course, who may well be the designer) if the DSS is to perform well. Already, therefore, differences in the desirable approach to designing a DSS as opposed to a transaction-processing system are emerging from this introductory outline. Emphasis on the attributes and thinking style of specific users, or, at least, classes of user is needed to a much greater extent in a DSS — to the point where the system's interface for each user may need to be 'custom built'. This, in itself, raises further issues, especially cost effectiveness ones, since the normal movement of managerial staff may enforce constant redesign.

Following a study of the decision-making process from the rational/economic, behavioural, and actual 'in practice' viewpoints, this chapter contains sections on the DSS design issues, principles, and practice.

13.2   THE DECISION-MAKING PROCESS

The allocation of scarce resources among competitive uses or activities is the classic decision situation faced by managers. These problems have prompted attention to the 'economic or rational man' concept, in which it is envisaged that the optimum decision can always be made by considering the most economic and rational of the alternative courses of action available.

While all decision makers do face such resource allocation problems frequently, they are rarely uncomplicated by issues of power play, emotion, and precedent. In addition, many responses to problems or new situations are derived purely from power or emotional conflicts. Does, for example, the love shown by a husband and father for his wife diminish when a child is born who needs to share this love? Love can clearly be an infinite resource. How much can (or should) a family tie influence the granting of extended payment by a credit manager? It is likely that the answer to this question would depend on the local custom in different countries. In Australia, the issue of the allocation of land rights for Aboriginal people is complicated by differences in culture. Land is deemed to be 'owned' by individuals in Anglo-Saxon law, while people 'belong' to areas of land in Aboriginal custom. Decision making on this type of issue obviously involves considerations which are not economic or based on a purely rational analysis.

13.2.1   Decision-making Stages, Decision Analysis, and Decision Style

An understanding of the decision-making process is an obvious prerequisite for effective DSS design. The best known early contributions to decision theory were made by Herbert Simon (e.g. 1957, 1958). He postulated three distinct stages in the making of a decision which he titled Intelligence, Design, and Choice. In the intelligence stage the decision maker gathers information on the problem area which informs about its scope and implications. During the design stage, the alternative courses of action are identified and the outcomes or consequences of each alternative are determined. Choice involves the selection of one alternative action based on the decision-maker's preferences for its associated consequences. The Simon approach and related work have formed the basis of the 'economic man' concept in decision analysis. This involves three conditions:

- In any decision situation the decision maker is faced with a number of different identifiable alternative courses of action.
- To each alternative there is attached a set of outcomes or consequences.
- The decision maker has a preference system which facilitates the ranking of the outcomes — thus resulting in the making of a right decision.

The technique of decision analysis — see Howard (1968, 1980) or Keen & Scott-Morton (1978) — is a methodology for decision making which has developed out of this three-part concept. It is a way of determining a set of possible choices, preferences, and information needs; and it provides rules and guidelines for making this determination and for the subsequent evaluation which ranks the choices. Unless a problem is fairly simple and deterministic, a good deal of associated modelling and other analysis, external to the specific problem, is likely to be needed to establish relative costs, priorities, etc. Proponents of decision analysis believe that human beings cannot adequately assess the probabilities and the risks associated with complex problems without formal modelling or other evaluative assistance. Hence, all aspects of the problem should be formalized and made as explicit as possible.

From the DSS designer's viewpoint, the decision-analysis concept gives a way of establishing the types of information required for a particular problem environment. It is not part of the designer's task to make decisions — or even to perform decision analysis — but an understanding of the principles involved can be of considerable help. It must be recognized, though, that decision analysis is concerned with specific problem situations (and often at one instance of time), whereas the DSS designer is usually required to create a system which supports decision making in a range of problem areas, possibly by a class of individuals, over an extended time period.

Decision or cognitive style has also been an area for detailed research, associated with decision theory. This work is based on the principle that a decision-maker's thinking style influences the choice of one from a number of alternative actions. Although there are many different ways of classifying behavioural characteristics in relation to decisions, the two-dimensional framework proposed by Jung (so-called Jungian topology) — see McGuire (1970), and Mason & Mitroff (1973) — is frequently used. This distinguishes two dimensions which describe the information acquisition method and the data-processing mode employed by the individual decision maker.

The first dimension can range in a continuum from 'sensation' (i.e. absorbing concrete facts in detail through sensory faculties), to 'intuition' (i.e. evaluating situations as a whole with little regard for factual detail). 'Sensation' individuals prefer a structured, deterministic environment to work within (a possible example being a builder or mechanic), whereas 'intuitive' persons are more comfortable in a less structured, non-routine environment (say, as an artist). The second dimension is a similar continuum, ranging from a processing mode involving 'thinking', i.e. a rational and logical evaluation of the available information, with little regard for emotional factors; to the 'feeling' individual whose evaluation is based on emotional and personal values with scant consideration of logic.

Combining these two dimensions yields four possible extremes of decision-making characteristics. These are usually referred to as:

ST   Sensation — Thinking
SF   Sensation — Feeling
NT   Intuitive — Thinking
NF   Intuitive — Feeling

Considering these classifications for the management role yields the conclusion that, when faced with a problem, an ST manager would exert control based on logical analysis of hard facts, an SF manager would impose value judgments on the available facts, an NT manager would perform an overall, but logical, assessment on an impression of the whole environment, while an NF manager might select an alternative intuitively (without being able to explain why) or even deny the need for any decision at all! From this argument, it becomes clear that any DSS ought to provide an interface with its users which matches their individual cognitive styles. For example, an NT manager would have little use for detailed reports, and any system which provides them would probably be ignored as a source of decision support. Many systems analysts seem to prefer a formal, rational approach to their design, and assume that their systems should also exhibit these characteristics. However, many managers are not ST types — see Chapter 12 and its references, and also Argyris (1971). Consequently there is a real danger that a DSS designed without regard to these factors will not suit its users, and thereby be unlikely to achieve its objectives.

13.2.2 Decision Categories

Problems originating within an organization cover a wide spectrum of complexity and affect different groups or levels of personnel. It has also become common to consider a two-dimensional categorization for decisions (Gorry & Scott-Morton, 1971).

The first decision dimension relates to the part of the organization affected by the particular problem. Anthony's (1965) triangular representation, as depicted in

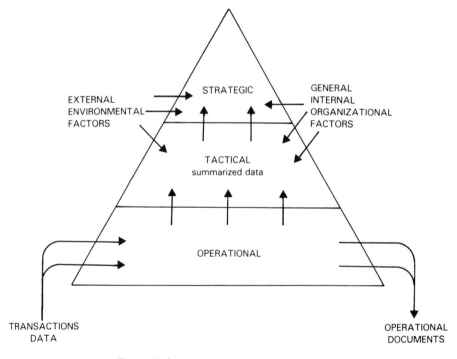

Figure 13-2   Decision levels in an organization

Figure 13–2, is usually used for this. While the boundaries between operational, tactical, and strategic management are not as precise as indicated in the figure — and in a small organization one person may assume more than one role — most problems can be classified into one of these levels. The operational-level manager has a fairly standardized decision-making task, much of which can be automated. For example, in an inventory management situation, typical operating-level decisions relate to the reorder of stock, the correction of errors or omissions, expediting suppliers who are late in delivering goods, informing other parts of the organization when deliveries have been delayed, etc. At this level there is typically a large flow of detailed data into, within and out of the organization.

The tactical manager is concerned with short- to medium-term implications within the tactical area of the organization, taking account of performance at the operating level and also of those general activities both inside and outside the organization which are likely to have an effect in the medium-term future. Using an example from an inventory system once more, the tactical manager is likely to be concerned with setting new reorder points based on: expected production-level changes within the organization, possible price rises, changes in delivery patterns likely to be occasioned by a regional war or a shipping strike. Most factual-type data relevant to tactical decisions are derived from summaries, or the like, of data used at operating level.

The strategic-level manager concentrates almost totally on the wider range of issues involving the performance of the organization in the medium-to-long term. Naturally, this manager is even more concerned than the tactical-level manager with external influences and the strategy decisions relate more to the future of the organization. Thus factual data derived from operating activities are less relevant in this situation than for the operational and tactical managers. Instead, external data are likely to be more useful. In the inventory management situation, strategy decisions might include limitations on total inventory holdings based on: working-capital restrictions, government regulations, or decisions on stocking policy based on a desire to obtain a competitive advantage in an area entirely removed from the inventory management activity.

The second dimension is related to the degree of structure, and hence the amount of uncertainty, involved in the problem. This introduces the concepts of complexity and probability into the decision analysis and alternative selection tasks. Uncertainty can originate from a number of sources, e.g. when the interrelationships between relevant variables are unknown or change with time, or if important external factors are unpredictable. Complexity is usually associated with the number of relevant parameters or variables in the problem environment and/or the manner in which they are interrelated. In practice the levels of complexity and uncertainty are seen to rise or fall in unison, reflecting the fact that little is known about many complex areas of organizations. Three levels of structure can be used to describe the range of complexity and uncertainty relevant to decision making: mostly structured, semi-structured, and mostly unstructured.

The 'mostly structured' category includes those decisions which are virtually automatic and where appropriate rules can be defined — e.g. deciding to reorder goods which fall below a fixed safety level of stock, or the decision to present a gold watch to an employee of 25 years standing (in accordance with company practice). It is apparent that many of these decisions can be automated within clerical or other operational-type transaction-processing systems, and the name DSS is probably inappropriate in these situations. Operations-research or financial-modelling techniques are also effective tools for this type of problem where uncertainty is low.

A 'semi-structured' category is normally considered to include the 'decision making under uncertainty' situation, where complete knowledge is not available and/or rules and objectives are not specific — e.g. deciding whether to accept or reject a supplier's tender on the basis of possible poor financial standing even though the tendered price is lowest. Most decisions which interest DSS designers fall into this category.

Decisions are said to be 'mostly unstructured' when there are almost no rules, guidelines, or precedents available to assist the decision maker — e.g. designing a company logo. DSS can be relevant in these situations in detecting problems and calculating the implications of alternative actions being contemplated as decisions.

Combining both dimensions yields a 3 × 3 matrix. This is sketched in Figure 13-3 with examples of appropriate decision situations in each box.

Discussion in the remaining sections of this chapter are focused on the semi-structured decision and problem category.

Manager level / Decision type	OPERATIONAL	TACTICAL	STRATEGIC
MOSTLY STRUCTURED	PAYROLL PAYMENT AUTHORIZATION	SCHEDULING PRODUCTION IN AN EXCESS CAPACITY SITUATION	SETTING POLICY ON STAFF NUMBERS
SEMI-STRUCTURED	BANK TELLER DECIDING WHETHER TO CONFIRM A CASH CHEQUE VALIDITY	SCHEDULING PRODUCTION IN A DEFICIT CAPACITY SITUATION	TAKEOVER/MERGER PROPOSALS
MOSTLY UNSTRUCTURED	JUDGING WINNERS IN A 'N 25 WORDS OR LESS' SLOGAN COMPETITION	DETERMINING A RADICAL NEW PRODUCT'S ADVERTISING PROMOTION	ESTABLISHING A NEW RESEARCH PROGRAM

Figure 13-3   The decision level/type method

13.2.3   The Practice of Decision Making

Most of the material presented so far in this section has been of a theoretical or descriptive nature. However, the empirical research work of Mintzberg and others has shed a good deal of insight into how managers actually make use of the various sources of information open to them. A summary of results published by Mintzberg (1975) indicates that managers' real activities differ significantly from those proposed in many textbooks. Investigating the commonly held view that 'a good manager is a reflective, systematic planner', Mintzberg reported from a number of different experimental studies:

- Foremen averaged 583 activities per 8-hour shift
- 50 per cent of the activities of senior executives lasted less than 9 minutes
- Only 10 per cent of senior executive activities lasted longer than 1 hour
- Senior managers operated for half an hour or more uninterrupted by subordinates or telephone calls only once every 2 days
- Only 1 per cent of their time was spent in open-ended tours of the organization without a specific purpose in mind
- Only 1 out of 368 activities was unrelated to a specific issue — was this the time spent in planning?

These results lead to the view that the manager — at whatever level — is data driven (in real time?). It follows that the planning activities and the construction of models with which to interpret information are mostly performed in the manager's mind, since there is usually insufficient time for a full and reflective view or analysis of any particular problem.

Mintzberg also considered the statement, often accepted by designers of information systems as being correct, that 'managers require, in fact need, aggregated information such as is provided by a formal management information system to support their decision making.' His reported findings included:

- Managers and chief executives spend approximately 75 per cent of their time in verbal (oral) communication
- All managers exhibited a strong preference for 'soft' information such as gossip, hear-say, and opinions, rather than for hard factual information contained in reports
- The chief executives surveyed were required to make an immediate response to only 2 of 40 routine MIS reports
- Of the total mail and reports crossing an executive's desk, only 13 per cent were of immediate use

It follows that the formal MIS, at least as it existed within the organizations surveyed, is of little relevance to the decision-making process; it seems that managers do not rely on this source of information and, indeed, they probably do not have the time to seek and digest it. A conclusion which Mintzberg reached was, therefore, that 'the strategic database of an organization is in the minds of its managers rather than the data banks of its computers'. A further conclusion may be that, when the soft information sources contradict those based on formal systems in either numerical or descriptive textual form, the manager tends to believe the former.

13.3 DSS DESIGN

13.3.1 Design Issues

In Section 13.2, a number of issues which need to be considered by DSS designers are defined. They are summarized in this section. While it is not usually possible for all these questions to be fully answered in the course of a project, both the user and the designer need to be aware of shortcomings which may exist in the resulting DSS.

Predicting the future with historical, numerical data

Most decisions of significance to the DSS designer require the prediction of future courses of events, hence the need to evaluate the consequences of actions as discussed in Subsection 13.2.1. However, the systems designer has historical data, usually of a numerical type, available. These data are only useful to the decision maker in so far as they can be used to predict the future with adequate accuracy. Thus, a set of figures on costs incurred in a manufacturing plant may show the information given in Figure 13–4. Although these figures are an indication of poor cost control, they are of little use for predicting September's results or for determining if action is needed now. Of much more significance would be a memo from the plant superintendent, stating in part:

> . . . the adverse costs over the past three months have been the result of a series of unexpected plant failures, necessitating overtime wages and high maintenance charges. Normal costs should be incurred in the following months.

Or, alternatively:

> . . . the work-to-rule action of the maintenance services union has caused production losses and increased costs due to plant malfunctions and overtime. Action must be taken, otherwise the low level of maintenance efficiency will lead to more breakdowns and even higher costs in the future.

DURABLE STEEL CO.

Slab Production Costs — September 1 ($000)

	May	June	July	August	TOTAL
Actual	550	610	720	650	2530
Budget	600	600	600	600	2400

Figure 13–4   Example of historical, numerical data

Users and designers of a DSS must therefore work closely together to ensure that the numerical database, and the reporting therefrom, permits an acceptable level of support. Also, the reports, their content, and timing ought to complement the other sources of information open to the decision maker.

Text-based data and soft information

Mintzberg's experiments, and other analyses of the way managers work, have highlighted the great reliance placed on verbal communication as opposed to formal MIS. Although the opportunities are still limited, there are ways that textual data — such as the plant superintendent's comments — can be incorporated within a computer-based DSS, for example, by allowing free text 'remarks' fields or including reference to the file number of the correspondence with other details.

Office automation systems, especially the combination of word processing, electronic mail, and text-storage systems, provide a more general, and potentially very sophisticated, tool for the DSS designer. When integrated with systems which use numerical databases, there is a good deal of scope for an effective design.

Formalizing the informal

It is well known that personnel in every organization communicate at both a formal and informal level. Examples of formal processes include routine reports, the procedures manuals which describe how tasks are to be performed, and the routine paperwork which describes detailed progress of services, orders, accounts, etc. Informal processes can cover a wide spectrum, examples being:

- Unofficial changes to procedures which suit operators and/or management
- Exchanges of information not included in the formal reporting or paperwork systems; these are usually oral communications (i.e. telephone) and can be entirely within the organization or involve outsiders

Obviously the existence of these informal processes has an effect on decision making, and the DSS designer often believes it necessary to make them explicit by incorporating them within the formal computerized system (Argyris, 1971).

No precise guidelines can be given to resolve the question of how to balance the informal and formal arrangements, since so much depends on the individual case. Certainly all the important informal processes must be identified (as, indeed, must the formal ones as well), and the impact on organization performance and user satisfaction assessed for each alternative design approach.

Uncertainty

There is a high level of uncertainty surrounding each DSS project. A design approach must therefore be adopted which minimizes the risk of substantial cost overruns, or simply the waste of resources on incomplete projects. Uncertainty may originate from a number of aspects, including:

- The project objectives may be unclear or be subject to radical change. This can lead to wasted effort if the wrong, or a subsidiary, problem is attacked.
- The feasibility of achieving all or even some of the objectives may be unclear. Each DSS design becomes a kind of research and development project with the design team exploring ways of presenting information, collecting data, etc. which will assist the decision making sufficiently to justify the project's costs.
- User preferences for reporting from, and interaction with, the system will shift over time, and with a change in management personnel. Although the individual decision-maker's needs should be met within a DSS design (compare the discussion on decision style in Subsection 13.2.1), the costs likely to be incurred if changes are needed in the user interface areas must also be taken into account. Perhaps the three major areas where difficulties arise are:
    1. The user/inquiry interface, especially the type of dialog used (see the sections on dialog specification in Chapter 9)
    2. The reporting process, including use of exception reporting and graphics, and the frequency of availability
    3. The database specification, which naturally governs the size, ease of access, complexity of reporting/inquiry supported, etc.
- It is often not clear when the project is complete and work should stop! Except in the most deterministic situations, there are always changes, enhancements, etc. which can be carried out, although with gradually diminishing economic returns.

13.3.2 Design Principles

The principles for DSS design proposed in this section are derived from considering a model of the decision process and its interface with computer-based data. The assumptions made to describe this model are:

- The systems which are the subject of this study are aimed at supporting semi-structured decision situations, i.e. those for which broad guidelines, rules, or precedents exist, but where complexity, uncertainty, or risk is significant.
- Most decisions of this semi-structured variety are made to improve the likelihood of a particular objective, or set of objectives, being achieved in the future. Objectives are not only seen in economic terms, but encompass a range of behavioural and social concepts.
- The information system of an organization, or a part thereof, is equivalent to the instrumentation and control system of a complex process. Therefore, the control systems theory approach is relevant to a study of decision making (Beer, 1975), provided that appropriate consideration is given to the individual nature of each person's selection process, as evidenced by the

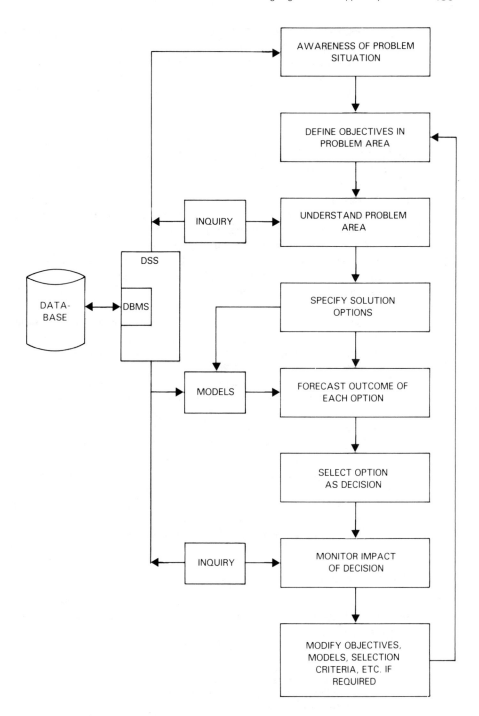

Figure 13-5 A 'black-box' view of the DSS/decision-maker interface

results of research into the effects of decision analysis and cognitive style (see Subsection 13.2.1).

A 'black-box' representation of the DSS/decision-maker interface is shown in Figure 13–5. The figure depicts the steps in the economic man type of decision analysis, the main differences from Simon's model (comprising intelligence, design, and choice phases) being the inclusion of a monitoring role as a tailpiece, and the feedback loop which indicates that an iterative approach is sometimes required. In practice this tends to be a continuous process, with solution options being suggested and outcomes forecast even while the decision maker is attempting to understand the problem area more completely. However, this representation is oriented towards the decision-maker's thought processes, and is not of great help to the DSS designer.

The model discussed in the rest of this section is intended to promote discussion of the types of assistance likely to be of use to a decision maker. Much of this material was originally published in a paper presented at the DSS-81 conference (Brookes, 1981) and published in the proceedings by Execucom Corporation. It is reproduced here with permission. The model is segmented into several sections comprising:

- The decision environment, or real world, which is the subject of the decision-maker's span of control
- An objective-setting process, which normally is a decision-maker's mental process, although it may utilize the output of formal, explicit, modelling tools such as linear programming or financial planning models.
- A problem-discovery phase, during which the decision maker becomes aware of a problem or identifies a situation which needs a response
- A problem-confirmation and information-interpretation phase; this is the stage in which the decision maker seeks more information from the DSS at greater depth, and determines implications
- An analysis or adaptive experimentation phase in which the designer seeks a solution which optimizes the expected performance of the real-world process
- A monitor-setting phase is the final step; it is needed to allow the decision maker to establish a monitoring role for the associated DSS

The decision environment

In our representation, the 'real world' — the target decision environment — sketched in Figure 13–6 may be a part or the whole of an organization. It is the area of interest to or responsibility of the decision maker. The environment is considered to be a process having the following parameters or sets of variables:

- *State variables, S* (which describe the current status of the environment), e.g. balance sheet items such as stock levels, number of employees, outstanding customer orders
- *Output variables, O*, e.g. goods or services produced, cash outflow
- *Input variables, I*, e.g. cash receipts, goods inwards, orders

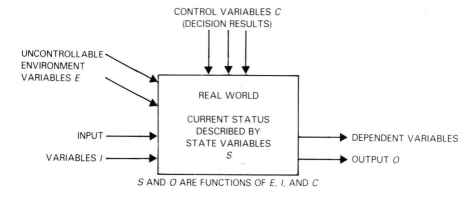

Figure 13-6   The decision environment

- *Environment or uncontrolled variables, E,* e.g. inflation or interest rates, taxes, government regulations, policy determined at a higher level
- *Control variables, C,* e.g. staff numbers, pay rates, prices, marketing policy, investment policy

Thus the process is seen to transform input variables, I, to outputs, O, with the transformation depending on both environmental and control variables. While the set E is outside the decision-maker's span of control, the controls C can be adjusted as desired. The selection of appropriate values for C can be considered to be the result of the decision-making process.

Performance evaluation and objectives

There is at least one measure of performance associated with the operation of this 'real-world' process. Normally, there is also a set of objective function parameters P_d which the decision maker seeks to achieve by manipulating C. The performance measures and objectives P_d are complex functions of S and O (S and O are themselves complex functions of I, E, and C). While these interrelationships can be expressed in deterministic form in simple structured cases, in the semi-structured decision environment the objective-setting and performance-measurement process followed by the decision maker may not be described in such simple terms. For example, they involve concepts of time-dependence and robustness (i.e. degree of inconsistency to unexpected changes). Nevertheless, the process of determining values of P_d can be considered in broad terms, as sketched in Figure 13-7.

The inputs to this process include:

- Overall organization objectives — note that in a strict sense these could be considered as part of the set E
- Previous values of P
- Summarized values of I, E, C, S, and O
- Projections of 'achievable' values of P, derived either from formal models or as a result of problem-solving analyses

- Soft information of a strategic nature relating to the degree of 'achievability' of various levels of P, competitors' likely plans, economic projections, and assessments of levels of P which are likely to be 'acceptable' to others

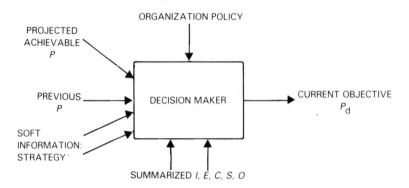

Figure 13-7   The objective-setting process

Problem discovery

The instrumentation of the real-world process must make it easier to detect problems, either by a direct warning or by providing sufficient information for the decision maker to determine an 'out-of-specification' condition. In this context a problem is considered to exist and a need for action arises when there is a degree of mismatch between the current expected or forecast value of P and the desired objective P_d. The degree of perceived mismatch determines the magnitude of the action required and the significance of the problem. Figure 13–8 shows this aspect. Note that it is impossible for the decision maker to monitor continually all the data which form the sets I, E, C, S, and O. Consequently it is essential that these values be condensed, filtered, or attenuated. Stafford Beer (1975) introduced the term 'attenuation' in relation to the problem-discovery task, and Keen (1977) has illustrated the types of 'operation' which could constitute this function.

Using these attenuated values of key variables and a personal perception of the real-world process, the decision maker must project future values of S and O. The perception of the real world is almost certainly a 'mental model' formed in the decision-maker's mind — as has been observed by Mintzberg. Naturally, the process of attenuation may include the use of explicit models, e.g. a financial-planning model, where this is appropriate. From the projected values of S and O the decision maker determines an expected value of P, and is able to compare it with P_d.

Some of the possible attenuation function operators available to the DSS designer to support the discovery phase include:

- Summarize — to condense the detail into summaries covering extended time periods, etc.
- Average, etc. — to generate statistical functions of the data sets, e.g. means, medians, limits, or sophisticated time series analyses

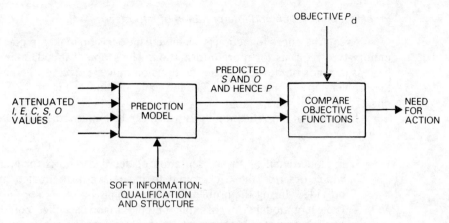

Figure 13-8   Problem discovery

- Compare — to compare the attenuated data sets with like variables, e.g. match against budget, last year, last month, best case, worst case; often seeking significant differences to highlight
- Project — to forecast likely future events, performance indices, or implications of previous actions
- Alert — to observe the raw data streams, or statistical derivatives of them, watching for specific circumstances to arise; in its simplest form this function includes exception reports, but the scope open to the designer (especially using time-series statistical analyses) is very great
- Monitor — although similar in meaning to Alert, this operator is here intended to be used as a temporary watchkeeper on specific variables, or combinations of them; it is frequently used to observe the response of the real-world process to earlier control actions

In addition, there ought to be a soft information component in the DSS if the decision process is to be supported fully. Several types of soft information are useful in this context. First, the supplied values of I, E, C, S, and O need qualification if their true meaning is to be understood. For example, a sales figure below budget, contained in an exception report, may or may not be a real problem depending on the reasons and explanations given by the manager in charge. Similarly, a report which indicates an on-target situation can be discredited with a few words of critical comment. Second, soft information dealing with the interrelationships between variables affects the structure of the predictive model used by the decision maker. Typical examples may be advice or opinions about future productivity rates in a manufacturing firm, or forecasts of a change in the rate of government funding per student in an academic institution. It follows that a soft-information input at this stage can cause a problem to appear by altering the predicted levels of S and O, even though no significant change has taken place in the numerical details presented by the DSS.

Problem confirmation and interpretation of information

As soon as a need for action is perceived, the decision maker frequently triggers inquiry-type requests for more information. The scope of this data-amplification process depends on how complete the decision maker perceives the knowledge of the problem environment to be. The left-hand portion of Figure 13–9 shows this phase.

The relevant amplification tools which can be employed by the DSS designer include:

- Explode detail — the presentation of detailed reports (or graphics, etc.) which describe the background to the relevant attenuated information provided during the problem discovery phase
- Project or model — use of explicit models to forecast likely consequences of existing or possible scenarios, or to determine the sensitivity of specific variables to changes in other parameters
- Compare — a comparison of the current situation with that applying to similar time periods
- Find precedent — scanning the database for historical details of earlier situations which are identical to the current one, including action taken and the outcome
- Find related — scanning the database for situations which are similar or are related through common parameters to the current position: this process can highlight other undetected problems and help explain the significance of the current circumstances
- Ad hoc inquiry — a 'catch-all' technique to permit investigation of details, or overall summaries, as desired by the decision maker

The decision maker must evaluate the results of the amplification process, and should then be able to use a (presumably?) more complete mental model of the real world to predict more accurately the future values of S and O, and hence P. Thus the degree of significance of the problem is confirmed (or rejected), and the decision maker is well on the way to specifying alternative settings of C and predicting their outcomes.

Clearly, a major role is played by soft information sources during the confirmation phase. The effect of these sources covers:

- Qualification of numerical values as outlined during the discovery phase discussion in this subsection
- Establishing an appropriate structure for the decision-maker's mental model
- Estimating the degree of statistical stability of parameters, particularly I and E; this measure of uncertainty plays a major part in determining the degree of robustness or insensitivity which the decision maker seeks in an optimal setting for the control parameters
- Reference details about potential sources of other data or information, both soft and numerical, which could be useful in this problem environment

Analysis or adaptation

The process of selecting optimal values for the parameters C is either a straightforward analysis of the information considered to be relevant (in a mostly structured environment), or a combination of analysis with mental experimentation — the nature of which depends on the decision-maker's style of reasoning (the semi-structured case).

The experimentation involves testing various scenarios, each with a different value of the C parameters. The decision maker evaluates the expected outcome of each scenario, calculates the expected value of the objective function P, and compares this with the desired objective function value P_d. This process of testing various alternatives for C and evaluating their consequences and implications continues until either (1) a set of control settings is found which causes the expected value of P to be sufficiently close to P_d, or (2) an optimal set of C is determined which minimizes the perceived difference between the value of P and P_d. This second situation may then result in re-evaluation of the objective-setting function, since the current P_d is clearly, in the mind of this decision maker at least, unachievable.

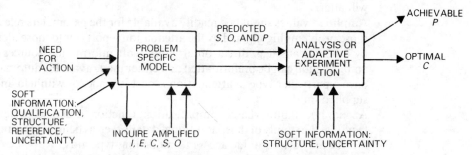

Figure 13-9 Confirmation and analysis or adaptation

In this phase of the process, shown as the right side of Figure 13–9, most of the numerical information would have been evaluated for its relevance to the problem, although some inquiries may be necessary. Some use of management science and modelling techniques generally would be expected in cases with many variables where enough is known of the interrelations between them. However, soft information would continue to be used since the experimentation process is influenced by structural considerations and, particularly, the degree of statistical uncertainty anticipated in the values of I and E.

Implementation and monitoring

Adjusting the settings of the C parameters can also be considered to be within the scope of a DSS. Appropriate instructions must be sent to those persons involved, and may be accompanied by some soft information giving reasons for the change in policy.

In addition, the decision maker may decide to augment the problem-discovery attenuation process by establishing new monitor functions to report on the response of the real-world process to the altered controls.

The integrated model

Since each of the phases described interact continuously with all of the others, an interconnected model as shown in Figure 13–10 can be constructed. It can be seen that there is at least one set of integrated decision-making phases for each decision maker. Further, these sets interface with those of other decision makers, thus forming what is termed in cybernetic theory a 'meta-system' (Beer, 1975). The main links are through the E set of parameters and soft information exchanges.

DSS interface

From the foregoing it follows that the key principles governing the interface specification between the DSS and a decision maker are (see Figure 13–11):

- It is necessary to supply attenuated values of all parameters I, E, C, O, and S to suit the problem-discovery phase particularly and the objective-setting function. Most of the reports will be preformatted as a result of the DSS design project, although threshold values for 'alert' or 'monitor' functions will alter.
- Amplified values should be readily available for the parameters relevant to those problems highlighted by the attenuation reports, or to those identified by other means (e.g. direct observation, soft information sources). This amplification can be preformatted and either made available automatically once a particular type of attenuation report is made, or withheld and only supplied on demand.
- An ad hoc inquiry-based amplification function must be designed to facilitate the supply of those additional details seen as being important. This facility may also provide access to modelling-type aids.
- A way of setting threshold values and time limits for 'monitor' and 'alert' reporting is required.
- A means for disseminating the new control-setting values to relevant parts of the organization should be established or formalized.
- An interface with the text storage/office automation environment may prove beneficial.

Soft information categories

The analysis of information needs has highlighted the importance of textual soft information as a source of decision support. In this section five categories of soft information are identified as being of particular relevance. With examples, these five categories are:

- *Qualification* — adds meaning to values of numerical information/data, e.g. explains that low sales are due to a customer's holiday, or an on-target budget item is really unfavourable due to the masking of real trends by a once-only event
- *Reference* — identifies a potential source of additional numerical or soft

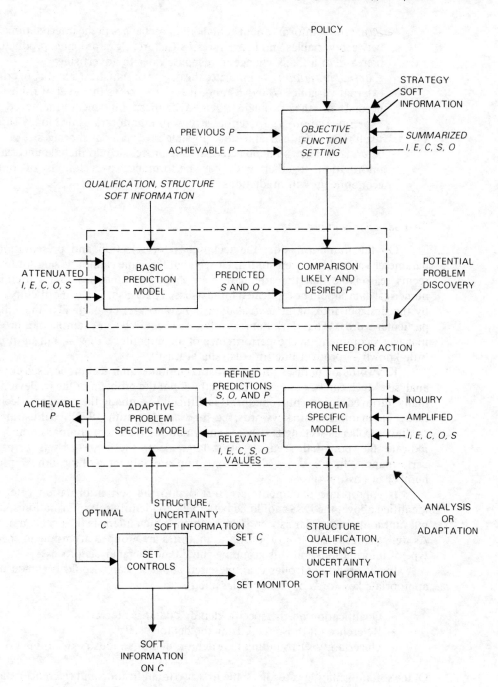

POLICY

STRATEGY
SOFT
INFORMATION

PREVIOUS *P*

ACHIEVABLE *P*

*OBJECTIVE
FUNCTION
SETTING*

*SUMMARIZED
I, E, C, S, O*

*QUALIFICATION, STRUCTURE
SOFT INFORMATION*

ATTENUATED
I, E, C, O, S

BASIC
PREDICTION
MODEL

PREDICTED
S AND *O*

COMPARISON
LIKELY AND
DESIRED *P*

POTENTIAL
PROBLEM
DISCOVERY

NEED FOR ACTION

REFINED
PREDICTIONS
S, O, AND *P*

ACHIEVABLE
P

ADAPTIVE
PROBLEM
SPECIFIC MODEL

PROBLEM
SPECIFIC
MODEL

INQUIRY

AMPLIFIED

I, E, C, O, S

RELEVANT
I, E, C, S, O
VALUES

STRUCTURE,
UNCERTAINTY
SOFT INFORMATION

OPTIMAL
C

SET *C*

STRUCTURE
QUALIFICATION,
REFERENCE
UNCERTAINTY
SOFT INFORMATION

ANALYSIS
OR
ADAPTATION

SET
CONTROLS

SET MONITOR

SOFT
INFORMATION
ON *C*

Figure 13-10   Integrated decision model

information, e.g. indicates that a specific person holds information on a
topic, or cites a situation which was similar to a current problem area

- *Structure* — informs about actual or likely changes in the interrelationships between variables and hence model structure, e.g. a probable productivity increase, or a likely change in response rates to advertising
- *External uncertainty* — indicates the degree of statistical stability of critical external variables (I and E) and, therefore, shows the level of robustness needed in the problem area dynamics; influences the need for experimentation, e.g. potential swings in inflation rates or money supply, likelihood of industrial action, possible raw material shortages
- *Strategy* — affects the objective-setting process; could include uncertainty information together with e.g. performance expectations of others, economic growth predictions

Text selection and presentation

On the numerical side, the techniques for selection and presentation of parameter values have been studied closely, but the same cannot be said for text. It seems reasonable that the attenuation/amplification functions found useful for numerical data should be replicated for text-based data also. The real difficulty faced by the designer looking at textual data is how to ascribe particular meaning to particular words. 'That dark horse is a fair cow' could be an example of a product manager's comment on the performance of a competitor's new — but until now, little-known — product line (in Australia at least!).

Keywords or phrases are the most common search technique used for text analysis. Much can be done with this method, but the problem of the irrelevance of many retrieved documents remains. It is difficult to embody the concept a decision maker has in mind within keywords; see, for example, Smith (1976). To illustrate, if a credit controller is seeking text-based information on a client company which will indicate the potential security of a large debt, the keyword-sets 'expected performance', 'future earnings', 'asset position' are only three of the almost infinite number of possibilities.

If appropriate documents are sorted into the soft information categories identified above, the DSS should be better able to identify soft information sources relevant to the particular aspect of the problem which interests the decision maker. As well, the responses from the DSS to inquiries are grouped according to specific type of information, and this grouping should aid the analysis process.

In the credit-controller example cited above a search could be made using appropriate keywords on data preclassified as:

- Qualification on the specific debtor's database records
- Reference on those records or the debtor itself
- Uncertainty surrounding that debtor, debtor's industry or product

Of the soft information categories, the first two (qualification and reference) may be cross-reference to related sets of numerical data. This, in Figure 13–11 the interface between the numeric and text databases would maintain this linkage. These qualification and reference categories can be labelled as 'dependent', meaning that

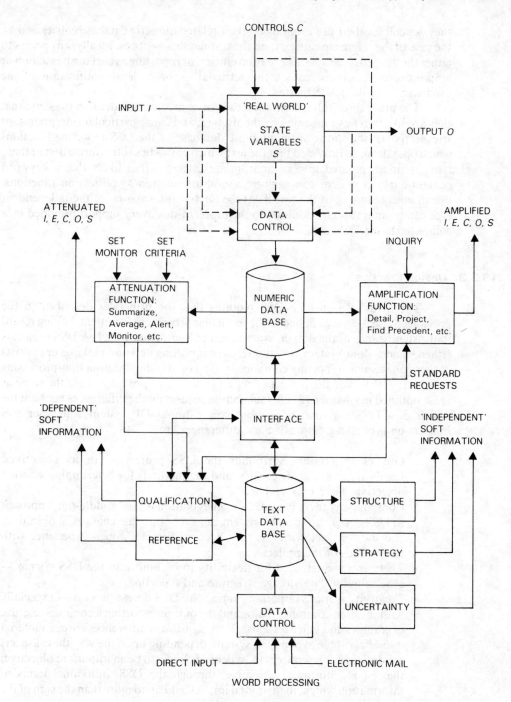

Figure 13–11   DSS interfaces

they depend for their full meaning on their related numeric database entries and, in the case of the reference category, on the text database entries. Ideally, any access to either the numerical or soft information entries, or reporting as part of attenuation or amplification functions, causes the retrieval — or at least notification of the existence — of the related items.

The other three soft information categories are 'independent' in the sense that they are likely to have meaning by themselves, and cause particular interpretations irrespective of the status of the numeric database or the DSS-reporting functions which operate on it. Provided that the text which embodies soft information of these types is first separated into its appropriate category, it is likely that a keyword content-analysis system can perform useful attenuation/amplification functions. Continuous scanning of the text database for soft information of the independent type can be an important addition to the problem-discovery support provided by a computer-based DSS.

13.3.3   Design Practice

The actual design of a DSS requires that the principles described in the previous subsection are applied to the particular project environment, having regard to the significance of the design issues raised in Subsection 13.3.1. A DSS project is either a stand-alone system aimed solely at supporting decision making, or consists of the management-reporting component of a conventional transaction-processing system. In either case the project selection criteria and procedures are the same as those outlined in Chapter 12. This subsection focuses on the differences between the design of a DSS and that of a more conventional DP system which services transaction processing. Some of these differences are:

- Greater uncertainty surrounds the DSS project — in its objectives, feasibility, user characteristics, and the methods for determining whether objectives have been reached.
- Consequently there is a need for an evolutionary or 'middle-out' approach to DSS design, so that the system can accommodate changes in objectives and user characteristics as they become firmer through experience with early stages of the project.
- There is a greater need for flexibility to be built into the DSS system — especially for data-storage structure and reporting.
- Creativity is more important during the DSS design process — especially with the user/computer dialog and the output/reporting techniques, e.g. use of graphics and voice response. Very significant differences are encountered in user acceptance of a DSS system, depending upon the way these aspects are designed. The concept of 'synergy' is likely to be an important objective; that is, attempting to assemble, through the DSS, individual items of information which, in their total impact, add up to more than the sum of the effects the individual items would have separately.
- The greater emphasis in a DSS is on output and data-storage aspects with relatively less attention to input, edit/validation and input controls — since

much of the data needed are already available within the corporate database.

- The requirement that the DSS system coexist with other sources of information, including text-based systems and informal exchanges in meetings or by telephone, is not shared by a conventional DP system.

In conventional EDP systems design it is usually possible to complete the project in one iteration (unless a large mistake is made!) through the project lifecycle. However, in a DSS design it is necessary to allow the evolution of a final system after several passes through the logical and physical design stages. The steps in a typical project would include:

1. Defining the project scope
2. Advisability study
3. Logical and physical designs
4. Programming and implementation
5. Post-implementation review

Definition of project scope

- Identify key design areas, with users specifying the objectives as far as they can be identified and described
- Using decision-analysis procedures, establish the types of information required to support problem solving and objective setting in these key decision areas
- Perform a preliminary cost-effectiveness survey in sufficient detail to establish the relative benefits of each set of information
- Determine appropriate stages of project evolution by selecting a series of individual subprojects, each of which is a step towards realizing the overall goal, taking the relative economic benefits into account; this may either result in a pilot project being established, or simply require completing a subsection of the total system

  Pilot projects can be a useful evolution tool when it is difficult to subdivide an overall project; they are designed to work on restricted subsets of the data flow, users, and problem types

Advisability study

Before detailed work on the project commences a review of resources and options available for the design approach should be made. Although this is equivalent to the feasibility study in a conventional DP project, the feasibility of a DSS project cannot normally be assessed until much later, because of the uncertainty factors.

1. Resources. The three resources which are important in a DSS project are data, processing capability and equipment, and people (both designers and users). Contrary to the problem of designing transaction-based systems of an operational nature, where the system tends to be driven by events such as arrival of documents, goods, or similar entities, the decision support system tends to be controlled by the data which are available. As discussed in Subsection 13.3.2, the data attenuation and amplification operations occupy a key role in the system's activity. Thus the key resource is the set of data, which either is available as the by-product of other systems, or can be made available, at reasonable cost, as the result of system design, additional data input, or access to external databases.

The processing capacity and equipment configurations are also an important resource for the system, to the extent that they establish the timeframe within which responses can be made. They are also likely to govern the accessibility of data, as well as having a significant impact on the user/system interfaces and the provision of specialist-supporting techniques such as graphics.

The way the personnel resource affects the project is that the experience of the system's designers and users affect the rate at which the project can be implemented. If the designers have little experience in the area under consideration, or with the data structure types, or with the equipment, then it is necessary to move at a slower pace, making use of pilot projects, etc. The same situation applies if the users have little experience in working with decision support systems.

2. Design options available. In determining the options available it is necessary to examine the available resources and to consider the different approaches which the designer can take to provide support for the decision-making process. The design associated with each option needs to be carried to a point where it is possible to determine whether adequate data-processing capacity and personnel are available to satisfy the tentative objectives, and also to determine the level of each resource type required.

3. Advisability study report. The study report needs to comprise:

- A review of the overall problem statement, including a discussion of the key areas involved, the constraints, and the ways in which the computer system may relieve or remove these constraints
- A statement of the business/organizational issues involved in or arising out of the project
- A discussion of the solution options available and the alternative approaches open for evolution towards completion of the total project
- A nomination of a recommended option from these possible solutions, which is covered in slightly more detail, with updates on costs and benefits
- A discussion on the effect that this new system is likely to have on the information-processing parts of the organization (i.e. requirements for additional equipment, terminals, communications lines, data, etc.)

Logical and physical design

Once the advisability study is complete, the designer's attention needs to focus on achieving the initial objectives set for the DSS, be they pilot project or subset of the total system. It is normal practice for a designer working on a conventional data-processing system to concentrate initially on the logical design aspects of the system — i.e. user-related details of the design (often called the user specification).

Following completion of the logical design, attention is then focused on the physical design aspects, which detail the way that the logical design is to be implemented physically on the computer system. When considering the design of a DSS the same tasks must be done, but it is usually desirable to design both logical and physical aspects of the system at the one time — using a series of tightly coupled iterations. This is because the design tends to unfold, in the sense that later aspects of the design frequently present ideas to the analyst and user which affect earlier aspects, and thus a cyclical or evolutionary process is clearly desirable. The steps by which a typical project would progress are:

1. *Decision analysis.* Review, and extend where necessary, the decision-analysis type study of key decision areas initiated during the project scope definition. This results in anticipated problem situations and the information needed to support decision making being defined.
2. *Attenuation report specification.* Using the attenuation-type functions suggested in Subsection 13.3.2 as a checklist, preliminary logical and then physical designs should be carried out with the objective of meeting the problem-discovery support needs of the users. An assessment of the relative utility of some available options is shown in Figure 13-12.

    The increasing functionality of colour graphics devices, and their decreasing cost with the greater sophistication of software support, mean

Function \ Technique	PRINTED REPORT	VIDEO DISPLAY DEVICE	GRAPHICS	DISPLAY PANEL	VOICE RESPONSE
ATTENUATION					
SUMMARIZE	5	3	3	1	2
AVERAGE	4	4	5	1	3
COMPARE	2	3	5	2	2
PROJECT/MODEL	3	4	5	1	1
ALERT	3	3	4	5	4
MONITOR	3	4	3	2	3
AMPLIFICATION					
DETAIL	5	4	2	1	2
PROJECT/MODEL	3	4	5	1	1
COMPARE	2	3	5	2	2
FIND { PRECEDENT / RELATED	5	4	2	1	2
AD HOC INQUIRY	3	5	4	1	2

Scale: 5 = very appropriate
4 = appropriate
3 = useful
2 = potentially useful
1 = unlikely to be useful

Figure 13-12   An assessment of the relative value of alternative **DSS** output media

that this medium should always be considered closely during this phase of the design. In most cases, graphics devices can double as VDUs and so they are appropriate for most attenuation functions; the main exception is summaries, when printed reports are often desirable. The usefulness of voice response increases dramatically in environments where access to reports or terminals is restricted, e.g. mobile users with radio-linked headphones.

3. *Amplification report specification.* While the design of attenuation reports is relatively straightforward — providing users know how to discover their problems — the specification of amplification reporting is a much less structured task. However, the designer should again concentrate on the relevant functions and seek to provide output in line with reasonable forecasts of information needs. There is always the fallback to ad hoc inquiry as the source of amplification reporting. In fact, many managers appear to prefer operating this way.

   The difficulty with this is the response time. For example, an ad hoc inquiry to find all customer orders due after a certain date, on which a major maintenance shut-down is to commence, could require a lengthy database search — unless the relevant records are indexed in some way. Consequently an hour or more could elapse before a report was available, whereas the automatic initiation of such a report program under certain attentuation reporting circumstances could mean the information being immediately available. The processing of large financial or other models is a similar situation, which could warrant unsolicited initiation as a DSS-amplification function.

   It should be realized that it is not necessary to actually produce amplification reports when they are available. They may be held in abeyance until called for. Thus there need be no great information 'deluge', only a large amount of precautionary processing, a good deal of which may never be used. Figure 13–12 also shows an assessment of the relative utility of alternative reporting media for amplification purposes.

4. *User interface.* Most often the ad hoc inquiry interface is largely determined by the system software environment available to the project team. However, its utility for the project should be reviewed at this time, particularly the important factors: ease-of-use, security, robustness, recovery after failure, and flexibility. Of particular importance may be the range of devices supported by the software, since matching the reporting method with individual decision styles frequently requires particular output or input media.

5. *Database specification.* This is a similar phase to that performed in conventional systems design, except there is a need to ensure that the structure, accuracy, timing, and logical/physical locations are appropriate for the reporting envisaged.

6. *Input design.* Frequently the data needed for a DSS already exist within the database, and hence no data input is needed. However, where necessary, the data sources, media, edit/validate rules, security checks, and timing issues must be specified and designed.

7. *Design walkthrough.* It is most desirable to walkthrough the resultant logical/physical design work with users — reviewing objectives and determining that they are adequately met. A check should also be made to ensure that future subsystems or extensions of the project will not involve extensive reworking.

Programming and implementation

These two phases are broadly equivalent to similar tasks in conventional DP systems work, since most uncertainty should have been resolved by this time.

Post-implementation review

Since most DSS projects are subdivided into a series of small systems, or are preceded by a pilot system design, the review of performance at the completion of each subsystem is a vital checkpoint. The feasibility and advisability of continuing must be the initial concern. Then follow reviews of objectives, justification, the development sequence of subsystems, and the suitability of the techniques employed for attenuation and amplification reporting.

13.3.4 An Example of Attenuation and Amplification Report Design

Apex Building Supplies is a medium-sized supplier to the construction industry. It has an annual turnover of $20 million while last year gross profit amounted to $7.2 million. It has been decided to use DSS design principles to assist management in the accounts-receivable section, especially the critical area of credit control, where sizeable losses are being encountered. To demonstrate concepts, reporting for the credit manager could follow the examples illustrated by Figures 13–13 to 13–17.

Summary (printed or displayed)

This might be as the accounts status summary in Figure 13–13.

APEX BUILDING SUPPLIES

ACCOUNTS STATUS — SEPTEMBER — $000

	Total	Current	60 days	90 days	over 90 days
September	2418	1606	309	201	302
August	2732	1801	328	197	406
Budget	2200	1600	350	150	100
Last year	1908	1552	121	128	107

Figure 13-13   Accounts summary

Alert, or exception, report

Manager's request: Monitor the debtors records and highlight slow payers. Criteria for reporting are 60 day balance greater than $30 000, 90 day greater than $20 000, over 90 days greater than $20 000. All figures rounded to nearest $1000. This report is illustrated in Figure 13–14.

APEX BUILDING SUPPLIES

SEPTEMBER DEBTORS EXCEPTION REPORT — AGED

Company	30 days	60 days	90 days	over 90 days
ARBU Decorators	15 000	22 000	25 000	27 000
Jackson Kitchens	-(2 000)	10 000	15 000	38 000
Maxi Interiors	150 000	35 000	11 000	4 000
Smith Designs	25 000	31 000	40 000	29 000

Figure 13-14   Exception report

EXTENDED DEBTORS EXCEPTION REPORT — SEPTEMBER

SMITH DESIGNS

12-month average monthly turnover	$26 000
12-month maximum monthly turnover	$38 000
Average O/S amount over last 12 months	$120 000
Maximum O/S amount over last 12 months	$138 000

MAXI INTERIORS

12-month average monthly turnover	$10 000
12-month maximum monthly turnover	$150 000
Average O/S amount over last 12 months	$28 000
Maximum O/S amount over last 12 months	$200 000

STOCK MARKET PRICE MONITOR — SEPTEMBER

	Today	Last month	3 months ago
Maxi Interiors	0.89	1.20	1.35
Smith Designs	1.79	1.75	1.58

Figure 13-15   Amplification report — detail

Comment: It appears from these figures that ARBU, Jackson, and Smith are consistent problem debtors, whilst Maxi Interiors is a larger, but not yet troublesome account. Nevertheless, the manager calls for amplification reports on both Smith and Maxi.

Amplification reporting — detail expansion

For expanded detail, an extended debtors exception report and a stock market monitor are given in Figure 13–15.

Comment: The extended debtors report shows that Smith Designs is simply a poor payer — and has been consistently. This fact will have been obvious to the manager from previous reports. However, in view of the size of the business generated by this account in a competitive market, no critical action — other than strong requests for faster payment — appears justified. This conclusion is backed by the stock market report.

However, the Maxi Interiors case is entirely different. The initial report did not appear too significant, but it becomes a problem situation when the sudden nature of the debt increases, in terms of previous history, is made clear. The problem reaches crisis proportions when the slump in stock price is taken into account. Thus the three sets of information on the company together present a picture which is more significant than that indicated when taken individually.

Amplification — comparison

These reports are given in Figure 13–16.

```
        DEBTORS COMPARISON REPORT — SEPTEMBER — $


                       30 days    60 days   90 days   over 90 days
Average for
all customers          15 000     10 000    8 000       5 000
Most active customer
(12-month basis)       70 000     28 000    19 000      18 000
```

```
    EXTENDED DEBTORS COMPARISON REPORT — SEPTEMBER — $


        Average for
        all customers
            12-month average monthly turnover     16 000
            12-month maximum monthly turnover     19 000
            Average O/S amount last 12 months     39 000
            Maximum O/S amount last 12 months     42 000
```

Figure 13-16   Amplification report — comparison

Comment: Thus the credit-restriction decision will cut gross profit by about 2 per cent, if the debts are paid by Maxi Interiors. Since this is significant, it may be that a less forceful approach is justified.

Amplification — projection

A projection report is given in Figure 13–17.

GROSS PROFIT CONTRIBUTION REPORT — SEPTEMBER — $

	Last year	This year to date
Maxi Interiors	36 000	43 000
Percentage of total	0.5	2.1

Figure 13-17 Amplification report — projection

Comment: Thus the credit-restriction decision will cut gross profit by about 2 per cent, if the debts are paid by Maxi Interiors. Since this is significant, it may be that a less forceful approach is justified.

Text-based soft information

The interpretation to be placed on the Maxi case appears all bad at this point. Consider the further impact of an internal memo from Bill Davis, the technical director, to Fred Blake the credit manager:

September 2

Fred,

I had lunch with Dave Brown of Durable Plastics today. He said that they were putting Maxi on to a 'cash only' basis from today because of their poor payment record, and of rumours of a cash shortage. He'd heard that others had already done the same thing, including our competition! Call Dave, he has the details.

Bill.

Comment: Of course, this memo is likely to add great weight to the case against Maxi; in fact, it would be a very useful attenuation, or problem discovery, trigger and even may justify action in the absence of any other indicators. The importance of soft information as a source of decision support can be emphasized by changing the critical portion of Bill Davis' memo to:

He said that Maxi had just landed a huge military order for office interiors and were having trouble getting the credit to place orders. They have to play it close to the chest as it's still very hush-hush in government circles.

Naturally, this nullifies much of what has been indicated by the other reports.

In this series of reports, Fred Blake has been satisfied with relatively little detail, but he has looked for printed reports. Options including graphics, greater details including product categories, further history, more comparisons, etc. are all possible — it all depends on the decision style of the users.

REFERENCES

R.L. ACKOFF, 'Management Misinformation Systems', *Management Science*, December 1967, B147-B156.

R.N. ANTHONY, *Planning and Control Systems: A Framework for Analysis*, Division for Research, Graduate School of Business Admin., Harvard University, Cambridge, Mass., 1965.

C. ARGYRIS, 'Management Information Systems: the Challenge to Rationality and Emotionality', *Management Science*, February 1971, B275-B292.

S. BEER, *Platform for Change*, Wiley, New York, 1975.

C.H.P. BROOKES, 'Incorporating Text Base Information within a Decision Support System', *Proc. DSS-81 Conference*, Execucom Corp., Austin, Tex. June 1981.

J. DEARDEN, 'Can Management Information Systems be Automated?', *Harvard Business Review*, March/April 1964, pp. 134-9.

G.A. GORRY & M.S. SCOTT-MORTON, 'A Framework for Management Information Systems', *Sloan Management Review*, Fall 1971, pp. 55-70.

R.A. HOWARD (ed.), *IEEE Transactions on Systems Science and Cybernetics*, Special Issue on Decision Analysis, September 1968.

R.A. HOWARD, 'An Assessment of Decision Analysis', *Operations Research*, vol. 28 January/February 1980, 4-27.

P.G.W. KEEN, 'The Intelligence Cycle — A Differentiated Perspective on Information Processing', *AFIPS National Computer Conference*, June 1977, pp. 317-20.

P.G.W. KEEN & M.S. SCOTT-MORTON, *Decision Support Systems: An Organisational Perspective*, Addison-Wesley, Reading, Mass, 1978.

W.M. MCGUIRE (ed.), *C. Jung Collected Works — Six Psychological Types*, Princeton University Press, Princeton, N.J., 1970.

R.W. MASON & I.I. MITROFF, 'A Program for Research on Management Information Systems', *Management Science*, May 1973, pp. 475-87.

H. MINTZBERG, 'The Manager's Job; Folklore and Fact', *Harvard Business Review*, July/August 1975, pp. 49-61.

A. NEWELL, J.C. SHAW & H.A. SIMON, 'Elements of a Theory of Human Problem Solving', *Psychological Review*, May 1958, pp. 151-66.

H.A. SIMON, *Administrative Behavior*, Macmillan, New York, 1975.

L.C. SMITH, 'Artificial Intelligence in Information Retrieval Systems', *Information Processing and Management*, Pergamon Press, 1976, pp. 189-222.

CASE STUDY — SALES FORECASTING AT HOUSEHOLD FRIEND LTD

Introduction

Household Friend Ltd (HFL) is a large company with 1400 employees producing and marketing a range of household goods sold largely through supermarkets and chemists. HFL has four divisions: Cleanser, Health and Beauty, Pharmaceuticals, and Food. The company's total sales are around $150 million a year. Production is centralized in Sydney, with the one production facility responsible for catering to the needs of the four divisions. HFL has been experiencing steady but solid growth for the past five years and its management could be characterized as conservative.

Two types of sales forecasting are routinely prepared and used at HFL, the annual 12-month budget and the monthly production-planning forecast. All forecasts are based on the four week, four week, five week accounting period. The annual forecast is built up on a state/product basis and accumulated for the national sales forecast. State sales managers provide the major input into the state/product forecast and the national product managers interact at the national level. The budget forecast, once set, remains fixed for the year and provides a reference point for sales comparisons. The rolling production-planning forecast, prepared on a national basis for the next six months' sales, is revised monthly. At the start of the year the production-planning forecast is typically the same as the budget forecast but, as the year progresses and sales deviate from budget, the production forecast is revised to reflect the actual sales situation.

Sales are forecast by the production-planning department each month delivering to product managers a set of black books containing the forecasts for the productions under their responsibility. The product managers record any modifications to the forecast in the black books, and the black books are, on completion, forwarded to the production-planning unit to be consolidated for production-planning purposes. The system did not work entirely satisfactorily, as production planning faced great difficulties each month getting the updated forecasts back from the product managers, who tended to sit on their black books and not get around to doing anything until pestered in person by a representative from the production and planning unit. Difficulties with keeping this manual system running motivated the production-planning personnel and the product managers to discuss whether a computer-based approach might not be more satisfactory.

Forecasting — Mark I

In 1972, HFL management felt that a computer-based forecasting approach could help not only to provide more reliable and accurate forecasting but also could reduce much of the tedious work involved in budget preparation and forecast revision for production-planning purposes. The project team was set up involving the users and EDP with the objectives of providing:

- An annual budget by state in quantity and value for financial budgeting purposes
- Up-to-date national quantity forecasts for the purposes of planning production and determining the disposition of stocks in depots
- Amended projections on the end-of-year situation for management-reporting purposes
- The means for inquiring on sales-forecasting information for purposes of improving future forecasts and retrieving useful management information.

A number of computer-based forecasting approaches were investigated. The means used to test the accuracy of the forecasting approach was a database of five year's history of both monthly sales and the manual production forecasts. Three years of the data were used to set the computer-forecasting technique at initial conditions, and the remaining two years used to roll the forecast forward, simulating the technique. The accuracy of the computer-prepared forecast and the accuracy of the manual forecasts were compared. The computer technique would be expected to have had trouble providing the same accuracy as the manual forecasts, as manual forecasts would have been made by sales and marketing management in full knowledge of the past sales performance of the products, and influenced by their judgment of the future and of their knowledge of planned marketing promotions and other events likely to affect sales. On the other hand, a computer forecast is based only on a projection of past data, although in practice the computer forecast could be revised to include the potential effect of marketing plans and the salespeoples' special knowledge of the marketplace. However, the simulation revealed that the computer forecasts (using a simple trend projection technique) yielded more accurate forecasts than the manual forecast. The actual technique consisted of:

1. Massage the sales history to remove the effects of extraordinary events like strikes, large customer returns, etc.

2. Remove the seasonal component by means of a 12-month moving average
3. Smooth the deseasonalized sales history by averaging out large random fluctuations
4. Calculate the slope of the sales trend for the past one, two, and three years of history; this yields three different sales-trend slopes and the most conservative is adopted as the trend line for forecasting purposes
5. The (deseasonalized) projection is calculated by extrapolating the most conservative trendline forward the requisite number of months
6. Apply seasonal factors calculated earlier to produce the actual forecast of sales

Given there was no manual correction of the computer forecasts, the fact that they were more accurate than the manually-prepared forecasts raised expectations that computer forecasting would provide an excellent starting point for sales forecasting at HFL. This project lasted over a year, with a team of a full-time user representative, who had previously been closely associated with the manual- forecasting activity, and an analyst/programmer. The computer-based forecasting system finally developed provided the following facilities:

1. An annual budget forecast by product within state, printed together with four years of sales history to enable easy checking by the sales force and modification if needed
2. A means of modifying sales history to remove the impact on sales of extraordinary events
3. Monthly tracking exception reports which reported those products within a state having actual sales deviating from forecast by more than a given amount; this amount could be controlled by the sales force on a product-by-product basis; the exception report contained for each product reported a new suggested forecast for the approval or modification by sales management
4. The forecasts by state accumulated on a national basis and the production- planning figures printed
5. For products with insufficient history or excessively erratic history, the system reported that the computer forecast could not be calculated and requested a manual forecast

It can be seen that the monthly production-planning forecast remained unchanged except when the actual sales deviated excessively from forecast. This meant that each month only those products appearing on the tracking report needed the attention of sales management. Around 500 products were forecast and maintained by this system.

Forecasting — Mark II

By late 1973 the forecasting system was mostly ignored by the users. A new project was commissioned to identify the users' problems and rectify them.

An experienced systems analyst was assigned to the project, and although no formal project team was established, the systems analyst worked closely with a number of users in diagnosing the source of the problems. The major area which concerned users was that the tracking report was on a state basis. This had been arranged at the specific request of the marketing manager, who had wanted all forecasts, including revisions, built up from a state basis. This marketing manager had left the company soon after the implementation of the forecasting system. The replacement had decided that sales revisions during a year would be made by the national sales staff in Sydney. As the production-planning forecast was only required on a national basis, the sales staff objected to the amount of time it took to check all the new suggested state forecasts. In addition, their major orientation was national not state sales. As a consequence the sales force tended to ignore the voluminous tracking reports, which meant that the suggested forecasts became the operating forecast by default. Occasionally some of these forecasts were quite unrealistic and caused significant problems in either short stock or excessive inventories.

A six-to-nine month project, completed in mid-1974, resulted in the Mark II forecasting system. This preserved the forecasting technique from the Mark I system but modified and enhanced the user interface, and produced tracking reports on a national sales basis. This had the effect of greatly reducing the volume of the monthly tracking reports to around 100 products. However, the changes made to the forecasting system appear to have done little to change the underlying user attitude to the system. In the period 1974–1976 the system slowly fell into increasing neglect by the sales and marketing people although its forecasts continued to be used by production planning. This inevitably led, at times, to bad forecasting data being used by production. The result was that the system was abandoned around 1977, except for the Cleanser division, which continued to use it for a further two years. This was due to the efforts of one of the users who felt that the system had a particular benefit for the Cleanser division.

The EDP Point of View

The EDP view on the demise of the system was that the users did not invest enough time in completely understanding the system and the way forecasts were prepared. Furthermore, they did not play their role in checking and modifying the computer-prepared forecasts where necessary. With a knowledge of the forecasting technique, EDP felt the users would have been able to anticipate the products requiring modifications readily, and they would have been able to check the forecasts prepared on the tracking report rapidly and identify those needing to be changed. The forecasting technique has been proved to be more reliable than the manual approach and thus offered a potential benefit to the company if properly used.

It was believed by EDP that a significant factor contributing to the lack of user involvement in the ongoing use of the system was the relative absence of incentive for sales and marketing personnel to prepare good forecasts. Responsibility for inventory levels and forecasting accuracy was very diffused so that no user allocated sufficient time or priority to forecasting.

The Users' Point of View

The main user criticisms of this system were:

- The system benefits are not easily seen to be worth the effort keeping the system going
- The 5–10 cm tracking report produced each month is an excessive burden on product managers, who see themselves as creative marketing people
- The forecasting system is too slow to react to changing marketing conditions
- After the tracking system has detected deviation, the trend-based forecast of times continues to produce forecasts out of line with the actual
- The four week, four week, five week accounting months play havoc with the seasonal months, as customers tend to purchase following a calendar cycle influenced by calendar-month payment terms; thus, a customer who orders on the first of the month may, some years, be in one accounting month, and other years be in another accounting month, and may even occasionally double up in a five-week accounting month
- Metrication contributed to problems with the forecasting system
- The forecasting system gives no attention to the scale of product sales; the relatively few high-turnover products warrant much more careful attention than the low-turnover products, yet the system treats all the same
- Seasonal items are a problem as some sell only in certain months
- The sales of health and beauty products are so significantly affected by marketing promotion plans that historically-based forecasts are of little value
- Manual forecasting does not take a great deal of time

Case Study — Sales Forecasting at Household Friend Ltd

Third Time Lucky?

A new forecasting project has been recently commenced with a project team drawn from sales, marketing, and EDP. The objective of the project is still in the definition stage, but it appears likely that it will be to develop a system to:

- Accept manual forecasts for the key products and produce computer forecasts for the non-key products
- Track forecasts and notify when significant deviations occur
- Calculate seasonal factors
- Accumulate the state sales budget forecasts to produce the national budget
- Reduce to an absolute minimum the system inputs from marketing

The EDP project leader has defined project success as dependent on the forecasters accepting accountability for the accuracy of their forecasting. To ensure this accountability the project proposal will include this item as a necessary policy decision for the project to succeed.

ASSIGNMENT

1. (a) What do you believe were the key factors responsible for the difficulties HFL experienced with their forecasting system?

   (b) How might they be avoided in the development of future decision support systems?

2. What, desirably, is the role of the user in the development of systems such as this?

3. Do you anticipate that a policy decision on forecasting accountability will increase the likelihood of project success? What can be done to salvage the system?

4. Had this system been under the control of the user, do you believe the outcome would have been different?

5. To what extent do you feel that the question of the accuracy and suitability of the model technique selected is an issue?

6. One division at HFL used the system successfully for a number of years after it was abandoned by the rest of the company.

If DSSs have to fit the cognitive and management style of the decision makers, what hope is there (a) of developing a common system for a number of decision makers, and (b) given that managers change jobs every few years, will these systems require constant maintenance?

7. What future do you see for the role of management science models in enhancing the value of the information provided by the DSS? Which particular areas do you see most likely to benefit?

8. How important for the success of a model-based system is it for users to understand the underlying model?

CASE STUDY — PATRICK MURPHY LIMITED

Patrick Murphy Limited, that well-known Irish-based department store firm located in Australia has recently acquired a new point-of-sale computer system which enables this store to collect on a central database details of all sales transacted. The information collected includes type of sale (e.g. cash, credit account or bankcard), category of goods sold (e.g. hardware, childrens' clothes, menswear etc.), salesperson identifier, department location, value, number of units. In addition, the computer is able to identify the date and time of sale and to maintain an up-to-date inventory file of stock, since receipts etc. of goods are also entered to the database via a warehouse system.

The store's promotions manager, Sean O'Flaherty, is keen to make use of this new database to provide himself and the general manager, Michael Murphy, with a vastly expanded range of up-to-date management information. In an interview with Angus Campbell, the expatriate Scots systems analyst, O'Flaherty remarked 'with all this competition from Grace Bros and David Jones we need to be right on the mark with respect to our promotions policy. Our decisions in the area of promotions cover the amount of floor space we are going to allocate to departments, the amount of advertising we plan to spend in each area on each type of product, the number of sales staff we allocate to departments and, of course, the desirable inventory level of each item'.

Campbell went on to ask O'Flaherty what types of report and information would be appropriate for these kinds of decisions, and O'Flaherty replied 'we need to know what is going on; I figure we need at least weekly reports giving us full details on sales by department, by product category within department. These should be compared with last week's and last month's sales and the sales for the same period last year; I'd also like to know if the sales trend in one store is similar to stores in other parts of Sydney and I'd like this tied in some way to the advertising budget that the company has'.

In response to Campbell's question regarding the desirability of exception reports, O'Flaherty said 'I don't know much about exception reports; I have never worked with them. However, in this case I guess the amount of data which the computer could provide would be so voluminous that we wouldn't be able to handle it, so maybe that's a good idea. Perhaps you could sketch out some drafts of these reports so Michael Murphy, son of our illustrious founder, and I can go over them'.

ASSIGNMENT

Assuming for the moment that you are Angus Campbell:

1. Prepare a draft of one alert type report which might help Sean and Michael in their quest for improved management information. Indicate the reasons behind your choice of report layout and what types of exception condition would have to arise before a particular department or sales category was mentioned in a report (that is, hypothesize a decision situation and explain how your report will service it). Include consideration of the user dialog.
2. Indicate what type of back-up information might be made available in case the managers raised further questions about the exception report details, and support your choice with reasons related to the decision environment.
3. Identify the areas in which you believe your knowledge is inadequate to permit the initiation of a DSS advisability study. Frame a list of questions for O'Flaherty which should enable you to clarify the situation. Outline your objective in asking each question.
4. Compare the use of graphical and printed reports using examples.

CASE STUDY — INTERNATIONAL TRANSPORT COMPANY

Note: For background information, first read the International Transport Company Case Study in Chapter 1. This case is set in 1981; that is, two years after the events covered in the Chapter 1 case.

The International Transport Company is in the process of redesigning its costing system from the level originally implemented in the early 1970s. The Finance Director, Mr Hendricks, is interested in seeing the new costing system developed in such a way that a fully integrated system can be subsequently developed which will greatly improve the availability of financial information about the company's products, services, and customers. He has employed a systems consultant, David Brown, to consider the issues likely to be important in the design of the costing system and the subsequent financial decision support system.

The following interview between Mr Hendricks and Mr Brown gives some indication of the Finance Director's intentions for the new systems.

DAVID BROWN: What is ITC's objective with respect to the new costing and information system?

MR HENDRICKS: Our objective in designing the new costing system is to give us the control that up till now we have been sadly lacking. You will know, of course, that the company's costing systems have been poorly designed and singularly inappropriate for the needs of many divisions, particularly the requirements of Mr Green's Long Distance Haulage Division. So we want to implement a new costing system which will collect details of all expenses incurred in all divisions, and allow us to report on them both for control purposes and also for analysis and projection purposes on the part of senior management.

DAVID BROWN: Can you tell me what you expect should be the scope of the information-reporting system?

MR HENDRICKS: Well, in this area we have a number of fairly precise requirements and a number that are more vague. Certainly I have the idea, and this is shared by the Managing Director, Mr. Turner, and all the general managers, that we should be able to obtain a consistent set of figures from the costing and general ledger systems which allows us to report by three different categories.

Firstly, we want to produce reports of both revenues and costs by profit centre — that really means the divisions at this point in time, though we may also want to carry it down to subsubsections of divisions; secondly, we want to be able to report by type of revenue and type of expense so we can find out how much we're spending on fuel across all divisions — on vehicles, on maintenance, what revenue we're getting in such areas as small packages, large packages, steel, drugs, and other types of commodity which we transport. We also want to know what expenses and revenue we're getting by using the railways and airlines for transportation media. And then, thirdly, we're looking at the reporting in a geographical sense so that we can reintroduce some state control functions, and identify the geographical regions where we're having more-or-less success and where more-or-less of our business is coming from.

Case Study — International Transport Company

DAVID BROWN: Much of this information is already available, isn't it?

MR HENDRICKS: Yes, certainly we are obtaining quite a lot of this information now through recently developed automatic invoicing systems which seem to be working fairly well, particularly in the long distance haulage area. But we're looking for a set of reconcilable figures. One of our greatest problems is that the numbers we get from some systems just don't relate to the numbers we get from other systems which supposedly should add up to the same totals. So we find we're making decisions in particular areas on the basis of one set of numbers, and then we find others able to produce counter-arguments against those decisions, based on figures drawn from different systems. That's quite ridiculous.

DAVID BROWN: What sort of reporting systems do the managers like?

MR HENDRICKS: Well, you'll have to go round and talk to them individually, but essentially I believe that we need a set of regular reports in the three reporting styles I mentioned earlier, i.e. profit centre, nature, and geographic location. But we will also need a range of exception reports and other ideas which can be used to highlight, to the senior managers within the divisions and other sections, just what's happening in the trucking and transport business. We also need an inquiry facility so that we can get the bulk of the detail out of the system whenever particular queries arise.

DAVID BROWN: What about computing equipment?

MR HENDRICKS: Well, we've learnt our lesson there and we've certainly no intention of procuring any new equipment until such time as we've identified quite precisely what we want to do. Certainly, though, we have no problem with obtaining some new equipment for this application and providing the necessary inquiry terminals, communications lines, and that sort of thing, in order to make it work properly.

DAVID BROWN: So that information system is confined mainly to an analysis of costing data, etc., plus revenues where appropriate?

MR HENDRICKS: Well, not exactly. That's the bulk of the information I expect to be able to get from the system, but, naturally we want to be able to identify things like poor performance, in terms of sections of divisions as well as divisions themselves, and customers who either increase or decrease their credit standing, or rather their indebtedness, in a short space of time, and services which suddenly become fashionable in a particular area of the country; in other words, we'd like to be able to keep a window open on the entire organization through the computer terminals.

David Brown subsequently went to see the director of the Long Distance Haulage Division, Mr Green, to get some information regarding his objectives, arising out of the new costing and finance information system.

DAVID BROWN: What's your attitude to the proposals for development of a new financial information system?

MR GREEN: Well, we're very happy with the way the automatic invoicing system's developed and considering the fight that I had to obtain that, at the moment I'm not pushing too hard in the area of financial information. That system gives us largely what we need to know in terms of the usage of particular services, but, of course, all the data are locked away in some sort of computer file and it's very hard to get it out and relate it back to expenses being incurred in particular sections or parts of the organization. So I'm all in favour of some system which allows us to keep tabs on all these data, both revenue and costs, but I'm not terribly keen on the central head office being able to pry into any data which I have available, without first asking me what it means. As far as I'm concerned, the figures aren't worth a damn unless I'm able to tell them, or maybe my manager's able to tell me, why it is that he's performing so damn well or so poorly for that matter.

DAVID BROWN: Are you happy with the current data collection systems which have been introduced in the last couple of years?

MR GREEN: Yes, the idea of collecting data on a daily basis at the various freight centres has been adequately installed and the accuracy of our data is now a lot better than it used to be. Of course, we need this new costing system because the other one hasn't been any use to us at all and consequently the general ledger figures have been quite useless. If the system is properly designed along the lines Hendricks says it's going to be then we ought to be able to get some very useful control figures out of it.

DAVID BROWN: What sort of reports will you be looking to from the system?

MR GREEN: Well, I want to be able to identify significant movements in activity by customers, either up or down, and I want to be able to relate this to the costs being incurred to provide those services, like I mentioned earlier — mind you, it would be great if we could find some way of linking together the comments made by managers on their performance, some kind of a daily or weekly report, and the figures that come in from the various systems because that way I'd be able to get a complete look at the data, including the comments, without having to keep on ringing everybody up.

DAVID BROWN: What do you regard as being the importance of this ownership of data issue?

MR GREEN: Well, as far as I'm concerned the data belonging to my division shouldn't be available to Hendricks unless he has my OK to get them.

DAVID BROWN: Surely that's a bit unreasonable. Couldn't we put a time limit on the data?

MR GREEN: Yes, I suppose that's a possibility. We could say that any data which have been available for more than 24 or 48 hours would then be available to be accessed by the central finance department, or anyone else with the authority. That would give us the chance to get in and have a go at it first. However, a real problem we may have is when people carry out special analyses on the data, running their own programs, and suddenly pop up with a whole series of trend pictures which we hadn't realized occurred.

DAVID BROWN: Do you think that this information system will cut down on the need for interaction at senior executive level?

MR GREEN: No, I don't think that that's the case, in fact I have some reservations, thinking about it, as to just how useful this database and its associated reporting might be. You'll recall I said a little earlier that we need to have comments from the managers as to why figures are out of specification or budget and that I was also concerned that head office might go off and use this data generated about our divisions without previous reference to ourselves. To me, the computer is a great library and that's what it's good for.

DAVID BROWN: Is that because the computer doesn't work rapidly enough?

MR GREEN: Speed isn't really the important issue. The important fact is that when I'm listening to you I can detect an inflection in your voice or I can see your face change, and so I can understand more than is put into your words. All the computer can do is print words or numbers and I have no other source of information to decide whether or not the facts are reasonable, or to help me determine how much credibility I can place on the answer.

DAVID BROWN: Well, in spite of this you feel we should go ahead?

MR GREEN: Oh yes, let's go ahead by all means, but let's not get carried away with the total comprehensive nature of this system that Hendricks seems to have, and I'm going to want to pay particularly close attention to the access that Hendricks has to my data. We'll probably be wanting to argue this out at Board level.

ASSIGNMENT

Consider the issues arising out of the design of a DSS for the International Transport Company, including the following:

1. What guidelines need to be set to design database management and coding systems for the new costing system, the associated general ledger developments, and the database for the financial information system?

2. What principles should underlie the design of reporting procedures, i.e. how would the data attenuation/amplification functions be carried out?

3. Draft two reports — or user/computer dialogs (with or without graphics) — which could be proposed for use by managers of the corporate finance and long distance haulage divisions.

4. How can textual comments, such as those referred to by Mr Green, be incorporated in the reporting process?

5. What type of implementation plan would you propose for the installation of an
   information system as suggested?

6. Comment on the ownership of data controversy and indicate how you would
   handle it.

INDEX